# The Making of a State

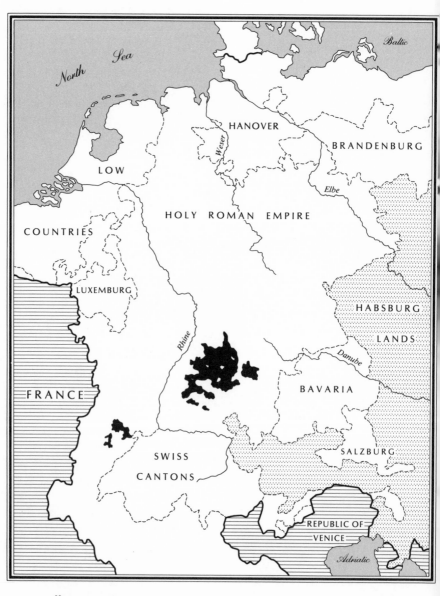

WÜRTTEMBERG IN THE HOLY ROMAN EMPIRE

# THE MAKING
# OF A STATE

## WÜRTTEMBERG

## 1593–1793

James Allen Vann

Cornell University Press

ITHACA AND LONDON

First published 1984 by Cornell University Press.
Published in the United Kingdom by Cornell University Press, Ltd., London.

International Standard Book Number 0-8014-1553-5
Library of Congress Catalog Card Number 83-18841
Printed in the United States of America
Librarians: Library of Congress cataloging information
appears on the last page of the book.

The paper in this book is acid-free and meets the guidelines
for permanence and durability of the Committee on Production
Guidelines for Book Longevity of the Council on Library Resources.

THIS BOOK IS DEDICATED
WITH RESPECT  AND GRATITUDE
TO
WILLIAM O. E. HUMPHREYS
WILLIAM A. JENKS
FRANKLIN L. FORD

# Contents

# Illustrations

[9]

# Acknowledgments

FRIENDS AND SCHOLARS on both sides of the Atlantic have assisted me in writing this book. In Germany the staff of the Hauptstaatsarchiv Stuttgart offered unflagging support during the eighteen months that I worked there. Dr. Eberhard Gönner, director of the archival system for Baden-Württemberg, welcomed me with all possible kindness and in the course of my stay became a close friend. I shall always be grateful to him and his wife, Eva. Hermann Tafel, also a friend and the owner of a comprehensive library on Württemberg history and art, provided similar encouragement and support. Wolfgang Böhm proved a stalwart companion in the archives and a great help in interpreting problems of documentation. I also thank the staff of the Landesbibliothek in Stuttgart and of the Universitätsbibliothek Tübingen. H.R.H. the Duke of Württemberg kindly allowed me to work in the confidential papers of his family's archive. Michael Graf Adelmann von Adelmannsfeldern, Michael Freiherr von Hornstein-Bussmannshausen, and Renata Freifrau von Massenbach provided sustained assistance, advice, and hospitality.

My debts in this country are equally numerous. The University of Michigan allowed me time off from my teaching duties for research in Germany and through the dean's fund and the Horace Rackham Foundation provided financial support. Mr. Derwin Bell, a cartographer in the Geology Department, University of Michigan, drew two of the maps. My colleague Michael Geyer read the entire manuscript and supplied trenchant criticisms that considerably sharpened my analysis. Four other colleagues—David Bien, Jacob Price, Raymond Grew, and Rudi Lindner—allowed me to consult them whenever necessary and took time off from busy schedules to offer useful suggestions. Hilton Root, a graduate student working on the final stages of his own dissertation, likewise contributed timely suggestions and support. Finally, Jefferson Adams of Sarah Lawrence College read each chapter and at every stage of the work gave valuable guidance on questions of style, organization, and presentation.

I have profited enormously from several years of discussion with Horace W. Brock of Menlo Park, California, a distinguished student of n-person multilateral bargaining theory.

Holde Borcherts of the University of Michigan Graduate Library worked generously to track down elusive research materials. Alice Gibson provided invaluable editorial assistance. Jeanette Ranta typed the manuscript, always alert to vagaries in spelling and citation. John Ackerman at Cornell University Press worked scrupulously to purge the final text of errors. My most sincere thanks go to these professionals.

The book is dedicated to three great teachers, men whose high standards and devotion to learning have shaped my life: William O. E. Humphreys of Chattanooga, Tennessee; William A. Jenks of Lexington, Virginia; and Franklin L. Ford of Belmont, Massachusetts.


JAMES ALLEN VANN

*Ann Arbor, Michigan*

# Abbreviations

| | |
|---|---|
| *AHR* | *American Historical Review* |
| *BWKG* | *Blätter für württembergische Kirchengeschichte* |
| GLAK | Generallandesarchiv Karlsruhe |
| HHSAW | Haus-Hof und Staatsarchiv Wien |
| HSAS | Hauptstaatsarchiv Stuttgart |
| *HZ* | *Historische Zeitschrift* |
| *JMH* | *Journal of Modern History* |
| LBS | Landesbibliothek Stuttgart |
| *PP* | *Past and Present* |
| SAL | Staatsarchiv Ludwigsburg |
| UT | Universitätsbibliothek Tübingen |
| *VSWG* | *Vierteljahrschrift für Sozial- und Wirtschaftsgeschichte* |
| *WJ* | *Württembergische Jahrbücher* |
| *WJSL* | *Württembergische Jahrbücher für Statistik und Landeskunde* |
| *WVJHLG* | *Württembergische Vierteljahrshefte für Landesgeschichte* |
| *WVJSLG* | *Württembergische Vierteljahrschrift für Landesgeschichte* |
| *ZWLG* | *Zeitschrift für württembergische Landesgeschichte* |

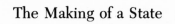

The Making of a State

# Introduction

THE GROWTH of government intrigues us all. Historians, political scientists, and sociologists are particularly concerned with the evolution of the modern state. The fact that professional bureaucracies now administer all the more advanced countries of the world has become so self-evident that we are inclined to assume this condition to be the natural outcome of the evolutionary process. And yet there was a time when things were otherwise. Power was more ambiguously allocated. Intelligent people, even those most involved with government, were unsure of the best way to distribute authority. This uncertainty prevailed throughout the early modern period as the men and women of seventeenth- and eighteenth-century Europe jockeyed in a complex, multilateral struggle to achieve a division of authority compatible with what they identified as their best interests. The problem was that their perceptions frequently changed. And since they lived in a corporately organized society that was itself in flux, environmental uncertainty compounded their difficulty.

What follows is a case study of an early modern state, the Duchy of Württemberg. I have selected this principality for a number of reasons, not the least of them being that, though Württemberg constitutes one of the richest, most influential polities in the German Federal Republic, few English-speaking persons understand its history. And yet Württemberg has contributed significantly to the shaping of German cultural and political life. Intellectual leaders as different in orientation and accomplishment as Philipp Melanchton, Johann Jakob Moser, Friedrich von Schiller, Christoph Martin Wieland, Georg Friedrich Hegel, and Friedrich Hölderlin have found nourishment there. And on a more restricted social but equally distinguished artistic plane, the eighteenth-century ducal court set a widely emulated

[17]

standard of aristocratic patronage. The quality of music, the distinction of the ballet and ballet school, and the beauty of the porcelain manufactured at Ludwigsburg, the splendid princely residence just north of Stuttgart, established high levels of artistic excellence. These traditions have continued into our own day and attracted admiring attention throughout Europe and North America.

Württemberg's religious and political traditions are equally noteworthy. Its rulers were among the earliest German princes to accept Martin Luther's religious teachings. By the middle of the sixteenth century they had secularized the Catholic ecclesiastical properties in the duchy, set up a state church, and imposed conversion upon their subjects. Württemberg thus became a Protestant bastion amidst a larger geographic region that remained predominantly Roman Catholic. Its venerable university at Tübingen trained generations of pastors who not only preached a militant Lutheran orthodoxy to the native Württembergers but fanned out across Germany to shepherd some of that nation's most important Protestant congregations. At a time when confessional allegiance determined eligibility for professional appointment, the university also supplied the various Lutheran urban and princely administrations with reliable cadres of trained civil servants who worked to centralize and rationalize German territorial authority.

Although Württemberg constituted one of the major kingdoms in Bismarck's Prussian empire and prior to the nineteenth century ranked as one of the more important principalities in the Holy Roman Empire, the duchy never attained the international status of Prussia, Bavaria, and Saxony. Nevertheless, within the second echelon of German sovereign power it played a substantial role. As the largest principality in the German southwest, Württemberg dominated one of the most politically important of the imperial provinces and in its dealings with Paris and Vienna functioned as a closely watched bellwether for the diplomatic alignments of the smaller German states.

Württemberg's ties to the empire operated on several levels. My own interest centers on one particular aspect of these relations, on identifying the consequences for a secondary German state of membership in the imperial federation. I am especially concerned about the effects of empire upon bureaucratic and administrative growth. To what extent, in other words, were the German territorial governments shaped by their membership in the old Reich? Recent scholarship has called attention to the empire as a far more vital political system than nineteenth- and early twentieth-century historians have assumed. An administrative case study enables us to test these

[18]

broader hypotheses in specific instances and to determine just how the empire influenced territorial government.

Württemberg entered the early modern period with an administrative structure that reflected in microcosm those of the larger European states. That is, the princely government was in place but its effectiveness was severely limited by the idiosyncrasies of the ruler and, more important, by the entrenched control of the local notables over public life. The town governments as well as the rural magistracies lay almost entirely in local hands. By the sixteenth century most of the incumbents were just professional enough to take refuge behind the fixed rules and procedures of their office but just amateur enough to have little desire for promotion, especially a promotion that would require them to leave home. Few of them showed any interest in enforcing directives from the crown that undercut their own authority or compromised their regional interests.

The Renaissance dukes reacted to this situation in much the same way as their royal counterparts elsewhere. Like the kings they lacked the strength to attack local interests directly and concentrated instead on streamlining the central administration. The key here was the old feudal council, an amorphous body drawn primarily from among the prince's vassals. By the end of the sixteenth century the dukes had turned away from the council and were relying increasingly upon an inner or privy council, a smaller consultative board with a personnel drawn from the ranks of the lesser aristocratic families of the region and from the dukes' own chancellery clerks. The privy councilor must be thought of as a new kind of administrative official more professional in orientation than either the local notables or the medieval councilors. University trained for the most part, the privy councilors made careers in government, where they acquired the knowledge and skills necessary for successful bureaucratic administration. As fulltime civil servants they had the opportunity to become well informed on matters of state and a greater reason to weigh their judgments carefully. Under their leadership the crown became more orderly and efficient in the conduct of its business.

These new professionals at the capital clashed frequently with the old corporate interest groups in the localities and on occasion also pulled in directions independent of the prince. In these terms three primary forces can be thought of as shaping Württemberg: the duke, the territorial estates dominated by the local notables, and the high officials of the privy council. And since each of these groups operated in the context of a larger society, their links to forces outside the government—and in the case of the prince and the councilors to

[19]

forces outside the duchy—become important sources for determining their relations to one another. Indeed, in the final analysis it was the organization of Germany that prevented a definitive resolution of these domestic rivalries and thus preserved the territorial government in a state of suspended growth. The case of Württemberg makes clear that the secondary sovereign powers in Germany simply lacked the capacity to develop fully as long as they were held in check by an imperial organizing force whose principal thrust was the preservation of traditional corporate interests.

Readers familiar with historical accounts of Württemberg will find that my approach has yielded conclusions somewhat different from those of the standard works. Events acquired new causal dimensions when I moved beyond single institutions such as the monarchy and the territorial assembly and attempted to view the state from the perspective of a fluctuating coalition of bargaining units. The same holds true with social analyses. Relations assumed a less static, more nuanced character when I placed the traditional corporate groups in the context of the political institutions that governed their lives. I found right away that they functioned under a set of imperatives that derived in part from outside their ranks, causing them on occasion to fracture into subgroups. These smaller units then crossed corporate lines in quite unexpected and remarkably supple combinations. In this broader—and I hope more interesting—sense, the growth of the state became a matter of sorting out the pressures and conflicts operative in all the several layers of government, from top to bottom.

Princes, estates, and bureaucrats shared areas of common interest as well as of conflict. Fluctuations in these overlapping ties produced complicated, often surprising alignments. My chief aim has been to allow these complexities to surface, for only then can we appreciate the uncertainty behind the decisions that shaped the emerging state. Linear explanations of bureaucratic growth or princely absolutism, like monolithic theories of state building or modernization, miss the point. They impart a wooden and misleading sense of inevitability to events and obscure the competition of human goals and the confusing sense of options that clouded the actions of individuals and groups.

A basic premise of this work is that historical change must be explained in terms of tensions between various individuals and groups. I believe that the study of human beings working out their conflicts illuminates historical change better than discussions of such abstract forces as religious interest, economic ambition, and social cohesion. It is not that these forces are unimportant. They are vital. But they can be grasped in their full complexity only as reflections and aspects of a bargaining process that involves both individuals and corporate bodies. Take, for example, economic ambition, clearly a powerful force behind the Württemberg dukes' assault upon the constitutional balance of the duchy. Their demands for greater revenue stemmed from a complex set of motivations that originated in cultural competitiveness. On their own the dukes could never sustain a military adventurism. Nor could they carry off an independent foreign policy. As much as they might strain in these directions, they had no choice finally but to act in some sort of concert with the other secondary powers of the Reich. But they jockeyed constantly with their fellow sovereigns for pride of place within the group.

A major tactic in this maneuvering was the effort to achieve increased status through a skillful exploitation of the conspicuous consumption and lavish military and cultural patronage that the kings of France had made synonymous with successful monarchy. The problem was that the Württemberg dukes quickly discovered that their private means could not support them in this enterprise. Any dramatic escalation in princely style demanded expenditure that could be sustained only through a restructuring of the territorial economy and tax system. Such a change in turn could be effected only by smashing through local privileges and bringing all subjects of the duchy under a program of aggressive taxation and military obligation. The result was that what began among the German sovereigns as a competitive cultural response translated within the duchy first into a clash between the prince and his estates over finance and ultimately into a struggle between crown, estates, and bureaucrats over the division of authority within the state.

The demand for revenue must therefore be seen as only one of several competing concerns held more or less strongly by differing segments of the population at differing times and places. To elevate it, or any other single force, to causal primacy ignores the rivalry of values operating within human beings. It is the competition between these values that determines the behavior of the very people whose responses to an uncertain environment ultimately explain everything. I might add that this perspective is fully compatible with the most general and advanced branch of the mathematical theory of games, n-person bargaining theory, which attempts to characterize rational behavior in multilateral bargaining contexts within uncertain environments.[1]

1. Interested readers should consult John C. Harsanyi, *Rational Behavior and Bargaining Equilibrium* (Cambridge, 1977), esp. chap. 11–14.

One final point needs to be made on the question of motivation. The Württemberg bureaucracy, as represented in the privy council, formed much earlier than we have heretofore assumed. And once formed, it developed, like the state itself, in corkscrew-like twists and turns rather than with a linear momentum. It is tempting to label the councilors as "state builders." They did not describe their efforts in such terms, nor did they think of themselves as builders. There were no "five-year plans," and they never spoke of the future as differing fundamentally from the present. On the contrary they discharged their duties in the firm conviction that traditional standards provided them with an adequate framework for their activity. And in their dealings with one another they frequently acted as if their aim was to secure the approval of their fathers.

But whatever their sense of history, the councilors were men of extraordinary diligence. Their long workdays, the volume and range of their business, and the virtual absence of vacation time all suggest an impressive commitment and enterprise. Too often it is the eighteenth-century portraits that shape our visual perceptions of early modern government. These graceful renderings conjure up visions of elegant dilettantes presiding languidly but effectively over the business of government. Such images have no place in the reality of high officialdom. At least in Württemberg—and it must have been the same elsewhere—the privy councilors carried on a staggering volume of business, much of it routine, much of it dull. For a good portion of the time period treated here, they met as a board at least once, sometimes twice a day. Between meetings the individual members worked on their own to discharge their particular duties and to digest the ever-swelling mound of petitions, briefs, memoranda, and reports that constituted their charge. In this way they expanded their responsibility—not so much by aggressive innovation as by dogged diligence. For whenever circumstances presented them with a new challenge, they met that challenge and then clung to the expanded authority that its resolution had given them. Slowly then, without sustained direction from the sovereign or conscious strategy by the collective board, the councilors created a central administrative office of remarkable efficiency. They may not have seen themselves as state builders, but they were. It was their somewhat conservative, diligent behavior that, in the context of a changed political environment, gave rise to the new state.

The ensuing chapters follow a chronological order. Chapter 1 describes the physical organization of the duchy: its geography, economy, demography, and general culture. Chapter 2 sets up the structure of the central government and defines its ties to the towns and villages of the countryside. Chapter 3 shows the three great seventeenth-century offices, monarchy, Landtag, and privy council, functioning in a classic period of constitutional balance. This balance is destroyed in Chapter 4. The dukes adopt new standards of kingship that call for massive expenditures. In order to raise unencumbered revenue they ally with their chief bureaucratic officials and toward the end of the seventeenth century move to exclude the estates from government.

Chapter 5 finds the bureaucrats on the defensive. The prince turns against the privy councilors by the end of the first decade of the eighteenth century and replaces these professionals with a cabinet government of courtiers. Then with Chapter 6 and the accession in 1733 of Duke Carl Alexander, the state takes a new direction. A novel, strikingly modern set of priorities comes into play. For the first and really the only time in these two hundred years, Württemberg politics move outside the traditional three bargaining categories. The final chapter reveals a return to course. Outside forces intervene by 1770 to reinstate a constitutional balance that lasts throughout the remainder of the century. The interesting point in this regard is that social change imposes an unexpected twist upon the settlement. The result is that Württemberg enters the nineteenth century with an ambiguous resolution of the conflict that has propelled the growth of the early modern state.

What particularly fascinates me is that at no time in my work on this book could I discover that the contemporary Württemberger—prince, estate, or official—regarded the outcome as inevitable. Each of them moved from day to day feeling only more or less secure. To follow the drama of their bargaining strategies is to grasp how and why they acted as they did.

# [ 1 ]

# The Shape of the Duchy

FRIEDRICH VON WÜRTTEMBERG entered Stuttgart in the late summer of 1593. Then, as today, the city served as the capital of Württemberg and in this instance Friedrich was returning as a reigning sovereign to take over the administration of a duchy that constituted the most important state in the German southwest. When he had left Stuttgart some twelve years earlier, Friedrich had had no idea that he would ever rule as duke of Württemberg, the principality that his family had constructed and governed for some 350 years. But on August 8, 1593, his cousin Ludwig had died childless, so that at the age of thirty-two Friedrich found himself head of the House of Württemberg, sovereign prince of the Holy Roman Empire, and sole Lord of Mömpelgard, the French county on the Doubs River some ninety miles west of Basel where he had been serving as appanage governor for his sovereign cousin.

At Stuttgart Friedrich encountered a ducal government whose administrative structure revealed both the inconsistency that we associate with the feudal principality and the more abstract impersonality of the modern state.[1] One can identify qualities characteristic of modern bureaucratic administration in the clearly defined responsibilities of the various branches of government and in the outlines of a small bu-

---

1. Of particular use in reconstructing the late-sixteenth-century Württemberg government are F. Wintterlin, *Geschichte der Behördenorganisation in Württemberg*, I (Stuttgart, 1902), 1–107; and W. Bernhardt, *Die Zentralbehörden des Herzogtums Württemberg und ihre Beamten*, I (Stuttgart, 1972), 1–106. See also I. Kothe, *Die fürstliche Rat in Württemberg im 15. und 16. Jahrhundert* (Stuttgart, 1938); H. Gmelin, *Ueber Herzog Friedrich I. und seine Stände* (Stuttgart, 1885); A. Adam, "Herzog Friedrich I. von Württemberg und die Landschaft," *WVJHLG*, 25 (1916), 210–229; and Werner Ohnsorge, "Zum Problem: Fürst und Verwaltung um die Wende des 16. Jahrhunderts," *Blätter für deutsche Landesgeschichte*, 88 (1951), 150ff.

reaucratic elite. But the fact that each branch discharged its duties in a relatively autonomous fashion reminds us that the principality had not yet emerged from the feudal world. With the exception of taxation, for which prince and territorial estates shared responsibility, decisions on all government business emanated from the private cabinet of the prince. There was no central administrative board staffed by professional officials; each department reported directly to the ruler, and he in turn imposed his will upon that unit.

It is true that the various department chiefs constituted a pool of high officials from which the duke obtained advice whenever he chose. Earlier in the century Friedrich's predecessors had sought to give these ranking officials a collegial identity by introducing the concept of a Geheimer Rat, a privy council made up of important officials who rendered advice as a collective board. But subsequent rulers had abandoned this system in favor of a looser pattern of consultation more in keeping with their personalities. Friedrich followed in this more recent tradition and during his reign gave a substantial boost to the notion of cabinet government.[2] Yet the idea of the privy council persisted, and under the dislocations of the Thirty Years War this office became a fixed institution of government.[3] Indeed, in the aftermath of the war, it displayed much the same sort of aggressive administrative energy that Friedrich himself had demonstrated. The growth of the council; the consolidation around it of a distinct social group; and the subsequent confrontation between this groups's commitment to the principles of bureaucratic administration and the more personalized conceptions of the prince form a process whose analysis is a basic concern of this book. The process must be understood as involving something more complicated than a series of institutional changes; for it occurred under a set of demographic, economic, and geographic constraints that influenced it at every point. Power politics was not the only factor that shaped the pattern of institutional growth; questions of attitude and value, and differing definitions of political and moral propriety were also important determinants of administrative dynamics. It seems fitting that the physical environment Friedrich encountered upon his reentry into Stuttgart itself reflected certain of these differences in attitude and emphasis.

2. Gerhard Oestreich, "Das persönliche Regiment der deutschen Fürsten am Beginn der Neuzeit," Die Welt als Geschichte, 1 (1935), 218–237, 300–316. Reprinted in Gerhard Oestreich, Geist und Gestalt des frühmodernen Staates: Ausgewählte Aufsätze (Berlin, 1969), 201–234.

3. For legislation setting up the privy council, see A. Reyscher, Vollständige, historisch und kritisch bearbeitete Sammlung der württembergischen Gesetze, II (Stuttgart and Tübingen, 1828), Nr. 54, 56.

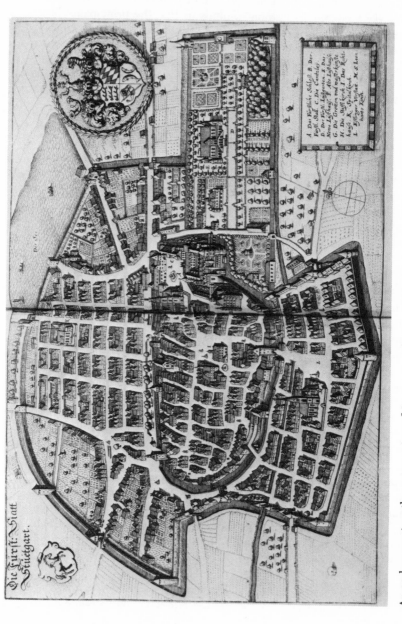

An early-seventeenth-century view of Stuttgart with its medieval moat and walls still guarding the original core of the city. Note the extent to which the duke's castle, flanked by government buildings, church, and pleasure grounds, dominated the landscape. The size and architectural distinction of these elements contrast sharply with the standardized, half-timbered houses of the town. Photograph courtesy of the Princeton University Library.

Friedrich found the city much as he had left it, chockablock with uneven rows of tall, half-timbered houses, many of them with barns and animal pens behind, with stylistic origins that lay in earlier centuries and an overall appearance that must have conjured up a sense of timeless sobriety.[4] To reach his family's residence, a turreted box-shaped fortress on the extreme eastern edge of the city, Friedrich had to pass through two rings of fortified walls. The first wall, as he entered from the Tübinger Strasse, opened at the Hauptstättertor, a late Gothic structure with two massive stone towers that led into a sometime suburb that had some hundred years earlier been absorbed into a city whose population now stood at about 9,000 souls.[5] Taking the street known to late-twentieth-century Stuttgarters as the Konrad-Adenauer-Strasse, he then entered a medieval gate, the Inneres Esslinger Tor, to reach the heart of the city and a road that took him past the old Gothic mint to the castle stables. The ducal fortress, like the town itself, preserved its medieval form; though unlike the town, where only one public building had gone up since Friedrich's departure for Mömpelgard,[6] the castle boasted substantial additions, among them a series of beautiful new gardens and a sumptuous casino of such architectural distinction that it was attracting European attention.

Contemporaries referred to the two-storied casino, designed by Georg Beer and finished only a few months before Friedrich's arrival, as the Lusthaus, thereby underscoring its principal function as one of pleasure and amusement. The building was of enormous proportions, standing sixty-four meters long, twenty-nine meters wide, and thirty-four meters high. Stairstep gables, composed of four stories of windows, framed its shorter ends. These gables, with their progressively smaller levels finished at each step with swirling volutes, gave the building the fanciful silhouette of a Spanish galleon in billowing sail and ensured that anyone visiting Stuttgart would identify the Lusthaus as a major element in the city's skyline. The interior was beautifully decorated and could accommodate the most lavish of entertainments. The sides of the barrel-vaulted ceiling supported elaborate landscape murals whose foliage and figures pointed the viewer toward

4. See illustrations on pages 26 and 71. Additional views and maps are found in LBS, Grafiker Sammlung: "Radierungen von M. Merian," and in the Landesmuseum, Stuttgart, "Radierungen von J. Sauter."

5. K. Weidner, *Die Anfänge einer staatlichen Wirtschaftspolitik in Württemberg* (Stuttgart, 1931), 9.

6. The building, completed in 1583, was a large stone structure erected by the territorial estates to house their offices and materials; see illustration on page 129. On construction, see HSAS, A36: Bü. 12.

FVRSTLICHER LVSTGARTEN ZV STVETTGARTT.

The Lusthaus and garden, engraving by Matthäus Merian, 1616. This fanciful complex was considered one of the most distinguished Renaissance creations in Germany. It attracted visitors from all over central Europe. Photograph courtesy of the Landesbildstelle Württemberg

the center of the roof where a series of frescoes reproduced the heavenly constellations. Two massive fireplaces, ornamented with carvings of grotesques, and several painted ovens contributed to the stately magnificence of the interior. The hall opened onto a raised terrace in each of whose four corners rounded towers with conical roofs provided indoor nooks for rendezvous and intimate conversation. Below the terrace an arcaded porch surmounted by a balustrade encircled the ground floor and offered space for promenades in case of inclement weather. A double outdoor staircase broke the line of this porch at the center of each long side of the casino and led up to the terrace, where a loggia with an enclosed upper story formed a kind of reviewing stand for the extensive parade ground on the casino's southern flank. Obelisks rising from classical capitals decorated the field and served to mark out boundaries for open-air tournaments and courses designed to display skill in horsemanship. Formal parterres—the typical Renaissance style of garden—opened off one end of the parade ground; two of its other flanks gave onto picturesque bosks, where shaded walks and small pavilions provided privacy in delightful natural settings. Everything in short combined to charm the senses, to impress, and to provide pleasure; and in conception, as in form and detail, stood in marked contrast to the cramped, old-fashioned buildings of the medieval town.[7]

The pastors, burghers, and lesser social orders who lived in the high-gabled houses and worshiped in the late Gothic churches behind the double walls of the city of Stuttgart and in numerous other smaller, even less cosmopolitan market towns had no immediate access to the impulses that had inspired the Lusthaus and little interest in subsidizing the balls, festivals, tournaments, and theatrical productions behind its walls. Indeed, insofar as the values behind such enterprises symbolized alterations in traditional political life or departures from conventional morality, the Stuttgarters, as well as their counterparts throughout the duchy, opposed them. This observation does not imply that the better-educated Württembergers lived shut up in a self-contained physical or intellectual universe. The point is rather that, unlike their rulers, their social and economic concerns tended generally to be local. Similarly, their theology and frame of moral reference took direction and nourishment from the theological

7. W. Fleischhauer, *Renaissance im Herzogtum Württemberg* (Stuttgart, 1971), 54–73, 163–170, 304–315, 326–337. Extant drawings by contemporaries of the casino and its gardens are found in HSAS, "Grundriss des Stuttgarter Lustgarten, 1609," von Heinrich Schickhardt und Zeichnungen von Gerhard Philippi und Salvator de Caus. See also Universitätsbibliothek, Stuttgart, Grafiker Sammlung: Lusthaus, K. F. Biesbarth and Friedrich Brentel; and LBS, Grafiker Sammlung: "Merian."

faculty at Tübingen, the duchy's historic university and the guardian throughout southwest Germany of Lutheran orthodoxy.[8]

Both geography and economics contributed to the intense localism of the Württemberg citizenry. The duchy lay in the southwest corner of the old Reich, flanked on the west by the properties of the Austrian Habsburgs and by the scattered territories of the various margraves of Baden and on the east by a screen of tiny principalities and city-states which separated Württemberg from the more coherent geographic mass of Bavaria. A busy mosaic of fragmented ecclesiastical, secular, and urban feudatories lay on the northern and southern borders. Finally, within the duchy itself a disconcerting array of sovereign enclaves—properties variously of city-states, imperial knights, crusading orders, Catholic monasteries, and Habsburg archdukes—provided havens of refuge for troublemaking Württembergers as well as stumbling blocks for any rational system of judicial, administrative, and economic direction from Stuttgart. Many of these little states had rejected the Reformation and remained loyal to the Catholic church, so that early modern Württemberg stood in the immediate proximity of a post-Tridentine Catholicism with an evangelical drive. In themselves, of course, such tiny feudatories posed no overt military threat, although there was always the possibility that they might become way stations for Austrian or Bavarian aggression. The real danger lay in the fact that their very presence posed intellectual and cultural alternatives that gave the militantly orthodox Lutherans of Württemberg a nagging sense of unease and stimulated them to zealous watchfulness and a suspicious mistrust of deviations from local custom.[9]

These Lutheran Württembergers inhabited a state that lay at the apex of a topographical wedge formed by two substantial mountain ranges. To the west the hills and mountains of the Black Forest (*Schwarzwald*) separated Württemberg from the Rhenish properties of the margraves of Baden and so determined the economic life of the southwestern and western portions of the duchy. In the long deep valleys scattered throughout this chain, late-sixteenth-century farmers

8. Weidner, *Die Anfänge einer staatlichen Wirtschaftspolitik*, 112–123; K. Pfaff, "Württembergische Zustände zu Ende des 16. und zu Anfang des 17. Jahrhunderts," *WJ* (1841), 312ff.; O. Borst, *Stuttgart: Die Geschichte der Stadt* (Stuttgart, 1973), 48–95; Gmelin, *Ueber Herzog Friedrich I. und seine Stände, passim;* Gustav Lang, "Landprokurator Georg Esslinger," *ZWLG*, 5 (1941), 34–87.

9. The best analysis of territorial growth in southwest Germany remains K. Bader, *Der deutsche Südwesten in seiner territorialstaatlichen Entwicklung* (Stuttgart, 1950). K. Weller and A. Weller, *Württembergische Geschichte im südwestdeutschen Raum* (Stuttgart, 1971), offer a general but useful summary of relations between Württemberg and these other smaller sovereignties. See also R. Oehme, *Geschichte der Kartographie des deutschen Südwestens* (Constance and Stuttgart, 1961).

followed a pattern of cultivation that still retained its medieval contours.[10] They lived for the most part in small, closely constructed villages out of which they worked the surrounding fields, fished the streams, and hunted through the forests. In addition to basic vegetable staples such as cabbage, beets, and beans, they planted crops of rye, hay, barley, and wheat and cultivated orchards of apples, cherries, and pears. Above them, on the slopes and plateaus of the mountains, farmers lived in isolated dwellings and worked primarily with livestock and timber. Local exchange flourished in these mountain pockets, so that in terms of foodstuffs the region seems to have been self-sufficient. This was not the case with finished goods, however; and when peasants came to the larger markets, it was not so much to acquire foods as to bring grain, hides, raw timber, and cured meat that they could exchange for such finished products as shoes and cloth. The mountain folk did not use their swiftly flowing streams and rivers to pump the mines or drive the machinery for textile production.[11] But while they fished their waters, enterprising burghers deep in the valley town of Calw had already begun to use the strong current of the Nagold River to drive the wheels and looms for a textile industry that in the seventeenth and eighteenth centuries supported a commercial enterprise of international importance.[12]

Similar economic patterns prevailed in the mountain lands along the southeastern and eastern borders of the duchy, where the Swabian Jura (Schwäbische Alb) rose just above Lake Constance and passed northward through the Hohenzollern principalities around Sig-

10. H. Jänichen, *Beiträge zur Wirtschaftsgeschichte des schwäbischen Dorfes* (Stuttgart, 1970), 29–159. Weidner, *Die Anfänge einer staatlichen Wirtschaftspolitik*, 7–23; K. Pfaff, "Württemberg nach seinem natürlichen und kommerziellen Zustand zu Ende des 16. Jahrds.," *WJ* (1841), 312 ff.; see also the report in 1599 of the mayor of Cannstatt in A. Adam, ed., *Württembergische Landtagsakten unter Herzog Friedrich I.*, II (Stuttgart, 1911), 106–107. K. -O. Bull, "Die durchschnittlichen Vermögen in den altwürttembergischen Städten und Dörfern um 1545 nach den Türkensteuerlisten," XII, p. 1, *Historischer Atlas von Baden-Württemberg* (Stuttgart, 1975), establishes the relative distribution of capital wealth for the mid-sixteenth century. For more general analyses of patterns of agrarian cultivation, see Wilhelm Abel, *Geschichte der deutschen Landwirtschaft vom frühen Mittelalter bis zum 19. Jhrd.* (Stuttgart, 1962), 138–238; Wilhelm Abel, "Zur Entwicklung des Sozialproduktes in Deutschland im 16. Jhrd.," *Jahrbücher für Nationalökonomie und Statistik*, 173 (1961), 448–489; Friedrich Lütge, "Die wirtschaftliche Lage Deutschlands vor Ausbruch des 30 jährigen Krieges," in Friedrich Lütge, ed., *Studien zur Sozial- und Wirtschaftsgeschichte* (Stuttgart, 1963), 336–395; Friedrich Lütge, *Deutsche Sozial- und Wirtschaftsgeschichte*, 3d ed. (Berlin, 1966), 196–321.

11. E. Gothein, *Wirtschaftsgeschichte des Schwarzwaldes und der Angrenzenden Landschaften* (New York, 1970; reprint of 1892 ed.), focuses on the Baden lands of the Black Forest, but his generalizations obtain for Württemberg as well.

12. W. Tröltsch, *Die Calwer Zeughandlungskompagnie und ihre Arbeiter* (Jena, 1897), 1–48; also Gothein, *Wirtschaftsgeschichte des Schwarzwaldes*, 518–565.

maringen to take in such Württemberg holdings as Urach, Münsingen, Blaubeuren, Teck, Heidenheim, and Herbrechtingen. Some mining for iron ore took place, especially in the mountains around Heidenheim; but these operations, like the gold and silver mines of the Schwarzwald, do not appear to have been notably lucrative, and most of the profit flowed into the hands of commercial traders from Ulm and Augsburg.[13] Long severe winters meant a shorter growing season for these highland areas. A continued use of the three-field system further compromised agrarian productivity. We have no trade statistics to measure the productivity of these broad mountain valleys; we know only that the markets at Tuttlingen and Herrenberg had a grain surplus sufficient to sustain an active export trade.[14] Other highland towns had to go long distances to obtain supplies adequate to local needs. Even a city as far north as Tübingen found local production unable to satisfy its food requirements and relied on far-distant farms to supplement local supplies. The city's needs were such that in 1574, when the peasants from the districts of Sulz, Rosenfeld, and Balingen refused to sell their grains on the Tübingen market, the municipal government was forced to declare a state of emergency and to petition the Württemberg estates for assistance to fend off starvation.[15] The three districts in question lay some forty kilometers southwest of Tübingen, whose population at that time was no more than 2,500 to 3,000.[16] While this figure made Tübingen the second largest city in the duchy, it did not constitute a population density such that farms lying closer to the city, had productivity been higher, could not have provided at least minimum cereal needs.

13. M. Schnürlen, "Geschichte des württembergischen Kupfer- und Silbererzbergbaus" (Tübingen: Ph. D. diss., 1921), passim; Gothein, Wirtschaftsgeschichte des Schwarzwaldes, 583–672; and W. Söll, "Die staatliche Wirtschaftspolitik in Württemberg im 17. und 18. Jahrhundert" (Tübingen: Ph. D. diss., 1934), 19–22 and 83–86.

14. H. G. von Rundstedt, "Die Regelung des Getreidehandels in den Städten Südwestdeutschlands und der deutschen Schweiz im spätern Mittelalter und im Beginn der Neuzeit," Beiheft 19, VSWG (1930), 59–78; Gothein, Wirtschaftsgeschichte des Schwarzwaldes, 457–518. The question of grain export is complicated by the fact that the ducal government, in order to keep domestic prices low, often attempted to prohibit grain export. These attempts generated bitter controversy and in each instance appeared to have been of only limited success. For illustratons of these regulations and the litigation surrounding them, see Reyscher, Vollständige Sammlung, XII (Stuttgart and Tübingen, 1942), 66 and 76; HSAS, Landtagsausschuss: Bü 1, 2, 3, 6, 8; and Weidner, Die Anfänge einer staatlichen Wirtschaftspolitik, 112–123.

15. HSAS, Landtagsausschuss: Bü. 8 (1573).

16. G. Schöttle, "Verfassung und Verwaltung der Stadt Tübingen im Ausgang des Mittelalters," Tübinger Blätter, 8 (1905), 5. By 1787, Tübingen, still the duchy's second largest city, had only 6,000 inhabitants; see Arthur Schott, "Wirtschaftliches Leben," in Herzog Karl Eugen und seine Zeit, ed. Württembergischer Geschichts- und Altertumsverein (Esslingen, 1907), 314.

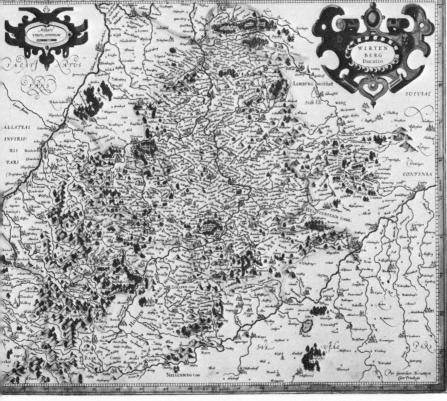

This late-sixteenth-century map by Georg Gadner shows the topography of the duchy. The effect is of an elongated, relatively flat landmass framed on the left by the woods and mountains of the Black Forest and on the right by the range of the Swabian Jura. Note the network of rivers that run throughout the area. Photograph courtesy of the Hauptstaatsarchiv Stuttgart.

Beyond the mountains north of Tübingen, Württemberg broadened out to embrace a broad hilly land mass that was the most fertile and agriculturally promising portion of the duchy. A network of rivers, the most important of which was the Neckar, crisscrossed this area, providing water for crops and abundant easy transportation. Though the Neckar, which rose outside the duchy, widened at the Imperial City *(Reichsstadt)* of Rottweil to permit barge traffic, the river had not yet been sufficiently cleared to allow continuous navigation from Rottweil up past Tübingen and Nürtingen to Cannstatt, an old Roman settlement functioning now as a port for Stuttgart. Plans were already in the air to open the river for barges. By the early seventeenth century these flat-bottomed boats passed uninterrupted to Cannstatt, where the river then accommodated yet more substantial craft which, by the end of that century, could sail north to Heilbronn and from there on to Heidelberg and then to the Rhine.[17] Smaller rivers like the Rems, the Fils, the Enz, and the Murr offered less extensive possibilities, but their waters facilitated an internal commerce and trade that gave the area an economic coherence.

It was the flourishing wine industry that distinguished this region most dramatically from the highland areas of the duchy. The steep slopes of the hills framing the Neckar north of Stuttgart and outlining the banks of the Rems and the Murr provided ideal settings for the cultivation of a strain of grapes that had already established a reputation for producing some of the most delicious wines in Germany. Otherwise the agrarian pattern differed only in emphasis from that in the highlands. Rye, barley, hay, and oats provided the principal grains, and cattle the chief form of livestock. But whereas sheep grazed in the highland meadows, horses were bred in the Rems, Fils, and Neckar valleys, where stud farms supplied the Württembergers' military and domestic needs.[18] Despite the north-central mass's milder climate and an agrarian potential greater than that of the highlands, grain production continued to be oriented toward local consumption with surprisingly little export activity except in the markets at Leonberg and Maulbronn.[19] The sixteenth century had indeed witnessed a steady growth in domestic market volume, reflecting a rise not only in local productivity but often in the income and assets of the landowning peasantry.[20] But in Württemberg this increased prosperity, with the partial exception of the wine trade which will be discussed later, had not yet been translated into an entrepreneurial effort that extended beyond the borders of the duchy. Nor did surplus agrarian capital go into the funding of industrial production.[21] As

17. During the early seventeenth century, the city-state of Heilbronn erected a mill on the banks of the Neckar, forcing Württemberg boats to unload at the city. On the controversy surrounding this mill, see HSAS, C10: 1156, 1156a. A French agent's report in 1669 on Neckar shipping is found in Max Braubach, "Eine Wirtschaftsenquête am Rhein im 17. Jahrhundert," *Rheinische Vierteljahrsblätter*, 13 (1948), 51–86.

18. Abel, *Geschichte der deutschen Landwirtschaft*, 165; W. Boelcke, "Bäuerlicher Wohlstand in Württemberg Endes des 16. Jahrhunderts," *Jahrbücher für Nationalökonomie und Statistik*, 176 (1964), 241–280.

19. See note 14 to this chapter. Maulbronn itself produced mostly timber and had to purchase quantities of grain. The grain negotiations appear to have been almost entirely in the hands of factors from the neighboring city of Pforzheim in Baden-Durlach; see E. Marquardt, *Geschichte Württembergs* (Stuttgart, 1962), 122–123.

20. Abel, "Zur Entwicklung des Sozialproduktes in Deutschland im 16. Jhrd.," 465; and Boelcke, "Bäuerlicher Wohlstand," 263–268 and 241–280.

21. Boelcke, "Bäuerlicher Wohlstand," 241–280; Weidner, *Die Anfänge einer staatlichen Wirtschaftspolitik*, 7–23 and 69–124; Hermann Kellenbenz, "Unternehmertum in Südwestdeutschland vom ausgehenden Mittelalter bis ins 19. Jhrd.," *Tradition*, 10 (1965), 163–188.

was the case in the highland regions, the active trade in raw materials and local produce in the north-central and eastern districts did not spill over into aggressive commercial or innovative industrial activity in the modern sense. An entry in a late-sixteenth-century diary, kept by a wholesale merchant in the tiny Imperial City of Weil der Stadt, spoke to the nature of contemporary economic life in Württemberg. The merchant noted that he had been building up a supply of tanned leather, shoes, and spun cloth (*Tuche*) in preparation for a trip into the duchy to the market town of Böblingen. From there he planned to visit other Württemberg trading centers, none of which handled finished goods for sale by the local Württembergers. In exchange for these products, he hoped to bring back to Weil foodstuffs and raw materials such as wool, wine, flax, and timber.[22]

Historical accident contributed to the lack of commercial and entrepreneurial activity in Württemberg. The state had no historical or geographic rationale beyond that of the energies of its ruling house. As that family had struggled to build its territorial base, it had been forced to accept compromises that now made it difficult for either the duke or the local entrepreneurs to take an aggressive posture on the national or European market.

The origins of the counts of Württemberg remain obscure, but archival records indicate that by the early eleventh century they had settled near Stuttgart on the mountain Rosenberg, where they erected a fortified structure that they called the Wirtemberg. Over succeeding generations they extended their influence locally to acquire a number of vassals and properties; but it was not until the thirteenth century that the collapse of Hohenstaufen power in the German southwest gave them the freedom to begin a sustained policy of territorial acquisition. Like so many descendants of Carolingian lords who built up large territorial units, the Württemberg princes expanded their holdings through a combination of purchase, treaty, inheritance, marriage, and brute force. But while in their case these tactics produced a power base of considerable scope, they never generated sufficient strength to enable the princes to absorb the rich, commercially active city-states of the region. Unable to subdue these Reichsstädte, the medieval counts had no alternative but to go around them, with the result that the territories of three sovereign city-states—Esslingen, Reutlingen, and Weil der Stadt—lay fully enclosed within Württemberg borders. Two others, Heilbronn and Rottweil, determined part of the outer Württemberg boundaries,

22. HSAS, Weil der Stadt: Bü. 3.

while the properties of Augsburg and Ulm occupied the immediate western vicinity and gave the merchants of those cities convenient entry to Württemberg lands.[23]

Armed conflicts with the Reichsstädte had more or less ceased by the late sixteenth century, but the urban powers had emerged from the long struggle with rights of commercial access into Württemberg. During the previous century, a period of great urban economic prosperity, they consolidated a kind of de facto monopoly over the flow of finished goods to the Württemberg peasantry and over the external marketing of these peasants' agrarian produce. Despite its sizable population, estimated in 1600 at something just short of 450,000,[24] Württemberg had not yet developed an urban economy vigorous enough to break this dependence, so that even as the Reichsstädte lost something of their political momentum, they preserved a strong commercial influence in the region around them.[25] Stuttgart, with some 9,000 persons, came closest to offering a territorial alternative to the Reichsstädte, but its industrial, commercial, and financial structure lacked the force to transform the duchy without the help of the other territorial towns, none of which possessed the strength to assist in the effort.[26] Tübingen had a lively book trade, but the town was

23. C. von Stälin, *Wirtembergische Geschichte*, 4 vols. (Stuttgart and Tübingen, 1841–1873), remains the most comprehensive history of the duchy down to 1600. K. Pfaff, *Geschichte des Fürstenhauses und Landes Württemberg*, 3 vols. (Stuttgart, 1839), is stronger on the seventeenth and eighteenth centuries, whereas C. Sattler, *Geschichte des Herzogtums Wirtemberg unter der Regierung der Grafen*, 4 vols. (Tübingen, 1773–1777), offers useful documentation on the earliest Württemberg counts and on their policies of territorial expansion.

24. Württemberg's borders encompassed a total land mass of 140 quadrate miles, with a population in the mid-sixteenth century of between 300,000 and 350,000 inhabitants: Söll, "Die staatliche Wirtschaftspolitik," 6. Söll estimates that figure had risen to 450,000 by 1618 (p. 48) and to 620,000 by 1790 (p. 101); cf. *Handwörterbuch der Staatswissenschaften*, II (Jena, 1924), 43. See also G. Mehring, "Wirtschaftliche Schäden durch den Dreissigjährigen Krieg im Herzogtum Württemberg," *WVJHLG*, 30 (1921), 58–89, who also estimates a population by 1618 of just under 450,000 persons. For a discussion of the sources for such estimates, see G. Mehring, "Schädigungen durch den Dreissigjährigen Krieg in Altwürttemberg," *WVJSLG*, 19 (1910), 447–452; and G. Mehring, "Württembergische Volkszählungen im 17. Jahrhundert," *WJSL*, 1919/20 (Stuttgart, 1922), 313–318.

25. Weidner, *Die Anfänge einer staatlichen Wirtschaftspolitik*, 24–50; see also, Reinhold Bührlen, *Der wirtschaftliche Niedergang Esslingens im 16. und 17. Jahrhundert* (Esslingen, 1927), 23–79; and H. Scheurer, "Wirtschaftliche Beziehungen zwischen der ehrmaligen Freien Reichsstadt Reutlingen und dem Herzogtum Württemberg, 1500–1800" (Tübingen: Ph.D. diss., 1959), *passim*. Aloys Schulte, *Geschichte der grossen Ravensburger Handelsgesellschaft*, 3 vols. (Stuttgart, 1923), goes only to 1530 but volume 2 is useful for pointing up the kinds of linkages between urban markets and the territorial economies. Hermann Kellenbenz, "Die wirtschaftliche Rolle der schwäbischen Reichsstädte in neuem Licht," *Esslinger Studien*, 10 (1964), 222–227.

26. Fritz Rörig, "Territorialwirtschaft und Stadtwirtschaft," in Paul Kaegbein, ed., *Wirtschaftskräfte im Mittelalter* (Vienna, 1971), 421–446; Günther Franz, "Das Ver-

oriented more toward education and administration than toward industry and commerce.[27] Most of the other towns, no one of which had more than 2,000 inhabitants, functioned as little more than centers of administration and local market exchange.[28] In this regard, Württemberg's economy was tied to the Reichsstädte much as that of the antebellum American South was tied to eastern industrial centers such as Boston and New York. The Weil merchant's diary demonstrated that the Württembergers, like the southern planters, produced raw materials that the Reichsstädte then used to fuel their own industrial production. In return the cities provided the duchy with finished products and, as the wine trade indicated, handled most of the external marketing for domestic agrarian surplus.

Wine production stood in marked contrast to other agrarian undertakings in that Württemberg vintners made a conscious effort to produce for export.[29] They did not try to break into the Rhenish or French markets but concentrated instead on the so-called Danubian region of the empire. There the light fruity wines coming out of the Neckar and Rems valleys offered a brisk competition to the sweeter, more bubbly vintages from Alsace and the middle Rhine. Three principal domestic markets gave the Württemberg grower an access to the export trade: Heidenheim for the Remsthaler wines; Geislingen for those from the Neckar region; and Blaubeuren for the Voralpland wines of the southeast. But even when they sold their goods at Württemberg markets, the growers found themselves dealing with commercial factors from the Reichsstädte rather than with local Württemberg merchants. These foreign traders took the wines to more cosmopolitan markets such as Esslingen, an important center for the Upper German market, and Ulm, a node in a network of commercial supply that followed the Danube to Regensburg and the great overland highway to Augsburg and Munich. There they could offer com-

---

hältnis von Stadt und Land zwischen Bauernkrieg und Bauernbefreiung," *Studium Generale*, 16 (1963), 558–564.

27. H. Jänichen, "Der Einflussbereich der Stadt Tübingen im Mittelalter," *Schwäbische Heimat*, 8 (1957), 82–84; Rudolf von Roth, *Das Büchergewerbe in Tübingen vom Jahr 1500–1800* (Stuttgart, 1880); Schöttle, "Verfassung und Verwaltung der Stadt Tübingen im Ausgang des Mittelalters," 1–34.

28. For populations in the various towns, see *Württembergisches Staatshandbuch* (Stuttgart, 1907).

29. W. von Hippel, "Bevölkerung und Wirtschaft im Zeitalter des Dreissigjährigen Krieges: Das Beispiel Württemberg," *Zeitschrift für Historische Forschung*, 5 (1978), esp. 424–426. See also W. Engelmann, "Der württembergische Weinhandel einst und jetzt" (Tübingen: Ph.D. diss., 1911); M. von Rauch, "Saltz- und Weinhandel zwischen Bayern und Württemberg im 18. Jahrhundert," *WVJHLG*, 33 (1927), 208–250; F. J. Mone, "Weinpreis zu Stuttgart von 1479–1576," *Zeitschrift für die Geschichte des Oberrheins*, 14 (1862), 37–39; Söll, "Die staatliche Wirtschaftspolitik," 8–9, 72–75, 103–106.

petitive prices that insured the factors a ready profit. In some instances they even charged the Württembergers for transport costs to these larger centers and then collected a brokerage fee for selling the wine on the national market.[30]

Late-sixteenth-century Württemberg, then, was a principality rich in raw materials and possessed of a diversified agrarian economy whose productivity in certain areas was rising, though in every case yields were lower than they would become in the second half of the eighteenth century. A lively local exchange system flourished but, with the exception of wine, little effort had been made to enter the larger German market system. Industrial production remained at a minimal level, and the Württembergers relied upon the neighboring Reichsstädte to provide them with most of their finished products. Merchants from these same city-states also controlled a portion of the commerce and took an energetic role in the domestic money market. The spectacular sixteenth-century failures of great banking houses in Augsburg and Ulm had forced something of a movement away from these cities, and recent scholarship has discovered the operation of an active credit system among the richer peasants which drew on domestic rather than foreign capital.[31] But much remained to be done before Württemberg could become a capitalistically aggressive, industrially vigorous state.

The peculiarities of historical compromise, like the geographic and economic organization of the duchy, supported in Württemberg a political system that in turn both reflected and shaped the contemporary social structure. This book focuses principally upon developments at the center of the political system, but since the Stuttgart administration rested upon local foundations, these more basic elements must also be considered. For local institutions contributed substantially to the formation of powerful interest groups that sought in turn to exercise their influence at the central level and in so doing created the political forces with which ducal administration had to reckon. The *Amt*, or *Vogtei* as it was sometimes called, constituted the most basic of these local political units and around that organization crystallized a powerful domestic elite known as the *Ehrbarkeit*. It was these local leaders who in the course of the sixteenth century gained control over the territorial diet and became the principal counterweight to ducal

30. Erwin Haffner, "Das Esslinger Kaufhaus" (Tübingen: Ph.D. diss., 1927), 47 ff.
31. Indeed, Hippel, "Bevölkerung und Wirtschaft," 429, states that by 1630 only 4.2 percent of the Württemberg population was engaged in industrial production. See also W. Boelcke, "Zur Entwicklung des bäuerlichen Kreditwesens in Württemberg vom späten Mittelalter bis Anfang des 17. Jahrhunderts," *Jahrbücher für Nationalökonomie und Statistik*, 176 (1964), 319–358.

power. Without the Amt they could never have developed the political and social cohesion that made them so significant a force in Württemberg history. Similarly, two other social groups, the imperial knights (*Reichsritter*) and the Lutheran prelates, evidenced deep roots in the localities, and their role in territorial politics, like that of the Ehrbarkeit, must be understood in terms of their relations to the broader levels of Württemberg society.

The fifty-eight Aemter varied widely in size and importance.[32] The Amt Ebingen, for example, consisted of little more than the town of that name, whereas Urach embraced not only that town but another sizable market center and some seventy-six outlying villages.[33] Regardless of scale every Amt contained a relatively substantial urban unit where the *Amtmann*, or *Vogt*, as the ducal commissioner was called, had his seat.[34] One can think therefore of local ducal administration as resting upon a network of market towns, within which officials appointed by the duke carried out his commands and from which they went out into the surrounding countryside to provide such services and to extract such resources as had been determined by the state. In both the town and the outlying villages (*Dörfer*) the Amtmann dealt with established administrative structures over which he had only varying degrees of control. Towns usually maintained two elective boards to carry out the responsibilities of local government: a *Gericht* that functioned as a criminal court of first instance for the entire Amt and handled civil litigation in the town, as well as appeals from the village courts; and a *Rat* that advised on the task of daily municipal administration.[35] Both committees were made up of members of leading local families, and by the late sixteenth century they were usually elected by these groups rather than appointed by the Amtmann.[36] The Amtmann, however, stood as the undisputed head of

32. The actual number of Aemter is less important for this study than an understanding of what the designation entailed. Throughout the history of the duchy, Aemter boundaries changed as new territories came into ducal possession and other divisions became more efficient. See W. Grube, *Geschichtliche Grundlagen: Vogteien, Aemter, Landkreise in Baden-Württemberg*, (Stuttgart, 1975), 10–21; E. Blessing, "Einteilung Württembergs in Aemter um 1525," Beiwort zur Karte, VI, 10, *Historischer Atlas von Baden-Württemberg* (Stuttgart, 1972), 1–4; and Wintterlin, *Behördenorganisation*, I, 112–114.

33. Blessing, "Einteilung Württembergs," 1.

34. K. Zimmermann, *Der Vogt in Altwürttemberg: Ein Beitrag zur Geschichte des württembergischen Staats- und Verwaltungsrechtes* (Marbach, 1935); Wintterlin, *Behördenorganisation*, I, 3–10.

35. R. Seigel, *Gericht und Rat in Tübingen* (Stuttgart, 1960), 11–26 and 117–121; H. Specker, "Die Verfassung und Verwaltung der württembergischen Amtsstädte," in E. Maschke and J. Sydow, eds., *Verwaltung und Gesellschaft in der südwestdeutschen Stadt des 17. und 18. Jahrhunderts* (Stuttgart, 1969), 1–22.

36. Grube, *Vogteien, Aemter, Landkreise*, 19–20.

the town government. He served on both boards and, assisted by a fiscal officer called the *Bürgermeister* and a town secretary (*Stadtschreiber*), regulated the town's finances and tax accounts and saw to the discharge of military obligations and to the administration of cases of judicial appeal. He also served as the conduit for the promulgation of ducal edicts and as the interpreter of instructions from the Stuttgart administration.

The Amtmann played a less direct role in the affairs of the Württemberg villages, most of which by the late sixteenth century regulated their daily business with little outside interference. Their chief administrative officer, the *Schultheiss*, had originally been an appointment of the duke (acting usually on recommendations from the Amtmann), but by the late sixteenth century most mayors were elected for life by a council of village elders called the *Gemeinde-Ausschuss* or *Gemeinde-Kollegien*, the rural counterpart of the town Rat, and only confirmed in that office by the Amtmann.[37] The village court, the *Dorfgericht*, also functioned autonomously as a court of first instance, exercising complete judicial authority in matters of local property disputes and civil litigation. Peasant villagers had rights of appeal, of course, and all criminal cases went in the first instance to the town courts. But even so, the Dorfgericht served most villagers as an adequate forum for justice and backed up its decisions, after consultation with the Schultheiss and other elders, with monetary fines and even physical confinement. In the more prosperous villages the elders elected yet another official, a fiscal officer similar to the urban Bürgermeister, who collected village taxes and kept the community accounts. This group of officials, all of whom owed their positions to local interest groups, saw to the daily affairs of the village community and, in consultation with the Dorfgericht and the town council, represented the community in dealings with the outside world.[38] In such a hierarchy the ducal commissioner remained a somewhat shadowy figure, customarily confining his participation in the rural communities to an annual sitting in each village where he examined accounts and heard appeals from the local civil court.

With its two distinct components of town and country, the Württemberg Amt might well have remained little more than a loosely organized administrative district with no sense of unity beyond a com-

37. Wintterlin, *Behördenorganisation*, I, 3–10; C. Grabinger, *Bernhausen* (Bernhausen, 1974), 47–48; W. Grube, "Aus der Geschichte von Stadt und Amt Güglingen," *Zeitschrift des Zabergäuvereins* (1958), 49–59; W. Grube, "Dorfgemeinde und Amtsversammlung in Altwürttemberg," *ZWLG*, 13 (1954), 194–219.

38. K. Bader, *Dorfgenossenschaft und Dorfgemeinde* (Vienna, 1974), 266–384; also Grube, *Vogteien, Aemter, Landkreise*, I, 12.

mon obligation to a ducal commissioner. But the Aemter developed in a quite different direction, and already in the early fifteenth century close ties had been formed between town and country. Archival records show peasant work forces coming regularly into town to assist with the maintenance of urban fortifications at the same time that officials were shuttling back and forth between the town and the various villages to work out the prorating of taxes levied in the Amt (*Amtschaden*) to improve local markets, to keep up the roads, and to set up projects of collective benefit.[39] That Württemberg brought into being this kind of local corporatism separated the duchy from many of the other west German territorial states, where sharp cleavages were opening between town and country. It also meant that these administrative units, intended originally as something of a convenience for the prince, possessed at least the potential for a political momentum of their own. They could not only carry out ducal commands but also oppose them. In point of fact the Aemter never demonstrated that kind of aggressive independence. There were occasions of friction to be sure, but at no time during the seventeenth and eighteenth centuries did the Aemter assert themselves as political rivals to ducal authority, no doubt in large part because no one of them singly could defy the might of the state. Furthermore, they had no institutional mechanism for collective action except the power of the duke himself. But if they failed to seize the political initiative, the Aemter nonetheless played a significant part in regulating the growth of central authority in the duchy. Their contribution lay not so much in political action as in the fact that they served as power bases for a group of families who in themselves constituted a political force of importance. For despite the balance between town and country within its boundaries, the Amt spawned an urban elite who used the integrated structure of rural and urban resources to become the principal counterweight to ducal authority.

This elite group, referred to already in the sixteenth century as the Ehrbarkeit, exerted political influence through control over the territorial estates, and it is in this context that these urban leaders appear here.[40] But since their base lay in the Aemter and it was there that

39. Bader, *Dorfgenossenschaft und Dorfgemeinde*, 322–334; Grube, *Vogteien, Aemter, Landkreise*, I, 21–22; Viktor Ernst, "Die direkten Staatssteuern in der Grafschaft Wirtemberg," *WJ* (1904), I, 55–90 and II, 78–119; and von Batzner, "Die Amtskörperschaftsverbände in Württemberg, ihre Entstehung und Ausbildung; ihre Aufgaben und Leistungen und die auf die Erreichung ihrer Zwecke verwendeten Mittel," *Amtblatt des kgl. württ. Ministeriums des Innern*, 8 (1878).

40. See H. Decker-Hauff, "Die Entstehung der altwürttembergischen Ehrbarkeit, 1250–1534" (Erlangen: Ph.D. diss., 1946), *passim*, for the origins of this group.

the dukes would seek to undermine their influence, the precise nature of their position in the Amt should be clarified. In setting up the Aemter, the dukes did not intend that either of the two principal elements should predominate. We have already seen that, except for a shared criminal court located in the town, town and village operated independently of each other, each with its own cadre of officials and hierarchy of administrative and judicial offices. But because the Amtmann, the man from whom the sovereign powers of the prince emanated, lived in the town and was required to visit the village only once a year, the town inevitably acquired prestige as the seat of ducal authority. The urban elite—and one must remember that this spectrum ranged from an oligarchy of farmer uncles in a small town like Güglingen to a cultivated, class-conscious patriciate in cities like Tübingen and Stuttgart—used this prestige to preempt a position of leadership on matters affecting the Amt. The ducal commissioner was usually selected from one of the most important town families. He reinforced the sense of urban leadership in that, in dealings with the prince, he consulted most conveniently with his friends and relatives in the municipal government and tended by temperament and inclination to support urban administrative interests.

During the early sixteenth century when the leaders of the villages and town, who were known collectively as the *Landschaften*, met together to elect representatives to the territorial diet, the Ehrbarkeit dominated the gatherings. To the profound irritation of the peasant leaders, the townsmen pushed through their own candidates and attempted to dominate the committees so as to assure themselves of control over the meetings.[41] Indeed, to a degree largely unappreciated by historians, these high-handed tactics by the local burghers contributed substantially to the Württemberg peasantry's decision in 1514 to enter the "Armer Conrad" revolt. In joining the uprising many villages made it plain that they were protesting not only the financial mismanagement of the young Duke Ulrich but also the assault by the Ehrbarkeit on village authority within the Amt.[42] This protest proved futile, however. In the aftermath of peasant defeat the Ehrbarkeit consolidated its position by setting up rules restricting election to outside bodies such as the territorial diet to those residents of the Amt who held offices controlled by the Ehrbarkeit.

41. See the typewritten manuscript on deposit since 1957 with SAL by H. Fink, "Zusammenstellung über das Landtagswahlrecht der altwürtt. Städte und Aemter." Also, F. Benzing, "Die Vertretung von 'Stadt und Amt' im altwürttembergischen Landtag" (Tübingen: Ph.D. diss., 1924), 40ff., 57ff., 80ff., 92–96.

42. W. Grube, *Der Stuttgarter Landtag, 1457–1957* (Stuttgart, 1957), 74–82, establishes this connection most convincingly.

At various moments during the seventeenth and eighteenth centuries the ducal government, and sometimes the peasant communities themselves, made efforts to break the hold that the Ehrbarkeit had secured upon the Amt. A favorite ploy was an attempt to strengthen the Amt Assembly, a gathering of the Landschaften in which the villages possessed a numerical majority and where, with skillful leadership, the peasants could circumvent the restrictions imposed by the Ehrbarkeit.[43] As will be seen, these efforts met with only limited success; over time the Ehrbarkeit developed a corporate solidarity that cut across district lines, and from a vantage point of control in the territorial diet its members could blunt the thrust of local assemblies.

It is something of a historical irony then that it was the structure of the Amt, a ducal administrative institution, that gave the town, and hence the Ehrbarkeit, a role in the powers of sovereignty that it could never have acquired on its own. Through this organization urban leaders extended their influence beyond town walls to construct a base for political maneuver which gave them territorial visibility. From that position they developed a corporate solidarity as a political force. They never constituted a class in the Marxian sense of that word, for wide economic variation existed within their ranks. Most small-town leaders possessed urban real estate of no great value and a sprinkling of allodial fields in the neighborhood. Thus they enjoyed an economic status little different from that of the village elders and markedly inferior to that of the wealthy patricians in the larger cities. Inevitably these economic differences were accompanied by distinctions in taste, custom, and style of life. What the Ehrbarkeit had in common was the fact that each member, in his own Amt, enjoyed a position of superiority that separated him from the mass of urban dwellers and assured his entry into the town magistracy, with all that such membership implied in terms of exemptions from taxes and service obligations and chances to exert political authority. The Ehrbarkeit constituted a political elite in the literal sense of that word; and it was the *Landtag*, or territorial diet, that provided the forum from which this group could perpetuate its position as spokesman for the Landschaften and make its bid for participation in the administration of the territorial state.

Parliamentary assemblies appeared relatively late in the German southwest. Despite the fact that diets had been held in Bavaria, Hessen, and the Tyrol since the second half of the thirteenth cen-

43. Grube, "Dorfgemeinde und Amtsversammlung in Altwürttemberg."

tury,[44] the institution did not take hold in the lands to the west until 1427, when Habsburg commissioners began to hold meetings with various magnates in the archducal possessions of Alsace and the Sundgau.[45] Some thirty years later, in 1457, the Württemberg counts followed up this initiative and summoned their own vassals, prelates, and townsfolk for consultation at Stuttgart and Urach. The diets met at a time when divisions in the comital house had split the principality into two counties with equally autonomous governments operating at Stuttgart and Urach. Domestic chaos attended this division, and the diets focused mostly on hammering out solutions to intricate problems of internal administration. Given the control that the estates subsequently won over taxation, it is surprising that finance scarcely surfaced as an issue. The orientation shifted, however, at subsequent meetings, where inheritance quarrels and a mounting military threat forced the counts to appeal more frequently on matters of finance and supply. At least once, and usually twice, during each of the remaining decades of the fifteenth century, they summoned assemblies and in exchange for votes of soldiers and revenue agreed to draw the attending churchmen, knights, and burghers more closely into the affairs of territorial government. By 1498 the estates were sufficiently mature politically that, working through the institution of the Landtag, they administered the reunited duchy as regents until 1503 when the young Duke Ulrich attained his majority.[46] Thus, despite its comparatively late beginnings the Württemberg

44. Armin Tille, "Die deutschen Territorien," in *Gebhardt's Handbuch der deutschen Geschichte*, 7th ed. (Stuttgart, 1931), II, 235–236; Fritz Hartung, *Deutsche Verfassungsgeschichte vom 15. Jahrhundert bis zur Gegenwart*, 6th ed. (Stuttgart, 1954), 63–92; Otto Stolz, *Die Landschaft der Bauern in Tirol* (Innsbruck, 1933), 34; Sigmund von Riezler, *Geschichte Baierns*, III (Gotha, 1914), 659–660; Eduard Rosenthal, *Geschichte des Gerichtswesens und der Verwaltungsorganisation Baierns*, I (Würzburg, 1889), 399–400; Hans Siebeck, "Die landständische Verfassung Hessens im 16. Jahrhundert," *Zeitschrift des Vereins für hessische Geschichte und Landeskunde*, 7 (1914), 11; Anton Brunner, *Die Vorarlberger Landstände von ihren Anfängen bis zum Beginn des 18. Jahrhunderts* (Innsbruck, 1929), 37; Peter Blickle, *Landschaften im Alten Reich* (Munich, 1973), esp. 7–24 and 439–475.

45. Nico Sapper, *Die schwäbisch-oesterreichischen Landstände und Landtage im 16. Jahrhundert* (Stuttgart, 1965), 47–64; Theodor Knapp, "Die schwäbisch-oesterreichischen Stände," *WVJHLG*, 25 (1916), 230–235; H. E. Feine, "Die Territorialbildung der Habsburger im deutschen Südwesten vornehmlich im späten Mittelalter," *Zeitschrift der Savigny Stiftung für Rechtsgeschichte, Germanistische Abteilung*, 67 (1950), 176–308.

46. In 1495 the Württemberg territories were declared an indivisible imperial fief and raised to the status of a duchy. See A. Adam, "Das Unteilbarkeitsgesetz im württ. Fürstenhause nach seiner geschichtlichen Entwicklung," *WVJHLG*, 6 (1883), 161–222; also HSAS, Württembergische Regesten 316, Nr. 16 and 20. On the fifteenth-century Landtag, see Grube, *Der Stuttgarter Landtag*, 11–73, and Friedrich Wintterlin, "Die Anfänge der landständischen Verfassung," *WVJHLG*, 23 (1914), 329–336.

Landtag blossomed rapidly. In the end it outlasted all its more elderly neighbors and by its extraordinary vitality attracted the attention of the celebrated late-eighteenth-century English politician Charles James Fox, who gave the Landtag international renown with his often-quoted remark that there were only two constitutions in Europe: the British and that of Württemberg.[47]

The Württemberg constitution, personified in the Landtag, rested on an agreement worked out in 1514 between the estates and Duke Ulrich (1530–1550) which became famous in Württemberg history as the *Tübinger Vertrag*.[48] Its specific terms were complicated and spoke in large part to details of only immediate concern, but it also assented to principles with long-term significance for political life in the duchy. In particular, the estates agreed to accept responsibility for liquidating government debts. They still expected the duke to live primarily out of his own purse, but the estates were aware that government expenditures could exceed the limitations of ducal resources and that at such a point the realm itself would have to contribute. At this time they assumed a ducal debt of some one million Gulden that Ulrich had contracted as a result of a combination of personal extravagance, fiscal mismanagement, territorial purchase, and military expenditure connected with the peasant uprising of 1514 and certain foreign ventures.

In exchange for this acknowledgment—the estates raised some immediate cash moneys and set up a permanent treasury for amortizing the remaining debt—the duke granted all subjects the right of free movement within the duchy. No Württemberger, in other words, could be bound to the land or denied the right to settle where he could make a living. In addition, Ulrich recognized the right of the estates to levy taxes and to participate in the supervision of the territorial administration. He also promised to consult the estates prior to any declaration of war. Finally, the estates acknowledged the sole right of the duke to summon the Landtag, though he in turn agreed to permit the representatives of Stuttgart and Tübingen to propose meetings. As is frequently the case in such declarations of general principles, the Tübinger Vertrag did not spell out the specifics of implementation and in succeeding centuries interpretations varied wildly as to the framers' original intent. Later champions of estates' rights, for example, claimed that the authority to levy taxes meant that no tax could be applied that was not voted specifically by the

47. C. J. Fox, "The States of Wirtemberg," *Edinburgh Review*, 29 (1818), 30.
48. Wilhelm Ohr and Erich Kober, eds., *Württembergische Landtagsakten*, I, *1498–1515* (Stuttgart, 1913), 163–240.

Landtag. The proper definition of the role of the estates in supervising the administration or in approving foreign policy proved equally controversial. But whatever the framers' intent, the concept of these rights had entered Württemberg's political consciousness. The Tübinger Vertrag set the rhetorical framework within which all negotiations between duke and estates were to occur and to a very large extent defined the basic issues upon which late-seventeenth- and eighteenth-century estates rested their opposition to the dukes' efforts to establish a strong central government under their own control.[49]

In the complex political jockeying that surrounded the formulation of this constitutional cornerstone, two points have a special significance for the present study: first, the absence of the imperial knights from virtually all negotiations; and second, the final consolidation by the Ehrbarkeit of its monopoly over the seats on the delegations to the diet from the Landschaften, that combination of town and villages making up each of the Aemter and representing the non-clerical, non-noble estates of the realm. Tradition stipulated that two delegates represent each Amt at the diet. One delegate was always the Amtmann who, though he usually belonged to the local establishment, held his office from the duke rather than by election and was regarded at the Landtag as a ducal creature. The other, as we have already seen, came from the ranks of the Landschaften. By law, representatives from both village and town could stand for election as delegates, but more often than not urban oligarchs managed to exclude their rural counterparts and to elect as second delegate a man from the Ehrbarkeit. In negotiations preceding the summoning of the 1514 Landtag, at the request of the elected estates and with the agreement of the duke, the Amtmann surrendered his position in the delegation, making way for a second elected representative.[50] The Tübinger Vertrag confirmed this procedure and by vesting the voting

49. L. von Spittler, "Historischer Commentar ueber das erste Grundgesetz der ganzen württ. Landesverfassung," Göttingisches Historisches Magazin, 1 (1787), 49–105. Reprinted in Sämtliche Werke, ed. K. Wächter, XII (Stuttgart and Tübingen, 1837), 89–141; L. Heyd, Ulrich, Herzog zu Württemberg, 1 (Tübingen, 1841), 269–322; Reyscher, Vollständige Sammlung, 1, 266–284; Reinhold Rau, "Zum Tübinger Vertrag 1514," ZWLG, 9 (1949/50), 147–174; E. Miller, "Die Bedeutung des Tübinger Vertrags," Tübinger Blätter, 42 (1955), 2–9,.

50. The Amtmann, if elected, could serve as a delegate until 1629, when further legislation excluded him even from standing as a candidate. See F. Carsten, Princes and Parliaments in Germany from the Fifteenth to the Eighteenth Century (Oxford, 1959), 24–60; Grube, Stuttgarter Landtag, 297–299 and 303–304; Wintterlin, Behördenorganisation, 1, 63–64; and C. Sattler, Geschichte des Herzogtums Wirtemberg unter der Regierung der Herzogen, VII (Ulm, 1774), 17–18.

of taxes and other administrative rights in the estates established the Landschaften as the basic political constituency of the duchy. Private negotiations with the duke, however, defined the instrumental procedure for elections from the Landschaften in such a way that, although the separate structure of town and village remained intact, the Ehrbarkeit was granted exclusive control over both seats in the delegation. The terms of the guarantee became explicit in 1515, when Duke Ulrich announced that in the future only members of the town magistracy (the Gericht and Rat) would be allowed to stand in the Amt for election as delegates from the Landschaften.[51] Representatives from the villages would no longer be recognized.

The disappearance of the imperial knights at the Landtag signified changes whose long-term importance equalled those occurring in the Aemter. Scattered throughout the Württemberg duchy stood the castles, farms, and villages of a group of nobles, never conquered as such by the medieval Württemberg counts, whose relations with Württemberg reflected an understandable mixture of suspicion, discomfort, and deference. Many of them owed feudal homage to the counts for the bits and pieces of privilege and property they had acquired from the Stuttgart princes as gifts or as payment for military services.[52] But all of them claimed allodial ownership over at least a portion of their property and stood in that sense like the Reichsstädte, free from any obligation or tie to the counts. Unlike the Reichsstädte, however, many knights took positions at the comital court and over the years involved themselves closely as advisers to the counts in the territorial administration and as allies in programs of common military enterprise. Indeed, when the Württemberg rulers first began holding diets, the knights participated in these meetings and, so long as the diets addressed themselves primarily to matters of statecraft and administration, took an active role in the discussions.[53] But by the end of the fifteenth century, as the diets' emphasis shifted more and more to matters of finance, the knights became increasingly uneasy. They began to absent themselves from the discussions and to insist that they had no fiscal obligation to the Württemberg state. Their ration-

51. Reyscher, *Vollständige Sammlung*, II, 56, Nr. 24; Stälin, *Wirtembergische Geschichte*, IV, 115; Grube, "Dorfgemeinde und Amtsversammlung in Altwürttemberg," 198.

52. See J. S. Burgermeister, *Thesaurus juris equestris*, II (Ulm, 1718), 622–627, for those knights who held property in fief from the House of Württemberg. Also, D. Hellstern, *Der Ritterkanton Neckar-Schwarzwald* (Tübingen, 1971), 21, Nr. 62, discusses links between the Ritterschaft in that area and the Württemberg dukes.

53. Grube, *Stuttgarter Landtag*, 11–73; Hellstern, *Ritterkanton Neckar-Schwarzwald*, 19–31.

ale was that they held noble rank as free subjects of the empire and recognized no sovereignty other than that of the emperor. They made so strong a case that they were not invited to the diet of 1514, summoned explicitly to cope with the question of ducal debt, but met instead at a later assembly of their own.[54]

The negotiations that followed between the knights and the estates proceeded with confusion and contradiction. The knights, for example, refused to contribute in any form to the taxes voted in 1514 at Tübingen. They did agree at a later time to assist Duke Ulrich in raising money for an imperial fine that he had incurred by fatally stabbing a rival in a dispute over a woman.[55] Matters reached something of a head in 1519 when the prelates and the delegates from the Landschaften called upon the knights to rally in the face of the military emergency confronting the duchy and to attend a diet. In letters to the knights, they stressed their belief that "prelates, knights, and Landschaft are united, true to one another, and obligated to band together in moments of emergency [confronting the state]."[56] The knights refused the summons and responded indignantly that they in no way constituted an estate of the duchy (*Kein Staind in der Wirtemberg Landschaft*) but functioned rather as independent nobles (*frey Edelleut*) without obligation to Württemberg.[57] The justice of this claim is not at issue here; what is important is that, in the fifteen years of chaos which followed Ulrich's abortive assault on the city of Reutlingen and subsequent banishment from the duchy, the Habsburg administrators who took over the ducal government acknowledged the knights' independence and institutionalized their liberties with imperial recognition of their *Reichsunmittelbarkeit*, or sovereign status within the empire.[58] By the time of Friedrich's accession, the sovereign independence of the knights no longer stood at issue; everyone recognized their constitutional position as vassals of the emperor and their personal independence from the claims of the state of Württemberg.[59]

This brief summary of their earlier ties is introduced only to underscore the history of close association between the knights and Würt-

54. Heyd, *Ulrich, Herzog zu Württemberg*, I, 369–374; J. Pfister, *Herzog Christoph zu Wirtemberg*, I (Tübingen, 1819), 39ff., and II (1820), 120; Reyscher, *Vollständige Sammlung*, XII, 17.
55. HSAS, A 34: Bü. 1c, Nr. 16. XIV.
56. Ibid.
57. HSAS, A 34: Bü. 1c, Nr. 16, XV.
58. Sattler, *Geschichte des Herzogtums*, IV, 141; Walter Grube, "Württembergische Verfassungskämpfe im Zeitalter Herzog Ulrichs," *Neue Beiträge zur südwestdeutschen Landesgeschichte: Festschrift für Max Miller* (Stuttgart, 1962), 144–160.
59. Hellstern, *Ritterkanton Neckar-Schwarzwald*, 32–112 and 184–199.

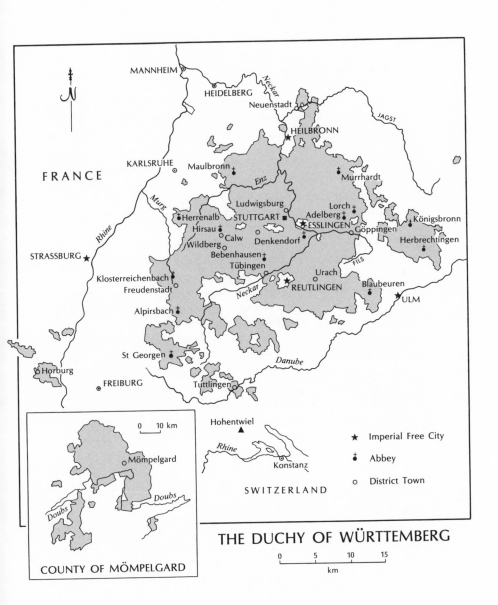

MANNHEIM

HEIDELBERG
Neuenstadt
Neckar

★ HEILBRONN

JAGST

KARLSRUHE
Maulbronn ‡
Murrhardt ‡

FRANCE
Enz

Ludwigsburg
Lorch ‡
Herrenalb ‡    STUTTGART ■    Adelberg ‡    Königsbronn ‡
Hirsau    ○ESSLINGEN
Murg
Göppingen
Rhine
Wildberg ○ Calw    Denkendorf ‡    Herbrechtingen ‡
STRASSBURG ★
Bebenhausen ‡
Tübingen
Klosterreichenbach ‡    Urach    FILS
Freudenstadt    ★ REUTLINGEN    Blaubeuren ‡
Neckar
Alpirsbach ‡    ★ ULM

St Georgen ‡
Danube

Horburg
FREIBURG ○    Tuttlingen ○

Hohentwiel
0    10 km    ▲    ★    Imperial Free City
Rhine
Konstanz    ‡    Abbey
Mömpelgard
Doubs    SWITZERLAND    ○    District Town

**THE DUCHY OF WÜRTTEMBERG**

Doubs    0    5    10    15

**COUNTY OF MÖMPELGARD**    km

temberg and to discourage too literal an emphasis on their constitutional status as sovereign powers. Throughout the early modern period the word *sovereignty* carried connotations unfamiliar to the twentieth-century mind and often lost in tidy historical generalizations about the structure of the Holy Roman Empire or neat colorations on maps depicting the territorial sovereignties of that polity.[60] Many of the knights, even when confirmed by the emperor in their Reichsunmittelbarkeit, still owed obligations to the Württemberg dukes for the privileges and properties that they held in fief from the House of Württemberg. By the same token they continued in their ancient tradition of military service at the Württemberg court and, as this book will show, they continued to take positions in the Württemberg administration. Sons often succeeded fathers in these positions; and as generations passed and branches of a noble family continued to divide, little more than a common name and title linked many of the nobles residing in Württemberg proper—or serving at court or in government—with the ancestral holdings that supported their family's claim to sovereign status. When these cadet branches acquired houses and farms in Württemberg, their members owed the same duties to the state as any other Württemberg property owner. Similarly, all peasants working such property looked to Württemberg, not to the sovereign noble who had bought the land, for the rendering of these services and responsibilities associated with territorial government.

Thus while those historians may be correct who stress the literal fact that Württemberg, unlike so many other principalities, had no indigenous territorial nobility, their emphasis on this point can be misleading. The knights whose holdings peppered the duchy did not live entirely free of obligation to and involvement with Württemberg. Indeed, in ways often missed in works that depict the imperial knights as self-contained sovereign elements within the Reich, this group—at least in its extended sense—was closely bound up in the affairs of the duchy. More interesting for this discussion than the stress on their sovereign status is the recognition that by giving up their position in the estates, the knights lost an institutional basis from which to conduct their inevitable participation in Württemberg politics. Afterward they could establish themselves only at court or in the administration, both of which positions committed them to working in the duchy for centralized authority rather than for local autonomy.

The withdrawal of the knights left the Württemberg prelates as the

---

60. On the subject of these complexities, see Heinrich Mitteis, "Land und Herrschaft: Bemerkungen zu dem gleichnamigen Buch Otto Brunners," in Hellmut Kämpf, ed., *Herrschaft und Staat im Mittelalter* (Darmstadt, 1956), 20–65.

second estate of the duchy; and this group, unlike the knights, participated in territorial politics from a base in the Landtag. Prior to the
Reformation the leaders of the Württemberg episcopate had used
their spiritual authority and the church's rich endowments to secure a
strong voice in the political life of the duchy. The Reformation ended
the financial autonomy of this group and radically redefined its composition. Bishops, as such, were dismissed, and the episcopal hierarchy abolished. Monastic houses suffered dissolution and the loss of all
endowment and political influence.[61] An exception was made for the
fourteen largest and most influential of the male establishments.
These houses continued to operate with their endowments more or
less intact, but they functioned in a quite different manner, serving
the duchy now as schools and preparatory colleges for advanced theological students at Tübingen. Two officials, appointed directly by the
duke, presided over each former monastery. One was a Lutheran divine who took the ancient title of prelate or abbot and supervised the
spiritual and intellectual life of the establishment. By virtue of his office, he also sat in the territorial diet as an estate of the realm. The
other official, technically subordinate to the abbot and referred to
originally as the *Klosterverwalter* and later as the *Klosteroberamt-
mann*, managed the farms, forests, and properties that made up the
endowment.[62] Relations between these officials could vary. The latter tended usually to identify with the fiscal interests of the central
government to whom he reported, whereas the prelates developed a
corporate solidarity among themselves and then with the other
estates.[63]

As opposed to the Aemter, whose delegates constituted the first estate and whose number grew in this period from forty-five to more
than sixty-five, the prelates remained constant at fourteen. A map of
late-sixteenth-century Württemberg shows the lands of these houses

61. H. -M. Maurer and K. Ulshöfer, *Johannes Brenz und die Reformation im Herzogtum Württemberg* (Stuttgart, 1975?), 119–123. Many of the former monastic properties were preserved as corporate economic units under state administration. The con-
vent at Oberstenfeld continued to function as a Lutheran house for gentlewomen. The
last abbess, Mathilde Alexandrine Duchess of Württemberg, died in 1913. For the
administrative personnel of these trusts, see W. Pfeilsticker, *Neues württembergisches
Dienerbuch* (Stuttgart, 1963), 3256–3521.
62. V. Ernst, "Die Entstehung des württ. Kirchenguts," *WJSL* (1911), 377–424;
Heinrich Hermelink, "Die Aenderung der Klosterverfassung unter Herzog Ludwig,"
*WVJHLG*, 12 (1903), 284–337; Heinrich Hermelink, "Geschichte des allgemeinen
Kirchenguts in Württemberg," *WJSL* (1903), 78ff.; Wilhelm Bofinger, "Kirche und
werdender Territorialstaat," *BWKG*, 55 (1965), 75–149; I. G. Kolb, "Zur Geschichte
der Prälaturen," *BWKG*, 29 (1925), 22–74.
63. Christoph Kolb, "Geschichte des Pfarrstandes in Altwürttemberg," *BWKG*, 57
(1957), 74–190.

snaking along the outer boundaries of the duchy like a serpentine wall.[64] Generally speaking, the properties of each house constituted a contiguous unit, the two largest of which were Bebenhausen and Maulbronn. Slightly smaller holdings characterized a second group made up of Königsbronn, Alpirsbach, Blaubeuren, Hirsau, Murrhardt, Herrnalb, Denkendorf, and Lorch; whereas those of the remaining four—St. Georgen, Adelberg, Anhausen, and Herbrechtingen—scaled down even further. Not surprisingly, the prelates of Bebenhausen and Maulbronn usually took roles of leadership at the diet and served as spokesmen for the other prelates, though the theological distinction of schools at Denkendorf, Lorch, and Hirsau also ensured prestige for their abbots.

In the aggregate, these Lutheran abbeys commanded an impressive economic strength. Fiscal records are too fragmentary to yield exact figures on their annual revenue, but two illustrations establish the relative standing of the abbeys prior to the Thirty Years War. In 1553, when ducal debts stood at 1,700,000 florins and the estates once again agreed to assume a large portion of the government's liability, they prorated contributions at 800,000 florins for the towns and villages of the Aemter and 400,000 florins for the prelates.[65] In the allocation of a smaller debt in 1583 the fourteen ecclesiastical foundations assumed one-half the total obligation of 600,000 florins.[66] Moreover, it is safe to assume that the burden reflected the prelates' economic capacity and not parliamentary manipulation by their more numerous colleagues from the Aemter. Relations between the two groups were exceedingly cordial; the prelates themselves almost always came from the Ehrbarkeit and often married the sisters and daughters of their colleagues at the diet. Furthermore, from the mid-sixteenth century onward the two groups met as one body rather than as separate houses and worked out mutually acceptable solutions to the problems confronting them. Similarly there were no subcommittees of the diet which did not include representation from both estates. On the Executive Committee (Kleiner Ausschuss), the governing board of the diet, the prelates occupied two seats; the burghers six. An identical ratio obtained on the larger council (Grösserer Ausschuss), where four prelates sat with twelve burghers.[67]

64. See map VI, 2, in Historischer Atlas von Baden-Württemberg (Stuttgart, 1972).
65. HSAS, tomus actorum, II, Fasc. 556–557, 579–580, 599–600, 633–635, 654–656 (13 Dec. 1553–8 Jan. 1554); also Reyscher, Vollständige Sammlung, II, 113, Nr. 36.
66. HSAS, tomus actorum, XI, Fasc. 248–250, 328–329, 463–464 (3–17 March 1583).
67. HSAS, tomus actorum, I, Fasc. 14–15 (7 Jan. 1551). Also, Sattler, Geschichte des Herzogtums, IV, 9–189; Grube, Stuttgarter Landtag, 197–223.

But if the assignment of fiscal responsibility caused little friction among the estates, the disposition of ecclesiastical revenues became a matter of nagging controversy between the estates and the prince, both of whom claimed control over portions of these funds. The legislation setting up the rules governing these revenues, the *Klosterordnung* of 1556 and the *Landtagsabschied* of 1565, stipulated that all income from the ecclesiastical trusts was to go first for the maintenance of church, schools, and the poor.[68] Once staff salaries and operating expenses for these concerns had been met, the remaining moneys could be used for the welfare of the duchy, for matters of defense and general charity. These funds were paid into a *Kirchenkasten*, a treasury set up for that purpose at Stuttgart, separate to be sure from the ducal treasury but administered nonetheless by government officials.

Each year Württemberg law stipulated that at least one-third of the ecclesiastical income go toward payment of those taxes voted by the estates and hence into their treasury.[69] But since the Kirchenkasten, controlled entirely by ducal officials, dispersed these funds and alone knew their total value—much of the income was paid in kind and had to be sold on the territorial market before acquiring a precise cash value—payments to the estates could be irregular. Then too, since the prelates themselves did not manage these properties, many held only vague notions about the receipts, and the possibility loomed that the estates received less than their fair share of the total. In actuality, prior to the Thirty Years War the dukes took little money from this fund. From 1568 to 1618 they received for government expenses a total of 1,071,669 florins or some 20,000 florins per year.[70] But when the late-seventeenth-century rulers required moneys for standing armies and other personal expenses that the estates deplored, the delegates quite justifiably suspected that aggressive ducal agents were subverting the ecclesiastical revenues. This feeling further exacerbated relations between the estates and the central government, hardening the former in their opposition to ducal policy.

The prelates, like their relatives in the towns and cities, constituted a social force that in the course of the sixteenth century had coalesced through a manipulation of the institutional structure of the duchy. This Ehrbarkeit should not be thought of as opposed by definition to

68. HSAS, A 34: Bü. 6a–c; Reyscher, *Vollständige Sammlung*, I, 323–326; Stälin, *Wirtembergische Geschichte*, IV, 729–732; Adam, *Württembergische Landtagsakten*, II, p. 1, 570ff. For a discussion of the work with the poor, see Arnold Weller, *Sozialgeschichte Südwestdeutschlands* (Stuttgart, 1979), 54–67.
69. Wintterlin, *Behördenorganisation*, I, 41–43 and 96–97.
70. A. Adam, ed., *Württembergische Landtagsakten unter Herzog Johann Friedrich, 1608–1620*, III (Stuttgart, 1919), 175 and 558, Nr. 2.

ducal rule. Indeed, Friedrich and his successors imparted legitimacy to the local structure that secured a position of territorial influence for the Ehrbarkeit. But the group manifested a specific kind of ducal loyalty. Its members regarded the prince in the constitutional terms spelled out in the Tübinger Vertrag and insisted that their territorial diet approve all innovations. They reinforced this insistence with a general set of moral assumptions that defined political leadership in custodial rather than progressive terms. Such definitions placed the prince squarely in the feudal tradition and called for him to rule as the protector of his children rather than as the director of their actions or as the single beneficiary of their energies.[71] As we shall see, the constraints implicit in such conceptions of authority operated as effectively as constitutional restrictions to limit the manner in which the dukes approached the various branches of their administration.

In the years prior to Friedrich's arrival, however, one can detect certain patterns of manners and customs at court which indicated shifts in ducal orientation consonant with the conceptions of strong monarchy which were gaining popularity in Tudor England and Valois France. Friedrich, as it turned out, gave a substantial impetus to the new direction and sought to exercise his will free from the constraints the Ehrbarkeit had imposed upon his predecessors. The dramatic contrast between recent architectural creations like the Lusthaus and the more traditional Württemberg styles called attention to the gulf widening between the self-conscious stylishness of the court and the inward-looking mores of the Württemberg people. Friedrich's orientation lay squarely with the new. In his youth he had traveled widely, first north to the Danish court and then east to the princely establishments of Silesia, Moravia, Hungary, and Austria. Later he had spent considerable time in France, where he supported the Huguenots in their struggle against the aggressive Catholicism of the Guise family and forged close ties with Henry of Navarre. He also visited Elizabethan England where he delighted in the opulence of the Tudor court. These experiences had widened his political horizons and left him—many of his countrymen felt—with a taste for crypto-Calvinist ideas and decidedly inflated notions about the perquisites appropriate to a reigning prince.[72]

Extensive travel had also awakened aesthetic inclinations that fur-

---

71. For a discussion of notions of late medieval monarchy, see Otto Brunner, *Land und Herrschaft* (Vienna, 1965), 111–164 and 357–440.

72. K. Pfaff, *Württembergs geliebte Herren*, ed. P. Lahnstein (Stuttgart, 1965), 41–43; Marquardt, *Geschichte Württembergs*, 125–126; and Sattler, *Geschichte des Herzogtums*, v (Ulm, 1772), 153–284.

ther underscored his apartness and prompted him to reinforce the physical contrasts already noted between court and country. Almost at once he summoned the Italian-trained building master Heinrich Schickhardt to begin work on a string of improved fortifications, hunting lodges, weekend retreats, and garden parks that wound throughout the Württemberg territories.[73] He also commissioned a thorough redecoration of the Stuttgart castle, where lavish refurbishing created a self-conscious sense of luxury and innovation.[74] In all of these undertakings, foreign taste and not Württemberg tradition provided the stimulus and determined the behavioral norm that placed so obvious a stress on grandeur and pleasure. Friedrich did not take his definition of propriety from conventional Lutheran orthodoxy but from an international cadre of monarchs who had adopted new modes of style and ceremony at their courts and were now insisting that these models constituted the *sine qua non* of royal status.[75]

In imparting this tone to his monarchy, Friedrich conjured up an ambience of power which in the fact proved ephemeral. Patterns of patronage, however discriminating, do not in themselves constitute a political reality; and as we have seen, powerful constraints in the fundamental organization of the duchy operated to restrict ducal maneuverability. Quite apart from the administrative drains in administering so irregular a geographic configuration and the limitation

73. Julius Baum, "Die Werke des Baumeisters Heinrich Schickhardt," *WVJHLG* (1906), 103 ff.; Berthold Pfeiffer, "Das Hauptwerk des Baumeisters H. Schickhardt," *Repertorien für Kunstwissenschaft*, 27 (1904), esp. 51–53. Also, Wilhelm von Heyd, *Die Handschriften und Handzeichnungen . . . Heinrich Schickhardt* (Stuttgart, 1902); and Fleischhauer, *Renaissance*, 276–300.

74. Fleischhauer, *Renaissance*, 316–326; W. Fleischhauer, *Barock im Herzogtum Württemberg* (Stuttgart, 1958), 123 ff.; and Sattler, *Geschichte des Herzogtums*, V, 180–194.

75. E. Schneider, *Württembergische Geschichte* (Stuttgart, 1896), 201–221; Adam, "Herzog Friedrich I. von Württemberg und die Landschaft." The recent two-volume edition of the Merian engravings of 1616, *Stuttgarter Hoffeste*, ed. Ludwig Krapf and Christian Wagenknecht (Tübingen, 1979), gives striking illustration of how the new iconography was taken over by the Württemberg court; cf. Ingrid Hanack, ed., *Die Tagebücher des Herzogs Johann Friedrich von Württemberg aus den Jahren 1615–1617* (Göppingen, 1972), 177–99. For an interesting perspective on the new iconography of kingship, see F. A. Yates, *Astraea: The Imperial Theme in the Sixteenth Century* (London, 1975), 1–28; F. A. Yates, *The Valois Tapestries* (London, 1959); François Gébelin, *Les châteaux de la renaissance* (Paris, 1927), 55–62, 68–74, 97–105, 131–141; R. G. Strong, *Splendor at Court: Renaissance Spectacle and the Theater of Power* (Boston, 1973), 19–119; Jean Wilson, *Entertainments for Elizabeth I* (New York, 1980); Jonathan Brown and J. H. Elliott, *A Palace for a King: The Buen Retiro and the Court of Philip IV* (New Haven, 1980), 141–192; Graham Parry, *The Golden Age Restor'd: The Culture of the Stuart Court, 1603–42* (New York, 1981), esp. 1–37 and 184–228; and H. C. Ehalt, *Ausdrucksforem absolutistischer Herrschaft: Der Wiener Hof im 17. und 18. Jahrhundert* (Vienna, 1980).

imposed by an essentially underdeveloped economy, social configurations in the territory militated against unilateral consolidation by the central government. Specifically the Ehrbarkeit provided a formidable domestic opposition to arbitrary expansion of the sovereign's prerogative. Rooted in the Aemter, the basic unit of territorial government, these local oligarchs rose from the scattered towns and cities to confront the duke as a powerful corporate force. Their social cohesiveness was secured in the constitutional structure of the realm; they controlled the rights of taxation and could counter ducal ambitions through parliamentary obstructionism at the diet.[76] Unless the monarch could circumvent these tactics with an effective administrative alternative, his claims of unchecked authority remained rhetorical and worked themselves out in whatever theatricals his private munificence could sustain.

To counteract this opposition Friedrich relied on a group of trusted advisers, men who would carry out his policies and work to coordinate the resources of the various Aemter. The group was a mixed lot. Some men came from the ranks of the *Ritterschaften*, that corps of knights entrapped by the end of the sixteenth century in a complicated nexus of multiple loyalties and cut off from any institutionalized participation in territorial government. Others surfaced as a new breed of professionals, men who were beginning to fashion their social identity around the central administration in much the way that we have seen the sixteenth-century Ehrbarkeit organize around the local Aemter. As it happened, Friedrich reigned for only fourteen years—from 1593 to 1607—and most of his radical innovations lost momentum under the traumatic dislocations of the Thirty Years War. The details of these abortive efforts at princely absolutism belong to the chronicle of historical failures. Friedrich's predilection for a strong central government controlled entirely by himself is mentioned here because this cabinet rule, like the cosmopolitan cultural influences that inspired it and the struggle with the Ehrbarkeit that fueled it, foreshadowed eighteenth-century developments that historians have heretofore depicted as peculiar to this later period. Like the bureaucratic formations discussed in Chapter 2, these late-Renaissance political maneuverings prefigure many of the creative tensions that in subsequent periods propelled the growth of the state. Linear notions of modernization which depict the growth of the state in terms

76. Gmelin, *Ueber Herzog Friedrich I. und seine Stände;* Adam, "Herzog Friedrich I. von Württemberg und die Landschaft."

of an irrevocable process distort the Württemberg reality. In this case at least, the road to strong, aggressive central government was filled with loops and twists; more than one start would be necessary before the ultimate direction became clear.

# [ 2 ]

# Central Administration

TURNING FROM the local to the central level of territorial administration, we find in late-sixteenth-century Württemberg interactions between personnel and offices similar in many ways to those encountered in the Aemter. But whereas the consolidation of the Ehrbarkeit resulted in a closed corporation opposed by temperament and interest to aggressive administration, developments at Stuttgart took a different turn. There we can identify the formation of a corporate group whose training was professional and whose functional raison d'être lay in the growth of central government. The consolidation of this bureaucratic elite depended in part upon the institutional structure of the central government and in this regard followed a pattern that recalls the links between the Ehrbarkeit and the territorial Aemter. There were, however, marked variations. The Landtag was already in place when the Ehrbarkeit consolidated its hold over the Amt, and it was participation in that larger institution which gave the group its corporate solidarity. The high civil servants shared this characteristic of political success in that they stood at the top of their respective departmental agencies. But in their case, no larger institution existed to give them a corporate shaping. The more dynamic among them received the title of privy councilor (*Geheimer Rat*) and, though there was no privy council as such, constituted a kind of talent pool into which the prince dipped on occasion to extract advice. These councilors did not function as a board; indeed they never met collectively. But in the course of the late-sixteenth and early-seventeenth century, they began to show signs of corporate solidarity. This chapter examines the Geheime Räte and sets the formation of this bureaucratic elite in the context of central administration.

The Stuttgart government had a structural organization similar to that of most German territories. Four central departments directed routine business: the chancellery (*Kanzlei*), the judicial council (*Ober-rat*), the treasury (*Rentkammer*), and the church council (*Kirchenrat*). Since these departments provided the institutional structure out of which the high civil servants evolved, some familiarity with departmental concerns and with the rules governing personnel will help to set in context the gradual formation of a bureaucratic elite in Württemberg. Equally important, an appreciation of the division of labor in the central government enables one to assess more accurately the strengths and weaknesses in ducal rule and helps to make the subsequent appearance of the privy council intelligible.

Not all departments participated equally in the affairs of state. For each of them a series of ducal ordinances from the mid-sixteenth century spelled out the categories of their competency.[1] These *Kanzleiordnungen*, all of which the territorial estates had ratified, also regulated the number and social composition of each staff, determining for example how many departmental officials would be noble and what sort of training would be required for a given position. Finally, they stipulated that ducal approval was necessary before any official could take office and that, as a minimum, this approval must rest upon the candidate's sworn acceptance of the *Confessio Wirtembergica*, a local adaptation of the Augsburg Confession established in 1551 as the official theological position of the duchy.[2] Though standard practice in all departments, especially at the lower levels, was to appoint without written contract and for an unspecified time period, case studies illustrate that by 1629, when military reverses drove the duke into temporary exile and prompted a subsequent reordering of the government, certain high-ranking officials had succeeded in defining their offices in ways that gave them greater security and in setting up criteria for recruitment that promoted a bureaucratic professionalization of central administration. They proceeded slowly and experienced many setbacks. An examination of the four principal departments points up the degree to which this uneven progress resulted both from conscious ducal policy and from the internal structure of the agencies.

1. Kanzleiordnung of 17 November 1550 in A. Reyscher, *Vollständige, historisch und kritisch bearbeitete Sammlung der württembergischen Gesetze*, XII (Stuttgart, 1841), 173ff.; Kanzleiordnung of 26 May 1553 in Reyscher, XII, 244ff.; Kanzleiordnung of 1569 in Reyscher, XII, 377ff. See also HSAS, A 17: Bü. 1, 2, 3, 16, 19, 22, 23, 25, 27.

2. HSAS, A 34: Bü. 16 a–c; Reyscher, *Vollständige Sammlung*, I (Stuttgart, 1828), 323–326; A. Adam, *Württembergische Landtagsakten*, 2 Reihe, I (Stuttgart, 1910), 570ff.; also J. Pfister, *Herzog Christoph zu Wirtemberg*, I (Tübingen, 1819), 523–550. See Ernst Bizer, *Confessio Wirtembergica: Das württembergische Bekenntnis von 1551* (Stuttgart, 1952), for a modern edition of the text.

The Kanzlei, with its origins in the thirteenth century, was the oldest of the four departments, and in many ways it is the most difficult to describe. Its medieval function was primarily secretarial; this was the agency for disseminating ducal commands and processing the business of state. The senior scribe took the title of chancellor and directed the six or more other scribes in their copy work and in the care and preparation of government papers.[3] In the course of the fifteenth century the chancellor's duties expanded to make him one of the two or three most important officials in the realm; in effect he became a top-level policy adviser. Because he was present whenever ducal business was transacted, the chancellor acquired a cumulative knowledge of government, and his proximity to the prince and other important officials seems eventually to have transformed his role from one of mere copying to one of active participation.[4] By the mid-sixteenth century he was assisted in this capacity by a vice-chancellor; under Duke Christoph (1550–1568) the two officials operated as the center of a group of policy advisers known as Geheime Räte. Though they did not constitute an officially recognized organ of government, the Räte acquired important responsibilities and, with the chancellor as prime mover, functioned as a de facto privy council for the prince.[5]

Toward the end of the sixteenth century, however, the chancellorship declined in importance. Duke Friedrich, for example, did not fill the office for the first ten years of his reign, relying instead upon Johann Jacob Reinhardt, whom he appointed vice-chancellor, to carry out the responsibilities of both offices. In 1602, when he finally promoted Reinhardt, a Württemberg lawyer whose career is discussed below, Friedrich left the vice-chancellorship vacant. It was not until two years before his death that he placed in that position Sebastian Faber, a distinguished Franconian lawyer who had studied at the University of Marburg and earned his doctorate at Basel.[6] The two offices stabilized only in the reign of Friedrich's successor, Duke Johann Friedrich (1608–1628). Faber continued as vice-chancellor until his death in 1624, and Baron Hans Christoph von Engelshoven,

3. F. Wintterlin, *Geschichte der Behördenorganisation in Württemberg*, I (Stuttgart, 1902), 15 ff.; and Gebhard Mehring, "Beiträge zur Geschichte der Kanzlei der Grafen von Wirtemberg," *WVJHLG*, 25 (1916), 339 ff.

4. W. Bernhardt, *Die Zentralbehörden des Herzogtums Württemberg und ihre Beamten, 1520–1629*, I (Stuttgart, 1972), 25–27; I. Kothe, *Der fürstliche Rat in Württemberg im 15. und 16. Jahrhundert* (Stuttgart, 1938), 25 ff.

5. Kothe, *Der fürstliche Rat*, 59–63; Wintterlin, *Behördenorganisation*, I, 25–27; Bernhardt, *Zentralbehörden*, I, 9–13; L. von Spittler, *Geschichte des wirtembergischen Geheimen-Raths-Collegiums*, in *Sämtliche Werke*, ed. K. Wächter, XIII (Stuttgart and Tübingen, 1837), 287 ff. See also HSAS, A 17: Bü. 27 and A 89: Bü. 3.

6. HSAS, A 202: Bü. 64. Faber was brother-in-law to Chancellor J. J. Reinhardt.

a nobleman who came from outside the duchy but had studied law at Tübingen, served as chancellor until 1626.[7]

Chancellery influence faltered primarily as a result of the increased power of the *Hofkanzlei*, a kind of mini-chancellery staffed with ducal favorites rather than with trained lawyers and concerned with the private business of the ruler.[8] As was the case in most German territories, the cabinet secretariat, which flourished first in the sixteenth century, formed the institutional basis for the aggressively personal rule of the Renaissance princes.[9] By 1545 the Württemberg secretariat consisted of a full-time private secretary (*Kammersekretär*), an assistant secretary, and two scribes.[10] Its influence fluctuated with the personal inclinations of the succeeding rulers, but in the reign of Duke Ludwig (1568–1593) the cabinet secretariat attained a central importance that contributed substantively to the weakening of the chancellorship and to Ludwig's successor's indifference to that office. By 1593 it was the cabinet secretary and not the chancellor or the chancellery officials who prepared all ducal instructions to the departments and to the various privy councilors. Both these groups, moreover, were instructed to deliver all their reports *only* to the hands of the secretary (*zu eigenen Handen*).[11] A decree of 1590 went on to stipulate that the cabinet secretary, in this instance Melchior Jäger von Gärtringen, should take precedence over the chancellor and that this latter official and all chancellery personnel should take their instructions from the "Lord Secretary."[12]

Jäger's career in the Hofkanzlei not only illustrates the importance of that office but also points out the degree to which personal contact with the prince outweighed administrative process in the prewar government. Jäger (1544–1611) was born into a respectable burgher family in the duchy, the son of an official in the provincial administration at Blaubeuren. At sixteen he entered the university at Tübingen. Without taking a formal degree he left the next year to travel abroad

7. HSAS, A 17: Bü. 72. H.C. von Engelshoven was the only nobleman appointed to this office. He worked primarily on legal matters, and the vice-chancellor supervised the daily operations of the chancellery.

8. HSAS, A 17: Bü. 35, 39, 72 and A 202: Bü. 511. Werner Ohnsorge, "Zum Problem: Fürst und Verwaltung um die Wende des 16. Jahrhunderts," *Blätter für deutsche Landesgeschichte*, 88 (1951), 150ff.

9. Gerhard Oestreich, "Das persönliche Regiment der deutschen Fürsten am Beginn der Neuzeit," in G. Oestreich, *Geist und Gestalt des frühmodernen Staates: Ausgewählte Aufsätze* (Berlin, 1969), 201–234.

10. Spittler, *Geheimen-Raths-Collegiums*, 313ff.

11. C. Sattler, *Geschichte des Herzogthums Wirtenberg unter der Regierung der Herzogen*, v (Ulm, 1772), 10, reproduced the report of Secretary Franz Kurz, dated 27 November 1570; cited hereafter as Sattler, *Herzöge*.

12. Reyscher, *Vollständige Sammlung*, XII, 447ff.

with the purpose of learning foreign languages. At the age of twenty-two he returned to Württemberg and in 1566 entered ducal service as a scribe in the cabinet secretariat. He rose to Kammersekretär in 1672 and ten years later, at the urgent prompting of Duke Ludwig, received a patent of nobility from Emperor Maximilian I. In 1586 he was named Geheimer Rat and given the title of director of the cabinet secretariat.[13] Despite the resentment of the departmental officials, who referred to him as "Duke Melchior," he held that post until his death in 1611. Though his influence declined markedly under Duke Friedrich, who resented Jäger's proprietary air toward the administration, Jäger maintained his directorship and with Duke Johann Friedrich's accession in 1608 returned to full favor as a ducal councilor.[14]

Like many of the Württemberg officials, Jäger made a series of marriages that paralleled the ascending fortunes of his career: in 1570 to the daughter of a city scribe; in 1586 to Anna von Berlichingen, daughter of one of the most distinguished Ritter families in the southwest; in the early seventeenth century to Barbara von Haugsleben, an aristocrat from the territorial nobility of the north.[15] In this sense his drive for upward social mobility was no different from that of other important departmental officials. And he shared with these men, including his "subordinates" on the chancellery (Reinhardt, Faber, and Engelshoven), the distinctive title of Geheimer Rat. Jäger's career was typical of the late-sixteenth-century shift in the political center of gravity from the territorial chancellery to the cabinet secretariat. And though Jäger thought of himself as an official rather than as a courtier, his success underlined the tentative nature of bureaucratic influence in the policy making of the prewar realm. As developments in the chancellery indicated, so long as the duke dealt individually with each department, he could elevate or suppress at will that department's role in his government.

The second of these central boards, the Oberrat, saw to the administration of territorial justice and as a judicial council contributed to the setting of governmental policy. Like the chancellery, the board was of medieval origin. Its name—literally Upper Council—derived simply from the fact that the judicial officials met upstairs in the

13. Title of appointment was "persönlichen Geheimen Rat vom Adel und Direktor der Hofkanzlei," HSAS, A 17: Bü. 48, Nr. 1.

14. Bernhardt, Zentralbehörden, I, 402–406; K. Pfaff, Württembergs geliebte Herren, ed. P. Lahnstein (Stuttgart, 1965), 38–39; W. Pfeilsticker, Neues württembergisches Dienerbuch (Stuttgart, 1957), 53, 1119, 1373, 1732.

15. F. Faber, Die württembergischen Familienstiftungen (Stuttgart, 1940), 69, c. 16; also H. Rath, ed., Stuttgarter Familienregister (Stadtarchiv Stuttgart) I, 256 and II, 867.

fifteenth-century chancellery building, while the prince, attended by the chancellor and his scribes, conducted territorial business from a chamber on the ground floor.[16] Late medieval rulers often assigned special commissions to the Oberrat, but by the late sixteenth century the board functioned principally as a court of first instance for all civil cases in which one or both parties were exempt from local justice. Such exemptions were held primarily by members of the duke's family, by courtiers, by high government officials (non-noble as well as noble), and by corporate organs of government such as the central departments and the Aemter. All disputes relating to vassalage and enfeoffed property (*Lehensachen*) likewise came before this council, as did charges of marital infidelity and property disputes relating to marriage settlements. The Oberrat also heard appeals from the territorial high court (*Hofgericht*) in cases involving fines of 200 florins or more. Finally the council had to grant permission before any local court could hear a case of capital offense and give written permission before that court could pronounce a sentence of capital punishment.[17]

Both in sociological makeup and in professionalism the personnel of the Oberrat reflected the growing complexity of territorial administration and the increased emphasis on preliminary training, especially in jurisprudence. By tradition the *Landhofmeister*, the ranking member of the duke's entourage, represented the ruler on the Oberrat and served as its director. But by the end of the sixteenth century his role had become primarily ceremonial. Because of the technical complications of Reformation property settlements and the expansion of government into areas of education and charity formerly reserved to the church, a legal expertise beyond the competence of the Landhofmeister became essential for active membership on the council. Accordingly the Landhofmeister began to deputize a lawyer to represent him. The chancellor or vice-chancellor usually filled this role and presided over the court. Council membership followed much the same rules. Earlier in the century the number of Oberräte tended to remain at nine, with seven of the members holding titles of nobility. By the turn of the seventeenth century, however, both the number of members and the ratio of their various positions in society had come to reflect a more decisive emphasis upon professional training. Between 1608 and 1628, for example, aristocratic members ranged in numerical strength from six to nine whereas non-noble Räte, all of whom were trained in law and many of whom held doctorates, stood

16. Kothe, *Der fürstliche Rat*, 62.
17. Wintterlin, *Behördenorganisation*, I, 28–30; Reyscher, *Vollständige Sammlung*, XII, 508ff.; HSAS, A 2: Bü. 1, 2, 3, 5 and A 17: Bü. 1, 3.

between nine and seventeen.[18] Furthermore, by 1613 noble Oberräte were required to pass the same entrance examinations as the
non-nobles. Whether noble or not, the candidate was expected to
submit a *Proberelation*, a legal brief in which he had analyzed a case
and tendered a recommendation based upon ample citation of territorial law.[19]

Given the increased emphasis upon professionalism in the Oberrat
during the sixteenth century, it is not surprising that many bureaucrats worked their way up the administrative ladder by serving on
this council. After all, this was the central agency most concerned
with the law and most rigorous in the setting of standards for appointment. Talented young lawyers eager for a career in the government
naturally focused on this board as the agency most likely to recognize
and reward their ability. The council inevitably attracted attention
from the duke, and the ambitious could therefore hope to rise to even
greater heights of influence by providing astute legal advice. Since
the council stressed education and professional expertise, its members provided the prince with a source of administrative talent. He
often turned to the Oberrat when he needed officials to represent the
duchy in intricate negotiations with neighboring powers or with the
Reich. Of the group of high officials who carried the title of *Geheimer*
or *Hofrat* between 1593 and the founding of the privy council in 1628
almost one-half (47 percent) had served in the Oberrat.[20] In other
words, whereas the board itself had little to do with policy making, its
membership constituted a pool of trained personnel whose professional skills made them indispensable to the ruler, whatever his pre-
dilections for cabinet government.

The Rentkammer, the government department responsible for administration of ducal properties, was a sixteenth-century creation. It
owed its inspiration to the innovative Flemish-Burgundian administrative techniques introduced into Württemberg by the Austrian

18. HSAS, Landschreiberrechnungen.

19. HSAS, A 17: Bü. 18, 22, 31; A 18: Bü. 6; A 202: Bü. 24, 168; A 237a: Bü. 385.
The Württembergers took the concept of a Proberelation from the Reichskammer-
gericht, which had required the examination since 1570. In adopting such a standard of
professionalism, Württemberg stood in the vanguard of the territorial states. Whereas
Württemberg began the practice in 1573, Bavaria did not take it up until 1600,
Brandenburg-Prussia until 1693–1709, and Electoral Saxony until 1718. See Rudolf
Smend, *Das Reichskammergericht* (Weimar, 1911), 304–305.

20. The title "Hofrat" went out of fashion in the 1550s when Duke Christoph abolished the council of that name. Geheimer Rat then became the customary designation
for ducal councilors. But toward the end of that century, records indicate a revival of
the Hofrat title, used interchangeably with that of Geheimer Rat. Service on the
Oberrat can be ascertained through Pfeilsticker, *Dienerbuch*, 1190–1292, and through
the biographical portraits in Bernhardt, *Zentralbehörden*, I and II.

Habsburg officials who governed the duchy between 1519 and 1534. During these years, Württemberg became a protectorate of the House of Austria while Ulrich, the hereditary Württemberg duke (1498–1550), went into exile as imperial punishment for his armed aggression against the neighboring city-state of Reutlingen. The Austrian occupation constituted something of a turning point in Württemberg history, for it not only necessitated a reorganization of the fiscal assets of the duke but also infused the Württemberg government with standardized principles of administrative process. The Austrians established rationalized procedure for all government business and to that end proposed a collegial advisory board to coordinate the central departments. Such a council would stand apart from both the court and the judicial system and serve as a centralized agency into which the various branches of government might feed.[21] The idea took hold slowly in Württemberg and will be discussed in connection with the creation of the privy council. But it should be noted here as one of the Austrian innovations, part of that same spirit of administrative rationalization which resulted in the establishment of the Rentkammer when Ulrich returned to Stuttgart in 1535.

Ulrich set up the Rentkammer to standardize the administration of his domain.[22] The department functioned more as a trust than as a bank; it did not handle ducal moneys directly. Income from properties continued to be paid into the *Landschreiberei*, a treasury in the literal sense of that word. Lines between the trust and the treasury inevitably crossed because the Rentkammer had to give permission for the officials in the Aemter to sell the produce from the ducal estates or to convert into cash those rents paid in kind by peasants holding leases on ducal lands. In this way the trust controlled the cash flow into the treasury and was responsible for policing the Aemter accounts. But no monies passed into the trust and it is best thought of as a property management board.[23] Administration of real estate and ducal regale, referred to collectively as the *Kammergut*, was somewhat peculiar in that by the end of the sixteenth century, with the exception of some sheep farms, a few lakes for commercial fishing, and several manors near Stuttgart that supplied the court with foodstuffs, the Württemberg princes had ceased to cultivate their estates. Super-

21. H. Puchta, "Die Habsburgische Herrschaft in Württemberg, 1520–34" (Munich: Ph.D. diss., 1967); W. Grube, *Der Stuttgarter Landtag, 1457–1957* Stuttgart, 1957), 114–174.

22. H. Hamburger, *Der Staatsbankrott des Herzogtum Wirtemberg nach Herzog Ulrichs Vertreibung und die Reorganisation des Finanzwesens* (Schwäbisch Hall, 1909); Wintterlin, *Behördenorganisation*, I, 30 ff.

23. Bernhardt, *Zentralbehörden*, I, 31–50; Kothe, *Der fürstliche Rat*, 8–56.

vision of these properties therefore meant an effort to standardize tenancy contracts and a systematic accounting for and supervision over the maintenance of castles, storage barns, farmhouses, mills, and other buildings on their land.[24] Most officials on the staff of the trust were technical experts, accountants, secretaries, supervisors, and lawyers specializing in real estate contracts. But the *Kammermeister*, who directed the trust and enjoyed the particular confidence of the duke, ranked as an important government servant. During the first two decades of the seventeenth century the Kammermeister carried the additional title of Geheimer Rat and in later years held a seat on the privy council.

The Kirchenrat, like the Rentkammer, was established only in the mid-sixteenth century. It emerged out of the Reformation and the setting up in Württemberg of a territorial church. At the most obvious level the substitution of a local for an international church involved the government in the administration of properties and ecclesiastical justice and in the responsibility for those services we understand under the rubric of health, education, and welfare.[25] These charges called for echelons of officials and generated new sources of income from which to fuel government growth.[26] Here, as with the creation of the Rentkammer, the territorial estates played no role at all: religious reform sprang entirely from ducal initiative, as administrative advances came from Habsburg officials. The estates continued to guard their powers of taxation but extraction per se does not appear to have been an issue in the Reformation settlement. The prince continued to provide for himself and to rely on the estates only for help in emergencies, so that the estates entered only peripherally into these changes.[27] As in most of Germany, princes and bureaucrats rather than traditional corporate units set the direction for this initial stage of government expansion.

The Kanzleiordnung of 1553 established the Kirchenrat as an official branch of the central government and divided the department into two agencies.[28] The secular arm, referred to as *politischer Kir-*

24. Wintterlin, *Behördenorganisation*, I, 31–41.
25. HSAS, A 17: Bü. 1, 2, 25; A 201: Bü. 66.
26. V. Ernst, "Die Entstehung des württembergischen Kirchenguts," *WJSL* (1911), 377–424; H. Hermelink, "Geschichte des allgemeinen Kirchenguts in Württemberg," *WJSL* (1903), I, 96 ff.; H. Hermelink, "Die Aenderung der Klosterverfassung unter Herzog Ludwig," *WVJHLG*, 12 (1903), 284–327; L. Heyd, *Ulrich, Herzog zu Württemberg*, III (Tübingen, 1844), 173–200; C. von Stälin, *Wirtembergische Geschichte*, IV (Stuttgart, 1873), 389 ff. and 734 ff.; Sattler, *Herzöge*, IV, 212 ff.; and Christoph Kolb, "Zur Geschichte der Prälaturen," *BWKG*, 29 (1925), 22–74.
27. Grube, *Stuttgarter Landtag*, 182–193.
28. Reyscher, *Vollständige Sammlung*, VIII, 42 ff. and 69 ff.; Wintterlin, *Behördenorganisation*, I, 40–43.

*chenrat*, supervised the clerical courts and administered ecclesiastical property. In this latter capacity the Kirchenrat maintained a central account (*Kirchenkasten*) into which all ecclesiastical income flowed and from which all expenses for the operation of the territorial church were paid. A separate entry was preserved for moneys from the fourteen great monastic trusts because, under the terms of the settlement, the duke and the estates were allowed to draw from the surplus on these properties for expenses incurred for military defense and for projects for the common good (*für das gemeine Landeswohl*). This particular board also regulated the practice of medicine in the duchy, took care of the poor, oversaw the curriculum and staffing of the University of Tübingen, and attended to the provision of instruments and musicians for the duke's chapel. A second agency, referred to in the Kanzleiordnung of 1590 as the consistory (*Consistorium*), guarded the purity of Lutheran doctrine and advised the duke on the staffing of the pulpits and schools of the duchy.[29]

Revenues from the ecclesiastical properties, like those generated by the Rentkammer, varied with the harvest and the price index. But whatever their fluctuating value, they constituted an important source of revenue. In 1551, for example, the ducal councilors estimated total government income, including the ordinary taxes of 32,000 florins, at 124,160 florins. They reckoned the yield from ducal lands that year at only 12,818 florins, or 10 percent of the total, so that we can assume an ecclesiastical contribution of 79,342 florins, approximately 64 percent of the income.[30] Much of the church's money went to defray its expenses, but in that the ruler could lay claim to at least a portion of the surplus—and the percentage of that portion was a matter of constant friction with the estates who also claimed rights over these moneys—the staffing of the Kirchenrat received careful ducal attention. A Kirchenrat director presided over both subcommittees of the department. Except for the secretaries, his consistory officials consisted entirely of theologians, most often the two court pastors and the chief pastor of the Stuttgart *Stiftskirche*. But members of the "political" board, like the director himself, tended to be lawyers who worked to guard ducal interests against the theologians, who resented their dependence upon the political board and bristled at any efforts except their own to regulate doctrine. Between 1584 and 1629 all the directors held doctorates in law rather than in divinity, and for all

29. Reyscher, *Vollständige Sammlung*, XII, 447ff.

30. HSAS, *tomus actorum*, I, Fasc. 285–313; I, A, Fasc. 318–344. Stälin, *Wirtembergische Geschichte*, IV, 721n1 and 727; Pfister, *Herzog Christoph zu Wirtemberg*, I, 535; Bernhard von Kugler, *Christoph, Herzog zu Wirtemberg*, I (Stuttgart, 1868), 284 and II (Stuttgart, 1872), 579–580 and 589–590.

but thirteen years of this period the director functioned also as a Geheimer Rat.

In addition to the four major departments, two standing committees assisted the duke in the central government. Neither committee functioned as a collegiate whole; the members performed other duties and participated in policy decisions primarily as individuals and only at the invitation of the duke. The first and least significant at this time consisted of a group, which varied in size, of military officers known as *Kriegsräte*. These officers, most of whom were imperial knights holding fiefs from the House of Württemberg, served as councilors on matters of tactics and supply in the event of war. They took no part in the direction of such regular military affairs as the ongoing supervision of the territorial fortresses and the maintenance of the ducal artillery, the only two permanent components of the territorial military effort. Rather they counseled as general advisers on those matters of interest to the duke.[31] The other, more important group was the Geheime Räte, also a pool of advisers rather than a functioning agency, though records survive of sporadic committee meetings in the first three years of the seventeenth century. Even on those occasions attendance fluctuated; the Landhofmeister, the chancellor, and the head of the Oberrat formed only a relatively stable nucleus. The other participants, all of whom came from the highest levels of service, attended or not, apparently at the discretion of the Landhofmeister.[32] At any event it was from this extended group that the privy council was constituted in 1628.

Prior to the creation of the privy council no office existed around which the high bureaucracy might coalesce as a group. We have seen how each department discharged its responsibilities through direct contact with the monocratic ruler; collective administrative energies fused only in his person. As a practical matter this architectonic administration ensured that only the prince, and those advisers in whom he chose to confide, possessed an overview of the affairs of state. Officials in an agency discharged their commissions with only an accidental knowledge of the activities in the other branches of government. One can assume of course that, in a small-scale setting such as early-seventeenth-century Stuttgart, the departmental chiefs saw one another almost daily and discussed common professional concerns. But since each official had sworn to protect the confidentiality of his agency's business, these ad hoc exchanges must have been in-

---

31. Wintterlin, *Behördenorganisation*, I, 44–45.
32. HSAS, A 204: Bü. 1 contains the protocolla for 1602–1603.

complete and could not in themselves have produced a coherent policy of administration. So long as their professional duties remained compartmentalized, it was difficult for the high officials to develop the comprehensive expertise that might enable them to participate as a force in the direction of territorial government.

The concept of Geheimer Rat provided the loose framework within which these high officials developed their corporate sensibilities. It is tempting to conceive of these early councilors in collegial terms, as an advisory board whose members were working their way toward comprehensive recommendations for the sovereign. But the fact was otherwise. The title carried with it no institutional membership; it was rather a designation bestowed by the ruler on those important officials to whom he wished to turn for advice. A man so named continued in his official capacity as a departmental chief or as a court official but in addition stood ready to supply the prince with whatever personal service that ruler might wish. A Geheimer Rat rendered his service as an individual and developed his links to the other Räte through common values rather than office. As a group the privy councilors came to share standards of professionalism and a commitment to rational principles of administration, and in this sense these early-seventeenth-century officials can best be thought of as personnel in the process of constructing an office.

Thirty Geheime Räte can be identified between 1593 and 1628. Only five of these dignitaries functioned strictly as courtiers—that is, as men who never engaged directly in the administration of central government.[33] They served as chamberlains or masters of the household and in such offices advised the duke on matters of domestic concern. They participated as "cronies" rather than as "professional officials" in the formulation of Württemberg state policy. This court group consisted entirely of noblemen, all but one of whom grew up outside the duchy. The exception, Count Johann Jacob von Eberstein (1574–1638), came from a family seated in Baden but with extensive Württemberg properties (held as fiefs of the ducal house) and with a long tradition of service at the Stuttgart court.[34] Whereas a university education prepared Eberstein for his career, the others rose to favor through personality or family influence; no evidence exists of

33. The five Räte holding only court office were Count Johann Jacob von Eberstein (1574–1638), Hans Georg von Hallweil (died 1593), Baron Hieronymus von Mörsperg und Beffort (died 1614), Baron Johann von Sprinzenstein auf Neuhaus (1551–1604), and Joachim von Trauschwitz (1561–1626).

34. Bernhardt, *Zentralbehörden*, I, 235–236; Pfeilsticker, *Dienerbuch*, 51, 209, 1087, 1127, 1525, 1526, 2409, 2952, 2984, 3052; O. von Alberti, *Württembergisches Adels- und Wappenbuch* (Neustadt an der Aisch, 1975), 144–145.

their having undertaken advanced studies. In these terms the group constituted an alternative to the more professionally oriented majority of high civil servants and fueled the momentum of cabinet rule.

The remaining twenty-five Räte served at one time or another as directors, vice-chairmen, or leading spokesmen in one or more of the central departments. Although their career patterns varied, each was a highly trained professional with expertise in law, foreign languages, or the military. Only one of them, Johann Magirus (1537–1614), rose through the Lutheran pastorate. He became a Geheimer Rat after he had been named provost of the Stuttgart Ecclesiastical Trust and had earned a reputation as a leading member on the consistorial board of the Kirchenrat.[35] The others held more explicitly administrative posts in the chancellery, the judicial council, or the ducal trust. The usual course in this regard was for the individual official to work his way up through the ranks of departmental service, although direct appointment to high office was not impossible. Records indicate that ducal command placed four noble and two non-noble officials in high office without their having proved themselves in prior administrative service. In each instance, however, the appointment could have been justified in terms of extensive professional training.

The two non-noble Räte who achieved their rank through direct appointment, Melchior Jäger and Matthäus Enslin (1556–1613), served the prince as private secretaries and are thus more properly described as personal rather than as professional officials.[36] Nevertheless both came to their posts with impressive credentials. Jäger, as mentioned earlier, handled several foreign languages; Enslin, prior to his arrival at Stuttgart, had been a professor of law at Tübingen. The careers of the four nobles appointed through personal contacts reflected a similar range of prior practical experience. The only native-born Württemberger in the group, Christoph von Laimingen (1568–1640), began his career as a page in the ducal household. But since his father served as Landhofmeister and in that capacity presided ex officio over the central departments, Christoph's appointment in 1609 to the Oberrat and Rentkammer must have surprised no one.[37] At any event, he had prepared himself for such office by extensive legal study at the Universities of Tübingen and Siena. While the other

---

35. Pfeilsticker, *Dienerbuch*, 2022, 2818; Bernhardt, *Zentralbehörden*, I, 482–483; HSAS, J 19: Bü. 68.

36. On Enslin's career, see Pfeilsticker, *Dienerbuch*, 1137, 1378, 2029, 2690, 2947, 2958. Also, Bernhardt, *Zentralbehörden*, I, 263–270; *Neue Deutsche Biographie*, IV (Berlin, 1968), 542–543; Faber, *Die württembergischen Familienstiftungen*, 40, 13.

37. Bernhardt, *Zentralbehörden*, I, 453–456; Pfeilsticker, *Dienerbuch*, 1196, 1653, 1708.

Stuttgart and its environs. Innovations in government must not obscure the fact that the capital city remained relatively small, with wild game roaming within sight of the outer walls. This painting by Hans Steiner (1589) captures the integration of town and countryside and conveys the comparative isolation of a city ringed on all sides by mountains. The town gallows stands just outside the duke's pleasure gardens. Photograph courtesy of the Landesbildstelle Württemberg.

three Hofräte enjoyed no such distinguised family tie to the Stuttgart government, they too had studied at both German and foreign universities and so arrived at Stuttgart with substantial linguistic and legal credentials.[38] For nobles as well as burghers, then, certain professional training determined eligibility even for direct appointment.

It is clear that by the late sixteenth century the very nature of government service in Württemberg was changing. We see the shift quite vividly in the marked differentiation surfacing between appointment to government office and employment at court. Prior to the Reformation, lines between court and government appeared blurred at Stuttgart, but by the end of the century chancellery documents distinguished routinely between members of the court (*Hofgesinde*) and administrative officials (*Räte und Diener*), and so between public and private service.[39] Concomitantly, the more important public servants sought to ground their employment on clearly defined terms of obligation and reward. In the case of the early-seventeenth-century councilors, for example, we find consistent examples of contracts drawn between duke and individual adviser which regulated the terms of the latter's appointment. Negotiations for these offices, so far as we can infer from the extant contracts, proceeded amiably and with great deference expressed by each official. Nowhere was there a hint of adversary relationships. Furthermore the duke retained full initiative in every case and regarded himself as the sole arbiter of administrative propriety. But despite the occasional ducal idiosyncrasy, the similarity of the contracts indicates that the officials were succeeding in stabilizing bureaucratic positions and in establishing conditions of service that would give them a cohesive identity in Württemberg society. At least eight Geheime Räte succeeded a fellow Rat to bureaucratic office; and in every instance but one the conditions and rewards of the office in question remained the same.[40]

The correspondence of 1602, naming Dr. Johann Jacob Reinhardt

---

38. Benjamin von Bouwinghausen-Walmerode (1571–1635) studied at Cologne and at universities in Italy, France, and Spain (HSAS A 153: Bü. 20); Bleickhardt von Helmstätt (1551–1636) studied at the Universities of Siena and Heidelberg (A. Schmidt, "Pleickhards v. Helmstätt Stammbäume süddeutscher Adelsgeschlechte um 1612," *Zeitschrift für die Geschichte des Oberrheins* NF 31 [1916], 53–64); Christoph Fircks von Nurmhausen (died 1649) studied at the Universities of Padua and Rostock (Oskar Stavenhagen, *Geneologisches Handbuch der kurländischen Ritterschaft* [Görlitz, 1930], 59 and 62–64).

39. Wintterlin, *Behördenorganisation*, I, 46–52.

40. On salaries, see HSAS, A 18: Bü. 9 (Kanzler); A 17: Bü. 14, 16 and A 201: Bü. 2a (Oberräte); A 17: Bü. 14, 16, 73 and A 282: Bü. 2251 (Kammermeister); A 201: Bü. 2a and A 282: Bü. 51 (Kirchenrat Director); A 64: Bü. 11, A 201: Bü. 16, A 282: Bü. 1600, and A 525: Bü. 31 (Propst of Stuttgart).

(1556–1609) as lord chancellor, spelled out the procedure followed in the appointment of high officials.[41] Reinhardt's career is interesting because it followed the pattern of training, experience, and professional orientation typical of non-noble Geheime Räte at this time. Like most of his colleagues Reinhardt was born inside the boundaries of the duchy, in this case in the little town of Steinheim, where his father held a managerial position in the provincial ducal service. In 1571 Reinhardt entered the university at Tübingen and took up the study of law. Upon completing his doctorate, he left Württemberg for a five-year apprenticeship as a lawyer on the Imperial Supreme Court (*Reichskammergericht*) at Speyer. There he not only widened his political perspective but also acquainted himself with the theories and practice of the common law of the empire. His command of imperial law brought him to the attention of Duke Friedrich, who summoned Reinhardt to Stuttgart and made him, at the age of thirty-seven, vice-chancellor and Hofrat. In the latter capacity he represented Friedrich at various imperial diets and traveled throughout the duchy on his master's business. In 1602 he became chancellor and served in that important position until he retired in 1608, just one year before his death. In the course of his career Reinhardt was married three times, on each occasion to a woman whose social rank mirrored his current position on the ladder of professional success: first to the daughter of a Heilbronn official; then in 1600 to the widow of a distinguished lawyer and Württemberg civil servant; and in 1607 to the daughter of an aristocratic family of knights.[42]

Official word of the ducal decision to name him chancellor reached Reinhardt in the form of a *Bestellungskunde*, a letter from Friedrich's private secretary which spelled out the terms of appointment and included a ducal gloss on the responsibilities listed in the most recent Kanzleiordnung. Reinhardt replied in writing with a *Revers*, a statement accepting the offer and setting down his own perception of the chancellorship and his expectations in terms of compensation and obligation. Friedrich combined these two memoranda in a document called the *Staat und Revers*, which Reinhardt signed as the article of appointment.[43] The details of this contract do not concern us, but

41. HSAS, A 202: Bü. 63.

42. Pfeilsticker, *Dienerbuch*, 1107, 1111, 1305, 1338, 1378, 1720, 2058, 2822, 2917, 3497; Bernhardt, *Zentralbehörden*, II, 553–554; Faber, *Die württembergischen Familienstiftungen*, III (Stuttgart, 1940), 137; Rath, *Stuttgarter Familienregister* (Stadtarchiv Stuttgart), II, 514; J. Kindler von Knobloch and O. von Stotzingen, *Oberbadisches Geschlechterbuch*, III (Heidelberg, 1898), 465.

43. HSAS, A 202: Bü. 63. For a general discussion of the Staat und Revers, see Wintterlin, *Behördenorganisation*, I, 50–51.

THE MAKING OF A STATE

certain points are of interest as indications of the contemporary status of the civil servant. For example, though the contract established the duke as the unquestioned authority in the administration and stipulated that all officials held office at his pleasure, it also stated that Reinhardt could not be dismissed (or resign) without three months' notice. Similarly, there were guarantees of compensation "in the event of physical or emotional sickness." No mention was made of a pension upon retirement, but other records indicate that, when retirement followed naturally upon the infirmities of old age and not ducal displeasure, high officials were receiving at least a portion of their salary.[44] Finally the contact guaranteed lifetime tenure in the office and gave Reinhardt a free hand in the internal supervision of the chancellery. A proviso with a nod to the possibility of later ducal displeasure reserved to the ruler full rights of revocation, preempting any tendency by Reinhardt to regard the office as a fief or to claim "squatter's rights" for himself and his descendants.

Two additional pieces of evidence carry us outside the Reinhardt case and strengthen the impression that his efforts to regularize his appointment reflected a growing self-consciousness among the high Württemberg officials. The first involved the career of Karl Carray, who in 1574 came to Stuttgart from Mömpelgard to serve on the judicial council. In 1588 Carray incurred disfavor and lost his position as *Registrator*, or principal secretary, to the council. Quite apart from the loss of salary and benefits, the social ramifications of Carray's disgrace were extensive. On the assumption that Carray had broken his oath of obedience to the duke, the municipal government of Stuttgart pronounced him a man of bad character and struck his name from the city rolls, thereby revoking his rights of citizenship. Moreover, despite the fact that his wife's family had served for generations in the municipal government, the magistrates denied him the right even to rent an apartment within the city walls until he should be granted pardon from the duke. Even when the duke changed his mind and appeared willing to reappoint Carray to office, the Hofräte continued to debate among themselves whether or not his character had been so tainted as to render him unfit to swear an oath of office. Their correspondence on the subject shows that their concern grew out of a belief that the right to swear an oath transcended the boundaries of ducal inclination and provided officeholders with a kind of moral cement

44. See for example, pension evidence in bibliographies on Sebastian Braunsteingen, Johann Büschler, M. Simon Keller, Rudolf Koler, Dr. Amandus Mögling, B. Rössling, Philipp Schertlin, Lorenz Schmidlin, M. Blasin Wagner, Sebastian Faber, Paulus Huldenreich, Melchior Jäger, and Konrad Schupp in Bernhardt, *Zentralbehörden*, I and II.

for their social order. The Hofräte wanted to stress the importance of loyal service as an effective device for setting them apart from the rest of Württemberg society.[45]

A memorial written in 1578 by Melchior Jäger, three years before he became a Hofrat, spoke to yet another element in the psychology of the high official. The accession of Duke Ludwig, who ruled from 1578 to 1593 and whom Jäger had tutored as a young prince, provided the occasion for the document, which Jager presented as a position paper on the nature of successful monarchy:

> An ideal governor should be the father of his country (*pater patriae*) . . . not reach his decisions unilaterally but with the advice of his officials (*Beamten*). . . . The prince should avoid flattering courtiers and, once having made a decision in consultation with his officials, should hold firm in his resolution so as to avoid generating feelings of distrust among his officials and disruptions in the orderly workings of the administration. . . . [The prince should] tolerate contradiction by his officials, when these objections are advanced with solid documentation, rational analysis, and becoming modesty.[46]

Jäger, as we have seen, served in the cabinet secretariat rather than in one of the central departments and therefore depended more upon the personal favor of the prince than did the departmental bureaucrats. His subsequent career as private secretary, moreover, worked often to undermine the influence of the other privy councilors. But on this occasion he wrote as a Beamte and not as a favorite and his emphasis on professional consultation and due administrative process found considerable resonance among the other civil servants. His tone was not unlike one that might be found in a contract for appointment. Like Reinhardt, Jäger indicated that there was a separation in his mind between the will of the prince and administrative office. The office remained subject to the prince, of course, but the official participated in the proper exercise of ducal authority.

Compensation for this participation was negotiated at the highest levels of the civil service between the official and the duke; for the lower ranks each appointment carried a fixed stipend.[47] Once again the early-seventeenth-century contract for Chancellor Reinhardt provides a useful index for these procedures. Reinhardt, like all officials, reckoned his salary in kind as well as in money. The salary, computed

45. HSAS, A 351: Bü. 3.
46. HSAS, A 201: Bü. 11a, Nr. 8a (Memorial of 8 October 1578).
47. Bernhardt, *Zentralbehörden*, I, 96ff. Württemberg salaries, according to Bernhardt, were lower than those paid in the neighboring principalities and city-states.

on an annual basis, was paid out in a lump sum, with produce payments forming by far the largest portion of the wage. Reinhardt had a cash stipend of 200 florins with a supplemental allowance of 34 florins 40 kreuzer to defray delivery charges on the clothing, grain, wine, and firewood that he also received. He took care to stipulate that these emoluments be subject to a fixed measurement rather than to current market value, so that regardless of price fluctuations he received two sets of court dress, three tuns of wine, 100 cords of wood, 100 bushels each of hay and spelt, and twelve bushels of rye. The total monetary value of these goods can be estimated at somewhere around 1,206 florins, ensuring Reinhardt of an annual equivalent of some 1,406 florins.[48] As chancellor Reinhardt earned considerably more than the other departmental officials but less than the provosts of the Stuttgart church properties.[49] Hofrat and Provost Magirus, for example, earned a total of some 1,588 florins, 300 florins of which were paid in cash. Other departmental officials fared less well. The director of the Rentkammer, Hofrat Martin Ludwig von Remchingen (died 1614), received a stipend whose total value, including payments in kind, did not exceed 573 florins.[50] Kirchenrat Director and Hofrat Balthasar Eisengrein (died 1611) earned only 510 florins worth of goods and cash.[51]

Landhofmeister Baron Eberhard Schenk zu Limpurg (1560–1622) received the highest wage of all: a yearly cash salary of 350 florins supplemented by payments in kind valued at over 1,300 florins and by free room and board for himself and six servants. In addition, in 1609 the duke awarded him a bonus as a sign of special favor (*Gnaden auf sein Person*). The bonus consisted of 300 florins in cash, one tun of the best ducal wine, food for two additional servants, and straw and hay for two horses.[52] The various contracts indicate that the discrepancies between salaries reflected differences in the importance of the office rather than personal distinctions among the officials. Geheimer Rat Reinhardt earned more as chancellor than his counterpart on the Rentkammer, the noble Geheimer Rat von Remchingen; the chancellorship was considered the more significant position. Departmental salaries in other words rested on office, though within that office values could vary. In 1606, for example, Remchingen left the Rentkammer to become Landhofmeister. His salary rose appreciably but fell

48. HSAS, A 202: Bü. 63.
49. HSAS, A 64: Bü. 11; A 201: Bü. 16; A 282: Bü. 1600; A 525: Bü. 31.
50. HSAS, A 202: Bü. 57.
51. HSAS, A 202: Bü. 243; A 282: Bü. 1877.
52. HSAS, A 202: Bü. 59.

far short of what his immediate successor, Baron Limpurg, was to earn.[53] Both these men were aristocrats: Remchingen came from the territorial service nobility; Limpurg from an ancient family of imperial knights. These nuances of pedigree might well have figured into Duke Friedrich's calculations, but the extant documentation suggests that the differential lay in personality rather than in gradations of nobility.

The Landhofmeister provided the link that joined vassals, court, and departmental administration and stood thus as the highest official of the land.[54] Although the office was reserved by territorial law for noblemen, the other high offices were open alike to noble and non-noble talent; in each instance compensation was negotiated without respect to social origin. Yet this generalization is not to suggest that social lines were losing all meaning. Indeed, in the early eighteenth century the pendulum swung back and gradations of birth loomed large. At that time dramatic differences obtained in opportunities for advancement in government and in the salaries paid to noble and non-noble officeholders, setting Württemberg in marked contrast to a state like France where each bureaucratic office carried a prescribed set of emoluments and responsibilities and conferred a status upon the holder without regard to his birth. It should be pointed out that prior to the Thirty Years War Württemberg preserved a semantic separation within the category of civil service between the aristocratic and common officials. The former carried the designation of *adelige Räte;* burghers were referred to as *gelehrte Räte*. But as the cases of Reinhardt and Remchingen illustrated, these distinctions had not yet promoted caste monopolies or discriminations in salary within the Hofräte. Both adelige and gelehrte Räte entered chancellery vocabulary as "Räte und Diener," and although their titles preserved a social differentiation, nobles and non-nobles moved with ease in government service and received equal (if sometimes separate) treatment.

Office therefore outweighed traditional considerations of birth in matters of salary, contract, and tenure. Biographical statistics on the privy councilors likewise reveal similarities in background and training and suggest an internal emphasis on professional rank which encouraged a loosening of traditional social distinctions. Nobility remained a highly desirable social category, but bureaucratic office was now bestowing its own status. In so doing, administrative rank determined educational and even marital patterns, thereby prefiguring in

53. HSAS, A 202: Bü. 57.
54. HSAS, A 202: Bü. 59. See *Staat und Instructionen* of 23 April 1609, the document spelling out the duties of Eberhard Schenk zu Limpurg as Landhofmeister.

the late Renaissance much that historians have associated with the growth of eighteenth-century bureaucracy. Like the late-eighteenth-century bureaucrats, the Württemberg Geheime Räte represented both aristocratic and burgher elements. Of the twenty-five professional privy councilors, fourteen came out of non-noble families and entered service as gelehrte Räte.[55] Two of the burghers, Melchior Jäger and Johann Kielmann (1568–1633), acquired titles of nobility in the course of their careers.[56] In the classic pattern of the upwardly mobile, they used their professional success to secure title and raise their families into the aristocracy. But in neither case did the "promotion" appear to have affected their careers in the bureaucracy. Kielmann von Kielmannseck continued to serve on the Oberrat, though now as a nobleman, and Jäger von Gärtringen pressed forward on a course whose success depended only upon ducal favor. Nor does the evidence indicate that the other gelehrte Räte, many of whom were just as successful as Kielmann, strove for ennoblement. In marked contrast to their eighteenth-century counterparts, these officials appeared to lay little stress on acquiring titles of nobility; high office conferred sufficient status.[57]

As a group the Räte shared certain basic characteristics. In the first place, they had a common geographical background. Sixty-four per-

55. Kilian Brastberger (1569–1614); Dr. Veit Breitschwerdt (1565–1631); Dr. Christian Dold (1550–1602); Balthasar Eisengrein (died 1611); Dr. Matthäus Enslin (1556–1613); Georg Esslinger (1560–1622); Dr. Sebastian Faber (1564–1624); Dr. Johann Jakob Haug (1553–1618); Johann Georg Hüngerlin (1551–1629); Melchior Jäger [von Gärtringen] (1544–1611); Johann Kielmann [von Kielmannseck] (1568–1633); Dr. Jakob Löffler (1582–1638); Johann Magirus (1537–1614); Dr. Johann Jakob Reinhardt (1556–1609).

56. Alberti, *Wappenbuch*, 397, states that in 1568 Johann Kielmann, father of the privy councilor and surgeon to the Württemberg duke, received confirmation of noble status from Emperor Maximilian II. But his son Johann entered the Württemberg Oberrat in 1590 as Johann Kielmann, gelehrter Rat. It was not until the 1620s that he appeared in the chancellery records as Johann Kielmann von Kielmannseck. See Pfeilsticker, *Dienerbuch*, 1137, 1209; and Bernhardt, *Zentralbehörden*, I, 428–429.

57. Dr. Balthasar Eisengrein, for example, was the son of a Württemberg official who in 1541 had received a patent of nobility from Emperor Charles V. Balthasar never used the "von" and remained a gelehrter Rat for his entire career in service. HSAS, A 17: Bü. 31 contains an interesting exchange between several gelehrte Räte on the financial disadvantages in accepting a title of nobility. These writers make clear that they regard professional distinction as sufficient for conveying the most desirable social status. See also a report from the Kirchenrat (1609) in A 282: Bü. 282 on the importance of office. In "Die Entstehung der altwürttembergischen Ehrbarkeit, 1250–1534" (Erlangen: Ph.D. diss. 1946), 33–47, Hans Decker-Hauff stresses office as central to definitions of status, and in his *Geschichte der Stadt Stuttgart*, I (Stuttgart, 1966), makes the repeated point that self-conscious solidarity among the established Württemberg families was such that the bulk of the sixteenth-century professionals showed little interest in acquiring noble rank, preferring instead to emphasize their links to the Ehrbarkeit. See also Spittler, *Geheimen-Raths-Collegiums*, 359ff.

cent of the officials came from Württemberg, and a sound majority of those born elsewhere claimed at least some family tradition in the duchy. It would therefore seem that, though physical place of birth did not determine a career, a strong regional identification increased professional visibility and facilitated a decision to enter the Württemberg government. The eleven adelige Räte comprised the most geographically diverse group,[58] and even in this instance a substantial core of five noblemen—Hans Wolf von Anweil (1544–1613), Christoph von Degenfeld (1535–1604), Ludwig Andreas Lemblin von Reinhardshofen (died 1635), Christoph von Laimingen, and Martin Ludwig von Remchingen—were born within Württemberg's borders. All but Lemblin, who came from a family of imperial knights seated outside Heilbronn, were the sons of men in ducal employ and followed their fathers into government service.[59] The remaining aristocrats, though technically "outsiders," belonged to families with connections that in several cases helped to explain their presence at Stuttgart. Baron Limpurg's family, for example, had put in generations of service at the Württemberg court, though Limpurg himself grew up at Heidelberg where his father was court chamberlain to the elector palatine.[60] Bleickhardt von Helmstätt (1551–1636), who succeeded Limpurg as Landhofmeister, likewise came from the Palatinate. But his family held numerous Württemberg fiefs and over the years had maintained close associations with Stuttgart.[61] The remaining four noble Räte, Benjamin von Bouwinghausen-Walmerode (1571–1635), Franz de Boys (1544–1615), Christoph Fircks von Nurmhausen (died 1649), and Hans Christoph von Engelshoven (1555–1626), migrated from Nassau, Frankfurt am Main, Kurland, and Alsace respectively. Neither of the first three had any prior connection with Württemberg, but Engelshoven's family had served in Mömpelgard so that, like Helmstätt and Limpurg, he came to Stuttgart through longstanding associations with the House of Württemberg.[62]

58. Hans Wolf von Anweil (1544–1613); Franz du Boys (1544–1615); Christoph von Degenfeld (1535–1604); Hans Christoph von Engelshoven (1555–1626); Christoph Fircks von Nurmhausen (died 1649); Christoph von Laimingen (1568–1640); Ludwig Andreas Lemblin von Reinhardshofen (died 1635); Eberhard Freiherr Schenck zu Limpurg (1560–1622); Bleickhardt von Helmstätt (1551–1636); Martin Ludwig von Remchingen (died 1614); Benjamin von Bouwinghausen-Walmerode (1571–1635).

59. Anweil's father studied at Tübingen and served on the Oberrat, 1595–1599; Degenfeld's father was Obervogt zu Göppingen; Laimingen's father held the office of Landhofmeister, 1579–1596; and Remchingen's father sat on the Oberrat, 1573–1576.

60. Stälin, *Wirtembergische Geschichte*, II (Stuttgart, 1841), 600–606; K. Müller, "Das Geschlecht der Reichserbschenken zu Limpurg bis zum Aussterben des Mannesstammes (1713)," ZWLG (1941), 215–243.

61. Schmidt, "Pleickhards v. Helmstätt Stammbäume," 53 ff.

62. Pfeilsticker, *Dienerbuch*, 505, 1105, 1117, 1193, 1300, 1388, 2804; HSAS, J 19:

The fourteen gelehrte Räte were even more alike in their origins. All but three of them were born in Württemberg, and two of the "outsiders," Christian Dold (1550–1602) and Johann Georg Hüngerlin (1551–1629), came there early in their careers to study law at Tübingen.[63] The other, Sebastian Faber (1564–1624), earned his doctorate at Basel but married the sister of Chancellor J. J. Reinhardt, who in 1606 recommended him to the duke for the position of vice-chancellor.[64] There are no discernible geographic subgroups among the native Württembergers. Surprisingly only two of the councilors came from Stuttgart: Kielmann, whose father had been personal physician to the duke; and Kilian Brastberger (1569–1614), son of the former Württemberg chancellor Johann Brastberger (1535–1581).[65] Tübingen, the duchy's second city, provided none at all. Instead, most of the gelehrte Räte grew up in one of the various Amt towns scattered throughout the duchy. No one was raised in a village or on a farm, so that one can think of the non-noble component as urban, but small-town in its origins.

As for economic status within their respective communities, the councilors composed a basically homogeneous group. Only Provost Magirus was of humble background; the other gelehrte Räte were sons or close relatives of provincial Württemberg officials, who ranked among the social and economic elite in their home territories. The aristocrats showed a similar economic profile: Baron Limpurg alone among the group could boast of extensive family wealth; the others were offspring of well-to-do Württemberg officials or middling courtiers in neighboring territorial services. Most Geheime Räte married at least once, usually before reaching the apex of their careers. Although details on these marriages are spotty, we have sufficient evidence for the aristocrats to say that, in every known instance of marriage, the bride was noble—most often a lady from one of the neighboring families of imperial knights.[66] The gelehrte Räte's choices

Bü. 43. Alberti, *Wappenbuch*, 166, gives the family's origins as Bavarian or Austrian; Bernhardt, *Zentralbehörden*, I, 260, cites his father as Amtmann zu Reichenweier and Hofmeister to Barbara Sophie von Württemberg.

63. Hüngerlin matriculated at Tübingen in 1570 (HSAS, A 17: Bü. 25). Dold, who grew up in the Landgravate of Hessen, entered Tübingen in 1570 and received his doctorate in 1582 (HSAS, A 17: Bü. 48 and A 274: Bü. 53). See also, Pfeilsticker, *Dienerbuch*, 1110, 2032.

64. For Faber, see HSAS, J 9: Bü. 44 and A 202: Bü. 64; also, Faber, *Die württembergischen Familienstiftungen*, XXIX, A and B. 2.

65. On Brastberger, see Bernhardt, *Zentralbehörden*, I, 184–186.

66. We have no information on du Boys and Lemblin; Fircks's two marriages took place after he had left Württemberg service. Five of the other nobles married while in office, and at least one of these marriages was to the daughter of a Württemberg offi-

were less homogeneous: of the seven non-noble officials who married while in office, four married noblewomen.[67] From the entire cohort of Geheime Räte, thirteen officials fathered children who lived to enter high government service or to marry prominent Württemberg officials. These marriages, it should be stressed, were not confined always to high officials, and the evidence for the group is by no means comprehensive. Nevertheless, at least seven marriages between the children or immediate relations of the gelehrte and adelige Räte can be documented.[68] This pattern suggests that, when plans were made for the second generation, status in government service might obscure those social distinctions that earlier had seemed more important.

Emphasis upon education provided yet another unifying bond among the councilors. They all, noble as well as non-noble, attended at least one German university[69] and in every case but one studied law. The exception, Provost Magirus, is an ambiguous case. We know that from 1553 to 1559 he was enrolled at Tübingen, where he held a fellowship.[70] It is not known what classes he attended—he took no advanced degree—but, given his subsequent career as a pastor, abbot, and provost, it seems most likely that he studied theology rather than law. In addition to a common curriculum most Räte shared a similar university experience: all but four of them took at least a portion of their study at Tübingen.[71] There they acquired the technical mastery of Württemberg law which enabled them to serve subsequently as administrative officials in the Stuttgart government. Work together in the small seminars and lecture courses must also have en-

---

cial: in 1579 Anweil married Maria Felicitas von Münchingen, whose father was ducal Kammermeister (HSAS, J 19: Bü. 19). The other nobles entered service already married.

67. J. J. Reinhardt, Melchior Jäger [von Gärtringen], Christian Dold, and Jakob Löffler.

68. Totals were compiled through an analysis of the genealogical charts in the biographical portraits contained in Bernhardt, *Zentralbehörden*, I and II. Karl E. Demandt, "Amt und Familie: Eine soziologische-genealogische Studie zur hessischen Verwaltungsgeschichte des 16. Jahrhunderts," *Hessisches Jahrbuch für Landesgeschichte*, II (1952), 77 ff., suggests that in sixteenth-century Hessen bureaucratic consolidation was even more advanced and that a clique of some twenty-five bureaucratic families monopolized 71.4 percent of the principality's administrative positions.

69. Firm documentation on university attendance exists for all but two officials, Degenfeld and du Boys. I assume that in both instances the men attended university. They each sat on the Oberrat, an office confined by this period to trained lawyers, and Degenfeld also served from 1560–1563 as a Hofgerichtsassessor at Tübingen, a position reserved exclusively for lawyers.

70. HSAS, J 19: Bü. 68.

71. G. Esslinger, S. Faber, C. Fircks von Nurmhausen, and L. A. Lemblin von Reinhardshofen.

couraged friendships and created something of a collegial network among the Räte in each age group.

Although none of the noblemen, and neither of the two gelehrte Räte ennobled in this period, earned an advanced degree, only Brastberger, Hüngerlin, and Georg Esslinger (1560–1622) among the remaining gelehrte Räte failed to obtain a doctorate in law. The standard experience consisted of several years' study at Tübingen, followed by a two- or three-year *Wanderung* to one or more of the neighboring Protestant universities. Basel, Strassburg, Marburg, and Heidelberg were the contemporary favorites, though Faber went as far north as Wittenberg, and Brastberger studied at the Lutheran universities of Denmark and Sweden.[72] In order to master Roman law, ten Württembergers even exposed themselves to Catholic Italy.[73] Viet Breitschwerdt (1565–1631) was a typical case. He entered Tübingen in 1582 and after some six years of study left Württemberg for Siena, where he spent at least a year under the legal faculty before taking his doctorate at Basel.[74] Two of the Räte, von Bouwinghausen-Walmerode and Jacob Löffler (1582–1638), visited Oxford and Cambridge and then made a circuit of the French universities.[75] Those who had gone outside Germany for study in Roman law often took positions in imperial service, where they could practice under the system of German public law before entering the territorial government. For over one-half of the gelehrte Räte, the standard practice was to spend several years at Speyer, trying cases before the Imperial Supreme Court.[76]

It may seem clear from the *curricula vitae* that, whereas appointment to high office still rested on ducal approval, late-Renaissance bureaucrats received that favor only in certain circumstances. The mid-sixteenth-century guidelines for hiring Räte—that they be "Men of open character, shrewdness, and bearing"—had definitely expanded.[77] Only two military figures (Bouwinghausen von Wallmerode and Helmstätt) entered the cadre of Hofräte without having served previously in one of the major administrative departments or

---

72. HSAS, J 19: Bü. 44; A 202: Bü. 168.

73. Those Räte studying in Italy were von Helmstätt, von Bouwinghausen-Walmerode, Lemblin von Reinhardshofen, Fircks von Nurmhausen, Laimingen, Haug, Faber, Kielmann, Breitschwerdt, and Brastberger.

74. Bernhardt, *Zentralbehörden*, I, 190–191.

75. von Bouwinghausen-Walmerode: HSAS, A 153: Bü. 20. Löffler: E. Niethammer, "Jakob Löffler," *Schwäbische Lebensbilder*, III (Stuttgart, 1942), 368 ff.; and HSAS, A 2021: Bü. 64.

76. Those Räte serving at Speyer were Breitschwerdt, Dold, Enslin, Faber, Haug, Kielmann, and Reinhardt. For a useful discussion of German public law, see Hanns Gross, *Empire and Sovereignty* (Chicago, 1975), 29 ff., 55 ff., 141 ff.

77. HHSAW, Württembergica, rote Reihe, Fasc. 66.

as a professor of law. And they were successful officers. For the others, even the aristocrats, the study of law constituted an essential preliminary to appointment. This study, moreover, was decidedly cosmopolitan; one cannot assume that these Württemberg bureaucrats brought only provincial perceptions to their offices. Admittedly their family origins were usually local and most of their studies had been undertaken at the territorial university. But virtually every one of them had spent several years outside the duchy; and for over one-half of the Räte (56 percent) that study had led them beyond German borders. After university at least seven Räte, in the fashion of Chancellor Reinhardt, worked for several years at Speyer, so that they came to Württemberg administration with a solid grounding in the principles and practice of public law. Finally it must be stressed that, while social differentiations were perpetuated in title, prior to the Thirty Years War non-noble birth did not constitute an obstacle to service. There were even signs that bureaucratic rank was lessening the importance of traditional distinctions and causing the high officials to identify as a social group. At the very least, central administration offered increased political opportunity to the sons of provincial and court officials and the promise of social advancement to burghers.

We have seen that the title of Geheimer Rat carried no institutional designation and that the Räte continued to work in their respective departments, rendering advice when called upon by the duke. Prior to the Thirty Years War the dukes consulted the Räte with varying frequency. Duke Christoph, who ruled from 1550 to 1554, leaned heavily upon his advisers and organized them into something like an unofficial executive committee. While the group had no constitutional status—that is, the estates did not recognize the board as an organ of government—its membership was fixed and included seats for the incumbents of the three most important governing offices: the Landhofmeister, the chancellor, and the vice-chancellor. In addition place was made for one gelehrte official from the Oberrat. Christoph assigned the Räte, whom he referred to as privy councilors, responsibility for advising him on all matters pertaining to the *Reservatsachen*, that collection of concerns that constituted the ducal prerogative. They included powers of high justice, regulation of enfeoffed properties and all matters of vassalage, control over ducal properties and finances, authority in matters of confession, rights of administrative appointment, approval of all laws and ordinances, and authority for disciplining administrative personnel.[78]

Following Christoph's death the administrative pendulum swung

---

78. Spittler, *Geheimen-Raths-Collegiums*, 284–290. On the Reservatsachen, see Kanzleiordnung of 1550 in Reyscher, *Vollständige Sammlung*, XII, 173 ff.

away from the Geheime Räte and back for the rest of the century toward cabinet influence. Duke Ludwig substituted his personal secretary Franz Kurz (1517–1575) for the seat reserved customarily for a gelehrter Rat from the judicial council and insisted that Kurz alone forward to him recommendations from the privy councilors. He also assigned to Kurz sole responsibility for all communications between the duke and the three administrative departments (chancellery, ducal trust, and church council).[79] Melchior Jäger, who succeeded Kurz as Ludwig's personal secretary, brought cabinet influence to even greater heights. By 1590 he had acquired the title of director of the court chancellery, as well as an imperial patent of nobility. As Geheimer Rat and Director Jäger von Gärtringen, he controlled not only the cabinet secretariat but also the territorial chancellery. He used his position to obtain exclusive right to convene the other Hofräte as a collegial board, so that these officials could not come together, much less forward recommendations or petitions, without his permission.[80]

The reigns of Duke Friedrich (1593–1608) and Johann Friedrich (1608–1628) carried forward the tradition of influential secretarial favorites though, with the possible exception of Mattäus Enslin, no Hofrat succeeded in attaining an influence comparable to Jäger's. The common pattern in the early seventeenth century was for the duke to summon one or more Räte for recommendations in the areas of their expertise and then to make his own decision in cabinet, forwarding the results to the various organs of government. Archival records convey little impression that the Hofräte met regularly as a collegial body. It must be stressed, however, that while the evidence is extremely spotty, committee minutes do indicate that, on those occasions when the Räte did assemble, they discussed a wide range of problems. Unfortunately, extant records speak only to a two-year period, 1602–1603, so that broad generalizations on the collegial function of the privy councilors are impossible to sustain. Nevertheless, according to the documentation, the early-seventeenth-century Hofräte discussed the entire spectrum of concerns associated with the Reservatsachen. They prepared, for example, recommendations for appointment to and promotion in the various bureaucratic offices. They analyzed reports of meetings of the Reichstag and forwarded suggestions for Württemberg's foreign policy. Similarly they handled disputes in matters of enfeoffed properties and processed petitions of grievance from ducal subjects. They also reviewed difficult cases from the Oberrat and the consistory and advised the ruler in ecclesiastical

79. Oestreich, "Das persönliche Regiment der deutschen Fürsten," 221.
80. Reyscher, Vollständige Sammlung, XII, 447 ff.

affairs and matters of property.[81] Indeed, if the items of business at these meetings constituted a typical work pattern, they reveal a considerably broader range of activities for the Geheime Räte than historians such as Gerhard Oestreich have recognized.[82] They suggest that by linking the Reservatsachen to the Hofräte, the Württemberg dukes kept alive the earlier Austrian notion of a central board, staffed by leading departmental officials, which could give professional advice on the administration of government.

Curiously it was the territorial estates rather than the ruler who provided the final impetus for the establishment in 1629 of a permanent privy council.[83] The details of that decision are part of the narrative of Württemberg history, and the specifics of the council's foundation belong to the storehouse of antiquarian lore; for shortly after its creation, sharp military reverses sent the young Württemberg prince Duke Eberhard III (1628–1674), attended by his elderly privy councilors, scurrying into exile at Strassburg. There the chief officials perished, and it was only when Eberhard returned to Stuttgart toward the end of the war that he reconstituted the council in the form in which it was to take shape. The point here is that the estates took advantage of Johann Friedrich's death and the minority of Eberhard, who at that time was only fourteen, to press for the abolition of the cabinet secretariat, an institution that they described as "most baleful." They envisioned the privy council as an administrative institution, staffed with professionals, which would link the departments collegially. Furthermore this linkage was to be of a precise sort. The estates specified in their resolution of 23 December 1629 that the privy council was not only to serve the prince, it was also to provide an institutional bridge between themselves and the departments of government.[84] The four Hofräte who composed the regency coun-

---

81. HSAS, A 204: Bü. 1.

82. Esp. G. Oestreich's influential essay, "Das persönliche Regiment der deutschen Fürsten." In this sense, the Württemberg evidence suggests certain similarities between developments in that state and those in Brandenburg as reconstructed by M. Klingenborg in "Ratstube und Kanzlei in Brandenburg im 16. Jahrhundert," *Forschungen zur Brandenburg-Preussischen Geschichte*, 26 (1913), 413ff., and in the same author's "Kurfürstliche Kammer und die Begründung des Geheimen Rats in Brandenburg," *HZ*, 114 (1915), 473ff. See also Otto Hintze, "The Origins of the Modern Ministerial System," in *The Historical Essays of Otto Hintze*, ed. Felix Gilbert (New York, 1975), 216–266; and Hintze's "Hof- und Landesverwaltung in der Mark Brandenburg unter Joachim II," in *Regierung und Verwaltung*, ed. Gerhard Oestreich (Berlin, 1967), 204–254.

83. Grube, *Stuttgarter Landtag*, 296–300. See also, Wintterlin, *Behördenorganisation*, I, 63–73; and F. Wintterlin, "Beamtentum und Verfassung im Herzogtum Württemberg," *WVJHLG*, 32 (1925/26), 4ff.

84. See Hauptlandtagsabschied of 23 December 1629 in Reyscher, *Vollständige Sammlung*, II, Nr. 56; also HSAS, J 26: Nr. 7.

cil—Landhofmeister von Helmstätt, Vice-Chancellor Löffler, and Oberräte Kielmann and Breitschwerdt—became the first permanent councilors, and each swore an oath to work for the joint good of the prince and the estates.[85]

The creation of the privy council marked the end of a period in territorial administration and set up the institutional framework within which the high Württemberg bureaucracy was to develop. Two points should be made in connection with this subsequent development: first, a sense of corporate consciousness was evolving among the high officials prior to the creation of the privy council. This consciousness crystallized around a set of standards and values we associate with professional or bureaucratic government. It is somewhat surprising that such attitudes should have antedated the institution that was to provide the means for the bureaucracy to participate aggressively and consistently in the direction of the Württemberg state. Such a reversal underscores the need to regard bureaucracy as more than institutional structure. The second point is closely related to the first: developments in Württemberg prior to the Thirty Years War suggest that the modern bureaucratic state grew in a more uneven fashion than has heretofore been appreciated.[86] It is useful to visualize its development as a number of waves rather than as the linear progression suggested first by Max Weber and subsequently incorporated into German historiography through the work of Hans Rosenberg. For Weber it was the alliance of the power of the absolute prince with capitalistic interests which called forth the bureaucracy in Western Europe, a thesis that Rosenberg supported through his analysis of events in late seventeenth- and eighteenth-century Prussia. He found in that state, under the guidance of a series of strong princes, a merging in government service of certain aristocratic and bourgeois elements to form a bureaucracy that first supported and then overwhelmed the Prussian prince, setting the state on a linear course toward an unhappy modernity. Both scholars assumed that the process of bureaucratic growth, once begun, proceeded toward the creation of the modern state with only minor interruptions and always at the expense of personal rule.[87] A look at late-sixteenth-century administra-

---

85. Spittler, *Geheimen-Raths-Collegium*, 333ff.; also T. Pistorius, "Die Ministerverantwortlichkeit in Württemberg," *WJSL* (1893), 17ff.

86. A comparison of these late-sixteenth-century developments with the late-eighteenth-century formations discussed in B. Wunder, *Privilegierung und Disziplinierung: Die Entstehung des Berufsbeamtentums in Bayern und Württemberg, 1780–1825* (Munich and Vienna, 1978), esp. 33–118, reveals that much of what Wunder discovered has been anticipated in these earlier events.

87. The notion of linear development underlies much of Weber's writing; for a specific discussion of bureaucracy, see his essay in H. H. Gerth and C. Wright Mills,

tion suggests a more circuitous path. We find in these governments bureaucratic enclaves that anticipated the patterns identified by Rosenberg as peculiar to the eighteenth century and that in this earlier instance led to quite different outcomes.

The bureaucracy in place in Württemberg on the eve of the Thirty Years War, one that had emerged in the previous half-century, had drawn firm lines of control between the embryonic order of bureaucratic officials and the autocratic prince. In that duchy, as elsewhere in late Renaissance Germany, the prince presided over a government that was at once personal and bureaucratic. It was personal in the sense that the prince's wishes determined all matters of policy: no appointment or program could pass without ducal consent. It was autocratic in that the prince, like his counterparts in the other territories, ruled his lands through personal favorites rather than by means of professional administrators. True, he employed trained officials in the service branches of his government. But all communications between the individual agencies and the ruler passed through the duke's private staff so that his favorites, who were not necessarily administrative officials, filtered and shaped policy decisions. Furthermore, departmental heads had no officially constituted board on which they could work together to marshal departmental energies behind a coordinated perspective. In this sense one can think of the Württemberg government as centralized in the concentration of political responsibility but compartmentalized in the carrying out of that responsibility.

Cabinet rule gave the Renaissance prince an aura of autocratic power that has lured historians away from the administrative officials and obscured significant developments within that body of civil servants. Yet certain of these men shared similar assumptions about the proper ordering of government and were beginning to build up a sense of themselves as constituting a functional if not a social caste distinct from the other elements in German society. They distinguished initially between themselves and the courtiers and then finally between themselves as a group and the departments that certain of them headed. Differences in social background mattered surprisingly little in their relations and not at all in their perception of their responsibilities and in the regulation of their salaries. In short the

From *Max Weber: Essays in Sociology* (New York, 1968), 196–244; and *Staatssoziologie*, ed. Johannes Winckelmann (Berlin, 1956). Hans Rosenberg, *Bureaucracy, Aristocracy and Autocracy: The Prussian Experience, 1600–1815* (Cambridge, Mass., 1958), esp. 9–45 and 137–238. See also Gustav Schmoller, "Ueber Behördenorganisation, Amtswesen und Beamtentum im Allgemeinen and speziell in Deutschland und Preussen bis zum Jahre 1713," in *Acta Borussica: Behördenorganisation*, I (Berlin, 1894), 15–143.

group contained both aristocrats and burghers and evidenced many of the characteristics that Rosenberg discovered in eighteenth-century officials: an emphasis on practical training and the study of law; a sense of professional identity; a determination to ground their services on principles of contract and to regulate the duties of office; and a conviction that the prince was best served by consultation with administrative experts rather than with his courtiers.

Nothing in these officials' efforts suggested a challenge to ducal authority; on the contrary they worked to extend the powers of the ruler. In this latter regard they anticipated early cameralistic concerns and, in the fashion of late-seventeenth-century practical theorists such as Johann Joachim Becher (1635–1682), saw all branches of government as parts of a larger whole. They did not think, for example, that fiscal concerns could be separated from those of justice, warfare, or public weal. And though they recognized that for purposes of daily administration particular agencies were required to oversee discrete concerns, they viewed such divisions as part of a collective harmony and symmetry. Society, as they perceived it, constituted an organic entity in which prince and subject were inseparably joined and all elements of administration were fused harmoniously to create the eudaemonistic state.[88] In their emphasis on coordinated responsibility and in their determination to regularize their advisory duties, these officials established themselves as an alternative to rule by the prince through his private secretariat. When cabinet government faltered under the strains of the Thirty Years War, both duke and territorial estates turned to these high bureaucrats and in 1628–1629 institutionalized their group by the creation of the privy council. That body then gathered together the administrative energies of the various departments to propel the postwar growth of the duchy and to accomplish its final transition from feudal principality to territorial state.

88. A particularly revealing illustration of this attitude can be found in the correspondence between the estates and the government during the years immediately prior to the setting up of the privy council. See esp. HSAS, A 34: Bü. 42; A 36: Bü. 32 and 33; A. E. Adam, "Württembergische Landtagsakten, 1620–32" (unpublished manuscript in HSAS), 339–431; and Niethammer, "Jakob Löffler," 368–393.

# [3]

# A Balance in Government

IN THE YEARS immediately following the Thirty Years War the primary governing bodies of the duchy experienced profound structural alterations. These changes introduced possibilities for new directions of growth and opened fresh options in the relations between crown, council, and territorial estates. Contemporaries were curiously slow to perceive the implications of these various innovations; their potential was obscured in large part by the old-fashioned tone of the ducal court. The personality of the monarch was such that a sense of continuity and adherence to traditional norms pervaded the government and imparted an aura of stability to domestic relations. The result was a forty-year period in which institutions matured and developed capacities for independence which were held in check by cultural assumptions of continuity and permanence. Profound tensions lay concealed behind the adherence to ancient mores: while the assumption prevailed that all was well, institutions were growing in ways that threatened to undercut customary patterns of government.

Conflict was by no means inevitable. Indeed, one of the most fascinating aspects of this period of Württemberg history is the sense of options conveyed by the documents. There were choices to be made; alternatives to be weighed, and Württemberg's development was neither consistent nor linear. Particularly in the areas of bureaucracy and government, the middle decades of the seventeenth century were marked by a reversion to older forms, a reversal of the transitional dynamics that we have seen gathering in the late-sixteenth- and early-seventeenth-century monarchies. Whereas the late-Renaissance princes strove to rule authoritatively and to free themselves from their territorial estates, the government of Eberhard III, who ruled as eighth duke of Württemberg from 1633 to 1674, took a different direction. Eberhard himself set the new course when he proclaimed that the prince and his estates were *corelativa*, the holders of a correlative power that bound them together indivisibly.[1] He accompanied this emphasis upon shared sovereignty with a reluctance to promote innovative policies over the opposition of his estates, so that his reign constituted a period of efflorescence for the Wüttemberg Landtag. At least on the surface prince and Landtag operated at a draw: just as Eberhard was unwilling (or unable) to impose bold new directions, so the estates resisted innovation and offered only a vigorous defense of a narrowly defined tradition. The result was a political stalemate: a period of reversion set in, in which central authority lost its unitary drive and the government moved increasingly toward a sharing of responsibility with the estates.[2]

At the most immediate level explanation for this apparent reversal centers on the personality of the prince. Eberhard was different in temperament from his predecessors and also from his more illustrious contemporaries. He lacked the elevated vision of monarchy which found such exalted expression in Charles I of England or Louis XIV of France. Nor was his dynastic ambition as sharply focused as that of his Hohenzollern cousin at Berlin, Friedrich Wilhelm the Great Elector.[3] Though not without some capacity for originality, he exercised his talents in an ad hoc fashion without discernible connection to a larger program of state building. He cherished his position as monarch, but he regarded that office as harking back to the terms of the Tübinger Vertrag, which held that a prince should rule as a *Landesvater*, a father of his people who governs with the consent and support of the territorial estates.[4] Nor was Eberhard the only Württemberger to base his views of government on that venerable document. Its emotional force endowed the concept of a balance of power with a sanctity that conditioned many of his subjects to oppose any effort at

1. HSAS, *tomus actorum*, XXXIX, 350–351 (3 November 1638).
2. W. Grube, *Der Stuttgarter Landtag, 1457–1957* (Stuttgart, 1957), 307–341, makes this point with particular vigor.
3. Eberhard's mother, Barbara Sophie, was the daughter of Joachim Friedrich Elector of Brandenburg and hence was great-aunt to Friedrich Wilhelm. The Württembergers made much of their Brandenburg connection and looked to that electorate to represent Württemberg's interests in the Electoral College of the Reichstag and at the Westphalian peace negotiations. There is no scholarly biography of Eberhard III. Interpretative essays are found in K. Pfaff, *Württembergs geliebte Herren*, ed. P. Lahnstein (Stuttgart, 1965), 49–52; and *Allegmeine Deutsche Biographie*, V (Berlin, 1965), 559–561. See also, C. Sattler, *Geschichte des Herzogtums Wirtenberg unter der Regierung der Herzogen*, VII–X (Ulm, 1774–1779)—hereafter cited as Sattler, *Herzöge*—and E. Schneider, *Württembergische Geschichte* (Stuttgart, 1896), 247–296.
4. See pages 45–46 of this book for a discussion of the Tübinger Vertrag.

This engraving of Eberhard III by Bartholome Kilian, 1674, depicts the bluff old monarch as a benign, though stern father of his people. Such a presentation differs markedly from the exalted renderings of monarchy that became the vogue with Louis XIV of France. Photograph courtesy of the Landesbibliothek Stuttgart.

political consolidation and that imparted to their opposition the moral imperative of constitutional legitimacy.

The economic upheaval and financial strain of the Thirty Years War combined with constitutional traditions and issues of personality both to retard and to deflect the earlier trends toward a centralization of power in Württemberg. The Stuttgart government came out of the war in an exceedingly difficult position. As in most early modern principalities, moneys for the ducal administration derived from two primary sources: the royal domain and regale, under the direct control of the prince; and public taxation, administered in Württemberg as the exclusive prerogative of the territorial estates. During the war both sources suffered devastation. But whereas the crown as well as the town and village properties sustained great damage, patterns of recovery were such that the properties subject to fiscal demands by the Landtag stabilized more quickly than those of the crown. As a result the postwar monarchy found itself in a vulnerable fiscal position. The duke depended more than ever upon the revenues voted by the Landtag and lacked the independent resources for an aggressive policy of centralization that risked antagonizing his estates.

Württemberg had entered the Thirty Years War as one of the most fertile, densely settled regions of Germany.[5] But even before fighting reached its borders, signs of economic contraction were discernible.[6] Recent scholarship has established that by 1630 agricultural production was unable to meet the dietary needs of the duchy. Conventional

5. W. von Hippel, "Bevölkerung und Wirtschaft im Zeitalter des Dreissigjährigen Krieges: Das Beispiel Württemberg," *Zeitschrift für Historische Forschung*, 5 (1978), 413–448; cf. Ingomar Bog, "Wachstumsprobleme der oberdeutschen Wirtschaft," in Friedrich Lütge, ed., *Wirtschaftliche und soziale Probleme der gewerblichen Entwicklung im 15.–16. und 19. Jahrhundert* (Stuttgart, 1968), 44–89; F. Koerner, "Die Bevölkerungsverteilung in Thüringen am Ausgang des 16. Jahrhundert," *Wissenschaftliche Veröffentlichungen der Deutsche Institut für Landeskunde in Leipzig*, NF 15/16, 178–315, 308f.; and Karlheinz Blaschke, *Bevölkerungsgeschichte von Sachsen bis zur Industriellen Revolution* (Weimar, 1967), 46.

6. K. -O. Bull "Zur Wirtschafts- und Sozialgeschichte der württembergischen Amtstadt Vahingen an der Enz bis zum Dreissigjährigen Krieg," ZWLG, 37 (1979), 97–140. Wilhelm Abel, *Agrarkrisen und Agrarkonjunktur* (Berlin, 1966), describes the German economy in general decline, a position affirmed for all of Europe by F. C. Spooner, *L'économie mondiale et les frappes monétaires en France 1493–1680* (Paris, 1956), 35, who asserts that the world economy in 1620 was operating "at partial speed." Cf. Friedrich Lütge, *Deutsche Sozial- und Wirtschaftsgeschichte*, 2d ed. (Berlin, 1960), 277; and Friedrich Lütge, *Studien zur Sozial- und Wirtschaftsgeschichte* (Stuttgart, 1963), 339ff. Three useful interpretative historiographic essays are: F. L. Carsten, "Was There an Economic Decline in Germany before the Thirty Years War?" *English Historical Review*, 71 (1956), 240–247; T. K. Rabb, "The Effects of the Thirty Years War on the German Economy," *JMH*, 34 (1962), 40–51; and Henry Kamen, "The Economic and Social Consequences of the Thirty Years War," *PP*, 39 (1968), 44–61.

agrarian techniques resulted in harvests that in good years could feed only 85 percent of the population.[7] Even with the income generated by textile and wine exports, it appeared that moneys available for food import barely met the minimum survival standards for those on the economic fringe of society. Under these constraints a period of demographic contraction had set in.[8] The currency was also weakening: as early as 1623 Alsace, Austria, and Württemberg had agreed to fix the Mark at 9 Reichsthaler or 13½ florins, a devaluation of 25 percent.[9] It was true then, as now, that such inflation benefited those persons with mortgages and debts—they could repay their loans in devalued currency—but at the same time inflation eroded the value of fixed investments and undermined the crown's purchasing power. The devastations of war accelerated these trends and, as we shall see, imposed severe fiscal constraints upon the government.

Württemberg's direct participation in the war can easily be summarized. Prior to 1634 the duchy remained out of the primary military theater. It contributed to the imperial cause through increased taxation and the assumption of the troublesome burden of winter quartering for those soldiers assigned to the region by the imperial general Albrecht von Wallenstein.[10] But in the late summer of 1634 fighting moved into the German southwest and Württemberg became a battleground. Duke Eberhard had reached his majority the previous year, and upon assuming control of the government he allied the duchy with the heretofore triumphant Swedish army.[11] The decision turned out disastrously: at the Battle of Nördlingen in August 1634, Swedish power was broken and Protestant allies such as Württemberg, two-thirds of whose army had fallen on the battlefield,[12] found themselves at the mercy of a victorious imperial army. For the next

7. Hippel, "Bevölkerung und Wirtschaft," 422. Drawing on research in 59 Aemter, Hippel estimates that by 1630 the grain and vegetable harvests supplied yields sufficient only for 280,000 persons out of a general population of 334,000.

8. Ibid., 419. Wine and textile exports yielded revenues sufficient to purchase food for an additional 38,000 Württembergers, leaving a deficit population surplus of 16,000 (Hippel, 425). Cf. Pierre Chaunu, *Europäische Kultur im Zeitalter des Barock* (Frankfurt, 1970), 332 ff.

9. HSAS, A 34: Bü. 40.

10. The first quartering of Wallenstein's Friedland regiments began in January 1628. For those and other subsequent quartering arrangements, see HSAS, A 34: Bü. 39–46.

11. Details of these negotiations are found in HSAS, A 36: Bü. 41–43. See also Theodor Schott, "Württemberg und Gustav Adolf 1631 und 1632," *WVJHLG*, IV (1895), 343–402.

12. Württemberg contributed an army of 6,000 men to the Swedish alliance; 4,000 of these soldiers fell at Nördlingen. See HSAS, A 36: Bü. 45; and Sattler, *Herzöge*, VII, 102 ff. and Beil. 32–33.

four years the duchy suffered occupation by Habsburg military forces. In 1638 when Eberhard returned from four years of exile at Strassburg, he confronted a ruined principality that not only had been bled through arbitrary taxation, forced billeting and requisitioning, and looting and burning by an ill-disciplined soldiery but also had lost some 50 percent of its territory.[13] A vigorous enforcement of the Edict of Restitution (1629) had resulted in a return to the Roman Catholic monastic orders of the fourteen great Württemberg abbeys with their attendant properties.[14] Once reinstalled the monks had renounced their allegiance to the Württemberg state and petitioned the emperor to grant them the constitutional status of Reichsunmittelbarkeit, which would free them from any secular control other than that of the empire.[15] Equally serious for the duke was the fact that during his absence the Habsburg governor, the future emperor Ferdinand III, had alienated large portions of the ducal domain, carving up these properties as fiefs for his own loyal retainers.[16] These lands were eventually returned: by 1650 Swedish diplomacy had rolled back all ecclesiastical boundaries to those obtaining in 1624 and restored ducal properties to the *status quo ante bellum*.[17] Nevertheless, the confiscations left their mark upon the duke and his treasury. Eberhard had lost his capital base at the very moment when his expenses were highest and was forced to depend almost entirely on the territorial estates. That the estates supported him during those years of deprivation doubtless contributed to Eberhard's loyalty toward the Landtag and to his reluctance, once better times arrived, to introduce policies offensive to that body.[18]

13. Missing were the properties of the fourteen great abbeys, a substantial portion of the remaining ecclesiastical lands, and over twelve secular Aemter, including the entire Herrschaft of Heidenheim; see HSAS, A 34: Bü. 49; and Sattler, *Herzöge*, VII, 200 ff. and Beil. 61, 62.

14. H. Günter, *Das Restitutionsedikt von 1629 und die katholische Restauration Altwürttembergs* (Stuttgart, 1901), 308 ff.

15. On the relations between these "restored" abbeys and the Wüttemberg Landtag, see Grube, *Stuttgarter Landtag*, 313–319.

16. HSAS, A 34: Bü. 50–51. A portion of these confiscated properties went to Habsburg retainers such as Graf Maximilian von Trautmannsdorf, who already held large Swabian fiefs, and to military commanders in the Spanish and Bavarian armies that occupied the duchy. The bulk, however, went to the Duke of Bavaria and to the Tyrolean line of the Habsburg family; see Fritz Dickmann, *Der Westfälische Frieden* (Münster, 1972), 31 f. and 382–383.

17. Properties were returned under the provisions of the Nürnberger Executionstages of 16 June 1650. Responsibility for implementation of the Order of Restitution was vested in Queen Christina of Sweden, who delegated her authority to her cousin Pfalzgraf Karl Gustav von Zweibrücken, the Swedish Generalissimus in Germany who later ruled Sweden as Charles X.

18. K. Pfaff, *Geschichte der Fürstenhauses und Landes Wirtemberg*, Teil III, Abteilung 2 (Stuttgart, 1839), 5, records treasury receipts establishing the annual interest on

Incomplete records preclude comprehensive figures on the extent of war damage or on losses in population and livestock. A comparison of population statistics for 1634 and 1655 reveals an average decline of 57 percent for sixty-four of the territorial districts.[19] Losses in these areas ranged from 31 percent at the lowest end of the scale to extreme cases of 77 percent. In at least eleven districts there were more destroyed and uninhabitable houses than there were inhabited ones. Throughout the entire principality over 41,000 houses and barns (43 percent) had been destroyed; four years after the peace, one-third of the farm land and 40 percent of the vineyards remained untended.[20] The districts that suffered most lay across major transportation routes and at strategic military points; mountainous regions such as the Black Forest were scarcely affected.[21] In Württemberg as elsewhere in Germany population and property loss was more extensive in the country than in the fortified cities; though it must be remembered that disruptions in the food supply, plagues, and psychological turmoil took their toll on urban fertility rates. In Stuttgart, for example, the birth rate had fallen some 48 percent below its prewar level by 1650.[22]

War costs in terms of military expenditure, looting, and property damage represented a staggering cash value. In 1654 a report to the estates from the government maintained that between 1628 and 1650 the duchy had sustained expenses of 118,742,864 florins.[23] This fig-

---

Eberhard's Strassburg debts at 300,000 florins. Upon Eberhard's return to Stuttgart, the Landtag assumed responsibility for over 800,000 florins of capital debt. In addition the estates voted to subsidize the duke with an excise tax on corn, meat, salt, wine, timber, commercial goods, and the sale of land and securities. See HSAS, A 34: Bü. 49, and *tomus actorum*, XXXIX, 17–27, 106, 125, 129–131, 151, 166–167, 170, 175–183, 188, 259–286, 405–412, 422–427, 532–541. Also, A. Reyscher, *Vollständige, historisch und kritisch bearbeitete Sammlung der württembergischen Gesetze*, XVII (Stuttgart and Tübingen, 1840), 162–165, Nr. 74.

19. Hippel, "Bevölkerung und Wirtschaft," 437. Günther Franz, *Der Dreissigjäh- rige Krieg und das Deutsche Volk* (Stuttgart, 1961), 42–44, posits an overall contraction of 50 percent in Württemberg. He cautions particularly against attributing all rural losses reflected in the 1650 survey to the war. In the Neckar Valley and in the Swabian Alb, for example, less than one dozen of the 1,400 sites reported as deserted owed their permanent depopulation exclusively to war (p. 85). Cf. E. Marquardt, *Geschichte Württembergs* (Stuttgart, 1962), 154, who estimates that population sank from 400,000 to just over 60,000 inhabitants.

20. G. Mehring, "Wirtschaftliche Schäden durch den Dreissigjährigen Krieg im Herzogtum Württemberg," WVJHLG, 30 (1921), 58–89; cf. Mehring's earlier article, "Schädigungen durch den Dreissigjährigen Krieg in Altwürttemberg," WVJSLG, 19 (1910), 449–452, and Pfaff, *Geschichte des Fürstenhauses*, Teil III, Abteilung 2, 1 ff.

21. Hippel, "Bevölkerung und Wirtschaft," 438.

22. Roger Mols, *Introduction à la démographie historique des villes d'Europe du XIVᵉ au XVIIIᵉ siècle*, II, in *Université de Louvain: Recueil de travaux d'histoire et de philologie*, 4ᵉ série, fasc. 2 (Louvain, 1957), 483.

23. The Stuttgart report estimated costs for 1634–1638 at 45,007,000 florins as op-

ure need not be accepted at face value; it included a 60,000,000-florin entry for looting and burning which was nothing but a vague estimate included for the explicit purpose of justifying a demand for larger tax subsidies from the estates. But even the estates' own more conservative computations revealed a crippling financial drain. The Landtag reported that between 1638 and 1650 billeting and war costs stood at 6,797,537 florins.[24] The calculations contained no estimates on the costs of looting, burning, and military exaction. More important, they did not reckon in the years from 1634 to 1638, a period when Spanish and Bavarian troops occupied the countryside and extracted contributions without consulting the estates. Confiscatory taxes for those four years alone totaled 45,007,000 florins, almost half the crown's inclusive figure for the entire war. Moreover the Reich owed Sweden a war indemnity of 7,500,000 florins, over 230,000 florins of which had to be furnished by Württemberg.[25] Even allowing for a certain exaggeration, then, the fiscal picture was a grim one. And the magnitude of these sums becomes all the more graphic when one realizes that in 1618 the sum necessary to supply the annual grain needs of an individual subject was reckoned at between 7½ and 10 florins![26]

It is important to bear in mind that recuperative capacity fluctuated within the postwar duchy and that these differences bore directly upon the comparative strength of the various governing bodies of the realm. Certain groups and geographic areas rebounded with greater resilience than others and so developed imperatives quite different from those whose capital base remained precarious. In particular the needs of the crown differed from those of the villages and towns, and these differences complicated relations between the central government and the Landtag. Recall that ties between the monarchy and the localities functioned on two distinct levels. While royal agencies such as the privy council negotiated with the diet and its committees at Stuttgart, the district Amtmann represented the monarch in his dealings with individual village and town governing bodies. As these

posed to 6,354,326 florins for 1628–1634 and 7,381,538 florins for 1639–1650. See Sattler, Herzöge, IX, 134; also F. Carsten, Princes and Parliaments in Germany from the Fifteenth to the Eighteenth Century (Oxford, 1959), 52–53; cf. C. von Stälin, "Württembergische Kriegsschäden im Dreissigjährigen Krieg," WVJHLG, VII (1899), 54 ff.

24. For the Landtag's report, see HSAS, tomus actorum, I, 2075–2095.

25. Dickmann, Der Westfälische Frieden, 473–477, discusses the problems of compensation by the Reich for the Swedish army. For the Württemberg obligation, see HSAS, A 204: Bü. 4 (minutes for 5 August 1650); cf. Sattler, Herzöge, VIII, Beil. 68 and IX, 32 f.

26. Hippel, "Bevölkerung und Wirtschaft," 440; also J. A. R. von Helferich, "Württembergische Getreide- und Weinpreise von 1456 bis 1628," Zeitschrift für die gesamte Staatswissenschaft, XIV (1858), 471–502.

various groups fought their way back from the devastation of war, their positions altered in significant ways that contemporaries seemed slow to appreciate but that worked to modify certain traditional political relationships.

The first point to note in this regard was the comparative weakness of the crown's recuperative fiscal capacities in the years immediately after the war. Ducal difficulties resulted primarily from an acute shortage in the labor supply for the royal domains. In part, of course, this shortage reflected the awesome demographic losses experienced by the Württemberg peasantry during the war years and spoke to conditions general throughout the duchy. But there was a dimension to the problem which worked to the particular disadvantage of the crown. During the 1650s the surviving peasantry distributed itself unevenly throughout the work force. In particular the peasants turned first for recovery to the cultivation of their own properties.[27] Those who survived the war succeeded in taking over abandoned farmland and thus expanding their agrarian holdings. Indeed, they were so successful that scholars now estimate that by 1650 the average Württemberg peasant was cultivating at least 100 percent more land than before the war.[28] Furthermore, the price of rye had risen during the war while meat prices, abnormally low for most of the period, fell after 1640; grain farmers could thus earn at least a small cash income as producers of consumable goods.[29] Then too, those among them who worked at construction or day labor profited from the widespread de-

27. Mehring, "Wirtschaftliche Schäden durch den Dreissigjährigen Krieg im Herzogtum Württemberg," 58–89.

28. W. Grube, Geschichtliche Grundlagen: Vogteien, Aemter, Landkreise in Baden-Württemberg (Stuttgart, 1975), 29; also Hippel, "Bevölkerung und Wirtschaft," 440. The fact that major disasters can bring benefits in their wake is noted by Fernand Braudel in Capitalism and Material Life, trans. M. Kochan (London, 1973), 46–91. The Württemberg case further illustrates this point, though it must be remembered that instances of splintering of large peasant holdings can also be documented for the German southwest; see Franz Riegler, Die Reichsstadt Schwäbisch Hall im Dreissigjährigen Kriege (Stuttgart, 1911); and Günther Franz, Der Dreissigjährige Krieg und das Deutsche Volk (Stuttgart, 1961), 89f.

29. M. J. Elsas, Umriss einer Geschichte der Preise und Löhne in Deutschland, II (Leiden, 1949), 14. Prices are a subject of enormous complexity, and great care must be exercised in using such generalized figures. Much of Elsas' data rests on ecclesiastical records; and since church establishments often bought in bulk, they often paid discount prices. Note also that in the late 1660s the grain market fell precipitously: Franz, Der Dreissigjährige Krieg und das Deutsche Volk, 86, asserts that between 1669 and 1673 rye prices on the Augsburg, Würzburg, and Munich markets stood at only 25–30 percent of their 1619–1624 value. My point is that those peasants surviving the disasters of 1634–1638 could market their rye at a time of rising prices and thus hold on at a moment of drastic upheaval when the crown was too weak to protect them. Franz's stress on the decline of the late sixties fails to take into account the restabilization in Württemberg society that had occurred in the intervening years.

mand for workers as well as from the low food prices. They managed to raise their purchasing power from three to four times its prewar value and thus to arrive at a position where they could purchase empty land.[30]

These conditions meant that the postwar peasantry was able to engage first in the reconstruction of those properties that carried the lowest rental and service obligations.[31] And since crown and ecclesiastical property carried relatively high rental burdens, these farms remained chronically short of workers.[32] Ducal revenues—derived principally from crown and church lands—declined accordingly, and the duke thus confronted the peacetime economy with priorities different from those of the Landtag, a body that turned for tax revenues to the villages and towns of the duchy. There too, of course, one found an acute cash shortage. But the more immediate effort at recultivation made the district (especially its rural component) a source of economic promise and enabled the Landtag to raise moneys at the modest rate of 6 percent, a clear indication that despite outstanding debts of almost five million florins the diet remained an attractive capital investment.[33] This ready access to money strengthened the Landtag's political hand and put the monarch at something of a disadvantage in the jockeying for position that took place after the war.

The Landtag's position, however, was complicated by two important structural changes that were taking place within that body: the final consolidation by the Ehrbarkeit of its hold upon the membership of the diet, and a redefinition of the political balance within the provincial districts. These innovations sprang in part from economic conditions and in part from pressures of a more sociopolitical nature. Their effect in each instance was to modify the links between the crown and the estates and to open new possibilities for conflict between those two forces. The first of these changes concerned the Ehrbarkeit. We have already seen how the sixteenth-century urban oligarchs succeeded in excluding village leaders from eligibility for election as district delegates to the Landtag. This victory had left the

30. Hippel, "Bevölkerung und Wirtschaft," 439.
31. W. Söll, "Die staatliche Wirtschaftspolitik in Württemberg im 17. und 18. Jahrhundert" (Tübingen: Ph.D. diss., 1934), 47–49.
32. Sattler, Herzöge, IX, 105–110; Grube, Stuttgarter Landtag, 321; R. Bütterlin, Die merkantilistische Geldpolitik im Herzogtum Württemberg von der Reformation bis Napoleon (Urach, 1966), 89.
33. On 18 August 1649 the estates registered a debt of 4,821,938 florins with annual interest payments of 241,096 florins (Carsten, Princes and Parliaments, 72n1). Hippel, "Bevölkerung und Wirtschaft," 441, notes that capital loans were negotiated primarily with the Swiss cantons; see also, F. Haug, "Die Einwanderung in die Herrschaft Friedberg-Scheer nach dem Dreissigjährigen Krieg," ZWLG, 5 (1941), 284–301.

Ehrbarkeit to share control over the delegations with the local ducal official known as the Amtmann. Though the Amtmann often belonged to one of the leading municipal families in the district, the urban magistrates feared that his explicit connection with the duke made him a dubious ally.[34] After all the Amtmann was a royal bureaucrat and as such represented ducal not local interests. Furthermore, by his ability to compete with the urban magistrates for election as district representative to the Landtag, he not only challenged the Ehrbarkeit's social control over the diet but also undercut that group's capacity for parliamentary opposition to the crown. Indeed by the early seventeenth century the ducal agents had succeeded in winning a good number of representative seats and were working actively at the diet to further crown policy. At the general diet of 1621, for example, twenty-five district officials were numbered among the 118 delegates, and these men reported regularly to Duke Johann Friedrich for instruction on the issues confronting the diet.[35] Three years later the ratio had tipped further in royal favor: twenty out of seventy-five representatives attending the Landtag—some 26 percent—were serving in the districts as ducal officials.[36]

The situation, though irritating, was by no means desperate for the urban leaders. They were always guaranteed one of the two seats in the district and in many instances controlled sufficient votes to defeat the Amtmann if he ran for the other. Nonetheless, alarmed by the possibility of a fifth column at the Landtag, they took advantage in 1628 of a regency government to launch an attack against the Amtmann's participation in the diet.[37] This official, they insisted to the regent, did not belong to the Landschaften but to the crown; as such he could never vote in the name of the estates. At best, the estates maintained, the Amtmann could sit at the Landtag only as an observer and in that capacity would not justify the expense of his travel

34. No comprehensive data exists on the social composition of the Amtmänner. Pfeilsticker's *Dienerbuch* treats only those officials in the Hof, Regierung, and Verwaltung and leaves out altogether the provincial officials. My own investigations in Nürtingen, Urach, and Vaihingen reveal that, though most Amtmänner came from prominent families in their districts, these officials moved about the duchy and thus could have no family connection with the local elites in the areas where they were working.

35. HSAS, A 34: Bü. 39; Sattler, *Herzöge*, VI, 163f.; Grube, *Stuttgarter Landtag*, 285ff.

36. HSAS, *tomus actorum*, XXXV, 350–356 and XXXVI, 683–694.

37. The regency government formed in 1628 after the death of Duke Johann Friedrich was headed by his brother Ludwig Friedrich, who came from Mömpelgard to carry out that responsibility. He died in 1631 and was succeeded by his younger brother Julius Friedrich von Württemberg-Weiltingen, who served until Eberhard's majority in 1633.

to Stuttgart and his room and board during the diet.[38] The regent, in need of fresh tax grants in order to meet current military expenses, gave qualified assent, and when the estates assembled in February 1629 no Amtmann appeared among the delegates.[39] The event apparently constituted a precedent: When the matter came up in subsequent years in the privy council, the consensus among the councilors was that the estates had won their point.[40]

Certainly the estates held this opinion. Their first order of business at the Landtag of 1651, the first general assembly since 1634, was to dismiss four delegates whose presence they found "unacceptable." The unambiguous criteria justifying these expulsions made explicit the Ehrbarkeit's determination to preserve its absolute control over the delegations, a control that the members tied to the preservation of Lutheran orthodoxy and to participation in the municipal governments of the various district towns. They dismissed one delegate because he was a "papist" and hence "unfit to participate." Two others received rejections because they belonged "neither to the urban court nor to the councils of the towns that sent them." A fourth was banned because he was a ducal official.[41] Confessional orthodoxy and membership in the urban magistracy: these were now the prerequisites for election from which no exceptions were to be made, and their elevation to the status of law meant complete control of the Landtag by the Ehrbarkeit. Except for the prelates,[42] the Württemberg estates now became virtually synonymous with the families who controlled the governments in the district towns.[43] The significance of this monopoly was crucial in terms of their ability to preserve both local power and their status as a privileged caste within the duchy.

38. F. Benzing, "Die Vertretung von 'Stadt und Amt' im altwürttembergischen Landtag unter besonderer Berücksichtigung des Amts Nürtingen" (Tübingen: Ph.D. diss., 1924), 33–39. Also, HSAS, A 34: Bü. 44–46; Sattler, *Herzöge*, VII, 4 and Beil. 2; Reyscher, *Vollständige Sammlung*, I, 362–364; and F. Wintterlin, "Beamtentum und Verfassung im Herzogtum Württemberg," *WVJHLG*, NF 32 (1925/26), 4ff.
39. Grube, *Stuttgarter Landtag*, 299f.
40. HSAS, A 204: Bü. 1 (19 March 1630).
41. HSAS, *tomus actorum*, XXXVIII, 91, 98, 102, 129, 175, 176, 394–396, 419 and XXXIX, 74–93, 106, 107, 129, 131, 159–160.
42. Although most prelates came from families of the pastorate or in territorial service, with strong ties to the Ehrbarkeit, there were instances of entry into the group by Württembergers of more humble origins. See Christian Kolb, "Zur Geschichte der Prälaturen," *BWKG*, 29 (1925), 22–74; Christoph Kolb, "Zur Geschichte des Pfarrstandes in Altwürttemberg," *BWKG*, 57 (1957), 74–190; Fritz Ernst, "Fünfhundert Jahre Stuttgarter Landtag 1457–1957," *ZWLG*, 17 (1958), vii; and M. Hasselhorn, *Der altwürttembergische Pfarrstand im 18. Jahrhundert* (Stuttgart, 1958), 24–38 and 81.
43. This control persisted throughout the history of Altwürttemberg. In 1799 the duchy contained 1,200 villages in which resided 75 percent of the principality's population; P. Röder, *Geographisches statistisch-topographisches Lexikon von Schwaben*, II

Victory for the Ehrbarkeit had several long-term consequences. Most importantly, the Amtmann lost his opportunity to function at the local level of the duchy in a dual role analogous to that of the English justice of the peace. Formerly, when elected as district representative to the Landtag, the Amtmann had served both as spokesman for local interests and as a royal servant, combining as it were the two dimensions of sovereign power in the duchy. His participation in the stormy debates of the early 1620s over coinage devaluation, for example, had worked to merge the interests of crown and estates in such a way as to promote a sense of commonality and to alleviate tensions between central and regional administration as well as between ducal and domestic concerns.[44] After 1629 he became strictly a royal official, identified in the district as a ducal agent whose allegiance lay with the government at Stuttgart. Thus, though the Amtmann continued his supervisory role in the internal affairs of a district such as Nürtingen, records indicate that the town magistrates no longer consulted him on matters of territorial taxation (*Landschaftsteuer*), a subject of great importance to his ducal master who depended upon the Landtag for all new taxes and who had relied upon the Amtmann to generate local support for ducal requests.[45]

Negotiations on tax matters fell to the town Bürgermeister, who now became the official link between the Landtag and the district.[46] As the central government soon perceived, so marked an exclusion of the Amtmann from the affairs of the estates eroded the government's ability to shape fiscal policy at the grass roots of the duchy. In the decade after the war the privy councilors sought to correct this imbalance by a series of confidential instructions to the chancellery, ordering the secretaries to forward all government communications on matters of finance directly to the Amtmann who was to open and then

(Ulm, 1801), 1177 and 1194. Only fifty of these villages sent their own delegations to the Landtag, where these representatives controlled ten of the eighty-six votes cast at that body; see W. Grube, "Dorfgemeinde und Amtsversammlung in Altwürttemberg," *ZWLG*, 13 (1954), 196. These ten votes in themselves represented no "progress" by the rural authorities against the Ehrbarkeit's monopoly. Rather they reflected the fact that ten districts represented by that time at the Landtag contained no towns: Asperg, Höpfigheim, Hoheneck, Kirchheim am Neckar, Maulbronn, Mundelsheim, Neidlingen, Pflummern, Reichenbach, and Steusslingen.

44. Grube, *Stuttgarter Landtag*, 285–291; see Hippel, "Bevölkerung und Wirtschaft," 435 ff., on the effects of the "Kipper und Wipper" upon the Württemberg economy.

45. Benzing, "Die Vertretung von 'Stadt und Amt,'" 61 ff. and 102–144.

46. HSAS, A 204: Bü. 1. See also H. Specker, "Die Verfassung und Verwaltung der württembergischen Amtstädte im 17. und 18. Jahrhundert," in E. Maschke and J. Sydow, eds., *Verwaltung und Gesellschaft in der südwestdeutschen Stadt des 17. und 18. Jahrhunderts* (Stuttgart, 1969), 1–22.

pass them to the elected officials of the district.[47] Such a precedure informed the Amtmann of the details of all government requests and ensured him of an opportunity to mold public opinion before the local leaders could develop a sense of the immediate response of the Landtag's leadership. The Landtag took offense at this policy and succeeded in persuading Eberhard to have the material sent first to the executive committee of the estates where it could be read and commented upon by those leaders before it reached the district. Local delegates could therefore ascertain their leaders' reactions before being required to discuss the matter with the Amtmann and the town magistrates. The duke's command, issued on 20 January 1657, brought reluctant compliance from his officials and prompted the privy councilors to draw up a memorandum outlining the dangers they foresaw in such a procedure.

The councilors noted that the insertion of the Landtag between the crown and the Amtmann in these fiscal matters further underscored the latter's separation in the districts from the affairs of the estates. Such a separation, the councilors suggested, sharpened local perceptions of the distinction between duke and Landtag and intensified the adversary nature of their relations.[48] Most of the privy councilors, as we shall see, were exceedingly conservative; and since many of them maintained close family ties with the estates, there could be no question of their writing such a report with the intent of attacking the privileges of the Landtag. The privy councilors recognized that the Tübinger Vertrag vested rights of taxation in the estates and were quite prepared to grant them their due in that area. But as professional administrators they feared that too rigid a separation of authority might compromise the administrative processes of the central government. And indeed judicial difficulties had already surfaced by the time of Eberhard's death in 1674.

One case from among the several hundred recorded in the privy council's minutes from this period illustrates the point. In this instance competing sets of jurisdiction made it possible for an insignificant miller by the name of Hanns Jerg Zigel to play off crown and estates in order to secure a favorable tax settlement. In April 1668 he first appealed to the estates for an adjustment on his tax rate. He claimed that he was paying too high a tax on wine to be served in the inn that he and his wife operated next door to his mill in the district of Backnang, a hilly region north of Stuttgart on the eastern edge of

47. HSAS, A 204: Bü. 1 and A 202: Bü. 2455.
48. HSAS, A 202: Bü. 2455 and A 204: Bü. 1 (Protocolla for 19 March 1630).

the duchy. A court of estates reviewed the case and decided against Zigel, who then brought the matter to the privy council without informing that body that the case had already come before the estates. The privy councilors referred the matter to the Oberrat where ducal lawyers ruled that Ziegel's complaint was justified and ordered his rate lowered.[49] The estates protested the right of the Oberrat even to hear the case and claimed that they alone could rule on tax matters. As late as February 1670 they were still complaining to the duke that the government had overstepped its authority and insisting that control over taxation gave the Landtag exclusive right to dispense justice in this area.[50]

Conflicts of this sort were part and parcel of the Württemberg political fabric and would doubtless have occurred with or without the Amtmann's involvement with the estates. The question was one of tone and degree. By excluding royal officials from the Landtag the estates had drawn a rigid distinction between themselves and the central government. Though rights of taxation constituted the technical definition that supported this separation, the proliferation of these judicial cases made clear that the Landtag's control over taxes could also erode the sovereign's control over justice. Eberhard's was not the personality to draw extreme conclusions from this possibility, but his successors proved men of quite different temperaments. They had no intention of sharing either judicial or fiscal power with the estates. In the conflicts that ensued over these matters, the Ehrbarkeit found its earlier victory over the Amtmann to have Pyhrric connotations. For while exclusion ensured the urban magistrates a caste monopoly over the Landtag, it denied them the contribution of an increasingly professional cadre of administrators and isolated them from the bureaucracy at a time when they desperately needed its support.

At the very moment that the Ehrbarkeit was excluding the crown from the internal workings of the Landtag, the pressures of war were stimulating political life in the territorial districts in ways that affected both the crown and the diet. Initially it was the crown's weakness that encouraged a greater political vitality in these regional units, administrative districts with a royal as well as a local component. The years of military occupation and ducal exile, followed as they were by a period of distinct impoverishment for the royal treasury, made it difficult for the central administration to keep in direct touch with the affairs of the villages, hamlets, and market towns of the duchy. Understaffed

49. HSAS, A 202: Bü. 2455.
50. HSAS, A 203: Bü. 13. For other such conflicts between the estates and the Amtleute, see A 202: Bü. 2455.

Stuttgart agencies, struggling simply to carry on routine business, had no enthusiasm for increased responsibilities.[51] Under these circumstances the Amt emerged as the level at which the wartime government found itself best able to carry out its administrative functions. Especially in more distant areas such as Urach, the Amtmann held the line for the duke and established in his master's name the liaison with local authorities on the regulation of markets, the administration of justice, the quartering of soldiers, and the maintenance of school, hospital, charity, and church. Local enterprise strengthened the institution of the district, and the Amt came increasingly to provide the framework within which the localities organized their political experience.[52]

As a result of this activity, the central government found itself at the end of the war in something of an anomalous position. The administration at Stuttgart was relatively enfeebled but reports to the privy council in the early 1650s indicated a greater vigor at the subordinate level of the districts. The Amtmann at Urach, for example, was traveling constantly throughout that Amt, presiding over the urban courts and consulting in the villages with those elders responsible for community justice. In addition he regulated property disputes, settled quarrels over inheritance, saw to the settlement of displaced peasants, and worked to stimulate a revival in the local markets. Extant correspondence to Stuttgart from the ducal officials at Schorndorf, Bietigheim, and Vaihingen indicates a similar activity in these Aemter.[53] Although the fragmentary reports preserved from the other districts are too incomplete to permit firm generalizations on their internal activies, the geographic, demographic, and economic diversity among the four districts already mentioned suggests that the pattern of regional administrative activity might well have been a common one. If so, it is useful to think of the monarchy's postwar efforts at strengthening the central government—efforts that centered particularly on the privy council—as a task of coordinating and channeling the energies of an already vigorous secondary level of territorial administration.

The threat of conflict in such a situation was obvious. One thinks at once of a power such as France, where at this very moment regional

51. During the late 1630s and 1640s, the Stuttgart government was chronically understaffed. The crown could not find—or afford to pay—sufficient qualified personnel and left large numbers of administrative posts vacant; see L. von Spittler, *Geschichte des wirtembergischen Geheimen-Raths-Collegiums*, in *Sämtliche Werke*, ed. K. Wächter, XIII (Stuttgart and Tübingen, 1837), 342–363, on problems of recruitment during these years.
52. HSAS, A 204: Bü. 4.
53. Ibid.

*parlements*, in alliance with the provincial aristocracy, were in rebellion against the crown. For the French Frondeurs district organization clearly constituted an alternative to central authority in ways that never developed in Württemberg, where the feudal nobility had already succeeded in separating itself from the territorial state and where the clergy was functioning as a branch of the government.[54] Furthermore, the distinction between Amtmann and Ehrbarkeit, as well as that between village and town, kept the Württemberg Amt from developing ultimately into a centrifugal force. Then too, stability was promoted by the fact that there was no institution except the monarchy that could weld the Aemter together. The Landtag had excluded the Amtmann and thus denied itself the possibility of serving as a forum that could unite regional administrative interests in a sustained struggle with the crown.

But if the Amtmann remained a loyal ducal official, and hence a crucial link between the crown and the localities, the Amt itself experienced internal realignments that raised the status of its rural component and allowed the village elders a greater political voice in regional affairs. Most important, peasant leadership gained the right to participate in elections to the Landtag. This participation by the rural elite in a decision heretofore reserved exclusively for their urban counterparts opened new possibilities of influence both for the crown and for the Landtag. Under the new arrangements opportunities existed for coalition politics that could either strengthen the Ehrbarkeit's position against the crown or provide the duke with an instrument of influence over the Landtag to replace the one he had lost with the Amtmann's exclusion from that body.

Again, it was a combination of war and economics that promoted the internal restructuring of regional influence. Records indicated that the Württemberg towns began a closer association with the surrounding villages of their districts during the trauma of military invasion. A common danger seemingly brought the district inhabitants together and forced them to pool their resources in order to survive. Under these circumstances the villages assumed a more active role in district affairs.[55] Their activity surfaced in reports to Stuttgart from various Amtmann who began to use terms like *Amtstandschaft*, a

54. The Reformation closed in Württemberg the classic alternatives to strong monarchy: the church and the *seigneurie*. The Württemberg church became a branch of the central government, and the territorial nobility took advantage of the general confusion to withdraw from the duchy and to incorporate as Reichsunmittelbar. Cf. Paul Logie, *La Fronde en Normandie*, 3 vols. (Amiens, 1951/52), for a detailed local study documenting the importance of the *seigneurie* as an institutional counterweight to central authority.

55. Grube, "Dorfgemeinde und Amtsversammlung in Altwürttemberg," 198 ff.

word with no direct English equivalent but one that carries the con-
notation of district solidarity.[56] The local assembly (Amtsversammlung), an ancient institution that had withered in the late sixteenth century but now began to revive,[57] provided the institutional
vehicle for increased participation by the villages; finance contributed
the fuel.

As the outlying villages assumed a larger portion of local expenditure, the village leaders demanded a greater voice in the affairs of the
district. They insisted particularly that rural officials participate in the
elections for delegates to the Landtag.[58] Already by 1638 we find evidence of such participation in the Amtsversammlung of Nürtingen, a
region northeast of Tübingen which had been especially vulnerable to
ravages by Bavarian soldiers.[59] This rural engagement continued to
gain momentum throughout the remainder of the century, and by
1737 village mayors (Dorfschultheissen) were taking part regularly in
the Landtag elections of virtually all the secular districts of the
duchy.[60] Rural officials never managed to modify the stipulation that
only members of the town magistracies could stand for election, so
that their participation never weakened the Ehrbarkeit's physical monopoly over the delegations.[61] But by active engagement in the selection process, the more powerful peasants moved into a stronger
position from which to defend their interests at the territorial level.
They could put pressure on their elected representatives to speak at
Stuttgart for rural concerns and could see to it that these delegates
championed no legislation that might undercut their own influence in
the villages.

Debates and discussions at the district elections are lost to us. One
must take care not to attribute undue importance to what, given the
limited pool of candidates, must have been relatively routine elec-

56. A Rieger, "Die Entwicklung des württembergischen Kreisverband" (Tübingen:
Ph.D. diss., 1952), 26; Reyscher, Vollständige Sammlung, XVII, 171.
57. On the earlier role of the Amtsversammlung, see F. Wintterlin, Geschichte der
Behördenorganisation in Württemberg, I (Stuttgart, 1902), 62: Viktor Ernst, "Die
direkten Staatssteuren in der Grafschaft Wirtemberg," WJ (1904), 74f., 80f.; and C.
von Stälin, Württembergische Geschichte, IV (Stuttgart, 1873), 723.
58. Benzing, "Die Vertretung von 'Stadt und Amt,'" 61ff.
59. Nürtingen Heimatbuches, II (Würzburg, 1953), xiii–xxii. Cf. Grube, "Dorfgemeinde und Amtsversammlung in Altwürttemberg," 204.
60. H. Lehmann, "Die württembergischen Landstände im 17. und 18. Jahrhundert," in Dieterich Gerhard, ed., Ständische Vertretung in Europa im 17. und 18.
Jahrhundert (Göttingen, 1969), 187. See also H. Fink, "Zusammenstellung über die
Landtagswahlrecht der altwürttembergsichen Städte und Aemter" (typewritten manuscript on deposit in SAL, 1957); and Benzing, "Die Vertretung von 'Stadt und Amt,'"
102–110.
61. See note 43 to this chapter.

tions. By the same token, an elected delegate usually served for life, so that opportunities for lobbying at elections occurred irregularly. A delegate's receptivity to domestic pressure groups must have been considerably less than would be the case today for one of our own, more frequently elected representatives. Still it is not unreasonable to suspect that the inclusion of the village elders in the election process offered the more powerful peasants at least a chance for increased influence in the Landtag and ensured at a minimum that the Ehrbarkeit would hesitate before ignoring the villages altogether.[62] Equally important, a wider role for the rural elite in an invigorated district assembly made possible a coalition of interests between town and countryside which strengthened the Landtag and enabled its members to resist more confidently those government policies that ran counter to their own concerns.

A dovetailing of rural and urban interests occurred shortly after the war when Eberhard attempted to regulate the economic recovery of the duchy. Both town and village responded with implacable opposition and used the Landtag to defend their interests. In their response to these cameralistic ventures, the estates contributed to the stalemate that characterized Württemberg politics in the years after the war. They frustrated the crown's efforts to introduce new policies but posed no new alternatives. We have already seen that the postwar economic priorities of town and village elites differed from those of the crown. The royal domain came out of the war more seriously compromised than the tax base of the Landschaft and therefore required a more aggressive program of rehabilitation. Under pressure to obtain peasant labor and operating cash, Eberhard undertook a series of programs aimed at stimulating the recovery of the state treasury. He proposed numerous mercantilist schemes for the creation of new industries—mining and beer making to name but two examples—and for resettlement of the lands left empty by war.[63] In each instance the programs were to have been funded by the crown through taxes voted by the estates and then protected with royal monopolies and government subsidies. The estates rejected these policies out of hand; they either refused funding or granted such meager allotments that the projects never got off the ground. Their position in these discussions always rested on a defense of the principle of free trade. Stuttgart, they steadfastly asserted, had no business interfering

---

62. Benzing, "Die Vertretung von 'Stadt und Amt,'" 110–139.

63. HSAS, A 204: Bü. 3, 4 and A 39: Bü. 39. Also Bütterlin, *Die merkantilistische Geldpolitik im Herzogtum Württemberg,* 91f.; Söll, "Die staatliche Wirtschaftspolitik in Württemberg," 46–68; and Hippel, "Bevölkerung und Wirtschaft," 442–448.

in the economic life of the principality and certainly no right to legislate such matters. They made both these points in the debates that took place in 1650 over the creation in Württemberg of a state brewing industry. The controversy provided a representative illustration of the estates' stand on such matters. In the 1640s Eberhard had tried to set up a chain of ducal breweries that would produce beer for domestic consumption. The estates denounced the move as "a dangerous innovation," pointing out that prior to the war "no one in Württemberg had even heard of brewing beer" and implying that Eberhard was forcing the Württemberg innkeepers to stock and sell his product to the detriment of local winegrowers and of the commercial interests that handled their wine.[64] The complaints reached a full crescendo at the general Landtag of 1651–1652, when the estates made suspension of these ducal efforts a condition for the grant of the additional moneys so sorely needed by the government.[65]

In their unsuccessful brewery negotiations with the estates, Eberhard and his advisers showed a mixture of irritation and disingenuousness. They presented the project as economically sound and as offering hope for the stabilization of government finances while at the same time providing employment and stimulating capital growth. Even as they stressed its advantages, they glossed over the implications of an increased power for the central government in the setting up and control of government monopolies. They also refused to recognize the impact of ducal brewing upon the peasant winegrowers who produced only for local consumption and upon the district markets, controlled largely by the Ehrbarkeit, through which vintners distributed their wine. Instead they denounced the estates as excessively parochial and accused them of ignoring the bright promises of the venture.[66] Their complaints were not entirely unjustified. For though the estates spoke loudly of constitutional freedom, their discussions revealed a mean-spirited defense of local interests and a palpable fear that any restructuring of the territorial economy might undercut their own power.[67] The estates persisted in this stance and throughout the rest of the century showed themselves resolutely opposed to all efforts to tamper with the economy of the state and hos-

---

64. HSAS, A 34: Bü. 50, 51. Cf. K. Weidner, *Die Anfänge einer staatlichen Wirtschaftspolitik in Württemberg* (Stuttgart, 1931), 112–121; P. Wiedenmann, "Zur Geschichte der gewerblichen Bierbrauerei in Altwürttemberg," *WJ* (1934/35), 47–58.

65. Grube, *Stuttgarter Landtag*, 323–324. On the sixteenth-century efforts at mercantilism, see Lehmann, "Die württembergischen Landstände im 17. und 18. Jahrhundert," 198n28.

66. HSAS, A 204: Bü. 4.

67. HSAS. A 34: Bü. 50 and 51; A 204: Bü. 4; *tomus actorum*, XLIX and L.

tile even to any cameralistic writing that treated economics as a branch of central government.

The merit of the Landtag's opposition is not at issue. As in the case of the crown, the estates doubtless acted with a mixture of public spirit and self-interest. More important is the opportunity to observe that the Landtag's position in this matter reflected more than simply an urban oligarchy's selfish commitment to its own commercial markets. Prosperous rural elements were also threatened by the prospect of an economy managed by the central government. Their interests too were served by opposition to policies that threatened competition for the more prosperous village landowners and interference in the agrarian markets that they controlled. The cameralistic challenge began in Württemberg at a time when rural participation in the district elections was increasing, and it opened up the option of a coalition in the district between village mayors and their urban counterparts. It seems fair to suggest that the Ehrbarkeit recognized the possibilities in coalition politics as a source of strength in its struggles with the prince. For we shall see that in the eighteenth century dukes with absolutist pretentions attempted to break the hold of the Ehrbarkeit upon the Landtag. Ducal strategy at that time centered upon the local assembly where royal agents strove to drive a wedge between villages and town. The attempt foundered upon the strong bond between the urban and rural interest groups, a coalition made possible by the opening up of the assemblies in the mid-seventeenth century to increased participation by the village notables.

The internal reorganization and increased political vitality in the districts found certain parallel expressions within the structure of the Württemberg monarchy. For whereas Eberhard deferred to the estates in their opposition to programs of cameralistic economics, he pushed through a reorganization of two important government agencies, the privy council and the treasury. The privy council is discussed at the end of this chapter; attention focuses here on the treasury. Eberhard introduced fiscal reforms in that office that bore directly on the distribution of political power. Though they were in themselves expediencies and should not be regarded as steps in a master plan, these reforms were to affect the Landtag and also to alter the House of Württemberg's relations with the territorial government. In particular they emancipated the ducal family from dependency upon the estates at the same moment that they tied the monarch more closely to the Landtag for the funds necessary to run his government. As was the case with the districts, the implications of these changes were not immediately clear to contemporaries. Eber-

A 1643 view of Tübingen by Matthäus Merian. The city was the stronghold of the territorial estates and the seat of the duchy's venerable university. Castle, church, and Rathaus—the architectural symbols of the division of political power championed by the estates—appropriately dominated the skyline. Photograph courtesy of the Princeton University Library

A. Das Fürstliche Schloß. B. S. Georgen Stifft. C. Der Universitæt. D. Das Fürstliche Seprendum. E. Das Rathauß. F. Die Burß.

Tübingen.

hard's determined commitment to a policy of cooperation with the estates meant that no one pushed these reforms to their ultimate conclusion and that they remained open-ended options in the Württemberg political drama. Like increased political activism, which might either have weakened or strengthened royal authority in the districts, so fiscal restructuring carried two alternative possibilities: it could further enhance the authority of the Landtag, or it could become the vehicle by which the dukes could escape that institution's control.

In structural terms the reorganization of the treasury proved a relatively simple matter. In the years immediately after the war the duke began to separate within the Rentkammer those properties and assets that he defined as belonging to the state from those holdings that he claimed for the House of Württemberg. The operative criterion for selection appears to have been a decision by the duke to describe as state property those lands and privileges in the royal domain over which the Landschaften had certain rights of supervision and whose income was liable for assessment in the case of taxes levied by the Landtag.[68] All other ducal holdings—primarily enfeoffed imperial lordships and properties purchased or inherited from the imperial knights, together with those estates incorporated into Württemberg through the dowries of ducal brides—were organized into a separate trust called the *Kammerschreiberei*. Under this arrangement ducal officials administered two separate treasuries: the Landschreiberei and the Kammerschreiberei. Income from the state properties under ducal control flowed into the Landschreiberei; and since these lands composed a portion of the tax base of the duchy, the Landtag exercised certain rights of inspection and administrative supervision over this account.[69] The Kammerschreiberei received all income derived from the private holdings of the House; accountability rested exclusively with the duke who controlled these properties and owed no Württemberg taxes on their possession.[70] By compact between the duke and the other members of the family, it was agreed that these "private" holdings would pass to the eldest male in the senior line of the family as a perpetual trust. The heir then used the income from

68. HSAS, A 204: Bü. 34.
69. Wintterlin, *Behördenorganisation*, I, 81–86; Schneider, *Württembergische Geschichte*, 286f.
70. Eberhard often delegated to the privy council responsibility for administrative supervision of the Kammerschreiberei. His instructions on these matters are scattered throughout the privy council records for the 1660s and early seventies. See also, HSAS, A 203: Bü. 8–13 and the letter from the executive committee of the Landtag (8 October 1666) in A 204: Bü. 34.

the trust to provide for the other members of the House.[71] Lest there should be disagreement as to what constituted a fair settlement for the daughters and junior cadets, Eberhard drew up precise instructions on the size and scope of appropriate dowries and spelled out in detail the style of residence, the furnishings, the transportation, and the hunting privileges appropriate for the princes of the House.[72]

Incomplete treasury records preclude any systematic reckoning of the assets or value of the Kammerschreiberei. We do know that by the time of Eberhard's death in 1674 the trust was furnishing sufficient capital for the fourteen children who survived him. Indeed, to the end of the old Reich the daughters and younger sons of the ducal House drew their support from its capital. More to the point for this analysis, however, is the fact that the Kammerschreiberei became a bone of contention between Eberhard and his estates, that the duke absolutely refused to compromise, and that the decision to reconstitute the royal domain precipitated a cash shortage for the government which led to a fundamental change in the duchy's traditional tax system.

This tax structure can be easily explained. Throughout the sixteenth and early seventeenth centuries the Württemberg Landtag had voted taxes only in order to raise moneys to pay off the debts incurred by the monarch in the running of the government. The estates never advanced funds directly to the sovereign; they expected him to borrow on his own those additional moneys required by his administration and then after the fact to seek redress for his debts from the Landtag.[73] This policy prevailed until 1638, when the young Eberhard returned from exile at Strassburg to find much of his domain alienated and his treasury on the point of collapse. In these circumstances he turned to the estates for an advance of money with which to carry on the government. The estates complied and by the end of the war had contributed more than 800,000 florins in direct subsidies to the crown.[74] But though the estates always insisted that these grants constituted an emergency action and that the primary role of the estates lay in continued negotiation on ducal debts, Eberhard re-

71. For the details of this family compact, see HSAS, Hausarchiv, G 1–8: 217.

72. The codicil of 1674 on Eberhard's last will and testament spells out these provisions in detail (HSAS, Hausarchiv, G 1–8: 221). A summary version of these provisions is found in Pfaff, *Geschichte des Fürstenhauses* (Stuttgart, 1839), 53–54.

73. Paragraph fourteen of the Landtagsabschied for 1629 contains a succinct description of the tax system and its philosophy (HSAS, A 202: 1861). A copy is also found in A 202: 1866.

74. Grube, *Stuttgarter Landtag*, 322.

fused after the war to return to a system of ducal borrowing. He never spelled out his reasons for this decision, but his discussions with the privy council suggested that an unadventurous temperament had combined with the realization that a chronic shortage of capital and an exhausted domain were not auspicious conditions for the raising of money from outside creditors.[75] In any event he firmly declined to borrow and insisted instead that the government operate out of current income.

But current income proved inadequate for the task. Quite apart from the problems discussed earlier in connection with the economic recovery of the royal farms, Eberhard's decision to redefine the domain and to assign a portion of these properties to a trust reserved exclusively for the upkeep of the ducal family further weakened an already compromised capital base. Funds generated by the Landschreiberei could not sustain the government and, in the face of the sovereign's refusal to borrow, the estates felt compelled to continue their wartime policy of advancing money directly to the crown. It is true that they remained adamant in their refusal to legislate any kind of permanent tax structure and that they confined their advance in each instance to pledges of one, two, or three years. But while they denounced the Kammerschreiberei as a dangerous innovation and considered the Rentkammer underfunded only because the duke had amputated a substantial portion of its corpus,[76] they had no legal grounds to challenge Eberhard's decision to establish an independent trust that would handle income from his own properties. They had to rest content with his bland assurances that these exhausted properties were contributing all they could to the ducal purse and hence to the government. Those accounts open to inspection by the Landtag did indeed project deficit balances so that monetary advances were necessary if the government was to function. The result was that, except for two years in the 1640s, the excise tax voted in 1638 when Eberhard returned to Stuttgart continued in effect until a reorganization of state finances took place in Württemberg under the impact of the Napoleonic invasions of Germany.[77]

The amount of these annual subsidies, or *Kammerbeiträge* as they

75. HSAS, A 204: Bü. 4.
76. HSAS, A 203: Bü. 11 (esp. the correspondence between the privy council and the executive committee of the Landtag for October 1666).
77. For the original excise legislation, see Reyscher, *Vollständige Sammlung*, XVII, 162–165, Nr. 74. The details of the tax varied over the years as new items were included and old ones deleted, but the basic staple remained the taxes on commercial goods, woolens, wine, salt, meat, and wood. On the abortive negotiations for 1642–1644, see Sattler, *Herzöge*, VIII, 30–71.

were referred to by the estates, varied under Eberhard from 12,000 to 40,000 florins; the average for the reign was 26,500 florins per year.[78] In themselves, of course, the advances were insufficient to cover government expenses, and it would be a mistake to assume that their presentation released the crown from fiscal pressure. The government continued to devour all revenues from the Landschreiberei—and whatever funds Eberhard chose to take from the Kammerschreiberei to pay the expenses of his court—as well as the bulk of the income from the ecclesiastical properties. On this latter score the estates protested vigorously that the crown consumed far more than its share of the church moneys. They regarded as a substantial victory Eberhard's affirmation in 1668 of their rights to a share in the church income and a pledge that henceforth the Landtag would receive its full third of these annual revenues.[79] Nevertheless, the decision to continue the wartime policy of direct grants to the sovereign marked an important step in the crown's dealings with the Landtag. The principle of regular taxation and direct subvention was established. The policy also meant that the crown was able to project an income over and above that of the domain and thus to embark on longer-term, more ambitious policies of expansion. Whereas Eberhard's general caution kept such plans to a fairly modest scale, later rulers pushed in the direction of military adventurism and roused the estates to full-scale opposition. And even Eberhard used the funds to establish a Cavalry Life Guard[80] and so to lay the groundwork for the great confrontation over a standing army for Württemberg that set the estates at loggerheads with the late-seventeenth-century monarchs.

As so often in this period, the lines of development remained am-

78. This average is obtained through an analysis of the levies voted over these years as recorded in Grube, *Stuttgarter Landtag*, 313–346. It is not at all clear that these sums were in fact collected each year and that all the moneys went unencumbered to Eberhard. Fragmentary records make verification impossible. But privy council protocolla for these years indicate that oftentimes a three-year grant was renegotiated the second year and that portions of the moneys were pledged to discharge obligations to the Reichstag or other imperial agencies.

79. HSAS, A 203: Bü. 12; Sattler, *Herzöge*, X, 149–151. Subsequent complaints to the privy council by the executive committee of the Landtag (A 204: Bü. 37 and 38) as well as petitions of grievances to the duke as late as 1674 (A 203: Bü. 15) indicated that Eberhard continued to retain more of the ecclesiastical income than the estates found appropriate. Nevertheless, he did affirm the principle that the estates were entitled to a full one-third of these revenues and thus provided them with a legal base from which to press their claims.

80. Eberhard commissioned a 100-man cavalry guard and paid for these troops from his own purse, diverting moneys from the Kammerbeiträge for this purpose. The Household Guard (*Leibgarde*) caused great consternation among the estates. See HSAS, A 202: Bu. 1861 (esp. the minutes from the privy council meeting of 14 December 1666). Also, Carsten, *Princes and Parliaments*, 72–82.

biguous: if the crown stood to benefit from the Kammerbeiträge, so too did the estates. The Landtag scrupulously maintained that the Kammerbeiträge were free gifts, not an obligation, a point that the estates returned to with a vengeance in their eighteenth-century struggle against absolute monarchy. They refused steadfastly to pledge any amount for more than a few years and thus ensured that the duke, who came increasingly to rely on these funds, would summon the Landtag on a regular basis. In marked contrast to such neighboring German states as Baden and the Palatinate, the Württemberg Landtag met regularly in the years after the war; once every two or three years was the pattern under Eberhard. And since the Kammerbeiträge constituted a primary item on each agenda, the estates were able to use the grants as a parliamentary weapon in their negotiations with the ruler. As the ducal concession on the ecclesiastical properties indicated, the estates secured important affirmations of their own historic rights and privileges. In this regard their postwar vigor produced results quite different from those achieved by the estates in Mecklenburg and Electoral Saxony, two other German principalities where frequent territorial diets secured powerful advantages for the territorial nobility at the expense of urban and village interests.[81]

The decision to create the Kammerschreiberei and thus to establish a *Hofkammergut* or ducal trust proved equally open-ended in its implications. Eberhard secured an independent fiscal base for the members of his family which freed them from personal dependence upon the estates and made possible the expansion of a capital exempt from territorial taxation. In this sense the family gained considerable mobility. But one must not forget that by transferring capital assets out of the state domain and into a special trust for private use Eberhard was sharply reducing the fiscal base out of which the routine expenses of administration had to come. By separating into parts what had heretofore been one large fund, he made the government more dependent than ever upon the tax revenue controlled by the estates. And surely Eberhard's decision revealed a perception of the state at odds with that of the traditional Landesvater in whose image his old-

---

81. For comparative references to the estates of the Palatinate and Baden, see Eberhard Gothein, "Die Landstände der Kurpfalz," *Zeitschrift für die Geschichte des Oberrheins*, 42 (1888), 1–76 (esp. 64ff.); and E. Gothein, "Die Landstände am Oberrhein," in *Fünfundzwanzig Jahre der Badischen Historischen Kommission* (Heidelberg, 1909), 29–51. For Saxony and Mecklenburg, see Fritz Kaphahn, "Kurfürst und kursächsische Stände im 17. und beginnenden 18. Jahrhundert," *Neues Archiv für sächsische Geschichte und Altertumskunde*, 43 (1922), 69ff.; cf. Carsten, *Princes and Parliaments*, 228–257, 340–347, 423–444.

fashioned piety and benign notions of sovereignty seemed so often to have been cast. The distinction between monarch and state was never drawn by the sixteenth-century patriarchs and was denied most emphatically by the more ambitious absolutists of a later period. But the language in Eberhard's last will and testament—a document subjected to frequent revisions in his own hand—made clear that his creation of the Kammerschreiberei reflected a basic philosophic commitment and not just a clever fiscal maneuver.[82] He spelled out for his heirs his firm conviction that the duchy constituted an indivisible entity distinct from their own persons and needs. The possessions of the state (Staatsbesitz), he asserted, stood above any private claims by the ducal family. The royal princes and princesses must be cared for, to be sure, but the proper source of that maintenance was a family trust and not the creation of appanages carved out of the territorial domain of the state.[83] Eberhard's thinking found considerable resonance in his discussions with the privy councilors and led to ideas of sovereignty quite unlike those of the late Renaissance rulers who governed in personal terms, reflecting their conviction that the state was but an extension of the monarch himself. The contrast with the L'État c'est moi of the eighteenth-century francophilic German monarchs is equally striking and points up once again the dangers of making linear growth projections for government.

The introduction of new elements in the privy council ultimately exerted a more far-reaching influence on the central government than did those in the treasury. Once the turmoil of war had subsided, Eberhard turned to the privy council and drew its members into a closer association for the direction of the Württemberg government. He also made structural changes in its organization so as to expand its administrative duties and to regulate the social composition of its membership. As with the other institutions examined in this chapter, the impact of these changes was not immediately clear and their subsequent resolution by no means a foregone conclusion. Council records for these years show the councilors hard at work on what appeared at first reading to have been routine matters given them by

82. HSAS, Hausarchiv, G 1–8: 217, 220, 221.

83. Eberhard's determination to prevent the carving up of state property into appanages built upon the earlier legislation by Duke Christoph (1550–1568) but with a much greater emphasis upon the distinction between the claims of the ducal family and those of the state; see B. Wunder, "Der Administrator Herzog Friedrich Karl von Württemberg," ZWLG, 30 (1971), 117–118. On the earlier legislation cf. J. Pfister, Herzog Christoph zu Wirtemberg, I (Tübingen, 1819), 584f. and 614f.; Stälin, Württembergische Geschichte, IV, 733f.; and A. Adam, "Das Unteilbarkeitsgesetz im württembergischen Fürstenhause nach seiner geschichtlichen Entwicklung," WVJSLG, 6 (1883), 161–222.

the prince or delivered for their attention by the district officials. Only on the rarest occasions did the councilors depart from their regular agenda to discuss substantive issues; and when they did so, dogged diligence rather than bold creativity characterized their remarks. Nonetheless an examination of council routine reveals certain subtle shifts in responsibility and perception which opened up a direction of growth not immediately perceived by the councilors, one much more far-reaching than their own conventional, slightly fussy temperaments would have anticipated or condoned.

The enactments of legislation to establish the privy council defined the board's duties in general terms, following the outline of a 1628 memorandum drawn up by a government official named Friedrich Rüttel.[84] Rüttel's list included seventeen categories. They ranged from obvious directives such as the coordination of relations between crown and estates and the administrative supervision of governmental agencies such as the treasury, the judiciary, the chancellery, and the church to more specialized concerns. The later included responsibility for handling certain petitions to the crown, for censoring (or curtailing the publication of) undesirable newspapers, tracts, and books, and for rendering advice on relations with neighboring nobility, city-states, other German principalities, and the imperial government.[85] A role of processing and advising rather than one of implementation was commended to the privy council, which served in this sense as an administrative clearinghouse.

The devastating sequel of invasion, exile, and economic collapse which followed the creation of the privy council brought the Stuttgart government almost to a standstill. As best he could Eberhard kept alive the earlier administrative momentum, replacing older councilors with men of his own choosing, but for the last years of the war the council functioned in the same hand-to-mouth fashion as the other central agencies.[86] After the war Eberhard issued a charter that built

84. Reyscher, *Vollständige Sammlung*, I, 362–364. See also the Landtagsabschied of 29 July 1633 in Reyscher, II, Nr. 29.

85. HSAS, A 201: Bü. 1. Friedrich Rüttel (1579–1634), though trained in medicine at Tübingen, supervised the ecclesiastical archives of the duchy and held the position in the central administration of Registrator bei Hof; K. O. Müller, *Gesamtübersicht über die Bestände der staatlichen Archive Württembergs in plannmässiger Einteilung* (Stuttgart, 1937), 18. Also, W. Bernhardt, *Die Zentralbehörden des Herzogtums Württemberg und ihre Beamten, 1520–1629* (Stuttgart, 1972), I, 13 and II, 587–588.

86. When Eberhard returned to Stuttgart in 1638 he maintained a privy council of three men: Baron H. J. von Reischach (1591–1642), who had accompanied him to Strassburg, Dr. Johann Friedrich Jäger (1596–1656), and Dr. Andreas Burckhard (1594–1651), who was serving as vice-chancellor. Reischach retired the next year and was replaced by Oberratspräsident Hans Albrecht von Wöllwart (died 1657). Not until 1641 were two new members added: Ferdinand Geizkoffler Freiherr von Haunsheim

upon the earlier generalities and made more explicit the council's organization and duties.[87] He defined council membership as consisting of the Landhofmeister, the chancellor, and at least three government officials, and he empowered these men to receive in his name all petitions to the throne.[88] No person or board was to approach the ruler directly; all reports and requests were instead to go to the privy council to be studied and then forwarded with advisory commentary to the duke. By the same token Eberhard announced that he would deal with both the central and the provincial agencies of his government only through the privy council, conveying all commands to the councilors who would pass them on to the appropriate subject, official, or board with guidelines for putting them into effect. In this way Eberhard turned the privy council into a mediating force between prince and principality and created for the first time in Württemberg a central college to which all agencies of the government reported. As with so much that Eberhard did, these reforms were not in themselves part of a larger program of state building. The council had no legislative power like that of the French *conseil d'État*. But its presence rendered the role of the monarch more effective and made possible a more systematic operation of the government. Council minutes demonstrate Eberhard's increasing reliance upon the board as a primary source of administrative energy for the task of rebuilding the government. Throughout the 1650s and 1660s he met almost daily with one or more of his councilors to provide the board with proposals, demands for information, and administrative commands. It is difficult to understand how popular Württemberg historiography perpetuated the image of Eberhard as ineffective, indolent, and given over primarily to the pleasures of the hunt.[89]

---

(1592–1653) and Johann Konrad von Varnbühler (1595–1657). From 1642–1645 the council stood at four: Geizkoffler, Jäger, Varnbühler, and Wöllwart. In 1646 Anthonii von Lützelberg (died 1662) came on as Hofmarshall and Geizkoffler, at the request of the estates, was removed. Burckhardt returned to service in 1647 and for the remainder of the war the council consisted of Burckhardt, Lützelberg, Jäger, Varnbühler, and Wöllwart.

87. See Reyscher, *Vollständige Sammlung*, XIII, Nr. 450 for the 9th Kanzleiordnung. Pars. II pertains to the privy council.

88. Council members in 1660 were Landhofmeister Wolfgang Georg Graf zu Castell (died 1668), Christoph von Manteuffel (1622–1688), Georg Wilhelm Bidenbach von Treuenfels (1614–1677), Dr. Johann Ulrich Zeller (1615–1673), and Dr. Nikolaus Müller (1610–1677). The office of chancellor was vacant at that time. On the number of members fixed by the Kanzleiordnung, see Spittler, *Geheimen-Raths-Collegiums*, 358.

89. HSAS, A 204: Bü. 4–38. The most recent general history of Württemberg, Marquardt, *Geschichte Württembergs*, 150–162, regards Eberhard more favorably, though the stress here is on Eberhard's ability to select wise councilors rather than on his active participation in the government.

In recruiting for the council Eberhard gave increasing weight to questions of social status. This emphasis upon rank, which ran counter to the late-sixteenth-century stress upon education, had significant consequences. Most important was that in making such a shift Eberhard deflected the council's growth as an agency independent of the traditional social orders. Instead, the council began to reflect the status quo and in so doing became a momentary force for stability rather than for aggressive consolidation in the duchy. We saw that prior to the war considerations of rank had been losing ground among the high officials in favor of an emphasis upon professional training and expertise. The sense of professionalism had developed to the point that when the privy council was created in 1628 no one had felt it necessary to raise stipulations as to the number, rank, or social origins of the members. The aristocratic Landeshofmeister Bleickhardt von Helmstätt served together with three non-noble lawyers—Johann Kielmann, Veit Breitschwerdt, and Jacob Löffler—in a fashion that suggested the council's indifference to social rank.[90] It was Löffler, for example, who represented the duke at the Landtag of 1629 and conducted negotiations between the duke and the estates on the constitutional position of the privy council. No one took offense when he took precedence at the ceremonies surrounding the opening of the diet, for his competence in these matters made him the obvious choice.[91] When an additional member was added to the council, the logical man for the position was Dr. Johann Sebastian Hornmoldt (1570–1637), a university-trained lawyer who headed the Kirchenrat.[92] No discussion surfaced in either the government or the Landtag on the need for equal representation of noble and non-noble advisers; the question of titles and rank, like that of the size of membership, remained matters of ducal convenience.

A similar attitude prevailed in the years just after Eberhard's return from Strassburg. Council membership stayed at three, with two of the three officials coming from non-noble families within the duchy.[93] But as Eberhard rebuilt the government and gradually in-

90. Spittler, *Geheimen-Raths-Collegiums*, 332.

91. Löffler delivered the speech from the throne at the opening of the diet and represented the duke in all dealings with the estates on this occasion (HSAS, A 34: Bü. 44–46; A 36: Bü. 34). On the ceremonial pageantry of the diet, see pages 128–132 of this book.

92. W. Pfeilsticker, *Neues württembergisches Dienerbuch* (Stuttgart, 1957), 1172, 1221, 2030; Bernhardt, *Zentralbehörden*, I, 391–392.

93. See note 85 to this chapter. The government's acute cash shortage made it difficult to recruit high officials. Indeed, the shortage of qualified personnel was one of the most profound of the problems plaguing the Württemberg government in the last years of the war and during the immediate postwar period. The crown found it impossible to attract qualified aristocrats from outside the duchy, and internal population losses seem

creased the number of councilors, nuances of rank colored discussions of appointment. The reasons for the new emphasis remain unclear; appointments to the council rested entirely with the duke, and he left no record of his thoughts on the subject. But as early as 7 November 1653 Eberhard wrote to his councilors asking them for suggestions in respect to a "well-qualified nobleman who could serve as chancellor and privy councilor." He also requested nominations for a "trained burgher" (subjectum) whom he could appoint as vice-chancellor.[94] So explicit a linking of social rank to administrative position represented a departure from the earlier custom of the duchy. While it is true that appointments as Landhofmeister had always gone to aristocrats (that official headed the ducal court as well as the administration), noble and non-noble officials had occupied the other Württemberg offices on the basis of qualification. Both wartime chancellors, for example, had been burghers: Jacob Löffler served from 1629 to 1633 and he was followed by Dr. Andreas Burckhardt (1594–1651), the son of a professor of logic at Tübingen, who held the post from 1641 until 1649[95] But now it seemed that eligibility for high office was beginning to be tied to social rank, a linkage that one might expect to compromise the corporate solidarity that had arisen from the earlier orientation around training and professional competence. One should not make too much of Eberhard's desire for a chancellor of noble birth, however. While gradations of rank might find ceremonial expression at his court, the tone of his government remained one of bluff cordiality.

The point is introduced here to call attention to the beginning of a trend in recruitment that in Württemberg, as in the rest of Europe, was to grow increasingly pronounced in succeeding generations. Indeed by the 1690s it was impossible in Württemberg for anyone without a "von" to serve even as vice-chancellor or as president of the Oberrat.[96] We find this same trend reflected in council membership.

---

to have made it difficult to obtain properly trained officials from within Württemberg borders. On the search for a Landhofmeister, see Spittler, Geheimen-Raths-Collegiums, 342–346; for discussions on recruitment within the privy council, see HSAS, A 204: Bü. 4 (Minutes from 8 May 1650 and 8 August 1650).

94. HSAS, A 202: 1861.

95. On Löffler, see Emil Niethammer, "Jakob Löffler," in Schwäbische Lebensbilder, III (1942), 369–393; and Bernhardt, Zentralbehörden, I, 472–475. On Burckhardt's career, see Pfeilsticker, Dienerbuch, 1104, 1105, 1110, 1136, 1171, 1209, 1338; cf. HSAS, A 204: Bü. 3 for council minutes showing Burckhardt's reentering the council in 1647. The minutes indicate that he was also active on the council in 1633.

96. Spittler, Geheimen-Raths-Collegiums, 360. See HSAS, A 204: Bü. 33 for an interesting discussion among the privy councilors on the importance of titles (minutes for 18 May 1657).

By the turn of the eighteenth century non-noble representation on the board had fallen to 9 percent. But contrary to general assumptions about the strength of aristocratic revival in eighteenth-century Europe, the pattern of noble preponderance did not become a fixed one in Württemberg. As the tables in the Appendix demonstrate, by the last quarter of the century the trend had reversed itself and non-nobles again made up almost one-half of the council. Enlightened despotism collided with reformist cameralism and aristocratic stubbornness in ways far more complicated than we have thought. Nevertheless, at least for the moment one can speak of the beginnings of a hardening of social lines that was to grow stronger during the next half century and to exert a quite unexpected influence over the working cohesiveness of the privy council.

A closer attention to questions of birth becomes even more noticeable in the changing social relationships between the non-noble Räte and the territorial Ehrbarkeit. There one finds a perceptible strengthening of ties and a concomitant sharing of values that eroded further the earlier corporatism of the board. No one spoke openly of these matters—at least not in the correspondence, papers, and official documents that have survived—but it was as if the non-noble officials had become more conscious of the circumscribed nature of their association with their aristocratic colleagues and thus more aware of the need to ground themselves in an established social order. Whereas the prewar councilors had had relatively few connections with the estates and had begun to marry either the aristocratic or the non-noble members of their own group, Eberhard's councilors cultivated an association with the Ehrbarkeit. In their marriages and in their efforts at recruitment they turned increasingly to the established families that dominated the pastorate and urban magistracies of the duchy. Of the ten non-noble Räte who served on the privy council between 1650 and 1670,[97] all but two officials belonged to families with close connections to the Ehrbarkeit.[98] Moreover two of the eight Räte with

---

97. Georg Wilhelm Bidenbach (1614–1677), Dr. Andreas Burckhardt (1594–1651), Dr. Johann Sebastian Hornmoldt (1570–1637), Dr. Daniel Imlin (died 1668), Dr. Marx Imlin (1606–1652), Dr. Johann Friedrich Jäger (1596–1656), Dr. Nikolaus Müller (1610–1677), Johann Konrad Varnbühler (1595–1657), Dr. Johann Ulrich Zeller (1615–1673), Dr. Georg Ludwig Zorer (died 1667).

98. Zorer and Dr. Daniel Imlin, the two exceptions, are ambiguous cases. Zorer, who served as director of the Kirchenrat from 1654–1659, appeared on only several occasions in the council minutes for 1657. Membership at that time was in a flux, and Eberhard customarily invited important officials to attend the council as guests. Zorer may well have been in this category. Similarly, Spittler, Geheimen-Raths-Collegiums, 364, described Imlin as a consultant rather than a full member of the council, a description not supported by council minutes for 1664–1667. They show Imlin attending regu-

demonstrable ties to the Ehrbarkeit had actually begun their professional careers in the municipal governments of the duchy's most important cities. Dr. Nikolaus Müller, who entered the privy council in 1657 and served until his death in 1677, had worked previously as the chief legal counsel to the estates (Landschaftskonsulent) and as the Bürgermeister of the city of Urach.[99] While Marx Imlin held a much shorter tenure on the privy council (1651–1652), he sat throughout the 1640s on the executive committee of the Landtag as a delegate from Stuttgart, where he was the Bürgermeister.[100]

The Räte's marital choices reinforced by and large their inherited connections with the estates. Information is fragmentary in respect to some of the officials, but at least six cases in which councilors married daughters of families with close connections to the Landtag can be documented. The most important of these marriages was that of Johann Ulrich Zeller, the councilor who guided Württemberg's relations with the Swabian Kreis during the last decade of Eberhard's reign. He married the daughter of the chief fiscal officer of the Landtag (Landschaftseinnehmer), Christoph Caspar.[101] The others all took wives whose fathers were influential pastors or government officials with family ties to the municipal officers of the district towns. Four of the ten non-noble Räte had received patents of nobility while in office: Georg Wilhelm Bidenbach [von Treuenfels], Dr. Johann Friedrich Jäger [von Jägersberg], Dr. Nikolaus Müller [von Ehrenbach], and Johann Konrad Varnbühler [von und zu Hemmingen]. Within these marriages one further point of interest can be noted. Although their choice of brides corresponded with that of their colleagues in the sense that these wives too came out of the Ehrbarkeit, the selection reflected a more circumscribed pool of candidates. Varnbühler, the most socially prominent and the most gifted politician of the group, married a grandniece of Dr. Veit Breitschwerdt, who had been an original member of the privy council.[102] First Jäger and

larly and working primarily on relations with the estates (HSAS, A 202: Bü. 59). At any event, Imlin, who was born at Heilbronn, may well have been related to the Ehrbarkeit family of Imlins from which Marx Imlin derived.

99. Pfeilsticker, Dienerbuch, 1138, 1139, 1225, 1331, 1447, 2031.

100. Ibid., 1139, 1222, 1310, 1423. During the 1640s Imlin also held the position of Landschaftsassessor for the estates.

101. Ibid., 1142. On his work with the Kreis, see J. Vann, The Swabian Kreis: Institutional Growth in the Holy Roman Empire, 1648–1715 (Brussels, 1975), 70–72.

102. Varnbühler married Suzanna Beck in 1628. On Varnbühler's career, see the essay by Friedrich Wintterlin in Allgemeine Deutsche Biographie, XXXIX (Berlin, 1971), 496–498. Also, O. von Alberti, Württembergisches Adels- und Wappenbuch (Neustadt an der Aisch, 1975), 902–903.

then after his death Bidenbach married Varnbühler's own daughter, Suzanna.[103] Although Müller's bride, the daughter of a Tübingen professor, evidenced no kinship with recently ennobled families,[104] it seems safe to suggest that the councilors with recent titles, while not marrying into the feudal aristocracy, were establishing internal connections within the Ehrbarkeit which tended to distinguish them as a group from their other non-noble colleagues.

These social alignments within the privy council contrasted with certain administrative shifts within the central government. For just as the councilors were developing closer administrative ties with the estates, so the prince was beginning to tighten the institutional bonds between himself and the council. He proceeded moreover in a way that enabled subsequent rulers to regard that body as an agency solely for the discharge of royal will rather than as a mediating force between crown and estates. Originally, of course, the privy councilors had sworn oaths both to the sovereign and to the estates, but this symbolic expression of their dual allegiance ceased with the Chancellery Ordinance of 1660.[105] In that document Eberhard stipulated that the councilors were to swear fidelity only to the duke. Although he followed that command with some general phrases charging the councilors to be active in the welfare of the estates, his stress on the oath left no doubt that these officials worked for him and that it was he who would determine what constituted the good of the estates.

Eberhard's conciliatory personality reduced the unpalatable effects of this redefinition of the council's loyalty and muted the difficulties inherent in charging a royal agency with responsibility for balancing royal authority with estates' rights. Relations between crown, council, and estates proceeded generally on an even keel, and for the rest of the reign the councilors were not required to confront their constitutionally ambiguous position directly. But under more aggressive rulers it became impossible to disguise these contradictions, and their overwhelming magnitude placed the late-seventeenth-century councilors in an exceedingly difficult position, one that is the subject of subsequent chapters in this book. A recognition of the commonality of values and traditions shared by the councilors and estates in the 1650s and 1660s makes even more startling the late-seventeenth-century councilors' resolution of these tensions. For at the moment of crisis

103. Pfeilsticker, *Dienerbuch*, 1139, 1206; cf. Bernhardt, *Zentralbehörden*, I, 406–407.
104. Pfeilsticker, *Dienerbuch*, 1331 (see Zobel).
105. Reyscher, *Vollständige Sammlung*, XIII, Nr. 450, Pars. II.

toward the end of the century the councilors supported the prince in his determination to curtail the power of the estates. In their discussions they showed themselves to have adopted definitions of sovereignty quite different from those of their relatives in the Landtag. Their stance in this regard points up the historiographical imperative of grounding social history in an institutional context. For we see that institutional loyalties pose alternatives to ties of kinship and caste and at certain junctures take precedence over these social criteria. These loyalties channel behavior in directions that become intelligible only when we recognize that the institutions within which people organize their careers have their own particular momentum and that on occasion this direction overpowers the pull of more conventional social ties.

Meanwhile Eberhard's council had not yet hardened into an independent institutional force. Its members still reflected the views of the group from which they were recruited. It was not until after Eberhard's death that the council became a distinct power on its own. Three representative illustrations taken from the papers of the mid-seventeenth-century council clarify the extent to which Eberhard's councilors shared the attitudes and values of their relatives at the Landtag.

The first instance involved a question of religious orthodoxy. In 1663 and then again in 1665 the estates submitted reports to Eberhard calling for a forcible resolution of the confessional heterodoxy that had surfaced in the duchy as a result of the war.[106] They pointed out that during the years of military occupation many Württembergers had converted to Catholicism. According to the estates, these recusants now refused all overtures from the established Lutheran church and thus constituted a serious threat to the spiritual well-being of the population. Equally alarming were the numbers of Calvinists whom the estates described as flooding into the duchy from the Palatinate to settle the deserted Württemberg farmlands. Supported enthusiastically by the officials of the Kirchenrat and Oberrat, the estates called for the expulsion by force of these heretics and a restoration of confessional purity in the duchy. Eberhard discussed the matter with his privy councilors, who declared themselves in complete agreement with the estates and urged a policy of confiscation and expulsion. Their only qualification was to recommend the

---

106. A confessional survey of 1660 revealed that some 3,000 persons (roughly 1.5 percent of the duchy's population) worshiped regularly as Roman Catholics or Calvinists (HSAS, A 203: Bü. 10). Cf. H. Tüchle, *Die Kirchenpolitik des Herzogs Karl Alexander von Württemberg, 1733–1737* (Würzburg, 1937), 4–6.

toleration of unmarried recusant day laborers, who possessed neither rights of citizenship nor privileges of property ownership, on the grounds that "the agrarian labor force remains inadequate for the duchy's needs."[107] To the dismay of both councilors and estates, Eberhard refused to act. An easy-going temperament doubtless inclined him to moderation, though his remarks in the privy council focused less on the relative merits of toleration than on the fear of a Catholic and Calvinist reprisal at the Reichstag if he offended his fellow sovereigns with unilateral action. Both estates and councilors deplored his passivity. And when visitation reports for the mid-seventies indicated thriving Catholic communities in the neighborhood of Sulz and a strong contingent of Calvinists over toward the Rhine in a Württemberg enclave near Bruchsal, a flurry of conferences and a rash of alarmist letters passed between councilors and estates as to how best they might persuade the new prince to carry out "just retribution" against these "dangerous deviants."[108]

The councilors and estates evidenced a similar likemindedness in their approach to foreign policy. The death of Emperor Ferdinand III on 2 April 1657 touched off a long series of debates and discussions in which the councilors shared completely in the fears, prejudices, and expectations of the estates in matters concerning other German powers and the institutions of the empire. At immediate issue was the question of succession, a decision vested in the Electoral College and hence one over which the Württembergers had no direct control. But the duke dispatched the privy councilor Georg Wilhelm Bidenbach to Frankfurt to lobby on behalf of Württemberg interests in the negotiations for the election contract (*Wahlkapitulation*). The details of the various concessions put forward for debate at Frankfurt and the lengthy policy discussions that ensued at Stuttgart need not concern us here.[109] More important was the unanimity between estates and councilors in their recommendations on the appropriate Württemberg posture for each of these issues. The underlying principles uniting councilors and estates were an unbending commitment to Lutheran orthodoxy and a translation of that commitment into a literal-minded defense of confessional purity on all imperial committees and in all discussions of imperial politics. They shared a pro-

107. HSAS, A 202: Bü. 59 (esp. minutes for 10 August 1666).
108. HSAS, A 204: Bü. 38. See also, Paul von Stälin, "Das Rechtsverhältnis der religiösen Gemeinschaften und der fremden Religionsverwandten in Württemberg und seiner geschichtlichen Entwicklung," *WJSL* (1868), 156 and 173ff.; and Sattler, *Herzöge*, x, 81f.
109. For a monographic study of the election, see A. F. Pribram, *Zur Wahl Leopolds I, 1654–58*, in *Archiv für oesterreichische Geschichte*, LXXIII (Vienna, 1888).

fessed loyalty to the concept of the Holy Roman Empire, an institution they defined in careful terms that made no provision for Habsburg aggrandizement. So long as the Habsburgs scrupulously observed the constitutional provisions of the Reich, the Württembergers were prepared to support the Habsburg claim to the German throne. But they balked at once at any hint of manipulation of the imperial structure for the power of the "Casa Habsburga."[110]

The councilors and estates viewed the great German princes in much the same way. They recognized the strength of Electoral Saxony and Brandenburg and looked to these Lutheran powers as their natural allies in the Reich. But once again they identified the territorial ambitions of these electoral monarchs and regarded their overtures with a somewhat jaundiced eye. Both councilors and estates saw as their best friends the smaller powers like themselves—Hessen, Ansbach-Bayreuth, and Baden-Durlach, in particular—and they urged Eberhard to unite with these governments in promoting a defense of the status quo. Any hint of military preparations or constitutional modifications threw them into consternation, and their letters to Bidenbach never failed to contain plaintive cries for *forschen und penetrieren*, that is, for Bidenbach to get behind the arrogant facades mounted by the powerful princes and discover their real motives. In the negotiations surrounding the formation of the League of the Rhine (*Rheinbund*) which followed the imperial election, estates and councilors again demonstrated a united front. They sympathized completely with the league's avowed purpose—a union of princes to frustrate Habsburg efforts to exploit the Reich for dynastic aims—but they eschewed diplomatic entanglements that might involve Württemberg in war. In this instance they urged a standpat policy upon Eberhard, but he ignored their advice and brought the duchy into the league.[111]

The fear of change and the slightly truculent defensiveness that the councilors and estates showed in their formulation of foreign policy spilled over into their responses to matters closer to home. Because

110. HSAS, A 204: Bü. 33 and 34 (esp. the minutes of the conference between Castell, Müller, and Zeller on 17 January 1659 in Bü. 34).
111. Ibid. (council instructions for 27 May 1657 and 12 June 1657 in Bü. 33 offer clear illustration of the Württembergers' defensive nervousness and their sense of conspiracies). On the Rheinbund, see Martin Göhring, "Kaiserwahl und Rheinbund von 1658," in Martin Göhring and Alexander Scharff, eds., *Geschichtliche Kräfte und Entscheidungen: Festschriften zum 65. Geburtstage von Otto Becker* (Wiesbaden, 1954), 65–83; and Roman Schnur, *Der Rheinbund von 1658 in der deutschen Verfassungsgeschichte* (Bonn, 1955), 34ff. Privy council minutes for 8 April 1657 (Bü. 33) contain a particularly clear presentation by Landhofmeister Castell on Württemberg's relations to the great electoral powers and on her "natural" allies in the empire.

of their proximity to the duke and their positions as royal officials, the privy councilors frequently were responsible for implementing ducal policies with which, as their papers demonstrated, they were not in sympathy. One instance in which they carried out a royal command in a literal but surreptitiously unsupportive manner concerned the duke's plan to construct an extensive new fortress near the mountain town of Freudenstadt in the Black Forest. Alarmed by the increased animosity between France and Spain and recognizing the possibilities of imperial involvement in the event of war, Eberhard in 1666–1667 decided to undertake an expansion of the Württemberg defensive fortifications and to enhance the duchy's level of military preparedness. The estates, ever hostile to any form of peacetime military expenditure, strenuously opposed the plans. The privy council provided the forum for the lengthy negotiations that ensued between prince and estates, and in these discussions the councilors faithfully discharged their instructions from the duke. Their memoranda to the estates and to one another, however, showed that their sentiments were those of the estates and that they encouraged the estates in their successful campaign to halt the project. In domestic as in foreign policy, they wanted Württemberg to make no move that might attract the attention of the larger powers or upset the internal balance of the duchy. *Tradition und Ordnung*, tradition and order: these were the words that surfaced most often in privy council papers; they were the lodestars against which all policies were charted.[112]

We shall see that in their supervision of the central administration the councilors proved considerably more aggressive than their rhetoric suggested. They were tireless in the discharge of their professional duties. Council minutes indicate that they sat in full session at least three times a week throughout the fifties, sixties, and early seventies; and for much of that time they met daily. Furthermore, when not in conference the individual members worked at digesting the agency reports and preparing the ducal memoranda that they presented to their colleagues for approval at the plenary sessions. A memorandum of 10 May 1670 from the councilors to Duke Eberhard set forth in detail their individual duties and described the officials as staggering under the volume and scope of their diversified responsibilities.[113] The cumulative effect of their diligence was not exactly as they perceived it; for like their relatives in the district towns, pulpits, and offices of government they regarded themselves as carrying on the traditions of

112. HSAS, A 204: Bü. 35-A. Also, Sattler, *Herzöge*, IX, 231; X, 10 and 123–124.
113. See Spittler, *Geheimen-Raths-Collegiums*, 366–378, for a full reproduction of this report.

the duchy and upholding the values sanctified by Lutheran orthodoxy and given political expression in the Tübinger Vertrag.

At least on the surface then Eberhard's long reign witnessed a shift in Württemberg political life away from the aggressive royalism of the late-Renaissance princes. In tone and style his government resembled that of Duke Christoph's, under whose mid-sixteenth-century tenure crown and estates worked harmoniously within a system of shared responsibility. Certainly Eberhard fostered a period of growth and prosperity for the Württemberg estates, so that their eighteenth-century representatives looked back to the middle years of the seventeenth century as a golden age. But beneath this political amiability that captured the fancy of later generations, military invasion, economic dislocation, dynastic ambition, and family concerns were producing structural alterations in the realm's three principal institutions. These changes in turn promoted significant shifts in the social forces behind these offices. Urban magistrates secured their monopoly over the Landtag just as increased village participation in elections to that body was reactivating local assemblies and bringing renewed vigor to the districts. The duke meanwhile had reorganized the treasury and redefined his family's relations with the estates so as to necessitate a change in the tax structure of the duchy. He also expanded the privy council's duties and fixed its membership in ways that differed from those of his predecessors and that encouraged new patterns of family connections. Close kinship ties to the Ehrbarkeit brought many of its values into the government and raised the possibility of a clash between the ducal officials and their master. But here, as elsewhere, the end result remained as problematical as that of the swells of the ocean. None of the changes in themselves led necessarily to conflict, and contemporaries perceived no imperative for collision. On the contrary, political life seemed to be following its customary, hence appropriate course. We find this sense of stability reflected in the pageantry surrounding the opening of the Landtag, one of the duchy's great state occasions.[114] The low-keyed ceremonial for 1672, easily accommodated the minor stresses of the reign and expressed the more general affability that prevailed between duke, council, and estates.

Early on a May morning in 1672 the bells of the Stuttgarter Rathaus began to toll, summoning the district delegates from the various inns and boardinghouses of the city to assemble at the Landschaftshaus, the high-gabled stone structure a few blocks west of the

114. Grube, *Stuttgarter Landtag*, 336–341, offers a fascinating reconstruction of Landtag ceremonial.

[128]

The estates' headquarters as they appeared in 1845. Only the first two buildings in the painting were standing in the seventeenth century. The ceremonies preceding the opening of the Landtag took place in the great hall of the decorated Renaissance wing in the foreground. Processions to the castle departed from that porticoed central doorway. Photograph courtesy of the Landesbildstelle Württemberg.

castle which served as headquarters for the Landtag. There the elder of the two prelates on the executive committee, the abbot of Murrhardt, greeted each representative and, as soon as everyone had arrived, delivered a short homily.[115] He invoked God's blessing upon the estates and passed on to a surprisingly detailed review of the rules of etiquette governing the day's festivities. He took particular pains with the gala banquet to which Eberhard had invited the estates after the initial presentation at the assembly—an invitation that must have caused some trepidation among the members of the executive committee. On earlier occasions of this sort the coarse manners of the delegates from the smaller market towns had embarrassed their more patrician colleagues, and the committee had obviously instructed the old abbot to make certain that these provincials did not disgrace them. His address stressed particularly that the delegates watch their drinking "in the presence of the prince and his distinguished attendants" (*in conspectu dess Landesfürsten und anderer vornehmer Herren*) and that they behave with "becoming modesty and decorum." After these remarks the *Landschaftskonsulent* broke the seal on the ducal letter and read aloud the order of precedence for the procession, a routine matter for the representatives but one that filled the prelates with apprehension. In previous years they had bickered so interminably over questions of seniority that Eberhard had adopted the practice of sending a sealed letter to the chief legal counsel assigning each prelate his place in that particular procession.[116]

Once the processional order had been announced, the estates walked over to the castle, where "humbly and in proper dress" they assumed their assigned places at the foot of the great stone staircase in the northwest corner of the courtyard. There they waited until the royal sergeant-at-arms had announced their arrival to the duke. Once Duke Eberhard, attended by the full privy council, had left his apartments and taken his place in the great hall of the castle (*Rittersaal*), the delegates entered to shake hands with the monarch and then with his privy councilors. All but the duke remained standing while the president of the privy council, Hofmarshall Christoph von Manteuffel zu Arnhausen (1622–1688), read aloud the *Propositionen*, a speech from the throne itemizing the business that had prompted the duke to convene the estates and offering royal suggestions for a prompt res-

---

115. The senior prelate on the executive committee served as titular spokesman for that body. Membership was fixed at two prelates and six representatives from the districts.

116. For quarrels over precedence among the prelates, see HSAS, *tomus actorum*, LXV, 740–751 and LXVII, 7–9 and 31–33.

olution. When he had finished the reading, Manteuffel offered a written copy of the speech to the abbot of Murrhardt, whereupon the Landschaftskonsulent responded with a short speech *per generalia*.[117] Afterward, the duke withdrew from the hall, once again shaking hands with the entire delegation.

The delegates proceeded next to the castle church to hear a sermon by the court chaplain, Christoph Wölfflin. As was customary on these occasions, Wölfflin preached on the Propositionen; and since Eberhard's desire for funds with which to honor the imperial request for military support constituted the chief item of business, Wölfflin took as his text Matthew 22:22, "Render unto Caesar the things that are Caesar's." The sermon that followed indicated that the chaplain was warmly sympathetic to ducal wishes, but, as Eberhard would have been the first to testify, such clerical cordiality was by no means a foregone conclusion. A few years earlier, at the opening of the Landtag for 1659, the court chaplain Zeller (also abbot of Denkendorf and a prominent member of the executive committee of the estates) had deplored Eberhard's desire to enter the Rhinebund. He took his text for that occasion from Proverbs 22:3, "A prudent man forseeth the evil and hideth himself; but the simple pass on and are punished."[118] At any rate all went smoothly in 1672, and after Wölfflin's sermon the delegates enjoyed a program of choral and organ music before a series of solemn drum rolls summoned them back to the Rittersaal for an afternoon of dining and drinking. Not until the next day would they begin serious deliberation.

Three long tables filled the great hall, and the delegates distributed themselves according to a seating chart drawn up by the privy council to conform to the gradations of power and influence among the guests. The duke sat at the center of the head table, flanked on one side by Manteuffel and on the other by Murrhardt. The guests at his table included the other prelates, the secular members of the executive committee, and the Landschaftskonsulent. The remaining privy councilors and courtiers in the ducal entourage presided over the lower two tables where the seats were filled by the district representatives. Once everyone had taken his place the duke rose, proffered a few cordial words of welcome, and drank the health of his guests. An elaborate meal accompanied by a wide selection of wines and interspersed with renderings of vocal and instrumental music followed. It

117. HSAS, A 203: Bü. 13 and 14 contain the Propositionen and preliminary negotiations by the estates.

118. On the Landtag sermons, see HSAS, A 203: Bü. 17 and *tomus actorum*, XLIX, 143; LVIII, 553–561; LXVIII, 387f.; LXII, 251.

was six hours later before the duke rose again, offered his carriage to the senior prelates, and together with the privy councilors departed from the hall. Remaining guests found their way home as best they could.

# [4]

## The Estates at Bay

IN THE LATE SEVENTEENTH CENTURY the Württemberg government once again altered its course. At the most fundamental level
the shift constituted a redefinition of the state. It was impelled by a
bitter, sustained controversy whose origins were cultural as well as
political. The political component centered largely on disputes over
taxation and military organization and on the institutional changes
that resulted from the ducal government's response to the French bid
for European hegemony. This chapter explores the monarchy's drive
for greater central control through the conflict with the estates over
the formation of a standing army for the duchy. This struggle had a
cultural as well as a political dimension. After the death of Duke
Eberhard a new type of monarch occupied the Württemberg throne.
His concern was with power rather than stability, and he drew both
his cultural and his political aspirations from the French monarchy at
Versailles. The absolutist orientation of the baroque prince contrasted
sharply with that of the territorial estates, for the cultural and political
norms of the estates derived from Württemberg traditions and from
such constitutional settlements as the Tübinger Vertrag. Religious
sensibilities added to the problem. A revitalized Pietism that found
its most dramatic expression in the leadership of the Landtag challenged the Francophile worldliness of the ducal court and added a
moral ingredient to the political scene.

The privy council played a significant role in the conflict. External
pressure closed certain of the options that we saw opening up for the
council under Eberhard and set that body on a more direct course. In
particular the council redefined its commitment to the territorial
estates—and hence to the balance of power between crown and
Landtag—and became a driving force for centralized authority. The

[133]

impact of the council must be distinguished from that of the prince. The councilors worked for a strong monarchy but one that operated according to their conception of administration. Even by the end of the century signs were multiplying that their ideas of government might not be those of the prince. But in the battle with the estates the council sided with the prince, and the century closed with a Landtag in 1698–1699, the abrupt dissolution of which set the stage for the eighteenth-century ducal bid for absolute rule. Both its ceremonial aspects and its abortive deliberations point up the extent to which some thirty years of sustained conflict over the military had redefined the balance of Württemberg power and transformed the nature as well as the substance of political discourse.

This seminal Landtag had its origins in a series of long-standing disputes that only gradually clarified the difference between prince and estates and polarized the principal institutions of the realm. These disputes were of an intensely personal nature and should be understood in those terms. But as in all such conflicts the chief protagonists were responding to larger forces and should be thought of as articulating the basic political, social, and cultural options in their society. These options converged in the struggle over the institutional structure of the Württemberg state; personal motivations and concerns interacted with the demands of public office to shape that conflict. The first turn in a new direction had occurred some quarter of a century earlier as the result of an unexpected tragedy within the House of Württemberg. Eberhard's death on 2 July 1674 brought his son Wilhelm Ludwig to the throne. The twenty-seven-year-old prince was a man quite similar in temperament to his father and had Wilhelm Ludwig lived he might well have continued Duke Eberhard's commitment to shared sovereignty.[1] But a sudden stroke on 23 July, just three years after his succession, took his life and precipitated a crisis for the Stuttgart government.

The duke left as his heir a nine-month-old son, Eberhard Ludwig (1676–1733). Since Württemberg law stipulated that a prince might rule only after his eighteenth birthday, a regency government had to be formed at Stuttgart. Resolution of the bitter feud over the composition of the regency which subsequently broke out within the ducal family produced two important long-term consequences for the Würt-

---

1. In his dealings with his privy councilors, Wilhelm Ludwig linked his policies explicitly to those of his father (HSAS, A 204: Bü. 38). On his relations with the Landtag, see W. Grube, *Der Stuttgarter Landtag, 1457–1957* (Stuttgart, 1957), 347 ff. Karl Pfaff, *Württembergs geliebte Herren*, ed. by P. Lahnstein (Stuttgart, 1965), 53 ff., offers a generalized biographic portrait.

temberg state. The first was the triumph of Wilhelm Ludwig's younger brother Friedrich Karl (1652–1698), whom Emperor Leopold named as prince regent (*Administrator*) on 27 November 1677.[2] The second was Leopold's insistence on the binding validity of the clause in Eberhard's will which stipulated that in the event of a regency the privy council should assume the position of *Mitvormund* in the government. Such status gave the councilors unrestricted access to state papers as well as full rights of advice and consent on all policy decisions. It ensured in effect that no regent could act without council approval and guaranteed the board a central role in any interim government. Strong-minded councilors could exercise their influence without fear of losing their posts. Moreover, they had no reason to fear that their effectiveness would be diluted through a packing of the board with councilors overtly unsympathetic to their views. For Eberhard's will specified that a regent could neither fire nor suspend a privy councilor and that he could make appointments to the board only with the prior consent of the standing members.[3]

Werner Fleischhauer, the distinguished Württemberg art historian, has described Friedrich Karl as the duchy's first baroque prince.[4] The attribution did not derive from an architectural program; the relentless warfare of those years precluded extensive artistic patronage or building in the duchy. It spoke rather to the fact that Friedrich Karl imparted a tone to the regency markedly different from that of his father's court. In much the way that, in the earlier half of the century, Charles I of England had sought to impose a greater formality upon the bawdy court inherited from King James, Friedrich Karl consciously separated himself from the more boisterous of his father's retainers. He introduced an etiquette at the Stuttgart castle calculated to enhance royal dignity and to impart an air of stately grandeur to the throne. The long drinking bouts, around which so many of the Eberhardine festivities had centered, ceased. In their place came operatic performances, ballets, and balls—still somewhat rustic when compared with those of Versailles or Vienna but markedly more sophisticated than the hunting and feasting that

2. Materials on the struggle within the Württemberg family over the regency government are found in HSAS, Hausarchiv, G 2–8 CXXIV: Bü. 1–6. Emperor Leopold's role in settling the dispute testified to the increased imperial presence in the affairs of the seventeenth-century German states. In 1457, the last occasion of such a domestic dispute, the Landtag had settled the matter without consultation with the emperor.

3. L. von Spittler, *Geschichte des wirtembergischen Geheimen-Raths-Collegiums*, in *Sämtliche Werke*, ed. K. Wächter, XIII (Stuttgart and Tübingen, 1837), 380–381. Copies of Eberhard's 1674 will are located in HSAS, Hausarchiv, G 1–8: 221.

4. W. Fleischhauer, *Barock im Herzogtum Württemberg* (Stuttgart, 1958), 127–128.

had provided the staple entertainment for Eberhard's reign.[5] Not surprisingly the regent's efforts resonated in the manners of his closest advisers. His chief privy councilor and Hofmarshall Baron Heinrich Friedrich von Forstner-Dambenoy (1641–1687) was a man of considerable aesthetic refinement. The son of the Mömpelgard chancellor, he had grown up speaking French and brought something of the Paris milieu to Stuttgart. With his wife Claudia Maria, daughter of the former Württemberg Hofmarshall Anthony von Lützelberg, he presided over the city's first salon. There, to the utter horror of the estates, the assembled notables and literati were expected to converse in French and to show a knowledge of and a concern for the fashions current at Versailles.[6] Johann Eberhard von Varnbühler (1639–1722) shared fully these Francophile tastes. He held a series of important administrative and diplomatic posts in the regency government, including that of privy councilor.[7]

It is difficult to pinpoint the causes for this sudden shift in royal style. Late Renaissance princes had shown a decided preference for cosmopolitan values, and in this sense Friedrich Karl's inclinations can be thought of as a return to earlier standards. Certainly his education was considerably more elaborate than that which the upheavals of the Thirty Years War had permitted for his father, and it is reasonable to attribute Friedrich Karl's worldliness largely to his early training. The subjects in his curriculum as well as the stress on extensive travel encouraged an elegance of manner and a sense of self-confidence in handling the affairs of the world. A look at these educational particulars reveals the expanded scope of opportunities available to the German princes by the middle of the seventeenth century. In basic outline the prince's educational program conformed to the mandate drawn up by the north German cameralist Veit Ludwig von Seckendorff (1626–1692). As Seckendorff prescribed in his *Teutschen Fürsten-Stat* (1656), instructional emphasis for Friedrich Karl shifted away from the humanistic-theological concerns of traditional Württemberg education to focus upon the practical arts of government (history, language, political science, mathematics) and upon what the

5. B. Wunder, "Der Administrator Herzog Friedrich Karl von Württemberg," *ZWLG*, 30 (1971), 117–163.

6. After Forstner's death the regent erected a bust of him at Freudenthal and inscribed it *amico principis* (W. Pfeilsticker, *Neues württembergisches Dienerbuch* [Stuttgart, 1957], 5, 1118, 2952). See also O. von Alberti, *Württembergisches Adels- und Wappenbuch* (Neustadt an der Aisch, 1975), 194; and *Allgemeine Deutsche Biographie*, XVII (Berlin, 1969), 192.

7. Wunder, "Der Administrator," 158. See also Pfeilsticker, *Dienerbuch*, 9, 27, 199, 1117, 1193, 1300, 2409, 2876, 2918, 2952.

contemporary Germans described as *Exerziten* (dancing, hunting, swordsmanship). He also received lessons in deportment and public speaking. Classes met daily, except on Sundays, and there is every reason to assume that the prince was expected to develop a systematic mastery of the material.[8]

Travel occupied an important place in the curriculum. The prince's first opportunity to leave Stuttgart occurred in 1666, when he was thirteen years old. At that time the forum for his instruction shifted from the ducal castle to the *Collegium Illustre*, a celebrated boarding school at Tübingen attended by generations of Württemberg princes.[9] For three years he continued his studies there under the supervision of his governor, Georg Rudolf Marschall, and mingled with the European noblemen who were visiting the school as a station on their cavaliers' tour. On 1 July 1669 he set out on his own foreign travels, a journey that lasted thirty-three months and carried him through northwest Europe, England, and Scandinavia. To save expense and to avoid controversies over protocol, the sixteen-year-old prince traveled as Baron von Hellenstein;[10] he was chaperoned by Berthold von Bülow (1636–1690), a Brandenburg nobleman of pronounced Lutheran convictions who had been selected for this purpose and promised a seat on the Württemberg privy council upon his return.[11] They set out first for Geneva, and after eight weeks moved into France for five months of study at the Protestant cavalry school of Saumur and for a similar period at the famous college of La Flèche in Anjou.[12] Subsequent stops at the universities of Bordeaux and Tou-

8. Wunder, "Der Administrator," 120; cf. Georg Steinhausen, "Die Idealerziehung im Zeitalter der Perücke," *Mitteilungen der Gesellschaft deutscher Erziehungs- und Schulgeschichte*, 4 (1894), 209ff.

9. The origins of the *collegium* lay in the educational reforms proposed in the mid-sixteenth century by Duke Christoph. The building at Tübingen was completed toward the end of that century; see E. Schneider, "Das Tübinger collegium illustre," *WVJHLG* (1898), 217ff.

10. The reigning German princes and their families generally traveled incognito when they left the boundaries of the Holy Roman Empire. They followed this practice in order to save expenses and to avoid the possibility of slights to their status as "European" sovereigns. The French court, for example, recognized only the emperor as a full sovereign and refused to give the German "princelets" precedence over the French princes of the blood.

11. The privy council's instructions to Bülow are found in HSAS, Hausarchiv G 2–8 CXXIII: Bü. 1 (19 and 25 July 1669). On Bülow's privy council appointment, see A 17: Bü. 20 (Eberhard's decree of 30 March 1672).

12. Despite the fact that the college at La Flèche was a Jesuit institution, its excellence in mathematics and scientific instruction was such that the Württemberg estates raised no objection to the prince's study there (HSAS, Hausarchiv G 2–8 CXXIII: Bü. 1). Jesuit influence at La Flèche is analyzed in C. de Montzey, *Histoire de la Flèche et de ses seigneurs*, II (Le Mans, 1878), 46–122. On the Académie protestante de Sau-

louse were followed by a visit to the fortifications at Marseilles and a two-months stay in Paris before crossing the Channel for London and Oxford University. Friedrich Karl next proceeded through the Spanish Netherlands, pausing for a three-month sojourn at the University of Utrecht in the Dutch Republic. A month at Copenhagen and two months at Stockholm ended the foreign leg of the journey. The two men spent the remainder of the tour in northern and central Germany, stopping for extended visits at the Brunswick court of Celle and at the Hessen university of Marburg before returning to Stuttgart on 3 March 1672.[13]

But for the mounting threat of another war between France and the empire, Friedrich Karl might have ended his travels after this extensive grounding in French culture and his introduction to the major Protestant courts of Europe. Louis' invasion of Holland that spring had prompted a military alliance between Austria, Spain, Brandenburg, Denmark, and the Dutch Republic which brought active fighting to the Lower Rhine. Since the empire had not yet committed itself, the Württemberg estates were most anxious that nothing be done to draw French attention to the duchy. They shared the privy councilors' alarm when they learned from them that Friedrich Karl had approached his father that fall for permission to enter the Austrian military service. In consultation with the councilors the estates determined to deflect such a possibility by the offer of a trip to Italy at state expense. In a letter to Duke Eberhard of 22 November 1673, the privy councilors proposed a journey of several months for Friedrich Karl on the express grounds that "removal from the duchy would preclude any precipitous action such as might compromise Württemberg neutrality." The councilors expressed their fears at the prospect of so long an exposure for Friedrich Karl to a culture so flagrantly Catholic, "where many a young man has been known to change his religion and where the temptation to worldliness and unbridled luxury is so great." But they affirmed their confidence in the prince's "good judgment" and in his "respect for his father."[14] And so Friedrich Karl once again departed Stuttgart, this time in the company of his equerry Friedrich Christoph von Forstner-Dambenoy, the brother of the man who subsequently became his Hofmarshall and privy councilor. The two young men spent several months wandering

<hr>

mur, see P. -Daniel Bourchenin, *Étude sur les académies protestantes en France au XVIᵉ et au XVIIᵉ siècle* (Paris, 1882), 137–147 and 226–262.

13 . HSAS, Hausarchiv G 2–8 CXXIII: Bü. 1–5 contain Friedrich Karl's travel correspondence and the records of account for his various trips outside the duchy.

14. HSAS, Hausarchiv G 2–8 CXXXVI: Bü. 1.

through the Italian Peninsula, with lengthy stops at the baroque courts of Rome and Naples. They would doubtless have lingered longer but for the fact that the imperial declaration of war against France offered Friedrich Karl a long-awaited opportunity to take up active military service.[15]

Friedrich Karl's military interests were a response to expediency as well as to temperament. They merit attention here because they fused with his cosmopolitan values to give his subsequent career as prince regent its particularly aggressive thrust; his military entrepreneurship was to precipitate the final showdown between his nephew and the estates in the Landtag of 1698. A consideration of Friedrich Karl's ambitions as a soldier also provides an opportunity to understand the military arrangements in the smaller states of the Holy Roman Empire and to examine the status of younger sons in German sovereign families. Finally his activities illustrate how decisively a single personality can influence historical development. Like so many other leaders, Friedrich Karl was responding to situations arising from movements essentially beyond his control. But we shall see that it was because of his personal orientation that his response brought into play the larger social and institutional forces in his government. These forces eventually acquired their own momentum and in so doing lost much of the tentative character that had marked them earlier.

His father's will stipulated that, as a cadet prince of the House of Württemberg, Friedrich Karl should inherit no property that carried sovereign status.[16] The provision meant that, despite his illustrious title as prince, he was in effect nothing more than a territorial aristocrat. True, he enjoyed many of the trappings of royalty. He lived in fine houses and received a generous allowance. But he exercised none of the prerogatives of a sovereign: he dispensed no justice, collected no taxes, and commanded no subjects. His descendants, moreover, faced the dismal prospect of maintaining status without even the firm guarantee of a regular allowance from the ducal treasury. In a culture where all sons and daughters inherited the titles of their fathers, Friedrich Karl, like other German princes in his position, could foresee that his heirs might have to scramble for both bread and

---

15. HSAS, Hausarchiv G 2–8 cxxxvi: Bü. 2; see Forstner's regular reports on the journey to the privy council as well as his account receipts for travel expenditures.

16. Eberhard's final testament (1674) is found in HSAS, Hausarchiv G 1–8: Bü. 221. The will stipulated that Friedrich Karl was to live at ducal expense until he reached the age of twenty-five. At that time he was to receive the castle at Winnenden together with 6,000 florins for furnishings, full hunting rights within certain specified ducal forests, a capital sum of 50,000 florins (to be paid out of the Kammerschreiberei), and a yearly allowance of 8,000 florins (called a *Deputat*).

Duke Friedrich Karl, surrounded by the symbols of martial victory and princely power, presents an image that would have been unthinkable to Eberhard III. The regent's dress and look reflect standards of *gloire* that have nothing at all to do with the values of the traditional German Landesvater. Photograph courtesy of the Hauptstaatsarchiv Stuttgart.

status. And indeed, his vision was prophetic. Already by the third decade of the eighteenth century, a privy councilor at the Baden-Durlach court was suggesting that junior princes give precedence to the imperial knights. In considering questions of rank for the German courts, the councilor reasoned compellingly that an imperial knight, regardless of his relatively modest title of baron or count, possessed lands over which no one other than himself and the emperor held sway. As for the cadet princes, they "possess not one centimeter of free land and have no one to command other than their own hired servants."[17]

Nothing precluded Friedrich Karl's purchasing property with sovereign status. The problem was that such lands came up for sale only rarely, and when they did, they tended to be expensive. Moreover, competition on those occasions was exceedingly keen. Local rulers, always eager to round out or expand their borders and supported in these endeavors by their estates, could outbid any private buyer.[18] The readiest road to both money and the opportunity to purchase lay in imperial military services. Quite apart from the possibility of profiting from contracts for supply and recruitment, a successful commander might hope to receive a gift of a sovereign lordship. The emperor, chronically short of cash, tended to reward his most distinguished generals by presenting them with land or by making properties available to them at a relatively low cost. Since many of the Swabian knights held their estates as imperial fiefs, the extinction of one of these family lines often meant a reversion to the imperial crown and thus the chance of a sale or a new investiture in the southwest. But as Friedrich Karl had already learned before his father's death, entry into imperial service could mean domestic trouble. He was soon to discover that it could be expensive as well.

Even after the Reichstag had declared war, the Württemberg officials wanted no undue ties between their government and the House of Austria. Thus when Friedrich Karl returned to Stuttgart from Italy, he was not permitted to join the imperial army under Austrian control. Instead his father arranged for him to take a command with the Swabian Kreis, an imperial provincial organization within which Württemberg played a leading role.[19] Friedrich Karl's employment by the Kreis provides an occasion to define its military responsibilities. They are a matter of note in that the Swabian Kreis was the organization through which Württemberg discharged its military obligations to the Reich. Swabian institutions, as we shall see, provided a

17. GLAK, 233/3381 (C. D. Stadelmann's memorandum of 23 January 1738, entitled "Unvorgreifliche Gedanken und Gutachten von einer Rangordnung").

18. See for example the negotiations in 1665 between Eberhard III and the Deutsche Orden over the duke's purchase for 48,000 florins of the Order's Kommendenhof at Winnenden; Beschreibung des Oberamts Waiblingen (1850), 217f. Cf. Friedrich Karl's purchase for 35,000 florins in March 1685 of the Reichsritterschaftliche Gut und Dorf Freudenthal with its seventeen peasants in Beschreibung des Oberamts Besigheim (1853), 175.

19. J. Vann, The Swabian Kreis: Institutional Growth in the Holy Roman Empire, 1648–1715 (Brussels, 1975), 33–95.

useful arena for maneuver in the ducal determination to acquire a standing army.

Although imperial military arrangements varied in their implementation throughout the Reich,[20] the Swabian system can readily be summarized. Throughout the late seventeenth century the Reichstag levied its tax assessments on the Kreis rather than on the individual estates of the empire. The Swabian parliament (Kreistag) prorated the province's obligation among its constituent members according to a table approved by the Reichstag. The separate states then raised their contributions by recruiting and outfitting the prescribed number of infantry and cavalrymen. They also had the option of paying a cash equivalent to one of their larger neighbors such as Württemberg, where the government was better equipped to carry out complicated logistical arrangements of mustering and supply. An army so formed was under the command of the Kreistag, which appointed a staff of officers to carry out its orders in the field. In accord with instruction from the parliamentary leadership, these commanders deployed the troops for the defense of provincial borders or in support of the larger imperial army funded by the House of Austria and its domestic and foreign allies.[21]

The Kreistag also administered the distribution of the vexatious quartering assignments levied upon the region. Since none of the Swabian governments maintained a permanent military force, imperial generals regarded them as "unarmed" components of the Reich (nicht armierte Stände), and they demanded that Swabian lands provide wartime winter quartering for a portion of the standing armies of the emperor and his domestic and foreign allies. Between January 1675 and April 1679, for example, they called upon the Kreistag to find accommodation for an average each year, in addition to its own troops, of seven infantry and nine cavalry regiments, several artillery units, and at least three staff headquarters.[22] These soldiers were ex-

20. Five of the ten provinces remained more or less paper creations: the Austrian, Bavarian, Burgundian, Upper and Lower Saxon Kreise. General treatments of their stunted growth are found in Alois Brusatti, Die Entwicklung der Reichskreise während der Regierungszeit Maximilian II (Vienna, 1950), passim; Carl Erdmann, "Ferdinand I. und die Kreisverfassung," Historische Vierteljahrschrift, 24 (1929), 18–32; and Vann, The Swabian Kreis, 23–36.

21. "Landesverfassung im Herzogtum Württemberg," WVJHLG, 34 (1928), 244–245; and F. Carsten, Princes and Parliaments in Germany from the Fifteenth to the Eighteenth Century (Oxford, 1959), 90–91. P. -C. Storm, Der Schwäbische Kreis als Feldherr (Berlin, 1974), 71–295.

22. HSAS, C 9: 324. Exact totals varied with each assignment, but these appeared to have been the basic units that the Kreis was required to accept. In addition, the Swabians were responsible for the winter quartering of their own troops; see Vann, The Swabian Kreis, 271–277.

pected to pay their own way according to the terms of contracts drawn up each year between the Kreistag and the imperial commanders.[23] And there is no doubt that the soldiers spent money in the taverns and shops of the areas in which they were billeted and thus contributed to the local economies. Nevertheless, their presence was an anathema to the host governments. Records indicate that the scale of contract payments never fully covered the costs of upkeep for the soldiers. Moreover these payments were more often than not in arrears so that the Swabian governments were forced to levy extraordinary taxes to make up the deficits.[24] It was the Kreistag's responsibility to see to it that each member state bore its full share of this dreadful burden and that no territorial ruler used his strength to thrust his share upon a weaker neighbor.

Friedrich Karl's involvement with the Swabian military establishment followed a long-standing Württemberg tradition of active participation in Kreis affairs. The ducal monopoly of one of the two places on the Kreis Secretariat (Ausschreibamt), as well as the fact that the duchy formed the largest, richest, and most powerful single state in the province, ensured the Stuttgart government of a leading role in quartering and command assignments. True, parliamentary procedure at the Kreistag gave each member only one vote and stipulated that all decisions were to be made according to principles of majority rule. As a result Württemberg's leadership always remained a matter of persuasion rather than fiat and, as Swabian institutions gained in strength, was increasingly difficult to sustain. Still the Kreis offered the Stuttgart rulers a fertile field for political maneuver, and its military command positions, all of which carried stipends paid for by the Kreistag, were useful places for unemployed princes such as Friedrich Karl. By the same token the weaker governments of the tiny city-states and ecclesiastical principalities that dotted the region customarily relied on Württemberg for the recruiting and supply of their individual military contributions.

This procedure made it possible to build what were in essence private regiments. An enterprising prince like Friedrich Karl could put together a regiment and rent the troops to the smaller powers, thereby funding the soldiers without the necessity of protracted, unpleasant dealings with recalcitrant territorial estates. But as Friedrich

23. Contracts were drawn up at the so-called Einquartierungen Convente of the Kreistag: January–February 1675 (HSAS, C 9: Bü. 298, 299, 565); October–December 1675 (C 9: Bü. 310–312 and 565); September–December 1676 (C 9: Bü. 321–325 and 566); September–December 1677 (C 9: Bü. 330–332 and 566); October–December 1678 (C 9: Bü. 337–341 and 566).
24. HSAS, A 230: Bü. 16, 17, 18, 21.

Karl discovered to his chagrin, there was a fundamental drawback to the scheme: the Swabian estates, like those of the duchy itself, adamantly refused to maintain an army except in times of acute emergency. The Kreistag unfailingly voted to dismiss its troops promptly once a peace was signed, and on some occasions even before. Their determination left the regimental entrepreneur without a peacetime contract for his men and hence without funds for their maintenance. Under these circumstances he had either to pay them from his own purse, find a government willing to hire them, or persuade his own estates to assume the costs. These problems had not yet surfaced by the fall of 1677 when Friedrich Karl resigned his command and assumed the title of prince regent. But the possibilities of using the Kreis structure to achieve his own aims soon attracted his attention. His speculations in mercenary soldiering produced a policy in which the potential rewards emboldened him—at the same time that the constitutional implications forced him—to seek a confrontation with his government. It was in the working out of the ensuring conflict that the Württemberg central institutions acquired more definitive form, and their members developed an independent perspective on territorial administration.

The crown's position was the first to be defined, largely in response to the constraints of the regency; for while Friedrich Karl exercised the authority of a reigning duke, his power was circumscribed in ways that set him apart from an ordinary monarch. First there was the provision that he do nothing without the advice and consent of his privy council; second, he had to contend with the ambitions of Wilhelm Ludwig's widow, the Dowager Duchess Magdalene Sibylla (1652–1712), who connived with both privy councilors and estates to increase her governmental influence.[25] Finally, and perhaps most significant, there was a time limit placed on his rule by the presence of his nephew Eberhard Ludwig. Friedrich Karl, after all, was only regent; as soon as the young duke reached eighteen he would assume full powers of government. Friedrich Karl, by then a much older

25. The emperor Leopold's original decree setting up the Württemberg regency had named Wilhelm Ludwig's widow, Magdalene of Hessen-Darmstadt (1652–1712) as "Mitvormunderin," a rather vague designation that assured her of rights of participation in the regency without giving her a status equal to that of the prince regent. A Württemberg-Hessen commission was formed subsequently to work out the precise nature of her responsibilities. This board awarded her the title of "Obermitvormunderin," thereby distinguishing her from the privy councilors, and assigned her full control over the prince's education and *oeconomica*. She in turn surrendered her claims for direct participation in the administration of government, though the prince regent admitted her rights to information on all state business (*Informationsrecht*).

man, would again become a junior prince, dependent upon his nephew for his allowance and faced with the necessity of providing for his wife and any children she might bear him.[26] The military pressures generated by the continuous French assault upon the empire; the need to use his temporary powers so as to secure a permanent base for his family's fortunes; his attraction to the style and elegance of the French court and his fascination with what appeared to be the absolute rule of Louis XIV; as well as his early training in the practical arts of cameralistic statecraft—all these elements combined to set his regency in opposition to the standpat politics of the Württemberg government. His administration initiated a turning point in the direction of growth for the ducal monarchy and set the duchy once more on a course toward strong central rule.

Regental policies touched off two confrontations between the monarchy and the government. The first took place early in the 1680s and brought the prince regent into conflict with the privy council; the second occurred a few years later in a dispute between Friedrich Karl and the estates over the Württemberg military. In each instance the prince regent appeared to be the loser, so that when his term as regent ended it looked on the surface as though Württemberg politics were still frozen in the deadlock that had developed under Eberhard. But an analysis of the two crises shows them to have been important milestones on a new path toward absolutism; on each occasion confrontation clarified internal institutional ambiguities and brought to the fore a new kind of leadership. Lines of difference sharpened; positions hardened, making impossible for the future the good-natured compromises that had marked domestic politics since the Thirty Years War. Furthermore, the conflicts eventually led to the alienation of the Landtag from the privy council and turned the territorial estates against the administrative bureaucracy. In ways unappreciated by historians of Württemberg, Friedrich Karl shifted the balance of domestic power, albeit imperceptibly. The results of this shift became apparent when Eberhard Ludwig forced the question of a standing army at the end of the century. At that time interest groups were able to align themselves in an unequivocal manner that permitted a consolidation of power heretofore unknown in the duchy.

The narrative contours of the clash with the privy council are easily followed. At issue was Württemberg's stand on the Chambers of Re-

26. Beginning in 1684 Eleonore Juliane bore Friedrich Karl a total of seven children, five of whom lived to adulthood (four sons and a daughter). It was the eldest of these children, Carl Alexander (1684–1737), who established the line from which the eighteenth- and nineteenth-century Württemberg monarchs descended.

union. These tribunals, instituted in 1679 by Louis XIV, were commissioned to search out lands that had once formed part of the Left Bank lordships acquired by France since the Treaty of Westphalia. By 1680 the courts had determined that virtually all of Alsace belonged properly to France and sanctioned Louis' decision to send his troops to take possession of the affected properties, including by 1681 the city-state of Strassburg.[27] Friedrich Karl, acting apparently under the combined impulses of Francophilia and fear for his family's lordship over Mömpelgard, now well inside French territorial boundaries, was quick to recognize the legality of these tribunals. On 18 February 1681 he swore homage to Louis as liege lord of Mömpelgard and in October of that year traveled to Strassburg to welcome the French king as reigning sovereign of that venerable Lutheran polity.[28] In so doing Friedrich Karl acted in defiance of official imperial policy and without consultation with the Württemberg privy council.

The membership and responsibilities of the privy council had altered since the days of Eberhard and Wilhelm Ludwig. Particularly striking by 1681 were signs that the board was firming up as a self-directed agency of the government. It has already been noted that Eberhard's will placed the privy council at the center of the regency, in a position at once crucial to and distinct from that of the acting monarch. The councilors, acutely aware of their new-found independence, took seriously their right to participate in the formulation of Württemberg policy. Indeed, during the months of uncertainty that followed Wilhelm Ludwig's death, they had declared themselves the acting government and had gone so far as to deny access to state papers to the various claimants for the office of prince regent.[29] Final wording of the regental appointment had encouraged them to continue to cherish a sense of governmental responsibility even after Friedrich Karl became prince regent. Only four years after he had taken office they presented the prince with a position paper demanding in essence that he alter his foreign policy. A need for fiscal economy provided the ostensible excuse for the paper. But while the councilors couched their theme in terms of stricter economy at court, their words made it plain that much more was at stake. The specific

27. Georges Livet, *L'intendance d'Alsace sous Louis XIV, 1648–1715* (Strasbourg, 1956); cf. G. Livet, "Louis XIV et l'Allemagne," *XVIIᵉ Siècle*, 46/47 (1960), 29–53, and F. L. Ford, *Strasbourg in Transition, 1648–1789* (Cambridge, 1958), 28–54.

28. Margrave Friedrich Magnus of Baden-Durlach accompanied Friedrich Karl on this journey to Strassburg; see C. Sattler, *Geschichte des Herzogtums Wirtenberg*, XI (Ulm, 1780), 78; cited hereafter as Sattler, *Herzöge*. A report of their meetings with the various French royals appeared in the *Gazette* for Versailles of 8 November 1681.

29. Spittler, *Geheimen-Raths-Collegiums*, 381–383.

recommendations concerned the administration of the royal kitchens, where too many "hangers-on" were being fed at crown expense. By "hangers-on" they meant that there were far too many French visitors at court. These Frenchmen, the councilors explained, "offended Württemberg sensibilities." And equally serious, their large numbers encouraged the "false impression" at Vienna that Württemberg was "disloyal" to the House of Austria.[30] Nothing came of this warning, and the council raised no official objection to Friedrich Karl's subsequent demonstration of support for France at Strassburg. Privy council minutes indicate that the councilors' silence resulted from differences of opinion among the members rather than from a feeling that such matters lay outside their jurisdiction.[31] Indeed, as subsequent events proved, when these differences were resolved to the point of a working majority, the board acted in a forthright manner to force a change in policy.

In 1681 all but one of the privy councilors, Maximilian von Menzingen (1635–1708), were appointees of the regent.[32] Their professional qualifications were mixed. Only two of them—Jacob Friedrich Rühle (1630–1708) and Johann Jacob Kurtz (1621–1693)—had received legal training; and Rühle alone had earned his doctorate. Born in the Rhenish bishopric of Worms, he had served in the Hohenlohe government and as chief legal council for the city-state of Heilbronn before coming to Württemberg at the age of fifty to accept a seat on the privy council.[33] His professional expertise, as well as his shrewd judgment and his extraordinary capacity for work—virtually every council report for the next twenty years was written in his hand—quickly made him a powerful force on the council. The fact that he had entered the government without prior association in the duchy enhanced his capacity for judging domestic issues on their individual merits and for assessing foreign policy without being influenced by vested local interests. He took the lofty charges placed by Eberhard upon the privy council at their literal value and readily adapted to the increased responsibilities acquired by that institution under the regency. It was he who composed the letter to Friedrich Karl warning of excessive French presence at Stuttgart, and it was under his guidance that a faction developed on the council in opposition to Friedrich Karl's support for the Reunions.

J. J. Kurtz, Rühle's only other colleague with experience in the

30. Ibid., 389–390.
31. HSAS, A 204: Bü. 38.
32. Pfeilsticker, *Dienerbuch*, 33, 200, 1120, 1370, 2252.
33. Ibid., 1138, 1140, 1216, 1223, 1334, 2017, 2032, 2089.

law, lacked his leadership abilities but shared his commitment to the institution of the privy council. As vice-chancellor since 1678 he had dedicated his considerable legal talents to furthering the authority of the board. He came from Reutlingen, a city-state surrounded on all sides by Württemberg territory, and had studied at the University of Tübingen. There he was regarded as the most distinguished pupil of Professor Wolfgang Adam Lauterbach, Friedrich Karl's legal adviser in the dispute over the regency. It was Lauterbach who brought Kurtz, serving by then on the legal staff of the Landtag, to the prince regent's attention.[34] The other three men—Menzingen, Heinrich Friedrich von Forstner-Dambenoy, and Bertold von Bülow—were courtiers. As was the case with their non-noble colleagues, the three aristocrats were born outside the duchy, though Forstner, Friedrich Karl's staunchest supporter on the council, had grown up in Mömpelgard where his Austrian-born father held a high position in the government. Forstner's brother had been Friedrich Karl's equerry on his Italian journey; and Forstner himself, who shared the regent's attraction to French culture, had championed Friedrich Karl's marriage candidacy at the court of Brandenburg-Ansbach, where he was then serving as Hofmarshall.[35] Bülow, as we have seen, was initially called to Württemberg to serve as governor to Friedrich Karl on his first and most extensive foreign tour.[36]

Friedrich Karl's flagrant Francophilia polarized the council. For most of 1682 the members bickered among themselves as to how Württemberg could best conduct its foreign policy under the trying circumstances of the Reunions.[37] Menzingen was particularly horrified by the annexation of his native Strassburg, but he was timid by nature and conditioned by ten years of service under Eberhard and Ludwig Wilhelm to oppose any unilateral foreign policy for Württemberg. Forstner, on the contrary, felt that the future lay with France and that Württemberg would do well to ally itself openly with Louis. He was supported in this contention by the presence at Stuttgart that year of the French agent the Sieur de Bourgeauville, whose primary mission was to secure official recognition by the Swabian Kreis of French gains under the Reunions.[38] Bourgeauville's efforts to mobi-

34. Ibid., 1110, 1137, 1145, 1146, 2385. Upon assuming the regency Friedrich Karl made Lauterbach Kirchenrat-Director and appointed him to the privy council. He died, however, in 1678; see Spittler, *Geheimen-Raths-Collegiums*, 387–388.

35. Pfeilsticker, *Dienerbuch*, 5, 1118, 2952. Also Alberti, *Wappenbuch*, 194, and the biographical sketch of the family by P. Stälin in *Allgemeine Deutsche Biographie*, VII (Berlin, 1968), 191–192.

36. Pfeilsticker, *Dienerbuch*, 199, 1116, 2759, 3010, 3066.

37. HSAS, A 204: Bü. 40.

38. Bourgeauville's Swabian activities, as well as his reports to Paris on events at Stuttgart, are analyzed in B. Wunder, *Frankreich, Württemberg und der Schwäbische*

lize Kreis support—a task that received enthusiastic endorsement from Friedrich Karl—brought him into close contact with Rühle, by this time the chief architect of Württemberg's Kreis policy and a power at the Kreistag where he customarily represented the regent.[39] Rühle met that summer with the leaders of the Franconian, Bavarian, and Upper Rhenish Kreise and corresponded regularly with the other Swabian governments. He was convinced by their remarks that the German states were not yet prepared to accept French annexations in Alsace. By the fall of 1682 he had repudiated Bourgeauville. He began to argue in council meetings and at the Kreistag against any unilateral action by Württemberg or the Kreis that would isolate the southwest from the rest of Germany. Instead he urged a neutral course that would bind them neither to Habsburg nor to Bourbon interests.[40]

Word that December of Friedrich Karl's intent to enter into a formal alliance with France mobilized the privy council behind Rühle. The showdown occurred in the first week of January 1683, when Hofmarshall von Forstner, as the ranking member of the council, proposed a declaration of military support for France. He urged the confiscation of funds from the ecclesiastical treasury *(Kirchenkasten)* for the purpose of raising a Württemberg army under the command of the prince regent, who would enter the alliance as a full military partner of France. Rühle led the counterattack and obtained full support from Kurtz and Bülow in a vote of opposition. Menzingen, who would doubtless have joined in as well, was away at the time in Regensburg. Armed with this support, Rühle wrote to the regent reminding him that he was bound by the terms of his appointment not to enter into any alliance without the explicit approval of the privy council. Such approval, he stressed, was not forthcoming. The council stood firm against the alliance and was prepared to appeal to the emperor in the event that Friedrich Karl proceeded on his own initiative. As Rühle took pains to point out, the emperor's judgment was not a matter of doubt and Friedrich Karl therefore had no choice but to abandon his plans or to face removal from office.[41]

---

*Kreis während der Auseinandersetzungen über die Reunionen, 1679–1697,* in *Veröffentlichungen der Kommission für geschichtliche Landeskunde in Baden-Württemberg,* LXIV (Stuttgart, 1971), 20–70.

39. Vann, *The Swabian Kreis,* 115–117. See HHSAW, RWR Fasc. 12 for the imperial commissioner's report to Vienna on Rühle's influence at the Kreistag.

40. HSAS, A 204: Bü. 40.

41. HSAS, A 204: Bü. 38; cf. Bourgeauville's report to Paris of 12 January 1683, located at Paris in the Archives du Ministère des Affaires Etrangères, Württemberg 4, F. 46ff., and cited in Wunder, "Der Administrator," 128–130. Wunder accepted the report at face value.

The prince regent did in fact back down. His decision turned out to be relatively unimportant in itself; Louis' attention at that time shifted away from the German southwest to the Spanish Netherlands, and the immediate danger of war passed. The importance of the event lay in the fact that it initiated a substantial change in relations between Friedrich Karl and his administration. After this confrontation he began to take markedly less interest in the quotidian affairs of his government. Nothing in the council papers suggests that his indifference was conscious or that further harsh words passed between the prince and his councilors. But these same records do indicate that in subsequent years the prince ceased his regular attendance at the council meetings. Instead he demanded short written summaries of the proceedings and followed virtually without question the council's recommendations on domestic issues unrelated to the military.[42] Nomination for appointments to government office; suggestions on the organization and administration of civil departments; proposals for rulings on petitions and cases of judicial appeal; strategies for Kreis negotiations; dealings with the districts on matters of toll, road, market, church, and school—council memoranda on these subjects forwarded to the prince came back almost always with the terse affirmation *placet*. The volume and scope of council business rose accordingly. District officials, like those of the central agencies, began turning routinely to the councilors for guidance, and they perfected a correspondingly closer control over the direction and management of government.[43] This observation is not to suggest that the council, at least throughout most of the 1680s, was acting independently of the prince, for the councilors carefully sought his approval on all policies. The point is that this approval came more or less automatically. It was as if the prince regent, having recognized the privy council's capacity for organized resistance, had decided to shift his energies into other areas. He turned over to the council the business of administration in exchange for a relatively free hand in his efforts to build a personal fortune.[44]

42. Council minutes for 1683, written by Secretary Sigismund Benedikt Moser (died 1697), indicate that between 5 January and 13 August the prince regent attended only one council meeting (HSAS, A 204: Bü. 38); cf. Spittler, *Geheimen-Raths-Collegiums*, 390.

43. A comparison of council protocolla between 1682 and 1689 indicated a steady expansion in the volume and scope of privy council business. By the end of the decade the council routinely handled the coordination and supervision of the central departments and carried on a steady correspondence with the district officials (HSAS, A 204: Bü. 36–41). See also the privy council's report to the prince regent of 23 March 1692 in which the councilors summarized Württemberg's Kreis strategy over the previous decade (A 202: Bü. 119).

44. An illustrative instance of this "division of labor" can be found in HSAS, Hausarchiv G 2–8, CXXXVI: Bü. 7. See especially the negotiations between the privy council

As more of the business of state came to be centered in their hands, the councilors evidenced a gradual shift in philosophic orientation. Whereas the board had earlier shown itself a staunch defender of principles of correlative government, later councilors tended to show an impatient irritation with interference in what they regarded as correct administrative procedure. Enthusiasm paled for continuous consultation with the executive committee of the Landtag. Instead the councilors sought to use the estates for their own ends; they resented independent impulses from that body.[45] Again, this observation must be understood as characterizing a trend rather than describing an invariable situation. Councilors did not always work harmoniously with the regent nor were they inevitably hostile to demands from the estates. Especially on matters of foreign affairs they often worked closely with the Landtag, where Rühle's staunch convictions on the necessity of Württemberg's neutrality found strong support.

A concerted effort to persuade Friedrich Karl to turn down an imperial commission in 1684 illustrates how successfully the privy councilors could work with the estates to support the principle of neutrality. In March the councilors became aware through Bülow that for some months the imperial general Ludwig Wilhelm von Baden ("Türken Louis") had been trying to entice Friedrich Karl into active military service. The bait was the promise of a high military command which the regent, according to Bülow, was about to accept.[46] On 10 March Rühle wrote a stern letter in the name of the privy council, urging the regent to set aside such plans and to remain in the duchy. He stressed the dangers to Eberhard Ludwig if Friedrich Karl abandoned the government, and he called this military adventurism a "hazard" to the entire principality.[47] Menzingen, once again at Regensburg, added his voice to the cause. He wrote to his colleagues urging them to maintain the status quo at all costs and enclosed an emotional letter for the regent in which he described Europe as "on the brink of a cataclysm" and begged him to do nothing precipitous.[48] The council then let the estates know of these negotiations. Supported by the dowager duchess, who had carefully cultivated the

---

and the prince regent over the latter's efforts to secure perpetual rights of jurisdiction in the villages belonging to his estate at Winnenden.

45. The privy council resented particularly efforts by the estates to share in the administration of the duchy while the prince regent was absent on military campaigns. See, for example, HSAS, A 204: Bü. 41 for negotiations between the councilors and the Landtag's executive committee in the autumn of 1688.

46. HSAS, Hausarchiv G 2–8, CXXXVI: Bü. 8 (protocolla for 29 February 1684).

47. Ibid. (10 March 1684).

48. Ibid. (18 March 1684).

chief officials of the Landtag, the councilors were able to convince the executive committee that it should dissuade the prince from so "dangerous" an alignment by promising him a capital settlement of 50,000 florins when he finished his regency. They also raised the possibility of an increase in the regular allowance that, as a junior prince, would once more be Friedrich Karl's under the terms of Eberhard's will.[49]

But whereas this kind of cooperation reflected shared assumptions about foreign policy, it said nothing about an agreement between estates and privy councilors on the balance of domestic power. It was on this latter point that the councilors' position gradually hardened, until by the end of the century they openly identified themselves with a commitment to a powerful central government. The question of a Württemberg army proved to be the issue that consolidated their positions. As Friedrich Karl's entrepreneurial ventures led him increasingly toward the formation of a permanent Württemberg military establishment, the estates became increasingly strident in their opposition. Their determined refusal to support such a venture led them to adopt fiscal tactics that interfered more and more with the successful running of the central administration and in so doing drove the privy councilors to abandon the idea of correlative sovereignty. New voices sounded on the council calling for stronger central authority. These demands found support among the high officials who conceived of this authority in terms of a strengthened administration that they would continue to control.

The conflict between prince and estates again had its roots in cultural as well as political differences. Though the Landtag had supported Friedrich Karl's candidacy for the regency, the estates had taken immediate offense at what they called the "Frenchification" of his court. They worried particularly about Eberhard Ludwig's growing up in such an atmosphere and began immediate agitation over his education. A relatively trivial incident in the spring of 1681 demonstrated the intensity of their feeling. It also illustrated the kind of bickering over cultural considerations that alienated regent from estates and compounded the difficulties of compromise on the more substantive issue of the military. Fearing that the young prince would be tempted and then corrupted by "loose French morals," the estates in March 1681 launched a campaign to get rid of a French governess and her son, as well as a French dancing master whom Friedrich Karl had hired to teach Eberhard Ludwig and his sisters. The executive committee designated Prelate Cappel of Blaubeuren to approach the privy council on the subject. Supported by the elderly court pastor

49. Ibid. (esp. the minutes for 13, 15, 19, 22, 24, 25, and 26 March).

Wölfflin—the same man who had preached at the opening of the 1672 Landtag—Cappel appeared before the council to voice the estates' concern over the "degenerate" tone at court. The estates worried that "lascivious French ways" were now the norm and that the tender age of the royal children rendered them "vulnerable to conversation punctuated with obscene and evil jokes." In particular they were concerned lest the children be unable to resist "a style of manners that placed topics of erotic love at the center of polite discourse." And they were disgusted by the idea of teaching a future Württemberg ruler that "French style defined good taste" and that "the essence of elegance lay in risqué behavior."[50] After the privy councilors had discussed the matter and accepted Forstner's defense of the French entourage,[51] the prelate approached the dowager duchess. The results are not verifiable, but they can be inferred from an entry in the Landtag accounts. A few days after the appeal to Magdalene Sibylla, the books indicated a withdrawal of 3,000 florins. An explanatory note described the sum as a present for the dowager duchess "in thanksgiving for a Christian education for the royal children."[52]

The military speculations that brought Friedrich Karl into open conflict with the estates began in 1687. In its initial stage, the regent raised an infantry regiment that he leased on a two-year contract to Duke Ernst August von Hannover (1629–1698).[53] That monarch conducted a substantial mercenary business and needed the Württemberg troops to fill a contract with the Republic of Venice, then at war with the Turks. There was minimum domestic risk in this venture; for while the Tübinger Vertrag outlawed military impressment in the duchy, it placed no constitutional restrictions on voluntary recruitment. So long as there were sufficient volunteers the estates had no legal basis from which to oppose the regent's activities. By November, however, the scale of Württemberg's obligation had increased substantially and rumors of illicit dragooning of young men were beginning to circulate at Stuttgart. Friedrich Karl by that time had contracted directly with Venice to provide two additional infantry regiments, a commitment that he raised in December by another one and a half regiments. By the end of the year his total obligation stood at 4,544 men.[54] In his terse replies to the anxious queries that now

---

50. HSAS, LB: Bü. 225, particularly the executive committee papers for 11 and 17 March.
51. HSAS, A 203: Bü. 22.
52. Grube, *Stuttgarter Landtag*, 351–352.
53. HSAS, Hausarchiv G 2–8, CXXXVI: Bü. 8.
54. D. von Andler, "Die württembergischen Regimente in Griechenland 1687–89," *WVJHLG*, NF 31 (1922–24), 217–279; also HSAS, A 28: Bü. 92 and 93.

began to emanate from the privy council, the regent denied any illegal tactics and described his enterprise as purely financial.[55] But a report to Paris of 3 February 1687 from Jean Closier, Sieur de Juvigny, then serving as French envoy to Stuttgart, suggested a far more aggressive purpose. Juvigny informed the French government that Friedrich Karl had told him he was assembling troops that he could use upon their return from Venice "to provide his nephew with a military force so that he could suppress the Württemberg estates." Furthermore, Friedrich Karl had said that "he would advise his nephew to use his power to make himself independent and absolute in all his lands, something that Friedrich Karl would have already accomplished himself if he had only been given full sovereign powers."[56]

Friedrich Karl's papers are silent on this point. Nothing in his extant correspondence speaks directly to a drive for suppressing the Württemberg estates or for absolute rule. But even if Juvigny overstated his case, he was certainly correct in respect to Friedrich Karl's mounting impatience with and contempt for the "exaggerated fears" of the Württemberg Landtag and its committees. Evidence also exists to document the regent's growing concern that the privy council was becoming too powerful and his gradual conviction that the bureaucracy's influence over the government would have to be curbed. Once again it was foreign rather than domestic affairs that solidified these opinions. Military invasion sent Friedrich Karl onto the battlefield and strengthened his determination to press ahead with the creation of a Württemberg army. His policies alienated privy council as well as estates and precipitated an alliance between them which helped to bring down the regency. At that point it looked as though the constitutional forces had won the battle. But their victory proved ephemeral. Friedrich Karl had set the Württemberg monarchy on a new course and in the process had permitted the consolidation of an administrative momentum within the privy council. That board's drive for a strong, rationalized central government made it difficult for the councilors to sustain a prolonged alliance with the estates.

The temporary alignment between Landtag and privy council began in the fall of 1688. Louis' decision to invade the Palatinate in September of that year placed Friedrich Karl in an exceedingly difficult domestic position. Despite his galloping Francophilia he had seen a chance for fiscal profit in supplying soldiers for Louis' enemies and in so doing demonstrated that cosmopolitan, pre-nineteenth-century

55. HSAS, A 204: Bü. 46, 47, 48; A 203: Bü. 26; LB: Bü. 247.
56. Juvigny's letter is reprinted in Wunder, "Der Administrator," 149n62.

Europeans made no necessary connection between cultural affinity and the conduct of public and private affairs. That summer, without the knowledge of his privy councilors or estates, he had signed a contract promising to provide three cavalry regiments for William of Orange.[57] The Württemberg officials had learned of these dealings only in September when complaints began to pour into Stuttgart from the districts. The *Amtleute* and the district municipal and village governments protested against the arbitrary impressment of local lads by the regent's military agents.[58] At that point the horrified estates, backed by the privy councilors, insisted that all conscripts remain in the duchy until recruiting procedures could be investigated. But, though they managed to prevent the departure for Holland of six companies, they moved too late to detain the bulk of the troops; two regiments had already slipped over the borders. It was these regiments that now provided the pretext for a French assault on the duchy. The first blow came in late September when Louis' generals threatened an invasion "with fire and sword" unless the estates paid an indemnity of 150,000 florins. They defined this sum as a fine for Württemberg's having violated the terms of the Truce of Regensburg (1684) by supplying arms to the Dutch Republic. Friedrich Karl had no alternative at that point but to summon the estates to raise the moneys with which to pay the fine and prepare a defense of the duchy. For despite the heavy recruitment of recent years, Württemberg still lacked its own force: Kreis troops were in Hungary fighting for the emperor against the Turks and the thousands of Württemberg mercenaries were either in Greece fighting for Venice or on their way to Holland.

The infuriated estates, encouraged privately by the dowager duchess and the privy councilors, refused all requests for moneys. They were particularly affronted by Friedrich Karl's demands for a personal indemnification of 28,000 florins to compensate for his losses on the six cavalry companies retained in the duchy. The exchange of charges and countercharges which passed through the privy council in the succeeding weeks provided the Ehrbarkeit with the occasion to take a public stand against peacetime recruitment.[59] Debate also sharpened the Landtag's perception that issues more far-reaching than those of arbitrary bad judgment were at stake. As Landschaftskonsulent Dr. Johann Heinrich Sturm (1651–1709) formulated his successive me-

57. Renate Wiebe, "Untersuchungen über die Hilfeleistung der deutschen Staaten für Wilhelm III. von Oranien im Jahre 1688" (Göttingen: Ph.D. diss., 1939), 47ff.; Wunder, *Frankreich, Württemberg und der Schwäbische Kreis*, 81–92.

58. HSAS, A 203: Bü. 26; LB: Bü. 247.

59. Ibid., A 203: Bü. 25 and 26.

morials, his rhetorical emphasis centered ever more directly upon charges of improper domestic procedures that had violated the constitutional liberties of the Württemberg youth and on a denunciation of an irregularly conducted foreign policy that had jeopardized the safety of the duchy. He was careful not to attack the regent directly. Instead he blamed these evils on corrupt advisers—on military agents such as Kreigsrat Johann Tobias Heller (1644–1692), who had supervised the mercenary recruitments.[60] But his language had implications that turned the dispute from a debate over policy to a confrontation over the very nature of government. For Sturm this dispute was an occasion to reaffirm the time-honored principles of correlative sovereignty and it was on this principle that he rallied the committees of the Landtag.[61] Friedrich Karl's responses were equally revealing. He bitterly denounced the estates for "shocking expressions touching his gloire" and accused them of trying to drive a wedge between the prince and his subjects. And his words left no doubt but that the wedge in this case was that of estates' rights.[62]

A French invasion in December 1688 plunged the duchy into war and cut off further debate. In the ensuring campaign Friedrich Karl accepted a commission as a lieutenant field marshal (Generalfeldmarshalleutnant) in the imperial army, a step that the privy council was in no position to prevent as it had done in 1684.[63] Backed by imperial authority Friedrich Karl then instituted a program of full militarization for the duchy. Indeed, quite apart from troops raised for the Kreis, by the end of 1691 he had supplied a total of some 10,000 mercenaries to Venice, Holland, the emperor, and Spain.[64] Unpalatable as this mercenary recruitment was, the estates had no authority to stop it without proof that force was being used. They could only write repeatedly to the regent that he was "forfeiting the love of his overburdened subjects."[65] More cogent was their persistent refusal of all regental requests for additional military funding. They supplied the funds to enable the duchy to meet its obligation to the Kreis but, de-

60. Pfeilsticker, Dienerbuch, 1485, 2043, 2046.
61. HSAS, LB: Bü. 247 (esp. the executive and steering committee minutes for 25 October, 10 November, 12 November, 15 November, and 4 December).
62. HSAS, A 203: Bü. 26 (esp. the prince regent's letters of 6 and 23 November 1688).
63. Friedrich Karl acted without consulting the privy council. See letter of Friedrich Karl to Landtag dated 20 April 1689 in HSAS, LB: Bü. 249; cf. Beilage 1 in letter of Kriegsrat Heller to Baron Johann Rudolf von Ow, Hofmarshall to the bishop of Würzburg, dated 5 March 1689 (LB: Bü. 248).
64. Wunder, "Der Administrator," 142.
65. HSAS, LB: Bü. 247 (26 October 1688) and 249 (1 June 1689); A 203: Bü. 27 (6 June 1690).

THE ESTATES AT BAY

spite the emergencies of war, turned down all proposals for construction and supply such as might promote an independent domestic military posture. The next three years were characterized therefore by steadily deteriorating relations between Friedrich Karl and the Landtag.[66]

These years were also marked by a growing coldness between the regent and the privy council. The administrative boldness that had developed within the council allowed the regent to suspect the councilors of rewriting his commands from the field so as to reinforce their own particular policies.[67] Though archival records contain no evidence of such tampering, they do indicate that the councilors were writing to prince and emperor to deplore the Landtag's intransigence while secretly encouraging the estates in their opposition. One must be cautious in attributing long-term strategy to these apparent double-dealings. A reading of council minutes suggests that they stemmed in large part from personality conflicts on the board. In November 1689 Bülow had resigned from the privy council in protest over the regent's aggressive militarism. His retirement left the board with only four members, and Friedrich Karl chose not to fill the vacancy. He had already replaced Forstner, who died in 1687, with his longtime friend and confidant Johann Eberhard von Varnbühler, so that regental policies had a strong champion on the board. Rühle, who had emerged as leader of the opposition, was now spending a great deal of time away from Stuttgart on Kreis business, leaving only Menzingen and Kurtz to counter these policies. Menzingen represented the duchy at Regensburg and was frequently there, so that the board often swung from support of Friedrich Karl to the opposite extreme upon the return of Rühle and Menzingen to the meetings.[68]

In any event Friedrich Karl launched formal charges with the emperor against both the council and the estates. He accused the former of overweening pretension in the administration of the ducal government and of "doctoring" his orders as they were relayed to the council from the field. The estates he denounced for refusing to vote the money and supplies essential for the defense of the duchy. Both insti-

66. Grube, *Stuttgarter Landtag,* 354–362.
67. HSAS, LB: Bü. 248. See correspondence among Kriegsrat Heller, Friedrich Karl and Baron J. R. von Ow, 25 February 1689 to 10 November 1689. Spittler, *Geheimen-Raths-Collegiums,* 390, points out that, already in September of 1688, Friedrich Karl was excluding the privy councilors from state ceremonies. See also Hausarchiv G 2–8, CXXXVI: Bü. 6 for correspondence between the council and the prince regent over the possibility of raising loans for the duchy at Frankfurt am Main.

68. HSAS, A 204: Bü. 39, 41, 49; LB: Bü. 248 (esp. letters of 5 January 1689 and 17 May 1690).

tutions responded with appeals of their own and sent delegations and materials to Vienna in their defense. The emperor in each instance backed the prince regent; he needed Württemberg troops for the war with France and wanted as powerful a set of fortifications in the duchy as he could obtain.[69] Imperial support for the regent left the officials with no choice but to comply with his demands. They did so until May 1691 when Friedrich Karl announced the conversion (Transmutation) of the territorial militia into a regular standing army under his own command staff and instituted a policy of compulsory conscription. While Varnbühler held the council for Friedrich Karl,[70] Sturm led the executive committee of the estates into open opposition. They refused to vote the taxes to maintain the army and once more appealed to Vienna. As before, Friedrich Karl outflanked his territorial opposition by successfully manipulating imperial institutions, underscoring the potential for maneuver open to sovereign as well as territorial subject in a federal structure like the empire. First he secured a contract with the Kreis for three regiments of his army (some 3,000 troops).[71] He then obtained an imperial order commanding the Württembergers to maintain the remaining 3,000 soldiers as part of their defense obligation.[72] The executive committee was forced to consent to what the estates insisted were two emergency fiscal measures rammed through by the crown: a head tax (Kopf- und Familiensteuer) and an income tax known as the Trizesimen by which the government claimed one-thirtieth of the value of the fruit and wine harvest.[73]

As the war with France continued to escalate, Friedrich Karl mounted one final effort to obtain public support for his policies. In the spring of 1692 he summoned a general meeting of the estates. There he hoped for a ratification of the emergency taxes forced through the executive committee during the previous year and for a

69. Ibid., A 203: Bü. 26 and 27.
70. Ibid., A 207: Bü. 49 (esp. minutes for 23 January 1691).
71. Ibid., C 9: Bü. 396, 568, 691, 692 (Allgemeiner Kreistag, 8 March–15 June).
72. The constitutional rationale for this decision was a Reichstag decree (1654) forbidding territorial estates to withhold support for the defense of their territorial states. Otto Gierke, Rechtsgeschichte der deutschen Genossenschaft (Berlin, 1868), 812; Fritz Hartung, Deutsche Verfassungsgeschichte vom 15. Jahrhundert bis zur Gegenwart, 5th ed. (Stuttgart, 1950), 137; also F. Hartung, "Herrschaftsverträge und ständischer Dualismus in deutschen Territorien," Schweizer Beiträge zur Allgemeinen Geschichte, 10 (1952), 176.
73. HSAS, LB: Bü. 253; Sattler, Herzöge, XI, 201; E. Schneider, Württembergische Geschichte (Stuttgart, 1896), 308f.; F. Wintterlin, "Wehrverfassung und Landesverfassung im Herzogtum Württemberg," WVJHLG, 34 (1928), esp. 245–247.

repudiation of that committee's most recent protest to Vienna.[74] He personally selected the text for the sermon read at the ceremonial opening: ". . . and admonished His people, they will fight comforted unto death to maintain the law, the temple, the city, the homeland, and the government" (2 Macc. 13: 13–14).[75] But before the estates had even heard these words, Landschaftskonsulent Sturm had created an environment that turned the text into a battle cry for legitimate government and by implication a rallying point for opposition to the regent. Instead of the general remarks customarily rendered by the Landschaftskonsulent after the speech from the throne, Sturm delivered his own fiery sermon. He read the delegates his summary of what had transpired at Stuttgart over the previous eighteen months and in so doing painted a vivid picture of regental abuse. The regent, he said, had compromised Württemberg's ancient liberties by introducing taxes against the advice of the executive committee and by acting unilaterally to transform the militia into a permanent army (miles perpetuus). Such procedures not only violated the Tübinger Vertrag; they "mocked the very premises of a legitimate, Christian, German-oriented, non-Machiavellian polity" (aller rechtschaffen Christlich und teutsch gesinnten, ohnmachiavellistischer politicorum).[76]

Sturm's address crystallized the confrontation that had been building up for the previous decade between prince and estates. His words identified the issue as no longer one of policy and administrative procedure; the state itself was at stake. His reading of the Tübinger Vertrag and his denunciation of customs that he characterized as un-Christian, foreign, and Machiavellian spoke to a specific vision of culture and society as well as to a definition of the Württemberg state. The question was one of basic premises: was society a matter of power and expediency? Or was it a system hammered out over the previous centuries and resting on the covenants, treaties, and traditions from those earlier days? For Sturm the answer was clear. He regarded the foundations of state and society in terms of a contract in which the subjects—in this case the estates—shared certain inalienable rights.

74. The executive committee appealed to the Reichshofrat on 6 February, 1692. The estates protested the illegal conscription for the Württemberg army and called for the dissolution of that force. See HSAS, LB: Bü. 253; A 202: Bü. 119 (esp. letters of 27 and 30 March from Friedrich Karl to the privy council); A 203: Bü. 28 (letter from privy council to Friedrich Karl of 27 March 1692).

75. Grube, Stuttgarter Landtag, 362.

76. HSAS, LB: Bü. 259; A 203: Bü. 27 (Sturm's address to the prince regent of 3 June 1692).

The intensity of his convictions drew the Landtag to him and ensured him a commanding role in its deliberations.

Johann Heinrich Sturm stood at the very center of the Württemberg Ehrbarkeit. His family had long been active in municipal government and he was married to the daughter of the prelate of Bebenhausen, a leading figure on the executive committee of the Landtag. Their son served as legal council and secretary for the Landtag,[77] and their daughter Beata had achieved international fame as the "Württemberg Tabitha." Her piety made her a legend in her own lifetime; and her biography, published first in 1740, fused Pietistic theology with literary accomplishment in ways that made her life a model for the kind of moralistic writing that gained great popularity in nineteenth-century German literature.[78] Sturm grew up in Württemberg and studied at Tübingen, where he earned doctorates in both theology and law. He read the Bible in its original Greek and Latin texts and took as his guide among secular writings *The Contemplations of Marcus Aurelius* and Bossuet's *Discourse on Universal History*. Given his scholarly orientation it is not surprising that he found the secularism of the new politics repulsive and that he emphatically rejected the elevation of realpolitik represented in the contemporary popularity of Machiavelli's writings.[79] As an early follower of Philipp Jakob Spener (1635–1705), Sturm struggled to revive in Württemberg the pious fervor of primitive Christianity. In this sense his success as a leader provides one of the earliest examples in German history of the potent linkage that could be effected between Pietism and political activism. He realized that state, church, and society were so interwoven in Württemberg that territorial politics would have to be the vehicle for Christian reform. It was this emphasis upon politics that attracted him to the broader stream of political conservatism within the Württemberg Ehrbarkeit. But while his leadership provided the rallying point for the estates' reaction against the new directions at court, Sturm's final goal embraced theological as well as political concerns. He was a deeply religious man in quest of a heightened Christian awareness rather than simply a political traditionalist striving to hold on to a world that was lost.[80] He stood therefore as a

77. Pfeilsticker, *Dienerbuch*, 1149.
78. H. Lehmann, *Pietismus und weltliche Ordnung in Württemberg vom 17. bis zum 20. Jahrhundert* (Stuttgart, 1969), 80f.: cf. K. F. Ledderhose, *Beata Sturm* (Eisleben, 1854); and Ledderhose's essay in the *Allgemeine Deutsche Biographie*, XXXVII (Berlin, 1971), 2–4.
79. Gustav Freytag, *Bilder aus der deutschen Vergangenheit*, III (Leipzig, 1895), 255f.; Friedrich Meinecke, *Idee der Staatsraison* (Munich, 1957), 180ff.
80. Lehmann, *Pietismus und weltliche Ordnung in Württemberg*, 28–34 and 80ff.

counterpart to the absolutist prince. Like the prince he sought a cultural foundation for the state. But for Sturm that foundation lay in a radical reorientation of contemporary society and not in a centralization of political power.

Friedrich Karl was not the man to perceive such nuances, and his response to Sturm's address revealed the extent of the cleavage between the new politics and those of either Sturm or his followers. Friedrich Karl informed the Landtag that he had acted with "no intent other than that of promoting the best for the land and of advancing the true splendor of the ducal House." He saw the quest for *gloire* as a driving imperative in monarchy and felt that this quality had to reside in a strong state. To that end Friedrich Karl claimed the interpretation of the constitution as his own responsibility. The Tübinger Vertrag was simply a document drawn up to meet a specific set of historical circumstances. In its literal sense, it was "past history" (*alte historie*). As a monarch he could use it only as a point of analytical departure, as a set of general principles to be adapted to changing circumstances. And present conditions, he insisted, demanded strong military action.[81] Sturm replied that neither he nor his colleagues could understand how compliance with the law of the land could be construed as unproductive literal mindedness. "If the Law is nothing but past history," he wrote, "then no treaty, no compact, no legislation is valid. The world is ruled only by power."[82]

A sudden reversal on the military front cut short these exchanges and sent Friedrich Karl back into the field. His capture that September by the French and his removal to Paris, where he was received with elaborate courtesy and attention by Louis XIV, set off a chain reaction within the empire that culminated with his dismissal as regent in late January 1693. An invasion of Württemberg by the French army followed shortly upon that act and threw the duchy once again into the center of the military theater. It was not until 1698, after the war had ended, that a general Landtag could again assemble. Debate resumed almost at once and followed the direction that had produced the earlier deadlock. But though the arguments remained much the same, the balance of power within the government had shifted decisively. Friedrich Karl was no longer regent, and the estates now faced their own legitimate monarch. They quickly discovered that Eberhard Ludwig not only shared his uncle's perception of monarchy completely but carried it to new heights. Moreover, he was prepared to

81. HSAS, LB: Bü. 259 (esp. 26 May 1692).
82. HSAS, A 203: Bü. 27 (Sturm's memorial of 18 June 1692).

THE MAKING OF A STATE

use all the powers of his office to implement this vision. And this time there was no question of checks and balances in the government; he had assumed full control.

Two points stand out in the narrative sequence that surrounds Friedrich Karl's fall from power. The first is the imperial capacity to influence domestic politics in the German states. So much has been written about the moribund quality of the post-Westphalian Reich that students of this period of European history are inclined to miss the fact that these institutions exerted an extensive influence over the smaller polities. Württemberg provides a striking example of this continued imperial vitality. Archival records confirm that the decision to depose Friedrich Karl was made outside the duchy and that it had nothing to do with the recent complaints to Vienna by the territorial estates. Consultation with Stuttgart by the imperial commissioner Count Sebastian Wunibald von Zeil took place only after the emperor had decided to declare the sixteen-year-old prince of sufficient maturity to rule the duchy. And then the deliberations included only Zeil, Magdalene Sibylla, and Eberhard Ludwig. The estates played no role in the affair, nor did the privy council, at least as an institution. The prime mover throughout the entire sequence was the emperor Leopold. Friedrich Karl's warm reception at Versailles and his subsequent behavior at that court had convinced the emperor that the regent had entered into a secret alliance with France. Leopold acted to prevent Friedrich Karl's carrying Württemberg (and hence the Swabian Kreis) out of the imperial camp at the very moment when these resources were critical for maintaining the Reich's western defense.[83]

The second point further underscores the imperial influence by calling attention to the impact of the deposition upon the privy council and the Landtag. Although neither body participated directly in the coup, both took advantage of the situation to regain their institutional momentum. In so doing they weakened the earlier ties that had bound them together in opposition to Friedrich Karl's self-seeking militarism and moved in somewhat different directions. Chapter 5 analyzes the internal dynamics of the privy council in these years. At this juncture it is sufficient to say that Magdalene Sibylla, to whom Leopold granted coresponsibility for the government until Eberhard

83. The documents relating to the imperial proclamation of Eberhard Ludwig's majority, or *veniam aetatis*, are found in HSAS, Hausarchiv G 2–8, CLXXXIV: Bü. 12 and 13; and in A 204: Bü. 50 (see privy council protocolla for January 1693, esp. those kept by Secretary Obrecht). See also, Sattler, *Herzöge*, XII, 1ff. and Beil, 2; A. Reyscher, *Vollständige, historisch und kritisch bearbeitete Sammlung der württembergischen Gesetze* 1 (Stuttgart and Tübingen, 1828), 385; Schneider, *Württembergische Geschichte*, 310–319; and Wunder, "Der Administrator," 151–157.

Ludwig could take over completely, relied heavily upon the council.[84] She expanded it; she changed its membership. The death that year of Vice-Chancellor Kurtz and the forced retirement of Varnbühler as an unreliable crony of the former prince regent had left only Rühle and Menzingen active on the board.[85] On their advice the new government made three appointments: Johann Georg Kulpis (1652–1698), who had worked closely with Rühle on Kreis business and now became director of the Kirchenrat and privy councilor; Baron Johann Friedrich von Staffhorst (1653–1730); and Baron Joachim Rüdiger von Ostien (1603–1699).[86] The two noblemen, like Kulpis, came from outside the duchy. They were courtiers, great friends of the young prince, and received respectively the titles of Hofmarshall and president of the privy council. With its majority of new members and an ever-greater responsibility for administrative direction, the council once again entered a phase of institutional growth.[87]

The estates anticipated a similar opportunity. When informed by the dowager duchess of Friedrich Karl's fall, they declared themselves in a state "of no small consolation." They were even more pleased when she promised to disband the three regiments not being paid by the Kreis. Nothing was said about the ultimate fate of the troops still under contract, but Sturm expressed confidence to the executive committee members that they would carry their point and that the full, literal terms of the Tübinger Vertrag would once more provide the framework for Württemberg government.[88] In the summer of 1693, however, a French invasion ended these speculations. The most severe devastation wrecked upon the duchy since the Battle of Nördlingen (1634) instituted a period when all attention focused on survival.[89] Levies of more than 600,000 florins were imposed upon the estates; and Landschaftskonsulent Sturm, together with a group of prominent Württembergers which included two prelates and the

84. Privy council minutes for the installation ceremony (22 January 1693) record Zeil's explicit instruction that the dowager duchess serve as de facto ruler until the young prince was able to manage on his own (HSAS, A 204: Bü. 50).

85. Leopold had stipulated a purging of the privy council's Francophilic elements; see Zeyl's report of 24 January 1693 in HSAS, Hausarchiv G 2–8, CXXXVI: Bü. 13.

86. HSAS, A 202: Bü.70 (protocolla of 10 October 1693). Ostien resigned two years later and was replaced by Kammermeister Ludwig Philipp von Geissmar (1651–1699).

87. HSAS, A 202: Bü. 5 contains an unsigned table outlining the specific administrative responsibilities of each of the five councilors. See also the protocolla for 1693–1697 in A 204: Bü. 48–55.

88. HSAS, Hausarchiv G 2–8, CLXXXIV: Bü. 13 (24 January 1693).

89. Wunder, *Frankreich, Württemberg und der Schwäbische Kreis*, 164–190.

mayors of Stuttgart and Tübingen, were carried first to Strassburg and then to Metz as guarantors for this sum. It was not until 30 November 1696 that Sturm and those hostages who had survived the rigors of prison returned to Stuttgart.[90] During the imprisonment of these men, the estates had found themselves deprived of leadership and saddled with financial burdens beyond the capacity of the exhausted duchy.[91] Under these trying conditions relations with the government remained relatively quiet as both sides restricted themselves to minor skirmishes. Eberhard Ludwig made one attempt in 1694 to install a ducal official as inspector for the Landschaft's financial accounts, but he backed down when the executive committee protested. The estates engaged in similarly tentative fencing by sending a series of memorials requesting an official repudiation of the Trizesimen tax introduced so arbitrarily by Friedrich Karl. They also wanted assurance that the crown would make no attempt to create a standing army. Both subjects were dropped upon receipt of a sharp letter from Eberhard Ludwig which ordered them to cease raising "idle questions."[92]

The Peace of Ryswick (30 October 1697) ended hostilities between France and the Reich and precipitated the final crisis at Stuttgart. At that point the Swabian Kreis no longer felt it needed the 3,000 ducal soldiers and declined to extend its Württemberg contract beyond the spring of 1698.[93] A decision on the fate of the standing army could no longer be postponed: Eberhard Ludwig had either to dismiss the troops and return the duchy to traditional policy or press forward with arrangements for their permanent maintenance, thus institutionalizing a standing army under ducal control. Having now assumed full authority in his government, Eberhard Ludwig was determined to go forward, but he sought initially to win his point by compromise. In March 1698 he summoned the executive committee of the Landtag and proposed the discharge of about a thousand of these soldiers. He asked in turn that the estates support the remainder for one more year, "as a defensive measure until peace was assured." When the executive committee demanded that the entire army be dismantled *instantissime*, Eberhard Ludwig took his case to the larger council (Gr.

90. T. Schott, "Die württembergische Geiseln in Strassburg und Metz, 1693–1696," *Zeitschrift für allgemeine Geschichte*, 3 (1886), 583–602.

91. Schneider, *Württembergische Geschichte*, 16 ff., 123 ff., 318, estimates a population decline from 450,000 to 300,000 inhabitants and puts financial losses from plundering and damage to crops, buildings, and forests at 2,660,000 florins.

92. Grube, *Stuttgarter Landtag*, 366–367.

93. Ruth Gebauer, *Die Aussenpolitik des Schwäbischen Reichkreises vor Ausbruch des Spanischen Erbfolgekrieges* (Heidelberg, 1966), 61–148.

Ausschuss) of the Landtag. But under Staffhorst's advice (and with the tacit consent of the entire privy council) he drew up the agenda for their meeting so that the issue of debate was no longer that of the *quaestio an* (whether or not the troops would be retained) but that of the *quaestio quomodo* (how best to raise the money for their upkeep). Led by Konsulent Sturm, the Grösserer Ausschuss refused the bait and threatened to appeal to the emperor if Eberhard Ludwig did not suspend at once the emergency taxes his uncle had instituted to support these troops. At that point Eberhard Ludwig dissolved the meeting and announced he did not require their approval for the maintenance of his army. He would place his case before a plenary assembly, where he was confident a less "impertinent," "wrongheaded" view would prevail.[94]

Accusations of misconduct had begun to fly even before the estates could assemble at Stuttgart. Sturm particularly resented the behavior of the privy councilors, whom he accused of trying to stack the odds against the Landtag's leadership and of sabotaging the meeting. He supported these charges by pointing to the councilors' refusal to issue a blanket permission that would allow the smaller districts to grant proxy votes to the executive committee. This custom, he insisted, had been followed since the Thirty Years War. The council's reply that votes cast at plenary sessions were "freer votes" than "proxies administered by committees with preconceived opinions" must only have confirmed his suspicions that the councilors had gone over entirely to the prince. And the privy council's subsequent refusal to confer with the executive committee on the drafting of the agenda and the composition of the letters of convocation doubtless strengthened that conviction.[95] But despite this preliminary animosity some fifty-eight delegates and thirteen prelates gathered at the Stuttgart castle on the morning of 29 September 1698 for the opening of the Landtag.[96] Not even the most pessimistic of them could have guessed that this would be the last such meeting in the forty years of Eberhard Ludwig's reign.

Nevertheless, the opening ceremony must have startled the older delegates. Any one of them who had been present at comparable occasions under earlier dukes could not have failed to recognize that

94. HSAS, A 203: Bü. 34; LB: Bü. 283–284. K. Pfaff, *Geschichte des Militärwesens in Württemberg von der ältesten bis auf unsere Zeit und der Verhandlungen darüber zwischen der Regierung und den Landständen* (Stuttgart, 1842), 39f.

95. HSAS, LB: Bü. 285.

96. Only ten districts (the smallest number since the Landtag of 1662) issued proxies. The fifty-eight delegates represented a total of fifty-five districts (Grube, *Stuttgarter Landtag*, 368).

Eberhard Ludwig was casting his monarchy in a radically different image. The self-conscious emphasis on royal power marking every stage of the pageantry created an atmosphere that carried only the faintest traces of the unpretentious, almost fraternal camaraderie that had been perfected to such an art under Eberhard III. To an age accustomed to regarding symbols as concrete expressions of reality, these stylistic innovations must have revealed as much about the changes of the previous twenty years as did the issues themselves. When the delegates arrived at the castle courtyard they found it ringed with a military honor guard in new uniforms studded with sparkling silver decorations. Once inside the Rittersaal they advanced the length of the hall to bow before the twenty-one-year-old duke, who was standing alone on a raised platform covered with costly tapestries. A table draped with crimson silk stood behind him and beside it was a high-backed armchair upholstered in the same color and material. After Privy Councilor Rühle had read the Propositionen and Konsulent Sturm had delivered a perfunctory response, the prelates led the delegates once again to the dais where each man made his "most humble reverence" before the monarch, who was now seated in the great chair. As had been the earlier custom, a dinner in the Rittersaal, decorated for this event with tapestries and silk damask hangings, followed the sermon. But whereas Eberhard III had dined surrounded by his councilors and estates and remained well into the evening drinking and chatting with his guests, his grandson presided in conspicuous isolation. Eberhard Ludwig sat at a small table, where he was joined by members of his immediate family. After a dinner served to him with great ceremony, he departed immediately; by three o'clock in the afternoon he was already at the hunt.[97]

The substance of the debates that began the next morning and continued throughout the next four months need not concern us here. More important was the rhetoric; for it was in the formulation of the charges and countercharges that the essence of the confrontation was revealed. No one believed that so small a military force would in itself bankrupt the duchy. Nor could Eberhard Ludwig have had any illusions as to this army's ultimate defense capability against invasion by a power such as France. The question was much more subtle, ultimately involving the way in which the state was to be defined. Sturm held that the law, the intrinsic constituent of the state, resided in the treaties, compacts, and legislation of the past—and most especially in the literal terms of the Tübinger Vertrag. He read these documents

97. HSAS, *tomus actorum*, cvii, 1–602.

as "resting all upon the basic principle that the welfare of the people (*salus populi*) constituted the raison d'être of the state, the *suprema lex*." "The love of his subjects not the glory of his House was the chief concern of the ruler." This love must reassert itself against the "ambition" and "worldliness" *(Luxus)* that now characterized the Württemberg monarchy. There was also an institutional component to his argument. The Württemberg state rested upon both crown and Landtag; and the privy council, as the administrative arm of government, was created to serve both elements in this duality. But the reality had become otherwise: "The privy councilors no longer spoke for the country; they no longer defended the estates. Instead they stood ready to implement the 'absolute commands' *(Absolute Befehle)* of the duke."[98]

Eberhard Ludwig met these charges from a position differing fundamentally in its implications from that of most of the privy councilors. But the heat of debate obscured the nuances of difference so that crown and council presented a solid front. The basis for their cooperation was the shared conviction that the state was an organic phenomenon. It had to grow and shape itself to a changing world. This growth could be—and most of the privy councilors felt that it should be—guided by the terms of the constitution. But the government must be granted the authority to adapt these terms to contemporary constraints. The question of the defense posture of the duchy concerned the ruler and his government and not the prelates and Landschaften.[99] At this juncture Eberhard Ludwig carried the argument a step further. He insisted that the dissolution of the army worked to enhance neither the general welfare *(bonum publicum)* nor his own glory *(Reputation)*.[100] Whereas council discussion did not pick up on the implications of a government oriented around ducal *gloire*, the members revealed themselves as convinced of the government's unitary responsibility for interpreting such matters for the good of the state.[101]

As the lines of debate hardened, Sturm guided the executive committee in a two-stage strategy designed to force Eberhard Ludwig to abandon his military plans. First the committee presented Eberhard Ludwig with a petition, signed by various leaders from the urban magistracies and assemblies of the districts, calling for the dissolu-

---

98. HSAS, LB: Bü. 286–287. For Sturm's speech attacking the privy council, see A 203: Bü. 36 (26 January 1699).

99. Ibid., A 203: Bü. 34 (esp. privy council minutes for 26 July 1698).

100. Ibid., LB: Bü. 285 (11 July 1698).

101. Ibid., A 203: Bü. 35 (esp. minutes for November 1698).

tion of the army. The purpose here was to establish the committee's credentials as spokesman for the general population and to counter charges from Eberhard Ludwig and the privy councilors that the committee was a self-appointed oligarchy speaking only in its own interest. Sturm then persuaded the larger steering committee to support the sending of a delegation to the emperor in Vienna to place legal charges against the duke. Both attempts boomeranged and in so doing revealed that Sturm's fiery leadership was trying to carry the Ehrbarkeit farther than it was prepared to go.

The delegates were willing to follow Sturm to the extent of withholding their approval for new military taxes. They even agreed to defy the duke in January 1699 when he summarily dismissed Sturm from the Oberrat, where he had served since 1680. At that time they voted to continue his governmental salary and to fund his full pension benefits through private payments from their own secret treasury (Geheimen Truhe).[102] But when Eberhard Ludwig required each of them to declare himself individually, the delegates backed down on the question of a suit at law just as the local magistrates had reneged on the earlier petition. In the final analysis they remained too parochial to press forward with a concentrated program of positive action. Beyond the Ehrbarkeit of cities such as Stuttgart and Tübingen, the Württemberg notables lacked a window onto the larger world that would have enabled them to place Eberhard Ludwig's maneuvers in a larger constitutional perspective. They were perfectly capable of rallying to defeat any direct assault on their control over the towns and districts. But most of them lacked the broader vision necessary to sustain a concerted opposition to crown policies that left their local privileges intact but that challenged their influence over territorial government. Indeed interviews with crown officials on this subject made clear that few delegates and municipal officials grasped the full implications of Sturm's definition of the state. And among those who did so, only a handful found the matter of sufficient gravity to merit personal sacrifice.

The word that preparations were being made for an appeal to Vienna prompted Eberhard Ludwig to mount his assault. On 1 February 1699 he sent letters to all his district officials ordering the Amtleute to undertake an immediate survey of their districts. He charged each Amtmann with the interviewing of every muncipal and village official who had voting rights in the district assembly. Under oath (auf Pflicht und Eid) these men were to swear whether or not

102. Ibid., LB: Bü. 287 (31 January 1699); A 203: Bü. 36 (26 January 1699).

they had instructed their Landtag delegates to authorize the steering committee to institute legal proceedings at Vienna. If a man swore that he had never given such an explicit instruction, the Amtmann was to ask him to say under oath whether or not he now wished such an attack to be launched against the duke.[103] Only the municipal officials of Tübingen, that stronghold of the Ehrbarkeit, responded positively to both these questions. All others replying affirmatively to the first recanted when confronted by the Amtmann and answered no to the second query.[104] Meanwhile Eberhard proclaimed a new military tax and ordered its immediate collection with or without the consent of the estates.

Eberhard Ludwig next demanded the prompt return to Stuttgart of the junior Landschaftskonsulent Johann Dietrich Hörner (1652–1724), who was recovering from an illness at a spa in northern Württemberg. Hörner was instructed to report at once to the privy council.[105] There, on 31 July Hofmarshall von Staffhorst issued an ultimatum ordering that he both repudiate Sturm's leadership and refuse to forward the formal charges against the prince to Vienna. Hörner protested to the council that the duke's unilateral tax had violated all the laws of the duchy and had challenged the very base of the estates' *privilegiorum*. He deplored a culture that defined statecraft as an exercise in "trickery and violence" rather than as the cultivation of "justice and piety." In words that echoed those of Sturm he stressed tradition and insisted that the duke was "bound by the letter of the law." Staffhorst's replies struck an even more belligerent tone. He accused the committee of making false claims in the name of the people and of seeking to "prostitute the duke before the emperor and the world." As for Dr. Sturm, he was "nothing but an opportunist whom the Holy Ghost will teach a lesson." Hörner should know that the duke knew exactly who the troublemakers were and that he counted Hörner among them. If they did not cease their treason at once, the duke was going to ruin them and their families. Under this pressure (Staffhorst spoke for over an hour) Hörner agreed finally to delay the departure of the delegation until the committee had reconsidered the case.[106]

Armed with this respite Eberhard Ludwig turned on the prelates. He summoned them individually to sign a document stating that they had reconsidered the matter and decided that such an appeal was un-

103. Ibid., A 203: Bü. 36 (1 February 1669).
104. Ibid., A 203: Bü. 36.
105. Ibid., A 203: Bü. 36 (28 July 1699); on Hörner's career see Pfeilsticker, *Dienerbuch*, 1318, 1350, 1447, 1451, 2255, 3505, 3506.
106. HSAS, LB: 289 (Hörner's summary, 29 July 1699).

lawful. He also required them to take an oath that it would be illegal for them or their successors ever to countenance an appeal by the Landtag against the authority of the ruling prince. Seven prelates signed at once; all but one of the remaining seven—Provost Johann Wolfgang Dietrich of Denkendorf—signed subsequently when Privy Councilor Rühle, as director of the consistory, told them that Eberhard Ludwig was prepared to dismiss them from office. The thirteen signers then voted unanimously that all future contracts for appointment to the office of abbot contain a clause explicitly prohibiting any appeal outside the duchy, thereby making it impossible for any Landtag to seek recourse against ducal authority by appealing to the emperor.[107]

The estates had lost the battle. True, they had never voted the taxes that now made possible the upkeep of a standing army. Nor had they recognized the prince's right to levy without their consent. But with the defection of the prelates and their own repudiation by the district assemblies, Sturm and his party had lost their mandate. Unwilling to accept a policy that struck at their control over taxation, yet unable to launch a parliamentary lawsuit in the imperial courts, the estates dissolved without legislation or resolution. And since Eberhard Ludwig found them redundant and he alone possessed the power of summons, they never met again in his lifetime. One leg of the triangle upon which the Württemberg state had heretofore rested was severely impaired. Whatever correlative qualities might remain, they would now be shared between prince and privy council.

107. Ibid., LB: Bü. 289.

# [5]

# The Prince and His Officials

HAVING CURBED his estates, Eberhard Ludwig announced that he intended to govern "as a great prince."[1] Exactly what he meant by this term is unclear. It is tempting to equate it with absolutism and to read into his rhetoric a vision of the prince as the sole arbiter of the monolithic state. Certainly he behaved in a high-handed manner and, insofar as he was able, brooked no opposition to his plans, sponsoring policies that aimed to strengthen the central government at the expense of local interest groups. And like so many of his counterparts in the other European states, he referred constantly to the need for *eine gute Polizei*, the cameralistic dictum for the well-ordered state.[2] Citing cameralistic thinkers as models, Eberhard Ludwig created new institutions and championed administrative innovations. His immediate successor Carl Alexander (1684–1737) did likewise. The result was that, by the middle of the eighteenth century, from virtually any vantage point in the territory the ducal presence bulked larger than ever before.

That the crown extended the scope of its powers in eighteenth-century Europe is a historical commonplace; Württemberg only confirms the norm. The problem lies in clarifying the precise nature of this growth and in identifying its driving force. Here a study of Württemberg is illuminating. Events in the duchy make it clear that ducal power expanded ad hoc, often under contradictory impulses. Just as bureaucratic growth proved to have been less linear than had been

---

1. HSAS, A 230: Bu. 35 (22 April 1700); cf. G 2–8 CXXIV: Bu. 18 (privy council memorandum on the prince's relation to the law, 20 August 1709).
2. Marc Raeff, "The Well-Ordered Police State and the Development of Modernity in Seventeenth- and Eighteenth-Century Europe: An Attempt at a Comparative Approach," *American Historical Review*, 80 (1975), 1221–1243.

thought, so absolutism developed from more complicated motivations. It did not proceed from a systematic program of state building any more than it derived from a reaction by ducal authorities to what recent German social historians have posited as a vigorous tradition of independent industrial production in the early modern countryside[3] Proto-industrialization was tentative at best in early-eighteenth-century Württemberg. Independent producers, moreover, inclined to support rather than to challenge the duke. For in that the urban guilds provided the political and economic base for the Ehrbarkeit, the crown always championed the entrepreneur as a potential counterweight to the territorial estates.

It is not surprising that the dukes pushed the government toward absolutism. Their direction, however, was jerky and gave no impression of a cumulative strategy. Nothing in Eberhard Ludwig's policy indicated a conscious awareness of either of the two principal drives so often associated with state building: the primacy of foreign policy (*Primat der Aussenpolitik*)[4] and the need for social control (*Sozialdisziplinierung*).[5] He was fiercely loyal to the empire (*Reichstreu*) and wanted a military force that would ensure him a role in the imperial army and guarantee his leadership in the Swabian Kreis.[6] But beyond these concerns he entertained no ambitions for an independent, aggressive foreign policy. Nor did he consider expanding his holdings in any way other than through the occasional feudal reversion or fortuitous purchase. The same holds true for the concept of social control. Eberhard Ludwig sought control only in the sense that he was always eager to expand his authority. His enemies were not the socially restless or the politically deprived elements in Württemberg society. On the contrary, he fought against the power of the territorial elite, the estates and the officials. And in his efforts to circumscribe vested local interests he often allied with the disenfranchised peasantry.[7]

3. P. Kriedte, H. Mendick, and J. Schlumbohm, eds., *Industrialisierung vor der Industrialisierung: Gewerbliche Warenproduktion auf dem Land in der Formationsperiode des Kapitalismus* (Göttingen, 1977).

4. See especially, Otto Hintze, "The Formation of States and Constitutional Development" and "Military Organization and the Organization of the State," in Felix Gilbert, ed., *The Historical Essays of Otto Hintze* (Oxford, 1975), 157–216. Also, Kurt von Raumer, "Absoluter Staat, korporative Libertät, persönliche Freiheit," *Historische Zeitschrift*, 83 (1957), 79ff.

5. G. Oestreich, "Strukturprobleme des europäischen Absolutismus," in Gerhard Oestreich, *Geist und Gestalt des frühmodernen Staates: Ausgewählte Aufsätze* (Berlin, 1969), 179–197.

6. K. Weller, *Württembergische Geschichte* (Stuttgart, 1963), 180ff.; E. Marquardt, *Geschichte Württembergs* (Stuttgart, 1962), 172ff.

7. Cf. Michel Foucault, *Folie et déraison: Histoire de la folie à l'âge classique* (Paris, 1961); and Foucault, *Surveiller et punir: Naissance de la prison* (Paris, 1975). These same assumptions underlie T. K. Rabb, *The Search for Stability in Early Mod-*

What drove Eberhard Ludwig in his struggle for greatness? He needed money more than anything else. And he needed this money on a heretofore unprecedented scale in order to maintain his position in the cultural competition of European monarchy. Württemberg may well have appeared a provincial backwater to Paris and Vienna, but its dukes clearly thought of themselves as European royalty. They scrutinized their sovereign peers within the Reich—especially the Protestant rulers of Hessen, Saxony, Brandenburg, and Bayreuth— and took meticulous note of the resplendent Catholic centers at Versailles and the Hofburg. They internalized these standards and sought wherever possible to surpass them. In this sense their arbitrary demands for increased taxation, their elaborate building projects, and their cameralistic ventures are best seen in the context of cultural competition; they stemmed from an overriding concern with the forms of power that Europe was associating with contemporary rulers.

The construction of Ludwigsburg, the magnificent palace that rose in the countryside north of Stuttgart, stemmed from just this consideration. From the beginning of the project Eberhard Ludwig spoke frankly about his motives for building. When he first took over the government he informed his advisers that the Stuttgart castle no longer met the standards of elegance appropriate to a ruler's *gloire*.[8] He required a more modern setting, a refined architectural backdrop that enhanced the splendor of his monarchy. His bewildered advisers found such talk incomprehensible. Privy councilors as well as estates identified the castle with the monarchy and told the prince that it embodied all that was glorious in the ducal tradition. Indifferent, if not hostile, to the theatrical demands of baroque kingship, they informed Eberhard Ludwig that the old fortress provided a setting ideally suited to a German prince whose primary concern was to set an example of duty and piety for his loving subjects.[9]

---

ern Europe (New York, 1976), and Robert Foster and Orest Ranum, eds., *Deviants and the Abandoned in French Society* (Baltimore, 1978). The Württemberg case does not support this insistence that the drive toward *eine gute Polizei* was motivated by the need to contain social elements potentially destructive to the power structure.

8. At least one cosmopolitan contemporary shared Eberhard Ludwig's opinion; see C. von Pöllnitz, *Lettres et mémoires*, I (Frankfurt am Main, 1738), 322.

9. HSAS, A 204: Bü. 65. On the role of architecture in baroque kingship, see H. Sedlmayr, "Die politische Bedeutung des deutschen Barocks," in *Gesamtdeutsche Vergangenheit: Festgabe für H. Ritter von Srbik* (Munich, 1938), 126–140. More recent works building on this theme are Werner Hager, *Barockarchitektur* (Baden Baden, 1968), 16–22; Dieter Hennebo and Alfred Hoffmann, *Geschichte der deutschen Gartenkunst*, II (Hamburg, 1965), 153f. and 315f.; H. H. Hofmann, *Adelige Herrschaft und souveräner Staat* (Munich, 1962), 135f. Cf. Max Weber, *Wirtschaft und Gesellschaft* (Cologne, 1964), 665–695.

The young Duke Eberhard Ludwig and his hunting dogs. The duke wears the insignia of the Knights of the Great Hunt, a chivalric order that he founded to enhance the national prestige of his monarchy. Photograph courtesy of the Hauptstaatsarchiv Stuttgart.

But Eberhard Ludwig's values lay elsewhere. Unperturbed by the clash between his own vision of monarchy and that of his councilors, he pressed ahead with his building plans. His first steps were halting and indicated that he was unsure just what it would take to reach his goal. Initial plans called for a relatively modest country estate, and in 1697 he began buying up the lands around Erlachhof, one of his own farms and the center of his future building site.[10] He hired a local architect from Marbach, Philipp Josef Jenisch (1671–1736), to work up the designs and by 1700 had taken to spending as much time as possible in the hunting pavilion that Jenisch had constructed on the property. Ground-breaking ceremonies for the central wing of the main house took place with great fanfare on 7 May 1704. This was about a year and a half after Eberhard Ludwig had entered the field as a military commander in the Imperial Army of the Rhine, a time when both estates and officials were rallying behind the duke in defense of the Habsburg cause in the War of the Spanish Succession (1702–1714). During the campaigns, no doubt as a result of the evenings he spent with cosmopolitan connoisseurs like Prince Eugene of Savoy, Eberhard Ludwig came to regard his architectural plans as too old-fashioned. He decided to sharpen his comparative perspective by sending Jenisch abroad "to gain acquaintance with other architecture."[11]

Jenisch's subsequent sketches goaded Eberhard Ludwig's competitive instincts and gave him a heightened sense of architectural possibilities. In 1707 he hired a distinguished North German engineer, Johann Friedrich Nette (1672–1714), to carry the work to still more elaborate dimensions. Nette in turn advertised for craftsmen throughout northern Italy and went himself to Bohemia to hire skilled stonecutters for the project. The result was that by the end of the decade the construction camp rang with foreign names: Frisoni, Colomba, Soldati, Lucca, Retti, Carlone, Feretti, Corbellini, Kratochwyl, and Peschina.[12] These artisans rejected Jenisch's original designs and substituted an elaborate master plan that gave the architecture of the palace a European importance and dramatically extended its scale and scope. They called not only for a magnificent residence to rival the great palaces of Europe but for the construction of a complete town to service the ducal court.[13]

10. P. Lahnstein, *Ludwigsburg: Aus der Geschichte einer europäischen Residenz* (Stuttgart, 1968), 13 f.

11. C. J. Belschner, "P. J. Jenisch," *WVJSLG* (1935), 109 f.

12. W. Fleischhauer, *Barock im Herzogtum Württemberg* (Stuttgart, 1958), 137–238.

13. Hermann Ströbel, *Ludwigsburg: Ein Beitrag zur Geschichte der landesfürstlichen Stadtbaukunst* (Stuttgart, 1918), 20 ff.

The cost for so vast an undertaking horrified the territorial estates and disquieted the fiscally conservative bureaucrats. Reinforcing these anxieties was the resentment that both groups felt at the number of Catholics pouring into the duchy. To attract the Roman Catholic Bohemian and Italian builders, Eberhard Ludwig had guaranteed them free exercise of their religion. Moreover, since most of them brought their families with them, confessional toleration meant that government agencies had to make provisions for the education, welfare, and community life of a religious group whose very presence the Lutherans found offensive. Gradually, as expenses continued to mushroom, their resentment hardened. The palace, which had begun as an instance of cultural difference between themselves and their ruler came to be seen as a physical symbol of the bitter division between the prince and his officials. For after the war Eberhard Ludwig moved permanently to Ludwigsburg, where he installed his mistress as official hostess. The two of them gradually turned the palace into an administrative counterweight to Stuttgart, the home of the Landtag and the seat of the professional bureaucracy.

This chapter examines the evolution of Ludwigsburg from an improvised statement of cultural one-upmanship into an alternative system of government in which the crown was the driving force for innovation. It is interesting to note at the outset that cultural competition aligned the dukes and their supporters with the forces of political and economic change. In order to obtain the moneys for baroque kingship, the dukes promoted a whole range of fiscal, commercial, and industrial innovations. They also streamlined their administration in ways that cut through the vested interests of traditional elites. Meanwhile, the parliamentary and bureaucratic leaderships—the two elements usually identified with administrative rationalization, progress, and social liberalization—were busy defending the status quo.[14] The professionals and the Landtag championed an old-fashioned system that operated principally to preserve the established avenues of patronage, advancement, and administrative power. In specific terms this commitment meant an iron determination to maintain the medieval tax structure, a vehement defense of confessional orthodoxy and of a church in which they controlled the offices and income, and an implacable hostility to an international culture heavily influenced by French manners, taste, and notions of kingship.

14. This Whiggish notion finds its clearest expression for German history in F. Carsten, *Princes and Parliaments in Germany from the Fifteenth to the Eighteenth Century* (Oxford, 1959). Cf. F. L. Ford's review of this work in *Journal of Modern History*, 32 (December, 1960), 382; and Helen Liebel, *Enlightened Bureaucracy versus Enlightened Despotism in Baden, 1750–1792* (American Philosophical Society, 1965).

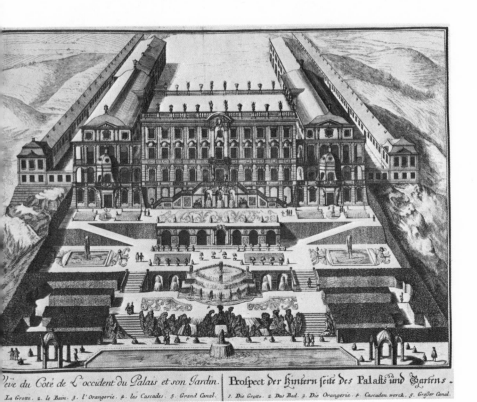

A 1710 engraving showing Nette's plans for the Ludwigsburg palace. Eberhard Ludwig occupied quarters on the second floor of the central wing and by the end of his reign had doubled the size of the palace. He extended the two side wings and then closed them at the end with a *corps de logis* parallel to the Fürstenbau in which he resided. Photograph courtesy of the Landesbildstelle Württemberg.

The formation of this opposition, as well as its intransigent conservatism, can be most readily grasped through an examination of the crown's domestic policies. The initiative for these policies, once the estates had been brought to heel, shifted gradually from the privy council to the prince. By the end of the war it was the duke and not the bureaucrats who was calling for innovations in government. The officials were left to deplore these moves, dragging their feet whenever possible. They stonewalled the duke's projects in large part because they regarded them as irresponsible. They conceived of administration in bureaucratic terms and resisted demands that ignored the principle of fixed jurisdictional areas ordered by rules. They also felt alienated, indeed shocked by Eberhard Ludwig's flagrant marital infidelity and by the luxury of his court, both of which the duke justified by references to French standards.

[177]

Though many of the high bureaucrats came from outside the duchy and were themselves of aristocratic rank, they shared with the territorial estates a hidebound Lutheran orthodoxy, an emphasis on the sobriety of life, and a resentment against the affectations and pretensions of the Frenchified court mores. In any case, they balked. And in dealings first with the estates over the funding of the military and then with the privy council over the servicing of the ducal debt, both Eberhard Ludwig and Carl Alexander moved toward a restructuring of the balance of power within the duchy. They sought to bypass the professional civil servants through the creation of new, court-centered administrative staffs into which they funneled the business of government. At the same time, they refused to summon the Landtag and sought to invigorate the local assemblies (*Amtsversammlungen*) in ways that would strengthen peasant participation and thereby undercut the power base of the territorial Ehrbarkeit.

Eberhard Ludwig's victory over Sturm and his party at the Landtag did not mean the end of that ancient institution. Eberhard Ludwig never intended to overturn the political system by destroying the parliament. His motives were at once less consistent and more naive. He simply wanted to rule as he saw best, to implement those policies appropriate to a great prince. He laid particular stress on the two most visible props of baroque kingship, the army and the palace. And for the next thirty years he spent most of his energies as monarch in acquiring them. Soldiers, he claimed, enabled him to defend his borders, to serve the emperor, and perhaps most important to take his place among the chief vassals of the Reich. He was determined that German diplomats no longer regard Württemberg as a quartering ground for imperial soldiers or its ruler as a military equerry to the sovereign commanders at Munich, Dresden, Berlin, and Hanover. Instead the duke of Württemberg was to be an *armierter Fürst*, a prince whose army gave him the status of an imperial general and the prestige of a ranking territorial power.[15]

Relations between crown and estates entered a new phase with the War of the Spanish Succession and Eberhard Ludwig's decision in August 1702 to enter the field as an active commander.[16] Military emergency eclipsed the question of a standing army. The soldiers of the duke could now be paid by the Swabian Kreis, the emperor, and

15. These themes recur throughout Eberhard Ludwig's early correspondence with both the privy council and the estates. For 1698–1699, see HSAS, LB: Bü. 286, 288, 289 and A 203: Bü. 34 and 36.

16. Eberhard Ludwig served as Römisch. Kaÿl. Mt. Generalfeldmarshalleutnant; see his first letter from the field in HSAS, A 203: Bü. 41 (13 August 1702).

the allies so that the army itself meant no additional expense to the duchy.[17] Instead, disputes focused on taxation as wartime obligations escalated. By 1704 annual military expenditure stood at 1,200,000 florins; and in 1705, the year when Eberhard Ludwig concluded a subsidy treaty with Holland for 300,000 florins, the treasury faced obligations of 1,300,000 florins.[18] Ignoring the isolationism of the estates, Eberhard Ludwig remained unwavering in his support for the emperor and pressed relentlessly for increased taxes to cover Württemberg's obligations to both Kreis and Reich. At the outset of each campaign he decreed a set of emergency levies: the so-called *Extraordinarii*, grants compounded on the customary tax base of the Aemter; and after 1703 the *Trizesimen*, an across-the-board tax of one-thirtieth of each season's wine and grain harvest. Though he made no initial effort to challenge the estates' right to supervise the collection of these taxes, the duke left no doubt that they would be raised with or without the estates' approval. Moreover, he refused to summon a plenary assembly and insisted instead on dealing with the *Grösserer Ausschuss*, the larger council of the Landtag, a board that he convened each summer and winter to ratify his proposals.

Eberhard Ludwig's steadfast refusal to summon a Landtag, a policy to which his nephew Carl Alexander also adhered, undercut the estates' capacity to influence the government. The larger council lacked the collective force of the Landtag and because of the membership's particular social composition tended to be narrowly self-serving. The larger council consisted of sixteen members, the eight executive committeemen supplemented by another eight delegates nominated by the executive committee and ratified for life terms by the collective estates. Although a pattern of limited rotation, especially among the prelates, is visible on the board, the overwhelming majority of delegates came always from the wealthier, more populous districts. There the cleavage between town and village was especially marked, and the municipal magistrates (from whose ranks the delegates always came) differentiated themselves more sharply from the general population of both town and countryside than did those in the lesser districts.[19] The wartime roster illustrates the point. In 1706

17. K. Pfaff, *Geschichte des Militärwesens in Württemberg von der ältesten bis auf unsere Zeit und der Verhandlungen darüber zwischen der Regierung und den Landständen* (Stuttgart, 1842), 41–52. Cf. J. Vann, *The Swabian Kreis: Institutional Growth in the Holy Roman Empire, 1648–1715* (Brussels, 1975), 280–283; and P. -C. Storm, *Der Schwäbische Kreis als Feldherr* (Berlin, 1974), 98–111.

18. Carsten, *Princes and Parliaments*, 109f.

19. On the potential implications of this differentiation, see M. Walker, *German Home Towns: Community, State, and General Estate, 1648–1871* (Ithaca, 1971), 34–72.

the executive committee consisted of the abbots of Bebenhausen and Adelberg, together with the Bürgermeisters of Stuttgart, Tübingen, Göppingen, Nürtingen, Vaihingen, and Schorndorf. They were augmented on the larger council by the abbots of Blaubeuren and Hirsau and by the Bürgermeisters of Böblingen, Heidenheim, Kirchheim unter Teck, Leonberg, Marbach, and Urach.[20]

Extraordinarii records document the comparative economic importance of these councilmen's districts and prelacies. Whereas the average tax base for the Württemberg ecclesiastical establishments was 1,259 florins, Bebenhausen and Adelberg, both with abbots on the executive committee, contributed respectively 6,272 and 2,508 florins. Their colleagues from Blaubeuren and Hirsau came from houses with below average rates, though in both cases personality appears to have had a great deal to do with election.[21] Johann Joachim Bardili (abbot of Blaubeuren), who served from 1699 to 1706, was a popular hero in the duchy. From 1693 to 1696 he was imprisoned by the French as a result of having volunteered himself as a hostage for the 600,000-florin indemnity that Louis XIV had levied upon the Württemberg estates.[22] Moreover, he was followed on the council by Ernst Konrad Reinhardt (1649–1729), the abbot of Alpirsbach, whose prelatal establishment carried a tax base second in value only to that of Bebenhausen.[23] The other prelate on the council, Johann Osiander (1657–1724), belonged to one of the leading families in the Ehrbarkeit and had earned a territory-wide reputation as a distinguished professor of theology at Tübingen prior to his appointment as abbot.[24] In any case, representation from the secular districts was even more heavily skewed in favor of the wealthy. For whereas the average tax base for the Aemter was 4,624 florin, all but one of the districts whose magistrates sat on the council paid many times that sum: Stuttgart 28,244 florins; Tübingen 18,580 florins; Schorndorf

20. HSAS, A 203: Bü. 49.

21. Ibid., LB: Bü. 298. Averages have been computed on assessments rounded off in each instance to florins. In computing the ecclesiastical averages, I included the four women's establishments (Liechtenberg, Pfüllingen, Reutin, and Weÿler) as well as Zwiefalten, the Kellerei Nellingen, and the Priory of Reichenbach. Blaubeuren paid 1,025 florins and Hirsau 1,254 florins.

22. Bardili was elected to the council in 1699; W. Pfeilsticker, Neues württembergisches Dienerbuch, (Stuttgart, 1957), 1407. On the hostages, see T. Schott, "Die württembergische Geiseln in Strassburg und Metz, 1693–1696," Zeitschrift für allgemeine Geschichte, 3 (1886), 583–602; and W. Grube, Der Stuttgarter Landtag, 1457–1957 (Stuttgart, 1957), 364–366.

23. In 1701 Alpirsbach's tax assessment stood at 2,979 florins. On Reichardt's appointment, see HSAS, A 204: Bü. 103.

24. Pfeilsticker, Dienerbuch, 1427, 2016, 2031, 3259, 3292, 3390, 3391. Osiander was elected in May 1702 (HSAS, A 204: Bü. 56).

17,510 florins; Kirchheim 15,052 florins; Urach 13,709 florins; Leonberg 11,253 florins; Göppingen 10,897 florins; Nürtingen 10,035 florins; Böblingen 9,094 florins; Vaihingen 6,582 florins; and Marbach 5,992 florins. Only Heidenheim with its 4,044 florins fell below the average.[25]

The preponderant weight given on the council to these more powerful towns and prelacies meant that the overwhelming majority of delegates came from the most firmly established element of Württemberg society, that wing of the Ehrbarkeit with the largest stake in the status quo. The oligarchs dominating the powerful municipal governments in such cities as Stuttgart, Tübingen, Urach, and Schorndorf had every reason to champion the traditional tax structure, since it placed the heaviest burden on the villages of the Amt. Again, the councilmen's vigorous defense of Lutheran orthodoxy dovetailed nicely with their loyalty to a territorial church in which the most prestigious and lucrative positions went generally to their own relations. This intimate involvement with the established system made the councilmen singularly ill equipped to deal with the fiscal pressures of war, to say nothing of the peacetime expenses of a standing army and the escalating costs of baroque monarchy. Though they could not help but see that it was beyond the capacity of customary taxation to produce sufficient revenue for such expenditures, they opposed any revision of the tax schedule. They feared that change might jeopardize their own guild and trade interests, and so they fought it with all their parliamentary strength. The result was an unproductive stalemate in which the estates rejected ducal demands for reform without offering counter proposals for easing fiscal pressure.

Negotiations in the winter of 1703 illustrate the point. At that time the councilmen refused to vote the tax increases demanded by the duke to wage the war. They withheld their consent on the grounds that more levies "placed an impossible burden on the shoulders of the already miserable subjects."[26] Eberhard Ludwig countered this pious sentiment with the contention that there was "no capital shortage in the duchy." He insisted instead that "the problem lay with the *modo collectandi*. . . . the villages are being bled white; while commerce, crafts, and industry are scarcely touched." He called therefore for a reform of the tax code that would shift more of the financial burden onto the towns and cities of the Aemter.[27] The council rejected that proposition and refused flatly to entertain any program of revision. A

25. HSAS, LB: Bü. 298.
26. Ibid. (letter of 9 January 1703).
27. Ibid. (26 January 1703).

delegation from the board (the Bürgermeisters of Stuttgart, Tübingen and Kirchheim and the abbot of Bebenhausen) called personally upon the prince to assure him that they "knew of no one who escaped taxation (*keine freie Leute*) other than the ducal civil servants." Somewhat self-servingly they pointed out that any increase of taxes on urban wealth would "deny relief to those very men of means already weighed down by taxes and only add further to their already intolerable burden."[28] In short, the council offered no alternative but declared itself unwilling either to vote additional funds or to revise the current system. Under these circumstances Eberhard Ludwig acted independently. Declaring a state of emergency, he announced the imposition of the Trizesimen, a tax that provoked the greatest alarm (*grösste Bestürtzung*) among the councilmen.[29] While their dismay doubtless had its roots in constitutional concerns, it must also have been nourished by the fact that the Trizesimen cut across their fiscal gerrymandering and subjected their own vineyards and fields to the same one-thirtieth assessment as those of the villages.

With the prelates pledged under oath to obstruct any appeal against the duke to Vienna and the Landtag in dissolution, the councilmen found themselves losing control over taxation, the cornerstone of the estates' political power. The duke not they now determined tax levies. Furthermore the Trizesimation undercut their control over these funds; for while the estates supervised both the collection and dispersal of the Extraordinarii, their commissioners only collected the Trizesimen. They then paid the amount directly into the *Kriegskasse*, a treasury set up by the duke for military supply. Under these conditions the council convened twice a year in meetings that more often than not degenerated into handwringing and lamentation. Extant minutes make it plain that, while the councilmen objected strenuously to virtually every demand by the duke, they themselves lacked either the vision or the initiative for positive action. Their discussions centered almost entirely on questions of their own self-interest and lacked even a pretence of concern for the general welfare of the duchy. Nor did they exhibit much in the way of corporate loyalty: the wishes of their less prosperous colleagues in the Ehrbarkeit left them unmoved.[30]

28. Ibid. (council minutes for 7 February 1703). In 1713 when the Grösserer Ausschuss finally revised the *Steuerfuss* (Eberhard Ludwig had been pushing for revision since 1698), the privy councilors regarded these revisions as perfunctory and overly protective of the Ehrbarkeit (A 204: Bü. 67 and 107).
29. HSAS, LB: Bü. 299.
30. HSAS, LB: Bü. 298–404 contain council minutes from 1702–1737; cf. Grube, *Stuttgarter Landtag*, 379–398.

The councilmen particularly opposed ducal hopes of stimulating industry in the poorer districts through the granting of state monopolies to local entrepreneurs or by the imposition of restrictions on trade.[31] They also took alarm at Eberhard Ludwig's aggressive imperial patriotism. When the duke led a military force in support of the emperor's efforts to curb the marauding of the Francophile Bavarian elector's soldiers, they denounced the action as dangerous meddling. They wrote to the duke deploring his "stirring up trouble against a powerful neighbor in campaigns miles away from your own lands," and insisting that "the duke of Württemberg's place is at home. . . . You must stand at the head of your possessions and rule like another Jehoshaphat!"[32] They returned to that famous Hebrew king in subsequent *Gravimina*, when they demanded that Eberhard Ludwig "rule his lands with the consent of his elders." There was no place in Württemberg, they maintained, for taxes levied "solely through absolute decree" (*bloss durch absolute decreta*). Instead, there must be "an imperative economy in the military as well as in the ducal government" (*Höchstnötige oeconomie, sowohl in militaribus als civilibus*).[33]

When the war ended Eberhard Ludwig ignored the council's wishes and kept his army intact. He supported the soldiers by continuing the Trizesimen, a tax that the councilmen now refused to ratify on the grounds that they needed a mandate from the general Landtag before they could fund a peacetime army. Eberhard Ludwig met this argument with an announcement that he intended to continue the levy with or without their consent. "Both natural and international law [*die natürlichen und Völkerrechte*]," he firmly told them, "define the preservation and defense of the fatherland as the chief duty of all subjects, indeed of all persons living in society [*alle in eine Societät stehenden Menschen*]."[34] After a decade of futile protesting, when it had become apparent to all that the council lacked the capacity for organized defiance, the estates' leadership settled finally on a compromise. In the autumn of 1723 the council agreed to approve taxation for a standing army on the condition that Eberhard Ludwig canvass the districts on the issue. The duke agreed and instructed his local officials to sound the Aemter on the following proposition: in ex-

31. HSAS, LB: Bü. 367 and 368 (papers from the conference on trade and commerce in the winter of 1724); see also A 202: Bü. 2831 (report of ducal trade commission, 18 September 1708).

32. HSAS, A 203: Bü. 42 (letter from the Grösserer Ausschuss, 22 March 1703).

33. HSAS, A 203: Bü. 49 (*Gravamina*, 15 April 1706); cf. A 204: Bü. 128 (*Gravamina* of 1719).

34. HSAS, A 203: Bü. 86.

change for the abolition of the Trizesimen and royal assurance that there would be no compulsory conscription, the estates would endorse the principle of military supply in the form of summer and winter Extraordinarii. In March 1724, after the proposition had received majority support from the districts, the council voted a three-year annual subsidy of some 360,000 florins for maintenance of a standing army.[35]

The vote, though binding for only three years, constituted a great victory for the duke. The delegates had accepted once and for all the principle of a permanent army. It remained now only to work out the terms of support. The final compromise—acquiescence in the principle but refusal to vote a permanent tax—said much about the balance of power within the middle-sized German states of the eighteenth century. Fifty years of domestic conflict over the army had revealed the limitations in the estates' capacity for resistance to determined ducal policy. Short of armed rebellion, they were simply not in a position to defy their sovereign unless they could obtain support from outside the duchy. Johann Osiander, abbot of Hirsau and by 1723 the leading voice on the council, recognized this point. In so doing he revealed an attitude toward monarchy quite different from that of earlier champions of estates' rights like Sturm and Hörner.[36] These men had venerated Eberhard III as the prototype of the ideal ruler and sought to steer his grandson along that same path (*Wiederum in den grossväterlichen Curs*).[37]

Osiander realized, without necessarily endorsing the fact, that Eberhard Ludwig had cast himself in an entirely different mold. He saw that if the estates were to retain an influence over the government, they would have to adopt a more flexible strategy in dealing with the prince. Osiander rejected outright the possibility of rebellion. The prince, he informed his colleagues, held an office that derived its authority from God. No subject could take up arms against the sacred person (*die geheiligte Person*) of his ruler (*Landesfürst*). "Tears and pleading are our only weapons!" (*arma nostra sunt preces et lacrimae*). But if armed resistance was out of the question, skilled

---

35. HSAS, LB: Bü. 366–377. Also, F. Wintterlin, "Wehrverfassung und Landesverfassung im Herzogtum Württemberg," *WVJHLG*, 34 (1928), 239–256; and K. Pfaff, *Geschichte des Militärwesens in Württemberg*, 44f. Note that this sum did not reflect the customary annual grant by the estates to the duke of 40,000 florins or the approximately 300,000 florins raised each year through ordinary taxation in order to amortize ducal debts and to cover the estates' share of the government budget.

36. See pp. 155–170.

37. Grube, *Stuttgarter Landtag*, 382.

Johann Osiander, abbot of Hirsau, proved an eloquent spokesman for the estates of Württemberg. His dress and manner recall the reign of Eberhard III and graphically illustrate the cultural differences that had grown up in the intervening years between the dukes and their chief subjects. Photograph courtesy of the Landesbildstelle Würtemberg.

political maneuvering was not. In particular Osiander urged the council to abandon its insular espousal of the literal terms of the Tübinger Vertrag. The estates would be far wiser, he maintained, if they sought to influence through a prudent assessment of each situation (*ex regulis prudentia*) rather than by blind adherence to the letter of earlier compacts. And for Osiander prudence meant identifying the areas of ducal inflexibility and steering around them so as best to preserve traditional interests.[38]

Osiander's strategy had merit. If the estates could not prevail against steadfast ducal determination, they nonetheless possessed considerable staying power. The territorial constitution guaranteed their rights and, short of a revolutionary restructuring of that instrument, assured them of at least a minimal participation in the government. Under these circumstances a German prince found it virtually impossible to ignore his estates altogether, and Eberhard Ludwig was not the man to make such an attempt. His tough stand on the military by no means implied a consistent aggressiveness in all areas of government. He had no intention of abolishing the Landtag or of recasting the state in his own image. He accepted the necessity of continuing the estates' privileges of taxation and demanded only that they support him on the specific issue of the army. Long after it had become clear that the estates could not block his single-handed imposition of the Trizesimen, he took care to observe the form of seeking their consent. His caution was more than just a matter of personality. Eberhard Ludwig's prudent avoidance of a final confrontation also calls attention to the checks imposed upon territorial authority by the structure of the Reich.

We are accustomed to thinking of the empire as being committed to the preservation of the territorial princes' sovereign liberties.[39] Eberhard Ludwig's restraint in victory reminds us that while the empire did indeed protect these rulers, it also upheld the rights and privileges of the corporate interests in their territories. Although Eberhard Ludwig enjoyed full sovereignty within his borders, he could not circumvent territorial law. Whatever the duke's opinion of

38. Osiander, son of the chancellor of Tübingen, Johann Adam Osiander, came from a family that stood squarely in the Ehrbarkeit. Educated at the Tübinger Stift, he went on to become a professor of theology at the university and then abbot of Königsbrunn (1696–1699) and of Hirsau (1699–1724). He was elected to the larger council in 1702 and to the executive committee in 1709. He also served as director of the consistory from 1709 to 1724. See Pfeilsticker, *Dienerbuch*, 1427, 2016, 2031, 3259, 3292, 3390, 3391, 3417, 3436; also Marquardt, *Geschichte Württembergs*, 168–169 and 182–183; Grube, *Stuttgarter Landtag*, 382–383; and Otto Schuster, *Das Lebenswerk Johannes Osiander* (Nürtingen, 1933), 189–196.

39. Leonard Krieger, *The German Idea of Freedom* (Boston, 1957).

the Württemberg constitution, both the emperor and the Reichstag had ratified the various compacts that guaranteed the Württembergers a ruler who would govern under their constraints. The same law that secured Eberhard Ludwig's princely liberties thus defined the parameters within which he ruled. He recognized that he could not push too far against local interests without jeopardizing his standing at the Reichstag and thereby providing his more powerful sovereign peers with a legitimate pretext for inserting themselves into his territories.[40] The House of Austria posed a particular danger since the Habsburgs, who continued to claim certain feudal rights of supervision over Württemberg, were always looking for an opportunity to intervene.[41] It therefore worked very much to Eberhard Ludwig's interests to obtain a compromise with the estates that preserved at least the forms of territorial law.

One final point needs to be made about the settlement: it eliminated the Trizesimen as the principal source of military funding. Recall that this tax fell upon every landowner in the duchy and went directly into the Kriegskasse—that is, the estates had no control over the ways in which the tax was spent. Under the terms of the compromise, however, the military derived its money from the Extraordinarii, which were assessed, collected, and administered by the estates. Indeed the rates for these taxes were computed from tables drawn up by the Landtag and weighted in favor of the urban interests that the delegates represented. In other words, the town magistrates who accepted the principle of estates' responsibility for military support were nevertheless able to prorate these costs under a system in which they enjoyed a favored status. Although the archival records surrounding the compromise contain no direct statements to this effect, we can assume that Eberhard Ludwig recognized the implications of shifting the burden of military support from the Trizesimen to the Extraordinarii and that he did so in order to secure the Ehrbarkeit's endorsement of the army. His district strategy points to this interpretation. Whenever possible, ducal officials sought ratification for the army through the Amt council rather than through the

40. Eberhard Ludwig and his privy councilors both recognized this point; see HSAS, A 204: Bü. 63 (26 October 1710).
41. In 1520 the Habsburgs purchased the duchy for 220,000 florins from the Swabian League. In subsequent negotiations with the ducal family, the Austrian archdukes retained certain supervisory rights. They reactivated these claims during the Thirty Years War and used them as a pretext for intervention in support of monastic claims against secularized properties. Austrian rights form a central theme in C. von Stälin, *Wirtembergische Geschichte*, IV (Stuttgart, 1873); and C. Sattler, *Geschichte des Herzogtums Wirtenberg unter der Regierung der Herzogen*, VII (ULM, 1774).

district assembly. Unlike the Amtsversammlung, where we have already seen that the peasant leadership was securing a larger voice for the villages, the councils remained dominated by the urban magistrates.[42] It was this group then that ratified the proposition of the standing army and instructed the Grösserer Ausschuss to vote taxes of supply.

During these years of jockeying with the estates, the duke also altered his relations with the privy council. The change was unplanned, and both sides contributed to its development; that is, the prince responded to impulses from the council just as the privy councilors reacted to demands from the crown. Alienation occurred gradually. As with the estates, the roots of the estrangement lay in differing moral or cultural perceptions and in what surfaced eventually as incompatible assumptions about the nature and purpose of government. Since these differences with the duke evolved in part out of the social structure of the council, this chapter examines the elements of its corporate professionalism—geography, rank, social origins, training, and philosophy. But before turning to these points we should remember that as these high bureaucrats lost their influence with the crown, they developed closer ties with the other Württemberg orders. These links formed slowly and were initially a result of the councilors' discovery that they shared with the estates and with lesser officials in the government a conviction that the moral tone at Eberhard Ludwig's court must be repudiated.

Policy differences obscured this sense of moral compatibility during the first decade of the reign. Under the leadership of Johann Georg Kulpis, the privy council sided squarely with the prince and on military matters as well as on foreign policy stood self-consciously apart from the territorial estates and from the ranks of the lower civil service where so many relatives of the Ehrbarkeit found employment.[43] Prior to his arrival at Stuttgart, Kulpis had held a professorship in imperial law at the University of Strassburg.[44] There he developed a great respect for the institutions of the Reich and became a staunch supporter of the imperial party that formed around Prince Ludwig Wilhelm von Baden ("Türken Louis") and Prince Eugene of Savoy.[45]

42. W. Grube, "Dorfgemeinde und Amtsversammlung in Altwürttemberg," ZWLG, 13 (1954), 194–219. Carsten, Princes and Parliaments, 120–121, misses the distinction between the Amt council and the district assembly.

43. On privy councilors' perceptions of these differences, see HSAS, A 203: Bü. 41 (15, 17, 20, 22 December 1702) and A 204: Bü. 65 (16 October 1702 and 17 May 1704).

44. Pfeilsticker, Dienerbuch, 1116, 1211, 1238, 2016, 2029, 2033.

45. Ruth Gebauer, Die Aussenpolitik des schwäbischen Reichkreises vor Ausbruch des spanischen Erbfolgekrieges (Heidelberg, 1966), 61–148; also Roger Wines, "The Franconian Reichskreis and the Holy Roman Empire in the War of the Spanish Succession" (Columbia University: Ph.D. diss., 1961), 75–104.

When he entered Württemberg service, Kulpis preserved his close ties with Ludwig Wilhelm and under his influence sought to guide Eberhard Ludwig toward ever greater involvement in the defense of the Reich.[46] With the backing of the privy councilors, he worked as Württemberg's representative at the Swabian Kreistag to join the southwest German principalities and city-states in a diplomatic and military alliance with their counterparts in the Franconian Kreis.[47] This association in turn organized much of the military defense for the empire and during the War of the Spanish Succession became the model for a larger association among the five western Kreise.[48]

The idea of Württemberg's taking so aggressive a posture in the Reich alarmed the parochial Württemberg estates and roused a stormy opposition from the lower civil servants, who bombarded the privy council with complaints about excessive expenditure and undue "foreign" influence in the duchy. Relations deteriorated completely in 1697, when word reached Stuttgart that Kulpis had committed the duke to the controversial Peace of Ryswick and thereby ensured the preservation in Mömpelgard of the Catholic establishments introduced there during the French occupation.[49] Personal charges against Kulpis of drunkenness, corruption, and atheism poured into the privy council from various municipal and clerical figures, whom Kulpis referred to contemptuously as the "unlearned," or *Nichtstudierten*. The councilors supported Kulpis against the denunciations and seconded his warning to Eberhard Ludwig that Württemberg had become a "kingdom of scribes and pharisees" (*regnum scribarum et pharisaeorum*).[50]

But with the death of Kulpis in 1697 and the ascendancy of Baron Johann Friedrich von Staffhorst (1653–1730), a quite different kind of leadership asserted itself on the privy council.[51] Whereas Kulpis had dreamed of a revitalized Holy Roman Empire, Staffhorst took office

46. See especially his dispatches to Stuttgart from Vienna in the fall of 1691 (HSAS, A 202: Bü. 2420).

47. Kulpis's pamphlet, "Unvorgreiflicher Vorschlag wegen Armir- und Associerung der sechs naechst am Rhein gelegenen Craysen," is reproduced in J. A. Kopp, *Gründliche Abhandlung von der Association deren vordern Reichs-Craysse* (Frankfurt am Main, 1739), 15f; see also Kulpis's published commentary on Pufendorf, *Commentationes Academicae* (Stuttgart, 1688).

48. Roger Wines, "The Imperial Circles, Princely Diplomacy and Imperial Reform, 1681–1714," *JMH*, 39 (1967), 1–29.

49. B. Wunder, *Frankreich, Württemberg und der Schwäbische Kreis während der Auseinandersetzungen über die Reunionen 1676–1697*, in Veröffentlichungen der Kommission für geschichtliche Landeskunde in Baden-Württemberg, LXIV (Stuttgart, 1971), 20–70.

50. HSAS, A 204: Bü. 55; cf. Marquardt, *Geschichte Württembergs*, 173–175.

51. Pfeilsticker, *Dienerbuch*, 7, 201, 400, 1123, 2345; also O. von Alberti, *Württembergisches Adels- und Wappenbuch* (Neustadt an der Aisch, 1975), 753.

with no higher principle in mind than that of carrying out his young master's wishes. A Hanoverian by birth, he had come south to serve as Hofmarshall for the ducal household. He entered the privy council therefore as a courtier rather than as a statesman, and he subsequently functioned on that board in a manner different from that of his colleagues. He regarded the government as an extension of the ducal household and, like that body, as existing only at the pleasure of the monarch. We have already seen that in dealings with the estates on the question of the army, he disregarded the constitutionality of their rights and asserted that the prince rather than custom or compact should determine the division of authority and responsibility within the duchy.[52] In 1700 he married Louise von Menzingen, daughter of his senior colleague on the privy council, and with the help of his father-in-law he managed in most cases to keep the councilors squarely behind ducal military policy. But while he held his colleagues on the army, an issue appropriate to their professionalism, he could not obtain their support for Eberhard Ludwig's domestic irregularities. On this point the councilors remained committed to traditional moral standards. They deplored Eberhard Ludwig's conduct and refused to endorse the high-handed policies through which the prince sought to obtain his ends.

At issue was Eberhard Ludwig's desire to marry his paramour, a Mecklenburg noblewoman named Christiane Wilhelmine von Grävenitz.[53] Shortly after she had arrived at Stuttgart in 1707 to keep house for her brother Friedrich Wilhelm (1679–1754), an equerry in the ducal household, the countess had attracted the attention of the twenty-nine-year-old monarch. By late 1707 he was so infatuated that he had begun to hint openly of marriage. Such talk precipitated a crisis in the government; for quite apart from questions of dynastic suitability, his privy councilors pointed to the incontestable fact that Eberhard Ludwig already had a wife. Some ten years earlier he had married with great pomp the princess Johanna Elisabeth of Baden-Durlach, and that lady was still very much alive. The prospect of a second marriage scandalized both church and government. Whatever the custom at more sophisticated courts—and Eberhard Ludwig countered all criticism by making references to Versailles, where Louis XIV had introduced a succession of royal mistresses—Württemberg had never experienced such behavior. Eberhard

---

52. HSAS, LB: Bü. 289 (Hörner's report, 31 July 1699); A 203: Bü. 35 (21 November 1698).

53. Pfeilsticker, *Dienerbuch*, 5, 209, 369; Alberti, *Wappenbuch*, 1089; Theodor Schön, *Monatsblatt von Adler* (1896), Nr. 183 (IV, Nr. 3).

Ludwig's post-Reformation ancestors had all lived in strict union with their wives and had, at least publicly, never violated their marriage vows. The thought that their ruler, the head of the territorial church, would have two living wives united the Württemberg clergy, estates, and officials in shocked resistance.

Landschaftskonsulent Hörner was the first to get wind of the duke's plans and raised the general alarm. Despite the fact that Staffhorst refused to allow the matter to appear on the privy council's agenda, the councilors began a series of private negotiations with the executive committee of the estates. Their first joint public action came with the New Year, when both groups refused to present themselves to the duke and to extend the customary good wishes for the coming months. By February they had authorized Konsulent Hörner to write a public letter to the prince denouncing his affair as an "unacceptable love." Any kind of morganatic marriage, in their eyes, constituted nothing short of bigamy and hence broke the law. The pastors on the consistory took a similar stand: supported by the privy councilors, they pronounced Eberhard Ludwig guilty of adultery and ordered the clergy to refuse him the sacraments. Not surprisingly such opposition infuriated the duke, who regarded these moves as "impertinent intrusions into his private affairs." As a Protestant prince he felt himself beholden to no moral authority beyond that of his own conscience; and his conscience, he informed his government, was clear.[54]

Faced with his willfulness, the estates and officials found themselves in a quandary. They realized that effective sanctions would have to come from beyond the territory but hesitated as to how they might best obtain them. Since the prelates had sworn never to seek redress outside the duchy, the estates' executive committee felt that, without a general Landtag, it dared not act. The dissident privy councilors took the lead at this point and made common front with Johanna Elisabeth, a woman of considerable spirit and determination. She agreed to mobilize her father, the reigning margrave of Baden-Durlach, for an appeal to the Reich; she also made a dramatic appearance before the executive committee of the estates. On that occasion she galvanized the committee members by announcing that Eberhard Ludwig was planning to convert to Roman Catholicism in order to secure an annulment of his marriage. She also announced that the duke intended to emasculate the estates by assuming for himself the full control and administration of all taxes. The executive committee, now thoroughly alarmed, threw its support behind her request and pro-

54. Grube, *Stuttgarter Landtag*, 380–382.

posed a joint appeal to the margrave by the duchess, the privy councilors, and the estates. Faced with the prospect of a national scandal that might well result in imperial intervention, Eberhard Ludwig backed down. "Die von Grävenitz," as she was now known to the disapproving Württembergers, departed for Switzerland; Baron von Staffhorst, her principal champion in the government, fell from office.[55]

The Grävenitz affair would be little more than historical anecdote but for the fact that it points up certain larger themes. At the most obvious level Eberhard Ludwig's retreat demonstrated once again the potential force of the Reich as a brake on arbitrary conduct by any territorial ruler. The incident also highlighed the differences in fundamental social customs between the prince and his estates and officials. Württembergers of all ranks in public life had opposed the marriage plans. In so doing they made it clear that they were unwilling to tolerate in their monarch behavior—however fashionable elsewhere—that flew in the face of local convention. But most important, the clash of values marked the first stage in a reorientation of relations between the prince and his officials. Just as the privy councilors discovered in the incident new grounds of commonality with the estates and the lower officials, so the prince recognized an incompatibility between himself and his administrators. Eberhard Ludwig took deep offense at what he regarded as the disloyalty of his privy councilors. In subsequent years he showed himself increasingly uncomfortable in dealing intimately with men whose cultural perceptions differed so markedly from his own. By the end of the decade he had virtually ceased to attend the privy council meetings. Instead, he required that the councilors submit their business in written reports which he approved, modified, or rejected from the comparative isolation of his private chambers.[56] And with ever greater frequency he began to surround himself with courtiers to whom he turned for the policy advice that his predecessors had sought from the privy council.

Christiane Wilhelmine von Grävenitz's subsequent return to Württemberg widened the gulf between court and government. In 1710

---

55. L. von Spittler, "Herzog Eberhard Ludwig und Wilhelmine von Grävenitz," in *Sämtliche Werke*, ed. K. Wächter, XII (Stuttgart and Tübingen, 1837), 318–350; E. Schneider, *Württembergische Geschichte* (Stuttgart, 1896), 332–337; Schuster, *Das Lebenswerk Johannes Osianders*, 105–116.

56. The first summary extracts appeared in 1696 (HSAS, A 204: Bü. 55). Thereafter, they were used irregularly. Then in 1708 Eberhard Ludwig deputized a Geheim Referendar from the Landkanzlei to transmit council reports on a regular basis, and by 1710 virtually all communication between the prince and the privy council was conducted in this manner; cf. A 204: Bü. 60, 66, 103.

she reappeared at Stuttgart, this time as the wife of one Count Johann Franz Ferdinand von Würben, an insignificant Bohemian nobleman whom Eberhard Ludwig had co-opted for the purpose by granting him a lifetime appointment to the office, title, and salary of Württemberg's Landhofmeister.[57] The conditions of the contract were that Würben never consummate his marriage, that his wife settle permanently in Württemberg, and that he never again set foot in the duchy. As the wife of the highest court official in the land, Christiane Wilhelmine resided at court where she took precedence over all but royal ladies. And since the duke lived apart from his wife, Countess Würben was able to serve as his official hostess for most of the reign. In that capacity she amassed an extensive personal fortune. Very like her more famous French counterpart Madame de Pompadour, she also took an active role in the formation of governmental policy.[58] Her insistence that Eberhard Ludwig live permanently at Ludwigsburg, away from the duchess who occupied the castle at Stuttgart, separated the duke physically from his chief bureaucratic officials. Since the privy councilors remained in town working at the chancellery, Eberhard Ludwig found it convenient as well as desirable to form an independent band of courtiers, sympathetic to himself and the countess, with whom he could confer daily on matters of policy and administration.

The uneasiness that had arisen as a result of the councilors' stand on ducal morals fused gradually with other, more serious political disagreements between the duke and his government. These differences developed without the benefit of any one decisive confrontation, such as characterized the military question that had polarized crown and estates. We find instead a growing sense in the monarch, first brought to consciousness in the Grävenitz affair, that his council was getting in the way. This feeling derived less from policy considerations than from frustration over what Eberhard Ludwig regarded as the privy council's excessive administrative fastidiousness in handling matters that touched his pride. In circumventing his council Eber-

57. Johann Franz Ferdinand von Würben (died 1719) came from an old, impoverished Silesian family (Wrbna); see Pfeilsticker, Dienerbuch, 1091, 1114, 1478, 2762; Alberti, Wappenbuch, 1089.

58. S. Stern, Jud Süss: Ein Beitrag zur deutschen und zur jüdischen Geschichte (Berlin, 1929), 45–47, indicates that in the 1733 settlement between Countess Würben and Carl Alexander, she received only 150,000 florins of the 340,000 florins claimed originally as compensation for her Württemberg properties. Cf. F. Dizinger, Beiträge zur Geschichte Württembergs und seines Regentenhauses zur Zeit der Regierung Herzogs Karl Alexander und während der Minderjährigkeit seines Erstgeboren (Tübingen, 1834), 19–21. Also, Pfeilsticker, Dienerbuch, 3044 and 3301.

A contemporary oil miniature of Christiane Wilhelmine von Grävenitz presents her as a somewhat conventional beauty. Only her unusually penetrating eyes suggest the cunning ambition that propelled her career. From the collection of the Württembergische Landesmuseum Stuttgart.

hard Ludwig showed a surprising unawareness of the administrative implications of his behavior. He simply wanted his own way. If the councilors would not agree with him, he would find others who did. Carl Alexander operated in a similar fashion. He shared his uncle's contempt for procedural routine and, like Eberhard Ludwig, sought

[194]

to circumvent the functional importance of his bureaucrats through a cadre of courtiers, Jewish financiers, and military advisers.

That these baroque monarchs found the procedural scrupulosity of their high officials so irritating speaks to their determined rejection of anything that might interfere with their image as mighty princes. But it also says something about the bureaucrats themselves. Estrangement developed when it did because the privy councilors were no longer cooperating as they once had. They had begun to resist ducal wishes, "foot-dragging" as Eberhard Ludwig described it.[59] In large part the councilors were balking because they resented their monarch's indifference to what they regarded as sound principles of administration. This cavalier attitude toward administrative procedure struck at the heart of their own world view, and their reaction can best be understood in terms of their political organization and personal values. The early-eighteenth-century privy councilors possessed administrative skills that gave them the collective confidence of experts. This confidence merged with a set of social assumptions to produce a corporate self-consciousness and pride in their administrative duties which made the bureaucrats sharply critical of any disruption in the orderly flow of government.

The councilors' behavior reflected a distinctly modern conception of officialdom.[60] They regarded officeholding as a vocation, a calling in which loyalty was devoted to impersonal or functional purposes. Economic and social differences lost their traditional importance in the face of a shared commitment to administrative tasks. In contradistinction to the courtier, who discharged official business as a secondary activity, the privy councilors believed that their role demanded their full working capacity. They focused their energies on social and political concerns which they set in the philosophic framework of Lutheran convictions and proposed to handle through rationalized administrative procedure. This vision caused them to reject the courtier's ideal of the gifted amateur and to deplore the growing emphasis upon material consumption which underlay the court's preoccupations with grandeur. One is tempted to associate their professionalism with what twentieth-century society defines as the middle-class virtues of thrift, discipline, and hard work. But in the Württemberg example the majority of these early-eighteenth-century bureaucrats be-

59. For examples of Eberhard Ludwig's growing frustration with his officials, see HSAS, A 202: Bü. 5 (31 March 1710, 2 July 1713, 27 July 1713); Bü. 1864 (19 April 1714); A 204: Bü. 114 (1 July 1715); A 202: Bü. 109 (12 September 1718); Bü. 5 (29 February 1724 and 17 March 1724).

60. Max Weber, "Bureaucracy," in H. H. Gerth and C. W. Mills, eds., *From Max Weber: Essays in Sociology* (New York, 1968), 196–244.

longed to the traditional aristocracy, an interesting counterpart to the historically more visible aristocrats who were gravitating to the princely courts and adopting the values of baroque monarchy.[61] These councilors sponsored a discrete service ethos and in so doing contributed substantially to the development of modern bureaucracy. Their participation in this development warns us against making too close an association of bureaucratic growth with an upwardly mobile, urban middle-class group.[62] At least in the Württemberg case, the old aristocracy contributed its share of the governmental standard-bearers. We must conclude therefore that bureaucracy is best understood as a set of values about the organization of power. These values could derive just as well from persons and social groups already considered by some as old-fashioned as from new, more immediately mobile elements.

This corporate world view was implicit in the style of life adopted by the early-eighteenth-century councilors. Between 1693 and 1709 fourteen men held the office of privy councilor.[63] All were married, and although their family assets differed widely, all of them lived at Stuttgart under similar circumstances. They tended to rent large apartments in houses near the chancellery where everyone worked for long hours six days a week. Except for Staffhorst, they took no significant role in court society. Their diaries and letters spoke only rarely of the balls, hunts, operas, and festivals so important to their monarch but dwelt instead on church sermons, reports of medicinal cures at nearby mineral springs, and lectures and literature dealing with such social problems as crime, education, and economic produc-

61. J. Freiherr von Kruedener, *Die Rolle des Hofes im Absolutismus* (Stuttgart, 1973), 43–72, provides an analytic model for assessing relations between the court and the aristocracy; cf. Otto Brunner, *Adeliges Landleben und europäischer Geist* (Salzburg, 1949), esp. 75–133; and Joachim Lampe, *Aristocratie, Hofadel und Staatspatriziat in Kurhannover: Die Lebenskrise der höhern Beamten an den kurhannoverschen Zentral- und Hofbehörden 1714–1760*, I (Göttingen, 1963), 143–334. More theoretical is the study by Norbert Elias, *Die höfische Gesellschaft. Untersuchungen zur Soziologie des Konigtums und der höfischen Aristokratie mit einer Einleitung: Soziologie und Geschichtswissenschaft* (Berlin, 1969).

62. W. K. Bruford, *Germany in the Eighteenth Century: the Social Background of the Literary Revival* (Cambridge, 1952), 234–269; cf. Hans Rosenberg, *Bureaucracy, Aristocracy and Autocracy* (Cambridge, Mass., 1958), 57–74.

63. Johann von Backmeister (1657–1711), Eckhardt von Dewitz (dates unknown), Johann Hiller von Gärtringen (1658–1715), Ludwig Philipp von Geissmar (1651–1699), Anton Günther von Hespen (dates unknown), Johann Georg von Kulpis (1652–1698), Maximilian von Menzingen (1635–1708), Johann Rüdiger von Ostien (1603–1699), Johann Wolfgang von Rathsamhausen (died 1711), Georg Andreas von Reichenbach (died 1710), Georg Wilhelm von Reischach (1673–1724), Jacob Friedrich von Rühle (1630–1708), Johann Rudolf Seubert (1653–1721), Johann Friedrich von Staffhorst (1653–1730).

tivity. Since all but Johann Rudolf Seubert (1653–1721) held patents of imperial nobility, we can assume that the councilors' restrained, professionally oriented lives reflected their conscious choice. There were no social barriers to keep them from moving in court circles; they lived as they did because they had a set of values and social priorities that inclined them in that direction.

In respect to their geographic origins, the councilors constituted a foreign element in Württemberg society.[64] They came from outside the duchy and, especially while in active service on the council, remained a bit apart from the traditional elements of territorial power. Not one of the fourteen early-eighteenth-century privy councilors could have called himself a native Württemberger. Indeed, only three councilors came from families settled in the region: Johann Hiller von Gärtringen (1658–1715) and Georg Wilhelm Freiherr von Reischach (1673–1724) were Swabian imperial knights with family properties inside Württemberg;[65] Johann Rudolf Seubert was born at Durlach, the son of a former Württemberg subject who had made his career in the Baden government.[66] The others had immigrated to Stuttgart from far-flung parts of the Reich: five from the Baltic (Holstein, Mecklenburg, and Pomerania); three from the Upper Rhine (Worms, Strassburg, and Alsace); two from Hessen; and one from Hanover.[67]

That these men moved so easily across territorial borders calls attention to three larger related aspects of eighteenth-century German life. First, we see in the Württemberg recruitment pattern strong evidence of a still vital national Lutheran network; the privy councilors came from neither Catholic nor Calvinist lands, only from those of the Augsburg Confession. Furthermore, most outsiders who took positions at Stuttgart came originally from comparable or smaller German states. That is, they were imperial knights or the sons of territorial aristocrats and commoners from the Lutheran states of the Third Germany. Whereas between 1593 and 1793 the Württemberg dukes named seventy-eight outsiders, only two of these men were natives of

64. The Württemberg pattern differed sharply in this regard from that of the other south German Protestant states; see B. Wunder, "Die Sozialstruktur der Geheimratskollegien in den süddeutschen protestantischen Fürstentümern (1660–1720)," VSWG, 58 (1971), 145–220.
65. Alberti, Wappenbuch, 316, 627–628.
66. F. Faber, Die württembergischen Familienstiftungen, x (Stuttgart, 1858), 25. On the father, Johann Christian Seubert, see Pfeilsticker, Dienerbuch, 1481 and 2033.
67. Backmeister (Rostock), Dewitz (Pomerania), Hespen (Holstein), Ostien (Pomerania), and Reichenbach (Holstein); Menzingen (Strassburg), Rathsamhausen (Alsace), Rühle (Worms); Geissmar and Kulpis (Hessen); Stafflhorst (Hanover).

Electoral Saxony and four of Brandenburg-Prussia.[68] Finally, these migrations point up how coherently the imperial structure continued to function as a cultural entity that strongly benefited its more accomplished subjects. By moving among the states of the Reich, ambitious officials could transcend the limitations of territorial particularism and find competing opportunities for advancement to high office.

Despite their geographic spread the councilors were a surprisingly homogeneous group socially. Ten of them came from families of the old nobility; the remaining four from urban professional families.[69] Of the burghers, only Seubert failed to gain an imperial patent of nobility in the course of his administrative career. The council membership therefore consisted overwhelmingly of men with noble status: hereditary aristocrats (72 percent); *Briefadel,* or newly created nobles (21 percent); and burghers (7 percent.[70] This aristocratic cast marked a departure from earlier Württemberg recruitment patterns. Throughout most of the second half of the seventeenth century council membership had been weighted toward commoners or recently ennobled officials.[71] But in the first decades of Eberhard Ludwig's reign the balance shifted in favor of the hereditary nobility. Between 1660 and 1720 that group contributed a total of sixteen privy councilors, twelve of whom entered the council after 1693. In other words, at the moment when the privy council was acquiring increased administrative responsibilities and becoming organized along more professional lines, its composition was increasingly weighted toward a class that is often presumed to have been indifferent to bureaucratic principles.[72]

68. Each of the native-born Saxons had family ties to Württemberg: Baron Johann Christoph von Pflug (1705–1772) married the sister of Duke Carl Eugen's morganatic wife, and the family of H. G. R. Röder von Schwende (died 1751) had a tradition of Württemberg service extending back before the Thirty Years War. The four Prussians were Johann Friedrich Goetze (died 1734), Baron Gustav Adolf von Gotter (died 1762), F. S. von Montmartin (1712–1778), and Baron Johann Nathanäel von Schunck (dates unknown). Please note that a career pattern for non-Prussians of moving from Brandenburg service to Württemberg was relatively common throughout the period. For example, Eberhard Ludwig's privy councilor Reichenbach, a native of Holstein, had served in both the Brandenburg and Saxon governments prior to his arrival at Stuttgart.

69. The four burghers were Backmeister, Kulpis, Rühle, and Seubert.

70. Cf. Wunder, "Die Sozialstruktur der Geheimratskollegien." Wunder missed this crystallization in early-eighteenth-century Württemberg of bureaucratic influence by the traditional nobility. In his data pool he also underestimated the number of councilors who were born noble.

71. Of the fourteen councilors who served from 1660 to 1693 only four (28.5 percent) belonged to the old nobility: Berthold von Bülow (1636–1690); Wolfgang Georg Graf zu Castell (died 1668); Christoph von Manteuffel zu Arnhausen (1622–1688); Maximilian von Menzingen (1635–1708).

72. A reverse pattern was followed in Brandenburg-Prussia, where between 1651 and 1688 the Great Elector appointed forty-two privy councilors of whom thirty-four

Nuances in the origins of their nobility, like differences in their economic status, apparently had little effect upon the councilors' interrelationships.[73] The title of privy councilor eclipsed more traditional distinctions and bestowed on the group a collective identity that distinguished its members not only from the municipal patriarchs of the Ehrbarkeit but also from the aristocratic elements at court. In part of course this separation rested upon function; the councilors' high government offices set them apart from the other Württembergers and contributed to a group cohesion resting upon similarities in education and training. All the councilors had studied at one or more of the German universities, where available evidence indicates that they pursued a common course of legal studies.[74] The only difference lay in their advanced degrees; only Kulpis and Rühle held doctorates. Since both men came from urban families and were two of the three officials ennobled while in Württemberg service, we may assume that the Ph.D. constituted a major asset for ambitious burghers but was not yet essential to the advancement of the born aristocrat.

But if they laid little stress upon higher degrees, the aristocratic professionals placed considerable emphasis on the importance of field training and practical experience. It is true that Staffhorst took office without prior administrative service outside the ducal household,[75] but the others joined the privy council only after long years in one or more of the Württemberg central agencies or in the higher administrative ranks of comparable territorial governments. Even the two Swabian knights did not think it beneath them to work their way up in the local bureaucracy. In 1683 Johann Hiller von Gärtringen married the daughter of Andreas Bardili, the director of Württemberg's Kirchenrat, and served an apprenticeship of several years on the

---

(81 percent) were noblemen (F. L. Carsten, *The Origins of Prussia* [Oxford, 1954] 258). Between 1688 and 1713, in those years when the Württemberg crown was hiring primarily from the nobility, Friedrich I of Prussia began to recruit primarily from commoners and Briefadel (Rosenberg, *Bureaucracy, Aristocracy and Autocracy*, 61). Rosenberg inferred from the Prussian pattern that, with increased professionalism, the old nobility withdrew in favor of a new social type. The Württemberg case suggests otherwise.

73. Cf. Wunder, "Die Sozialstruktur der Geheimratskollegien." Had Wunder considered behavior patterns he would have discovered for these decades ample evidence of collegial corporatism and, at least for Württemberg, a conscious downgrading of traditional distinctions.

74. Excepting Staffhorst, all councilors but Geissmar served on one or more of the territorial judicial courts in positions requiring legal training. Geissmar, who worked primarily with finance, studied law at Giessen (Pfeilsticker, *Dienerbuch*, 1118 and 2386).

75. Pfeilsticker, *Dienerbuch*, 7, 201, 400, 1123, 2345; also Grube, *Stuttgarter Landtag*, 372–373.

Oberrat before taking a seat on that judicial board. He worked for most of the 1690s as a legal assistant for the Württemberg delegation to the Swabian Kreistag and then for almost a decade more on the ducal legation at Regensburg before his appointment in 1709 to the privy council.[76] Georg Wilhelm Freiherr von Reischach had a similar career. After three years as a ducal equerry (*Kammerjunker*), he entered the judiciary, serving first as an apprentice on the Oberrat and then as an assistant judge on the territorial court at Tübingen. In 1706 he returned to Stuttgart where he became vice-president of the Oberrat and three years later entered the privy council. That same year Eberhard Ludwig named him president of the Oberrat.[77]

This marked emphasis upon career training and the commitment to officialdom as a way of life separated the noble councilors from their counterparts at court. They also remained apart from the territorial Ehrbarkeit, with whom they nevertheless shared confessional orthodoxy and social conservatism. Experience in other areas of Germany insulated them against the more provincial prejudices of the Ehrbarkeit, particularly against that group's indifference to all events outside territorial borders and its uncompromising attachment to the ancient compacts and treaties of the Württemberg constitution. The councilors' own regional dialects, native traditions, local customs and "foreign" dietary habits must have reinforced their sense of individuality; for of these fourteen councilors, only two formed attachments to local interest groups: Staffhorst was oriented almost entirely to the court, and Rühle married one of his daughters to a Landschaftskonsulent. In general the others kept to themselves and followed a course much like that of Joachim Rüdiger von Ostien, president of the privy council from 1693 to 1696. Ostien arrived at Stuttgart in 1693 and returned to his estates in Pomerania upon his retirement in 1696. Before entering Württemberg service he had served as a minister in the Pomeranian administration and as vice-president of the Royal Swedish Tribunal at Wismar. In that he had behind him not only a substantive administrative career but a family of grown children already settled in his native region, he was able to carry out his administrative duties in Württemberg without a need for local ties.[78]

Although few councilors sought links to the Ehrbarkeit, several in

---

76. Pfeilsticker, *Dienerbuch*, 1151, 1221, 1370, 1483, 1795; Alberti, *Wappenbuch*, 316; HSAS, A 202: Bü. 81.

77. Pfeilsticker, *Dienerbuch*, 36, 1113, 1115, 1121, 1199, 1295, 2484, 3011; Alberti, *Wappenbuch*, 627–628; HSAS, A 202: Bü. 43 (minutes for 3 September 1715).

78. Pfeilsticker, *Dienerbuch*, 1113; HSAS, A 204: Bü. 51 (minutes for 20 October 1693).

the group married along professional lines. Three of the four councilors who married while in Württemberg service selected their brides from professional families. These three married daughters of other high civil servants (two privy councilors and the director of the Kirchenrat); the fourth married a widow with no ties to the Ehrbarkeit.[79] The second generation followed a similar pattern. Those sons of an age to hold office usually took posts in the Württemberg central government. Then, when their fathers left office, they either surrendered these positions and sought their fortunes elsewhere in the Reich or remained in ducal service and married the daughters of other high Württemberg officials.[80] Thus Johann Friedrich Seubert, son of the privy councilor, made his career on the Württemberg Oberrat. His daughter in turn married the son of a privy councilor.[81] Even Rühle's children followed this pattern. Whereas one daughter had married a lawyer for the estates, each of his other two offspring married the child of a privy councilor.[82]

The councilors' political careers rested squarely upon their administrative expertise. As a group they entered the eighteenth century centered around a collegial board where each man had a clearly defined set of responsibilities. We have already seen that in the confrontation over the military the councilors supported the monarch. Eberhard Ludwig responded to this support by strengthening the board. Following the example of the Great Elector, he hoped to duplicate the Brandenburg system in Württemberg.[83] In particular he streamlined the councilors' operations so as to encourage each official to develop a specific area of administrative competence. By 1700 each councilor was working in one of five broad areas of government: (1) justice and Polizei; (2) imperial relations (Vienna, the Reichstag, the

79. Backmeister (the daughter of Privy Councilor J. C. Keller); Staffhorst (daughter of M. Von Menzingen); and Hiller von Gärtringen (daughter of Kirchenrat-Director A. Bardili). Kulpis married a Stuttgart widow by the name of Sophie Margaretha Kiefer.

80. The career of Friedrich Maximilian von Menzingen (1670–1730) typified a pattern: although his father was privy councilor, he served as an equerry at court (1693–1696) and then, after six years of travel and study abroad, entered the Oberrat, where in 1706 he became president. After his father's death in 1708, he joined the government of Hessen-Darmstadt (Pfeilsticker, Dienerbuch, 33, 1113, 1114, 1197).

81. Pfeilsticker, Dienerbuch, 1180.

82. His two daughters married Landschaftskonsulent Gerhardt Maienbusch and Privy Councilor J. A. Frommann; his son married the daughter of Privy Councilor J. V. von Bode.

83. Conrad Bornhak, Geschichte des preussischen Verwaltungsrechts, I (Berlin, 1884), 315–319; cf. Otto Hintze, "Der oesterreichische und der preussische Beamtenstaat im 17. und 18. Jahrhundert," HZ, 86 (1901), 401–444; and Josef Kallbrunner, "Zur Geschichte der oesterreichischen Zentralverwaltung im 18. Jahrhundert," VSWG, 33 (1940), 188–194.

Supreme Court); (3) finance and military; (4) estates, tolls, coinage, and commerce; and (5) church, education, and Kreis.[84] Under this system a councilor not only dealt directly with the subordinate central agencies in his area but also drew up all pertinent reports for the prince and the council. This "expert" then led council discussions on these matters and guided his colleagues into a consensus recommendation for the prince.

The councilors worked well under this system and exercised a close supervision over the various branches of the central government. Their steady flow of policy reports and administrative directives during these years indicates that, by the second decade of the century, the Württemberg central government was operating according to a fixed bureaucratic routine. On matters emanating from the crown, the privy council passed the charge to the appropriate agency. When problems came to Stuttgart from the territorial districts, the central agency handling the appeal referred its recommendations to the privy council, at which time the members reviewed the decision and, when appropriate, ordered changes. In such instances the council member in whose area of competence the problem lay researched the case, reported to his colleagues, and with their approval formulated a response. If the prince did not attend that meeting, he received a copy of the council's recommendation for final approval. In this manner the privy council served as the mechanism through which ducal consent was obtained from below and through which ducal authority asserted itself at the center. The councilors controlled the subordinate agencies and saw that boards such as the consistory and the Oberrat did not exceed their mandates or develop an administrative momentum independent of the prince's wishes.[85]

After the outcry over his plans for a morganatic marriage, Eberhard Ludwig turned away from his privy council. We have seen that he ceased to attend board meetings and demanded instead written summaries of council business (*extracti protocolli*). He found in this departure a way to exploit the councilors' knowledge without having to engage personally in their deliberations. But while such a procedure left him free to pursue the pleasures of palace and hunt, it placed him in the potentially awkward position of having to assert his personal wishes against the overpowering weight of expert opinion. Even before he left Stuttgart, his council marginalia revealed a growing resentment toward his administrators. He found to his chagrin that they

84. HSAS, A 202: Bü. 5.
85. See council papers for 1705–1708 in HSAS, A 204: Bü. 59, 60, 62; A 202: Bü. 79–81, 1861, 2831, 3039, 3096–3098; A 203: 48–55.

were adhering to procedure with a loyalty that seemed to take precedence over what he felt should be their primary concern—the prompt execution of his wishes. The councilors were in no position to challenge the monarch, and nothing in their papers indicates that they so intended. Unlike the Landtag delegates, who always claimed to represent larger constituencies in the duchy and whose privileges were secured by the constitution, the privy councilors held their office directly from the prince. They recognized that in a literal sense he was their employer. Their critical attitude in respect to certain of his policies stemmed not from a strategy of opposition but from differing perceptions about government. They were beginning to think more in terms of the state than in terms of the prince's person. Furthermore, their professionalism and command of administrative detail made them hostile to policies that ran counter to the principles of orderly, rationalized governance. When the duke advocated schemes that did, the councilors felt morally obligated to object. And when they accompanied their unwelcome words with delaying tactics, irritation propelled the duke to reorganize his government. Between 1708 and 1717 bad feelings sputtered around three primary issues: royal policy toward the Stuttgart municipal administration; court expenses; and Eberhard Ludwig's contempt for administrative routine. These issues should not be thought of as major battles, nor were they confined to specific moments or easily separable from one another. They nagged—sometimes in unison, sometimes individually—and had the cumulative effect of wearing down the confidence between the duke and his bureaucratic officials.

Eberhard Ludwig's relations with the Stuttgart magistracy offer a case in point. That he sparred constantly with the urban leaders comes as no surprise. After all, these men stood at the center of the territorial Ehrbarkeit and had failed to support not only the standing army but also Eberhard Ludwig's liaison with "the Grävenitz woman." The duke met this recalcitrance with a mixture of contemptuous indifference and truculence. He showed the magistrates what he thought of their political importance by assigning them a precedence in his first Table of Rank below that of the lowest commissioned army officer. The *Rang Regiment* stipulated that lieutenants should proceed the mayors of Stuttgart and Tübingen, the two most prestigious secular officials of the Landtag.[86] He also demanded that municipal deliberation be suspended in all cases involving the imple-

86. HSAS, A 202: Bü. 19 (8 May 1710).

mentation of royal decrees in the city and did everything he could to push through the election of his own men to public office.

In the winter of 1710, after several years of unsuccessful skirmishing with the city officials, Eberhard Ludwig ordered immediate reductions in the personnel and salary scales of the municipal government. The city council appealed at once to the executive committee of the estates, a board on which the mayor of Stuttgart also sat; the estates in turn referred the matter to the privy council. The prince, thinking of the council as his own, felt confident that the councilors would render in his favor. To his great chagrin, their chief concern was impartial justice. On 8 May 1710 they forwarded a detailed report to the duke in which they reviewed relations between the crown and the city over the previous two years. Both the tone and content of the report left no doubt that the councilors felt the duke had acted arbitrarily and had exceeded his authority.[87] They took an equally firm stand three years later when Eberhard Ludwig commanded the council to order the immediate execution of two women who he claimed had shouted insulting remarks at the countess and himself as they made their way through the city. The privy councilors responded that they doubted whether obscenities, however objectionable, merited the death penalty; in any event they felt obligated to require that due judicial procedure be followed. The case, in other words, would first have to be heard by the municipal court and then come before the Oberrat and finally be reviewed by themselves. No one, not even the prince, they informed Eberhard Ludwig, had the right to interrupt the prescribed course of justice.[88]

Incidents such as these, though annoying, were decidedly less serious than the privy council's steadfast repudiation of deficit spending. Whereas Eberhard Ludwig took a cavalier attitude toward money and assumed that his subjects would pay for what he felt appropriate to a monarch's style, the councilors focused determinedly upon the account books of the Rentkammer and on the constitutional limitations circumscribing ducal rights to taxation.[89] Already during the war Baron von Reischach had queried the duke on behalf of the council as to his plans for handling shortfalls in the budget. At that time Eberhard Ludwig thought it sufficient to reply with the hastily scrawled

87. HSAS, A 204: Bü. 103 (8 May 1710).
88. HSAS, A 204: Bü. 108 (18 October 1713) and A 202: Bü. 29 (10 July 1713). Cf. A 204: Bü. 66 (22 February 1710) and Bü. 67 (13 May 1713) for a comparable recommendation in terms of procedures for appointment to the duchess's household.
89. HSAS, A 204: Bü. 111 contains council papers assembled in 1714 to support the estates' constitutional rights of taxation. See A 204: Bü. 108 (15 September 1713) and Bü. 117 (11 September 1716) for council negotiations with the Rentkammer.

*Increase in ducal expenditure, 1693–1718*

| Account | Ducal expenses (in florins) | | Percentage of increase |
|---|---|---|---|
| | 1693 | 1718 | |
| allowances to members of ducal family (*Deputate*) | 25,162 | 40,948 | 63 |
| salaries for ducal court (*Hofstaat*) | 70,000 | 120,000 | 71 |
| salaries for ducal cabinet | 26,175 | 95,858 | 266 |
| stable, livery, etc. | 12,693 | 30,000 | 136 |
| Total increase | 134,030 | 286,806 | 114 |

comment, "by the Trizesimen" (*ex tricesimation*).[90] Peace, however, necessitated a more substantive answer. With rapidly rising deficits no longer connected even remotely with defense, the councilors reminded the duke that imperial law would never sanction the continuation of emergency measures that violated the territorial constitution. "Do not defy the estates and try to continue the extremes [*Extremitäten*] of the past," they warned. "In peacetime the people will not stand for excessive, arbitrary levies like the Trizesimen."[91] The councilors especially deplored the "staggering" costs of the construction at Ludwigsburg. "Cut back! Be reasonable [*moderate*]!" they repeatedly urged the prince, indifferent to the fact that Eberhard Ludwig apparently sought "greatness" not moderation. Since their own values were so far from his obsession with *gloire*, they did not realize how much their carefully reasoned demonstration that other German princes were not building on this scale (*Andere Herrn bauen nit so stark*) must have fed Eberhard Ludwig's sense of cultural one-upmanship.[92]

At any rate ducal expenditure continued to mount. Incomplete fiscal records preclude a comprehensive reconstruction of income and outgo for these years, but available figures certainly justify the worst of the councilors' suspicions. The table above, constructed from reports of the Rentkammer, offers some indication of the rise in personal obligations drawn by the duke against crown revenues.[93] These figures include neither sums paid by the monarch out of the

90. HSAS, A 204: Bü. 102 (24 May 1709).
91. HSAS, A 204: Bü. 109 (14 May 1714), Bü. 110 (30 May 1714), Bü. 111 (2 October 1714), Bü. 67 (23 October 1714), Bü. 113 (22 June 1715); also, A 203: Bü. 45 (24 May 1703).
92. HSAS, A 204: Bü. 63 (council minutes for 26 October 1710); cf. Bü. 116 (30 March 1716).
93. HSAS, A 202: Bü. 1866 (24 February–27 August 1718 and 4 February 1719).

ducal trust (Kammerschreiberei) nor contributions to these accounts from the estates.[94] They also take no account of the outlay for building and for the military. The scale of growth in ducal expenditure can best be appreciated by comparing these figures to those for 1717, when total expenses for the central administration, including 11,086 florins paid in pensions, ran to 82,415 florins.[95] Crown expenses far exceeded revenue, either public or private. Rentkammer records for 1716 indicate a deficit for that year of 350,000 florins.[96] An analysis of midyear reports preserved from 1717 projects a deficit for that year of an additional 450,000 florins.[97] The cumulative effect of this kind of spending was disastrous: on 27 August 1718 the Rentkammer reported that the crown owed a sum total of 3 million florins. One-third of this figure represented the compounded service interest on moneys borrowed over the previous decades by the duke to finance Ludwigsburg and to cover the shortfalls in his military and household budgets.[98] And certainly the sharp rise in the amount spent on the cabinet staff offered concrete proof of Eberhard Ludwig's creation of an alternative to the established bureaucracy.

Attempts to force a more realistic spending policy upon the duke backfired. His fitful schemes for economy never went much beyond proposals for cutting back the civil service, and he reacted with indignation to the councilors' suggestions that he reorganize the ducal household and curtail his building programs.[99] In the end, when finally confronted with fiscal crisis, he blamed the bureaucrats. On 5 April 1718 he wrote to the privy council from his residence at the mineral springs of Wildbad, absolving himself of all personal responsibility for the sorry state of his finances and accusing the councilors of disrespect as well as of mismanagement and the virtual sabotage of his affairs:

I have underlined certain phrases and expressions [in your most recent reports] that should have been couched with greater respect and re-

94. von Riecke, *Württembergische Jahrbücher für Statistik und Landeskunde* (Stuttgart, 1879), 84 ff., concluded from the Katasters that in the years 1713–1744 the estates raised 640,000 florins in annual direct taxes. Of this sum 360,000 florins went to amortize ducal debts and 280,000 florins went to the military.

95. Kanzlei accounts in HSAS, A 202: Bü. 1865 (esp. the reports of 20 September 1717).

96. HSAS, A 202: Bü. 1866 (report of 13 June 1717).

97. HSAS, A 202: Bü. 1866 (papers for June 1717).

98. HSAS, A 202: Bü. 1866 (17 August 1718). On ducal borrowing see A 204: Bü. 103, 126, 176; also K. Müller, "Die Finanzwirtschaft in Württemberg unter Herzog Karl Alexander (1733–1737)," *WVJHLG*, 38 (1932), 276–317, esp. pp. 283–284.

99. For various schemes to reduce expenses, see HSAS, A 202: Bü. 1861 (20 June 1698, 25 February–2 March 1699, 26 April 1704, 3 October 1707, 10 May 1708) and Bü. 1863 (February 1709).

straint [toward my royal person]. . . . If you had got the treasury office in better order, we would never have had this confusion and lamentable administration of our royal finances. . . . We have considered various policies of retrenchment compatible with our royal dignity and great reputation and find nothing more that we can cut back on. . . . You must look more sharply to our government—to the ecclesiastical as well as to the temporal sector—and root out the negligence, sloppiness, and rampant deception that you have permitted to compromise the orderly administration and economic well-being of my government.[100]

Eberhard Ludwig delivered this censure to a privy council he had already begun to restructure. His initial strategy after Countess Würben's return to Stuttgart had been to pack the board with courtiers. From 1710 to 1714 he made eight appointments to the council, only one of them a man with prior experience in the Württemberg government.[101] That official, Johann Andreas Frommann (1672–1730), had been a law professor at Tübingen and was married to the daughter of Privy Councilor von Rühle.[102] Though he had died prior to Frommann's appointment, Rühle had done much to advance his son-in-law's interest on the board.[103] Two other appointees had prior experience in the administrations of neighboring German states, and the remaining five were courtiers.[104] Two, in fact, were close relatives of Countess Würben: Friedrich Wilhelm von Grävenitz, her brother, and David Nathanäel von Sittmann, a notorious adventurer who had married her sister Eleonore.[105] It is not surprising that on

100. HSAS, A 202: Bü. 1866.

101. 1710: Friedrich Wilhelm Graf von Grävenitz (1679–1754), Justus Vollrad von Bode (dates unknown); 1711: Dr. Johann Andreas Frommann (1672–1730); 1712: Johann Heinrich Freiherr Schüz von Pflummern (1669–1732), Johann Franz Ferdinand Graf zu Würben und Freudenthal (died 1719); 1713: Adam Hermann Heinrich Freiherr von Thüngen (died 1723), David Nathanäel Baron von Sittmann (dates unknown); 1714; Johann Nathanäel Baron von Schunck (dates unknown).

102. HSAS, A 202: Bü. 81; Pfeilsticker, *Dienerbuch*, 1138, 1216, 1230, 1347, 2280.

103. Rühle placed his son-in-law on the Württemberg delegation to Vienna (1705–1707) and then in 1709 secured his entry onto the Oberrat. Frommann was also brother-in-law to Jacob Schäffer (died 1728), who from 1702–1712 worked as secretary to the privy council.

104. In 1714 Schunck came to Württemberg from Brandenburg, where he had served on the quarterly court of the Alt Mark (Pfeilsticker, Dienerbuch, 1122, 1367, 2761). Bode arrived in 1710 from Oels, a Württemberg appanage in Silesia, where he had been chancellor; see Pfeilsticker, *Dienerbuch*, 1115, 1228, 1370; and HSAS, A 202: Bü. 81 (papers dealing with his dismissal, 1713–1714).

105. On Sittmann, see Pfeilsticker, *Dienerbuch*, 39, 1123, 2165, 2322, 2736, 2931. L. von Spittler, *Geschichte des wirtembergischen Geheimen-Raths-Collegiums*, in *Sämtliche Werke*, ed. K. Wächter, XIII (Stuttgart and Tübingen, 1837), 408f., insists that, prior to his arrival at Stuttgart, Sittmann had been hairdresser and maître d'hôtel to a Countess Wartenberg in Berlin; cf. Grube, *Stuttgarter Landtag*, 383. On Grävenitz, see HSAS, A 202: Bü. 79 and 2832; Pfeilsticker, *Dienerbuch*, 17, 404, 1095, 1119, 1163, 2273, 2482, 2504, 2686, 2724, 2953, 3348; also biographical entries in *Allgemeine*

questions of policy these courtiers proved unable to prevail against the administrative expertise of the professional officials. As we have seen, the council continued in these years to take stands unpopular with the duke and to render advice dictated by the principles of rationalized governance. Its stance also ran counter to the prevailing ethos of the court. On issues such as the building of a Catholic chapel for the Italian workers at Ludwigsburg[106] and the toleration of Capuchin confessors for well-born Catholic courtiers,[107] the councilors adhered firmly to their time-honored convictions of confessional purity.

Under these circumstances the courtiers lost interest in the board. They followed Eberhard Ludwig to Ludwigsburg and gathered instead in the ducal apartments where they formed a kind of kitchen cabinet around the prince. In the spring of 1717, on the pretext that "We are no longer able to attend regularly our council meetings at Stuttgart," Eberhard Ludwig institutionalized these positions by instituting an official board called the Conference Ministry (*Geheimer Konferenz Rat*), which he endowed with an independent secretariat.[108] The four courtiers appointed to the ministry—Grävenitz, Baron Heinrich Schüz von Pflummern (1669–1732), Baron Adam Hermann Heinrich von Thüngen (died 1723), and Baron Johannes Nathanäel von Schunck—retained their seats on the privy council. But in reality the council at Stuttgart, now placed under the titular presidency of Baron von Sittmann, was reduced to an administrative clearinghouse. The two remaining professionals on the board, Seubert and Frommann, became little more than clerical workers.

The privy councilors continued to transmit the duke's commands to the various central administrative agencies. But whereas previously they had participated in the formulation of these directives, they now only processed them. Whatever discussion surrounded the policy at hand took place in the duke's cabinet. The councilors' role shrank to one of seeing that cabinet orders reached the proper administrative board and reporting on their subsequent implementation. The privy council also lost its status as the government's chief representative to the crown. In October 1718 ducal orders stipulated that, on all mat-

---

*Deutsche Biographie*, IX (Berlin, 1968), 616 and 617; and J. Zedler, ed., *Grosses Vollständiges Universal-Lexicon aller Wissenschaften und Künste*, XI (Halle and Leipzig, 1735), 511 and 512.

106. HSAS, A 204: Bü. 103 (12 May 1710); A. Heine, *Geschichte der katholischen Gemeinde Ludwigsburg* (Ludwigsburg, 1932), 5ff.

107. HSAS, A 204: Bü. 113; H. Tüchle, *Die Kirchenpolitik des Herzogs Karl Alexander von Württemberg, 1733–1737* (Würzburg, 1937), 9.

108. HSAS, A 202: Bü. 91; also F. Wintterlin, *Geschichte der Behördenorganisation in Württemberg*, I (Stuttgart, 1902), 66n2.

ters of importance to the duke, central directors were to report personally to the cabinet ministers.[109] While Eberhard Ludwig later required the directors also to deliver written memoranda to the privy council, the new procedure displaced the councilors' central position in the government.[110] Even on matters under their direct supervision, they were no longer permitted to deal with the prince but instead reported to his ministers. And since the cabinet ministers had their own secretariat, the privy councilors could not even be sure in what form their reports would be forwarded to the monarch.[111]

Under these conditions council business contracted sharply and became increasingly routine. Baron von Sittmann appeared on and off in the chancellery offices but took little role in daily affairs. Indeed for the next four years the content and volume of council business was such that Seubert and Frommann handled all matters themselves. The council ceased to meet as a plenum; and in 1721, when Seubert died and Frommann took leave, Eberhard Ludwig replaced them with two other professionals—Johann Philipp von Schütz (died 1744)[112] and Wilhelm Ulrich Smalcaldér (died 1739)[113]—who carried on the routine business. The duke obviously found the system satisfactory, for in 1724 he issued a Kanzleiordnung, the first such proclamation since 1660, making the cabinet ministry a matter of public law.[114] In that ordinance he appointed Grävenitz prime minister (*premier ministre*) and lord high chamberlain (*Oberhofmarshall*); charged Schüz von Pflummern with representing him in all dealings with the Reichstag (*Comitalgesandter*); and named two new ministers to the cabinet: the prime minister's son, Sigmund Victor von Grävenitz (died 1766), and Caspar Pfau (1686–1744), a Saxon who had risen to favor through his services as private legal counsel to the duke.[115] The ordinance stipulated further that "all state and private

109. HSAS, A 202: Bü. 109 (16 October 1718).
110. HSAS, A 202: Bü. 127 (13 February 1719) and Bü. 1866 (Schunck's letter of 8 April 1719).
111. Spittler, *Geheimen-Raths-Collegiums*, 408–415; cf. Stern, *Jud Süss*, 61–62.
112. Pfeilsticker, *Dienerbuch*, 1230, 2017, 2032. Schütz served on the Oberrat, 1712–1716, and from 1716 to 1721 sat as vice-president on the Kirchenrat.
113. Pfeilsticker, *Dienerbuch*, 1141; also HSAS, A 202: Bü. 82 (protocolla for 27 November 1722). Smalcader belonged to a patrician family in Schwäbisch Hall and prior to entering Württemberg service worked for the Reichskammergericht.
114. A. Reyscher, *Vollständige, historisch und kritisch bearbeitete Sammlung der württembergischen Gesetze*, XIII (Stuttgart and Tübingen, 1851), Nr. 875; also HSAS, A 202: Bü. 77 (Secretary Vollmann's letter of 4 May 1724) and Bü. 91 (4 May 1724).
115. HSAS, A 202: Bü. 77 contains the *vitae* for these appointees. On young Grävenitz, see also A 202: Bü. 79; and Pfeilsticker, *Dienerbuch*, 30, 1119, 1141, 1150, 1163, 1369, 2310, 2468. Pfau, son of the ducal treasurer of Saxe-Anhalt, arrived in 1712 to serve as private secretary to Duke Eberhard Ludwig. By 1714 he was handling the

business of the monarch, without exception, is to be handled by the ministry, except in those cases in which the ministers explicitly delegate their authority to one of the subordinate agencies." Finally, it vested the ministers with complete control over government appointments. Cabinet ministers, not privy councilors, would henceforth hire and fire the civil servants.

For the remaining nine years of his reign, Eberhard Ludwig governed entirely through his cabinet. His ministers dealt scarcely at all with the privy council, though each of them held a seat on that board. Their attitude was not one of hostility but of indifference: they rarely came to Stuttgart and when they did showed little interest in council routine. At one point Eberhard Ludwig thought to expedite consultation by moving the privy councilors to offices in the Flügelbau, a wing of the Ludwigsburg palace.[116] But neither he nor his ministers felt the matter to be of great consequence; and when the councilors, fearful of losing all contact with the subordinate agencies, petitioned to remain at Stuttgart, he willingly acquiesced. He decided instead to require a councilor to report one afternoon a week to the palace, where he would be available for questioning by the ministers.[117] On these occasions discussions about points of information and not policy debate were the rule; no effort was made to involve the privy council more closely in the running of the government.

Carl Alexander carried to even greater extremes his cousin's hostility toward bureaucracy and his desire for personal rule. He despised his government personnel and lumped privy councilors with lower-echelon workers as

> nothing but a group of kinfolks—fathers, sons, cousins, in-laws, brothers, godsons, and God knows what other relations. They measure everything by custom [auf die alte Observanz] and ceaselessly cite chapter and verse of the law. But their legal prattle says nothing at all about their love of justice. Quite the contrary! They fail to perceive that such canting results in bad administration and serves only to justify their own selfish exploitation of office.[118]

In 1735 he set up a cabinet ministry staffed with men whom he regarded as loyal to his person rather than as political experts.[119] Un-

---

legal affairs of the entire ducal family; see HSAS, A 202: Bü. 91 (report of 19 April 1724); Pfeilsticker, Dienerbuch, 1140, 1159, 1165, 1181, 1226, 2001, 2017.

116. HSAS, A 202: Bü. 109 (19 July 1727).

117. Ibid. (28 July 1727).

118. HSAS, A 202: Bü. 67 (letter postmarked Blaubeuren, 21 October 1736).

119. HSAS, A 202: Bü. 6 (16 June 1735) and Bü. 91 (16 June and 2 August 1735, 9 April 1736, 24 December 1736). Wintterlin, Behördenorganisation, I, 69–70, mistakenly reports as missing the papers surrounding the creation of the cabinet ministry.

der that board he placed a series of military, commercial, and fiscal committees through which he attempted to rule the duchy until his sudden death in 1737. Chapter 6 analyzes the implication of these procedures for the central government; the point here is that the professionals continued to be excluded from the center of government. The status of the privy council, however, now changed. Carl Alexander was a convert to Roman Catholicism and was married to a Thurn und Taxis princess who shared his religious convictions.[120] He had come to the throne only as a result of the unexpected deaths of Eberhard Ludwig's direct heirs, first his grandson in 1728 and then three years later his only son, Eberhard Friedrich (1698–1731). In order to secure the succession Eberhard Ludwig had required Carl Alexander to negotiate a religious settlement with the territorial estates known in Württemberg history as the *Reversalien*.[121] This agreement, modeled on the Saxon compact drawn up at the end of the seventeenth century when Augustus of Saxony had converted to Catholicism in order to obtain the Polish crown, guaranteed the rights of the established Württemberg church. It also restricted the appointment to prelacies and government offices to men prepared to swear an oath of loyalty to the Württemberg Confession.[122] And when he came to the throne, Carl Alexander sought permanently to allay Lutheran fears within both the duchy and the Reich by transferring to the privy council his episcopal rights as sovereign (*Landesbischöfliche Rechte*) and by vesting that board with full control over the properties as well as the doctrine of the territorial church.[123]

Such a decision meant that, even if it no longer functioned as a central source of ducal policy, the privy council's administrative importance was assured. Its ecclesiastical responsibilities alone precluded its ever falling again to the status of a secretariat. Nor could two men

---

120. In 1727 Carl Alexander married Maria Augusta von Thurn und Taxis, a zealous Catholic and a woman of political ambition. On Carl Alexander's religious policy, see Tüchle, *Die Kirchenpolitik*; cf. three older, more Protestant-oriented studies: F. Moser, "Leben und Ende des Herzogs Carl Alexander von Württemberg," *Patriotisches Archiv* (1784), 105–220; Dizinger, *Beiträge zur Geschichte Württembergs*; and P. Stark, "Zur Geschichte des Herzogs Karl Alexander von Württemberg und der Streitigkeiten nach seinem Tode," *WVJHLG*, 11 (1888), 1–28. See HSAS, A 202: Bü. 67 (esp. 4 November 1736) for ducal attitudes toward the Pietists.

121. HSAS, A 202: Bü. 2376 contains papers on the negotiations with the estates.

122. Text is reprinted in H. Mosapp, *Die württembergischen Religionsreversalien: Sammlung der Originalurkunden samt einer Abhandlung über die Geschichte und die zeitgemässe Neuregelung der Religionsreversalien* (Tübingen, 1894), 16–27. Fritz Kaphahn, "Kurfürst und Kursächsische Stände im 17. und beginnenden 18. Jahrhundert," *Neues Archiv für Sächsische Geschichte und Altertumskunde* (1922), 62–79.

123. The terms of investiture (30 March 1734) are printed in Mosapp, *Die württembergischen Religionsreversalien*, 27f.

carry out its charges. And since church administration involved complex, often quite technical supervisory duties, appointments would have to go to those trained to assume them. In short, the very charges that guaranteed the board's continued importance ensured the career official's domination of its membership. Carl Alexander's appointments reflected this fact. Excluding from consideration his cabinet members, most of whom held seats *ex officio* on the council but took no part in its deliberations, Carl Alexander named seven privy councilors in the course of his four-year reign.[124] These men were all highly educated bureaucrats with considerable experience in either law, scholarship, or administration.[125] Only Baron Johann Eberhard von Wallbrunn (died 1752) had not risen through the ranks of Württemberg service; and he arrived after a long career in the governments of Baden-Durlach and Hessen-Cassel.[126] Furthermore, whereas in the course of his forty-year reign Eberhard Ludwig had appointed only one native-born Württemberger (Frommann) to the privy council, Carl Alexander gave five of his seven appointments to native sons.[127] Council membership, in other words, had not only regained its professionalism but had acquired a distinctly local orientation. Since the monarch was not looking to the council for advice or close participation in his government, he no longer felt it necessary to recruit members from outside the duchy.

Eberhard Ludwig's decision to create an administrative alternative to the privy council marked the first step in what became a royal counterattack against bureaucracy. For the next fifty years his successors strove to establish in Württemberg a system of personal rather than bureaucratic government. In this effort they followed Eberhard Ludwig's lead and sought to replace the Stuttgart chancellery with the court as the directing center of the state. Just as Eberhard Ludwig had done, so these later dukes set up an authority parallel to the one that had developed over the course of the seventeenth century. They filled this auxiliary chain of administrative command with their favorites—a motley group of aristocrats, adventurers, and immigrant

124. Johann Conrad Abel (1665–1735), Georg Bernhard Bilfinger (1693–1750), Baron Christoph Peter von Forstner (died 1755), Friedrich August von Hardenberg (1700–1768), Johann Conrad Hellwer (1659–1738), Philipp Jacob Neuffer (1677–1738), Baron Johann Eberhard Friedrich von Wallbrunn (died 1752).

125. Abel, Forstner, and Hellwer had studied and practiced law; Bilfinger and Neuffer studied theology; Hardenberg and Wallbrunn had extensive administrative experience.

126. Pfeilsticker, *Dienerbuch*, 1124; HSAS, A 202: Bü. 80 (appointment papers of 28 November 1733).

127. Abel (son of a Württemberg medical doctor; place of birth unknown); Bilfinger (Cannstatt); Hellwer (Rechentshofen); Neuffer (Göppingen); Forstner (Mömpelgard).

Jewish financiers. The government's expenses rose accordingly. We have already seen that Eberhard Ludwig's cabinet expenditure mounted by 226 percent. By 1735 Carl Alexander had raised that total by another 14,618 florins (15 percent).[128]

Carl Alexander brought to the throne a set of political assumptions different from those of his predecessors. His absolutist policies carried the duchy into a new political dimension. But the point to note at this juncture is that it was cultural competition that had provided the initial force behind the expansion of taxes and state finance which produced this preliminary reorientation of the government. It had also prompted the clash over the morality of power between Eberhard Ludwig and his estates and then between the prince and his civil servants. For whereas the latter group regarded the state as an impersonal abstraction to be governed according to fixed rules, the prince had responded in strictly personal terms to the pressures of shifting international standards of kingship. He looked on his territories not as an end in themselves but as a source to provide him with the means for holding his own in the rivalry among the German courts. In their original motivation his politics were personal and cultural; they did not aim toward state building in any conscious sense of that term. But whatever their orientation, their implementation necessitated a restructuring of the domestic balance of power. The construction of Ludwigsburg, the most conspicuous physical testimony to ducal authority, illustrated the point. Both the chronology of its construction and Eberhard Ludwig's initial tentativeness of design preclude our regarding the building of the palace as part of a drive toward absolutism. It was not the decision itself but rather its implementation that necessitated a consolidation of the monarchy's power. A similar connection becomes evident in the tensions generated by the lavish building projects and the munificent patronage of ballet, opera, and theater by Carl Eugen, the duke whose fifty-year reign closes this book.

Another pattern of growth can be charted in the political changes attending this cultural competitiveness. On the periphery of princely absolutism heretofore distinct political forces, the estates and the high officials, were drawing closer together. Shut out for most of the first seven decades of the eighteenth century from the power of decision

---

128. K. O. Müller, "Die Finanzwirtschaft in Württemberg unter Herzog Karl Alexander," lumps together in his totals for government expenditure those moneys going to maintain the territorial administration and those used for the cabinet officials. These latter costs have to be extrapolated from Müller's figures; for privy council salaries in 1733, see HSAS, A 202: Bü. 79 and 1869; for salaries in 1739, see Bü. 57.

making, they continued nonetheless to carry out those duties assigned them by the constitution. And unlike the gifted amateurs at court, their continuity was secure. Over time they were to lose their separate identities and merge together as a single social group. Toward the end of the seventeenth century what was once a tripartite division of prince, high bureaucracy, and estates had dissolved. For a moment prince and bureaucrats worked together as a unit in opposition to the estates. Then in the mid-eighteenth century a new combination took shape as bureaucrats joined estates in isolation from the crown. Once this fusion occurred, the court found itself unable to solve the problems of government. A compromise became essential.

# [6]

# New Directions of Growth

O n 27 January 1734 Carl Alexander arrived at Stuttgart as reigning
duke. His tenure proved remarkably brief. Only three years and
forty-three days after his accession he died suddenly at Ludwigsburg,
leaving his nine-year-old son Carl Eugen (1728–1793) to succeed
him. The age of the child made the formation of a regency obligatory;
and in the years that followed the duke's death the balance of domestic power swung once more in favor of the professional administrators
and their allies among the estates. Under these circumstances it is
tempting to pass over Carl Alexander's government, to regard his unpopular policies simply as an extension of those of his predecessor,
and to focus instead upon the reaction that set in after his death.

This temptation must be resisted on three counts. First, and most
broadly, the resistance engendered by these policies pointed up an
intrinsic weakness in eighteenth-century territorial monarchy. For all
their absolutist rhetoric these German rulers still depended heavily
upon their subjects' active cooperation. Carl Alexander's innovations
were imposed unilaterally and lacked roots in the established structure of Württemberg society. His personal resources could not compensate for the absence of broader support. Like so many other monarchs he had not yet acquired that monopoly of men and supply
which would have allowed him to impose his will arbitrarily. Religion
posed a special difficulty for him in this regard. As a Catholic he could
not mobilize the popular following in the duchy that might have com-
pensated for his alienation of the established interest groups. Catholicism remained an unsympathetic force to the hometowners and villagers of Württemberg. Their confessional suspicions prevented the
monarch from capitalizing effectively upon the ingrained loyalty that
these men and women felt for the crown. Without a strong popular

commitment, the legislative and administrative powers vested in the sovereign were insufficient to prevail against a concerted opposition by estates and bureaucrats.

Second, the bureaucratic resurgence soon faltered. Once Carl Eugen attained his majority, he shifted the weight of authority back to the court and reinstituted certain of his father's policies. In this sense it was Carl Alexander's government and not the reaction to it which prefigured the primary direction of late-eighteenth-century politics. His efforts to create a state economy that could supply the crown with unencumbered operating funds were particularly prescient. Their failure pointed to a basic dilemma plaguing early modern rulers in their push for absolute monarchy: the relative unsophistication of cameralistic capitalism and the administrative difficulties inherent in attempting to create an alternative to professional bureaucracy.

Finally, Carl Alexander introduced a new dimension to Württemberg politics. He took no interest in the princely *gloire* so important to more conventional monarchs. Nor did he conceive of government in terms of the established Württemberg triangle of princes, bureaucrats, and estates. He operated outside traditional categories and thought of the state as a business, an instrument of financial power in which all of its inhabitants were channeled into the pursuit of money. He directed his government primarily toward financial profit and to that end ignored the corporate distinctions within which political life had operated. The result was a series of programs and reforms that pushed long-established groups toward internal realignments and new allegiances within the broader society. They also paved the way for the entry into the larger political arena of two new social forces: the peasants, a group heretofore restricted to the villages by the municipal Ehrbarkeit; and the evangelical radicals, a cultural force previously confined and contained by the established Lutheran church.

The duke's unusually firm sense of himself as an administrator stemmed in part from personality distinctions. He was by instinct a tougher, more sharply focused man than either Eberhard III or Eberhard Ludwig had been, or than Carl Eugen would be. His education and upbringing differed markedly from those of the former dukes and from those that would shape the character of his own son. Whereas they learned statecraft in terms of traditional Württemberg categories, he took his lessons from a reformed Catholicism with marked authoritarian tones and from years of colonial service on the imperial military borders. His foreign training doubtless shaped his perception of the state and his conception of the monarch as the sole arbiter of that enterprise. Certainly it compounded the difficulties that awaited him when he returned home as reigning duke and set about imposing his vision upon the Württemberg government.

Unlike most territorial sovereigns, Carl Alexander began life with the unpleasant knowledge that he would have to make his own way in the world. His father Friedrich Karl, prince regent during Eberhard Ludwig's minority, possessed only limited financial resources and under family law inherited no extensive sovereign territory that he could pass on to his sons.[1] With his nephew Eberhard Ludwig developing into a healthy, sexually aggressive young man, Friedrich Karl could have had no strong expectation that one of his boys would ever rule Württemberg. As a result he followed a classic pattern for cadet German princes and sent the boys off at an early age to seek their fortunes in military service. At thirteen Carl Alexander took an apprentice position on the staff of the great imperial commander "Türken Louis," where he showed a ready aptitude for tactics and a marked capacity for hard work.[2] From that time until he returned to Stuttgart as sovereign at the age of fifty, he lived essentially on his own. With few material assets beyond his name and social rank, he built an international reputation as a skillful commander and a resourceful military administrator.

Long years outside the duchy meant that Carl Alexander approached the Württemberg government with a comparative perspective that made him unique among the rulers discussed in this book. His years abroad had exposed him to a series of professional, personal, and intellectual encounters far more varied those than available to more conventionally raised Württemberg sovereigns. Four such experiences left lasting impressions that help to explain his particular conception of government. First, and most important for his professional career, was his friendship with Prince Eugene of Savoy. In 1699, after six years of successful apprenticeship under "Türken Louis," Carl Alexander arrived in Vienna with a letter of introduction from his old commander to Prince Eugene. The distinguished general took an immediate liking to Carl Alexander and placed him on his

1. Carl Alexander inherited Winnentals, an estate that Friedrich Karl had secured with sovereign status. Otherwise the Administrator had possessed no sovereign property; B. Wunder, "Der Administrator Herzog Friedrich Karl von Württemberg," ZWLG, 30 (1971), 161. Friedrich Carl's testament (1694) is deposited in HSAS, G 2-8, CXXXVI: Bü. 9; his (1724) is in Bü. 11.
2. Aloys Schulte, Markgraf Ludwig Wilhelm von Baden und der Reichskrieg gegen Frankreich 1693–97, II (Karlsruhe, 1892), 311.

personal staff in the War of the Spanish Succession. From that position the duke fought first in Italy and the East and then alongside his cousin Eberhard Ludwig in the Rhenish campaigns of 1712.[3] As Prince Eugene's protégé Carl Alexander perfected his tactics under one of the most brilliant commanders of the age. He also moved in the highest political circles of the Reich at a time when the Habsburgs were strengthening central authority in their lands and there was much discussion about a more effective imperial administration.[4] He formed at Vienna a set of loyalties and friendships which fused with his training as a soldier to place him firmly in the camp of those patriotic autocrats who were committed to the political revitalization of the empire. He developed especially close ties with Friedrich Carl von Schönborn (1674–1746), who was in Vienna as chief representative for his uncle Lothar Franz von Schönborn, archbishop elector of Mainz and imperial vice-chancellor. The Schönborns championed advanced notions of princely absolutism based upon a union of throne and Catholic altar at the same time that they called for a strong Reichstag within which the balance of political power would be held by the sovereigns of the secondary German states. Friedrich Carl drew Carl Alexander into active participation in the so-called *Deutsche Partei* that had coalesced around this commitment and that worked under the leadership of Prince Eugene and Lothar Franz to influence imperial policy. Like their respective patrons the two friends called for invigorated imperial institutions directed by German princes who had consolidated their territorial power and marshaled their domestic resources in support of a strong empire.[5]

Two other events built upon these emotional and philosophic commitments, the first occurring on 21 October 1712 when Carl Alexander converted to Roman Catholicism. His decision came at a high tide of zeal for evangelical Catholic reform, a moment when a victorious Catholicism had been linked expressly with the concept of a triumphant throne.[6] Reformed Catholicism had always contained an authoritarian element—as attested by the Habsburg reconquest of

3. Paul von Stälin, "Karl Alexander," in *Allgemeine Deutsche Biographie*, xv (Leipzig, 1882), 366–372.
4. C. W. Ingrao, *In Quest and Crisis: Emperor Joseph I and the Habsburg Monarchy* (Purdue, 1979), 7–30. Also H. F. Schwarz, *The Imperial Privy Council in the Seventeenth Century* (Cambridge, Mass., 1943) and John Spielman, *Leopold I of Austria* (New Brunswick, N.J., 1977).
5. Hugo Hantsch, *Reichsvizekanzler Friedrich Karl von Schönborn*, I (Augsburg, 1929), 288ff. and 71–77; cf. Ingrao, *In Quest and Crisis*, 34–38.
6. R. J. W. Evans, *The Making of the Habsburg Monarchy, 1550–1700* (Oxford, 1979), 117–134; R. A. Kann, *A Study in Austrian Intellectual History* (London, 1960), 50–115.

Bohemia—and the crusading spirit then in vogue at Vienna offered no exception.[7] Domination, by force if necessary, was taught almost as a sacred mission for Catholic rulers, who were to use their authority to strengthen the Holy Church. The conversion to Catholicism of a prince whose family had long been associated with Germany's most determined Protestant elements was therefore an occasion of considerable propagandistic value, and Carl Alexander's confirmation was celebrated with high state in the Hofburg chapel at a festive ceremony attended by Emperor Charles VI and his entire court. The emperor's obvious delight on that occasion contrasted sharply with the response to the news in Stuttgart, where the pastors and officials were horrified that a member of their reigning family had taken such a step. Even though no one thought at that time that Carl Alexander might come to the throne, the Württembergers' comments showed them to have identified and rejected in Habsburg Catholicism a commitment to authoritarian government.[8]

Following the reception into Catholicism the emperor named Carl Alexander imperial commander of the imperial fortress at Landau and in 1716 sent him as a field marshal to assist Prince Eugene on his drive through the Balkans. After the Treaty of Passarowitz (1718) had sealed the Austrian triumph in the East, Eugene managed to secure for him an appointment as *Statthalter*, or military governor, of the conquered Serbian provinces. For the next thirteen years the duke resided at Belgrade, where he organized and successfully administered the Habsburgs' colonial Balkan government. He gave detailed attention to the development of the state economy and to the construction of a regular system of taxation and supply.[9] Equally significant for his future Württemberg rule was the fact that, as military governor, he imposed these reforms by fiat and where necessary guaranteed their implementation by force. He needed no skill in jockeying within conventional political categories but was concerned

7. Robert Birely, *Religion and Politics in the Age of the Counterreformation* (Chapel Hill, N.C., 1981), treats in detail the authoritarian strain in early reformed Catholicism. On the later period see Karl Bertsche, ed., *Die Werke Abrahams à Santa Clara in ihren Frühdrucken*, 2d ed. (Vienna, 1961).

8. H. Tüchle, *Die Kirchenpolitik des Herzogs Karl Alexander von Württemberg, 1733–1737* (Würzburg, 1937), 22–28. Cf. K. Dizinger, *Beiträge zur Geschichte Württembergs und seines Regentenhauses zur Zeit der Regierung Herzogs Karl Alexander und während der Minderjährigkeit seines Erstgeboren*, I (Tübingen, 1834), 5ff.; and J. Schall, "Zur kirchlichen Lage unter Herzog Karl Alexander," *BWKG*, 4 (1900), 123–143.

9. Langer, "Serbien unter der kaiserlichen Regierung, 1717–1739," *Mittheilungen des K. k. Kriegs-Archivs*, III (Vienna, 1889), 155–248.

Within the engraving, the coat of arms and scrollwork bear the inscription:

CAROLUS ALEXANDER
Dux Wurtemb. et Tecc. Comes
Montispeligar, li. Dynasta Hei,
denhemii &c. Eques aurei velleris S.Ca.
sariæ Majestatis S. Rom. Imp. erict
melutti Circuli Suevici Generalis Campi Marc.
schallus, ac Chil. tam dua rum Cæsar quam duarum
Circ. Suev legionum equestrium ac pedestrium. &c.

Duke Carl Alexander displays none of the self-conscious Francophilia of his
two immediate predecessors. His aggressive posture and the set of his face
recall the spirit of the military camp rather than that of the drawing room. He
wears the Habsburg Order of the Golden Fleece, an affirmation of his Catholic loyalties that was not lost on the contemporary Württembergers. Photograph courtesy of the Landesbildstelle Stuttgart.

rather with colonial subjugation and with the channeling of indigenous energies in the service of the state.

Carl Alexander thus returned to Stuttgart a fully formed man whose fame devolved from traditions and experiences outside the ken of the duchy. In contrast to the other reigning dukes in his family, he showed no interest in personal luxury and defined rank in terms of achievement rather than status. Nor did he take particular pleasure in ceremony. He kept a modest court at Ludwigsburg and, unlike his son, remained indifferent to the liturgical splendors of baroque Catholicism. Power in the sense of disciplined control was his goal. He approached his government from that perspective and set out to make the state a well-run machine, one that responded immediately to the directives of its operator. He died before revealing the kind of ruler he might finally have become, but certainly the intermediate road was clear: the business at hand was the raising of money. And to that end he went to work at once.

His reign proved exceedingly unpopular; and when he died suddenly, under somewhat suspicious circumstances at Ludwigsburg, his subjects rejoiced openly.[10] A contemporary observer, Anton Weberous (1701–1803), recorded the reaction at Stuttgart, where the news of the duke's sudden stroke arrived about ten o'clock in the evening:

Lights began to show in the windows, the night was turned to day; friends and foes embraced indiscriminately. Only the sick stayed within doors that fateful night. Then suddenly the rumor spread that the duke had been brought round and lived again. Calamity of calamities, what horror was this? The lamps were doused and the crowds slipped unobtrusively back into their houses. But dawn confirmed the news of the death, and now the joyful cry rang out: "The duke is dead!" Plane and file, awl and shears were laid aside, and the day was turned into a public holiday. The pastry cook and haberdasher Benz, who lived at the outer city wall, made a transparency and displayed it in his windows. It depicted a devil flying through the air above a church with two spires and bearing off a man. Under it ran the legend: "Look how the devil in person carries off the apostate to his reward."[11]

10. The duke died of an apparent stroke on the eve of his projected departure for a medical examination in northern Germany. Though Catholic supporters suspected that his valet, a relative of one of the more important leaders in the opposition, had poisoned him, more reliable scholars have rejected this possibility. Cf. F. Moser, "Leben und Ende des Herzogs Carl Alexander von Württemberg," *Patriotisches Archiv* (1784), 105–220; Dizinger, *Beiträge zur Geschichte Württembergs*, I, 181f.; and E. Schneider, "Der Tod des Herzogs Karl Alexander von Württemberg," *Besondere Beilage des Staatsanzeigers für Württemberg* (1900), 65f.

11. Reproduced in C. Elwenspoek, *Jew Süss Oppenheimer*, trans. E. Cattle (London, 1931), 16. Even stronger sentiments are reflected in a contemporary poem by the

More established elements orchestrated these feelings of popular joy. Pastors gave public thanksgiving for deliverance from Catholic rule and prayed openly in their churches for a Lutheran prince.[12] Meanwhile the privy councilors joined with the estates in having the ducal "creatures" arrested and in restoring a correlative balance of political power such as had not been seen in the duchy since the days of Eberhard III. Both groups agreed to ignore the clause in Carl Alexander's will that called for the joint appointment of his wife and his old friend Friedrich Carl von Schönborn, now bishop of Würzburg and Bamberg, as regents for his young son. They turned instead to Protestant branches of the ducal House and appointed first one and then another well-meaning but politically ineffectual prince as regent.[13] In both instances the regents agreed to take no decision on domestic or foreign policy without prior consultation and agreement with the privy council. They accepted fully the principle that administrative authority was to be shared equally between the crown and the privy council.[14]

Whereas confessional prejudice fueled the popular reaction, those who stimulated and exploited these fears acted from more complex motives. Whatever their doctrinal convictions—and there is no reason to assume that they were insincere in this regard—they also acted to safeguard their own political and economic interests. In this broader sense it was not so much Carl Alexander's religion as his aggressive economic and domestic innovations that had antagonized the estates and civil servants and prompted their alliance under the regency.[15] His policies had threatened the Ehrbarkeit's domination of

---

Pietist pastor Georg Conrad Rieger, reproduced by K. Steiff and G. Mehring, eds., *Geschichtliche Lieder und Sprüche Württembergs* (Stuttgart, 1912), 648–655.

12. The privy council suspended two Pietist pastors from office for describing the duke's death in their sermons as *eine Erlösung Gottes;* see H. Lehmann, *Pietismus und weltliche Ordnung in Württemberg vom 17. bis zum 20. Jahrhundert* (Stuttgart, 1969), 86.

13. The seventy-year-old Karl Rudolph of Württemberg-Neuenstadt (1667–1742) served for one year and upon his retirement was succeeded by Karl Friedrich of Württemberg-Oels, senior prince of the family's Silesian appanage. For a comprehensive assessment of these men, see Dizinger, *Beiträge zur Geschichte Württembergs,* 65–88.

14. The privy council's invitation to Karl Rudolph spelling out the terms of the regency is preserved in HHSAW, Württembergica B. 20a. On the council's powers, L. von Spittler, *Geschichte des Wirtembergischen Geheimen-Raths-Collegiums,* in *Sämtliche Werke,* ed. K. Wächter, XIII (Stuttgart and Tübingen, 1837), 424.

15. Protestant historians of earlier generations have incorrectly stressed the possibility of forced conversions in the duchy. Though one need not accept at face value the Catholic apologia of Tüchle's *Die Kirchenpolitik des Herzogs,* it does seem clear that Carl Alexander himself had no interest in forcing Catholicism upon his subjects.

the Landtag and its exclusive control over and general exemption from taxation. They had also brought a new kind of personality into government, a cadre of fiscal speculators, commercial entrepreneurs, courtiers, and military officers—men who could in no sense be regarded as professional civil servants.[16] The most important of them came from outside the duchy with no formal education and no previous experience in territorial administration. And even those native Württembergers who before joining Carl Alexander's entourage had worked in government service or taken legal degrees gave no indication that they approached their offices with the professional values of the bureaucrat.

Supported exclusively by the favor of the duke, these men saw themselves as instruments of the prince rather than as administrators of a legally regulated system. The duke's needs determined their assessments of all problems and in their eyes justified riding roughshod over standardized procedures. But while often ruthless in their dealings and venal in their ambitions, the crown agents were not always the unequivocal villains that their opponents among the estates and in the professional bureaucracy maintained them to be. Much of their activity prefigured policies that later centuries accepted as desirable.[17] Yet their imperfect grasp of economic principles meant that many of their projects aborted or produced unanticipated dislocations. And since the best of them were Jews and Catholics and thus stood outside Württemberg's Lutheran culture, their critics found it all too easy to link their mistakes with the evils of religious, hence moral, error.[18]

Joseph Süss Oppenheimer (died 1738) pioneered most of the fiscal

16. On this new type of courtier as a European phenomenon, see Werner Sombart, *Luxus und Kapitalismus* (Munich and Leipzig, 1913), 2–44 and 77–111. On the Jewish component of the new group, see Heinrich Schnee, *Die Hoffinanz und der moderne Staat: Geschichte und System der Hoffaktoren an deutschen Fürstenhöfen im Zeitalter des Absolutismus*, 6 vols. (Berlin, 1953–1967). Volume IV (1963), 87–178, contains a section on Württemberg.

17. On the much-debated problem of the relationship that cameralist policies bore to the formation of a territorial economic system, see Georg von Below, "Der Untergang der mittelalterlichen Stadtwirtschaft: Ueber den Begriff der Territorialwirtschaft," in his *Probleme der Wirtschaftsgeschichte* (Tübingen, 1920), 501–620; Hans Spangenberg, *Territorialwirtschaft und Stadtwirtschaft* (Munich, 1932); and Friedrich Lütge, *Studien zur Sozial- und Wirtschaftsgeschichte* (Stuttgart, 1963), 281–335. On the nineteenth century, see Heinrich Heffter, *Die deutsche Selbstverwaltung im 19. Jahrhundert* (Stuttgart, 1950); and Ernst-Wolfgang Böckenförde, *Die deutsche verfassungsgeschichtliche Forschung im 19. Jahrhundert* (Berlin, 1961).

18. The superficiality of the contemporary understanding of these economic and fiscal experiments is made clear in the pamphlet literature; see the collection of these satires and commentaries in LBS, Hist. 2° Nr. 348, Süssiana.

innovations. Known as "Jud Süss," or Jew Süss, he first entered Württemberg history as Carl Alexander's resident agent at Frankfurt am Main. There he negotiated advantageous contracts for the bullion supply for the Württemberg mint and arranged the final financial settlement for Countess Würben, by that time a *persona non grata* in Württemberg.[19] In 1735 Carl Alexander summoned Süss to Stuttgart as his court factor and charged him with raising funds. The duke needed cash not only to stabilize the treasury after the extravagances of the previous reign but also to maintain the twelve thousand–man army he had determined to keep on active duty after the War of the Polish Succession (1733–1735). The larger council of the Landtag had emphatically refused its support for a peacetime force virtually twice the size of Eberhard Ludwig's standing army and was insisting that if the duke wanted a permanent army on that scale, he would have to pay for it himself.[20] Carl Alexander accepted the challenge. While governor of Serbia he had sponsored a series of successful projects to raise money for the government, and by hiring Süss he hoped to repeat the achievement in Württemberg.

Süss set up a series of schemes and programs aimed at strengthening the fisc. They differed only in detail from the cameralistic ventures then in vogue within the larger states of Austria, Prussia, and Bavaria, and they recalled many of the strategies employed some hundred years earlier by Charles I in his struggle to free the English monarchy from financial dependence upon Parliament.[21] Both Süss and Carl Alexander shared the cameralistic conviction that the treasury formed the heart of the state and that money constituted the driving force of the government; in other words they regarded finance as their primary area of battle. They launched their campaign on a number of fronts, the first of which involved an attack on the Württemberg tax structure. They did not assault the estates' control over

19. On the Würben settlement, see p. 193 n58. For Süss's childhood and early career, see S. Stern, *Jud Süss: Ein Beitrag zur deutschen und zur jüdischen Geschichte* (Berlin, 1929), 1–47; also Heinrich Schnee, *Die Hoffinanz*, IV, 109–125 and VI, 57–70.

20. F. Wintterlin, "Wehrverfassung und Landesverfassung im Herzogtum Württemberg," *WVJHLG*, 34 (1928), 239–256; W. Grube, *Der Stuttgarter Landtag 1457–1957* (Stuttgart, 1957), 391–392.

21. Werner Sombart, *Der moderne Kapitalismus*, I (Leipzig, 1902), 336; A. Small, *The Cameralists* (Chicago, 1909), 332–393; Schnee, *Die Hoffinanz*, I, 49–145; and Anton Tautscher, *Staatswirtschaftslehre des Kameralismus* (Bern, 1947). Cf. M. Walker, "Rights and Functions: The Social Categories of Eighteenth-Century German Jurists and Cameralists," *JMH*, 50 (1978), 234–251; J. H. Elliott, "Self-perception and Decline in Early Seventeenth-Century Spain," *PP*, 74 (1977), 41–61; and M. Barkhausen, "Governmental Control and Free Enterprise in Western Europe and the Low Countries during the 18th Century," in Peter Earle, ed., *Essays in European Economic History, 1500–1800* (Oxford, 1974), 212–273.

direct taxation but sought rather to circumvent it by imposing indirect taxes from which the revenue flowed directly into their own
hands. Accordingly Carl Alexander, acting on recommendations from
Süss, introduced a series of surcharges on such items as playing cards
and writing paper. He then farmed out their collection to foreigners,
most of whom belonged to Jewish firms such as the Frankfurt House
of Moses Drach and Partners.[22] It is not surprising that such measures infuriated the Württembergers, rich as well as poor. The Ehrbarkeit took particular alarm. For quite apart from the fact that these
indirect taxes applied to all consumers and thus took no account of
the customary exemptions on the basis of rank, the municipal and
prelatal leaders recognized that such levies undercut the estates' control over the collection of taxes and the administration of the tax
system.

Even more threatening to the Württemberg officials were the new
government agencies that Carl Alexander created and, to the chagrin
of the traditional officeholders, staffed with his own men. The duke
endowed these agencies with what amounted to prescriptive rights
against the numerous families in the Ehrbarkeit who had been using
their government offices to screen them from taxes. The *Fiskalamt*,
which he set up in 1736, became especially notorious. It was charged
officially with providing an instance of first hearing for those Württemberg officials suspected of financial improprieties against the state.
In reality, however, the board functioned more like a kangaroo court
than a grand jury. Under Süss's prodding the commissioners did not
wait for cases to be presented to them by the agencies. Instead they
initiated charges against mayors and local officials whom they suspected of avoiding taxes. Led by the director of the duke's cabinet, a
former professor of law at Tübingen, Dr. Johann Theodor Schäffer
(1687–1748), the commissioners in effect extorted moneys from those
civil officials who were otherwise exempt from taxation.[23] Account books showed fines ranging from one to thirteen thousand florins and recorded rural as well as urban "offenders." There were even
instances of retroactive prosecution, one of the most notorious of
which involved the heirs of a village official, a wealthy peasant Schultheiss named Rogler. His children paid the commissioners 3,000 flor-

22. Elwenspoek, *Jew Süss Oppenheimer*, 76–82; A. Reyscher, *Vollständige, historisch und kritisch bearbeitete Sammlung der württembergsichen Gesetze*, XVII
(Stuttgart and Tübingen, 1848), Nr. 74.

23. HSAS, A 202: Bü. 67 contains Schäffer's correspondence with Carl Alexander.
On Schäffer's career, see W. Pfeilsticker, *Neues württembergisches Dienerbuch* (Stuttgart, 1957), 1108, 1140, 1163, 1298, 1328.

ins and 10 Eimer of wine for crimes that the board claimed the old
judge had committed back in Eberhard Ludwig's reign.[24]

The *Gratialamt* was another, equally unpopular board. Its primary
purpose was to obtain money for the crown through what amounted
to the sale of public offices. Jacob Friedrich Hallwachs (died 1763),
who had been brought to Stuttgart by Süss, took the lead in this enterprise.[25] Under the pretext of collecting donations of gratitude to
the duke—hence the name Gratialamt—he and his commissioners
operated as official brokers for government appointments. Those who
desired confirmation or appointment were expected to donate to the
commission and, according to the size of their gifts, to receive varying
degrees of endorsement from the board. Since the duke acted in most
instances upon the recommendation of the commissioners, a letter of
unqualified support from the board became tantamount to appointment. When the records of the Gratialamt became public after Carl
Alexander's death, the commissioners were shown to have sold offices
and privileges ranging in importance from that of overseer of the public bathhouse in the town of Marbach (120 florins) to confirmation as
Bürgermeister of Stuttgart (7,750 florins).[26]

Aggressive fiscal politics hit the officials in other ways as well. Immediately upon his accession, Carl Alexander ordered all government
employees "to help meet pressing expenses" by contributing one-
eighth of their annual salaries to the Rentkammer. New and future
employees were to surrender 25 percent of their first-year wages.[27]
After Süss's arrival, the duke followed these preliminary levies with
an annual assessment called the *Besoldungs Groschen*, whereby officials contributed three kreuzer out of every florin of their salaries toward the establishment of a government fund for civil service employees.[28] The principle behind the fund was a solid one; namely, that an
endowment for salaries would guarantee the government's ability to
maintain regular payments in times of emergency. But to the officials
the tax appeared nothing short of robbery. They saw it as simply a
government measure to raise ready cash and were convinced that the
proceeds would go only to enrich speculators such as Salomon Mayer,

24. HSAS, A 53 I: Bü. 20, 21, 25, 41, 43. Also, Stern, *Jud Süss*, 99–104 and Akten
43; Elwenspoek, *Jew Süss*, 86–106; and Schnee, *Hoffinanz*, IV, 139f.

25. F. Wintterlin, *Geschichte der Behördenorganisation in Württemberg*, I (Stuttgart, 1904), 71. On Hallwachs, see Pfeilsticker, *Dienerbuch*, 2045 and 2835.

26. HSAS, A 53 I: Bü. 4, 6, 11; Stern, *Jud Süss*, 95–97; Elwenspoek, *Jew Süss*
86–106; and Schnee, *Die Hoffinanz*, IV, 138f.

27. HSAS, A 202: Bü. 1869 (esp. letters of 13 January and 8 April 1734); Reyscher,
*Vollständige Sammlung*, XVI, 444.

28. Reyscher, *Vollständige Sammlung*, XVII, 477.

a Jewish business associate of Süss, whose capitalist ventures the government was backing.[29]

More serious for the Ehrbarkeit as a whole was the mandate given to the *Pupillenamt*, a board charged with the care of orphaned children. Though the estates secured its radical restructuring under the regency, thereby ensuring that the board never functioned in any comprehensive manner, its creation marked another effort by the crown to bring the territorial officials under tighter fiscal control. Carl Alexander set up the agency ostensibly to manage the properties of those civil servants who died leaving orphaned children.[30] As with the Besoldungs Groschen the initial rationale was a sound one: such a system protected the orphan's inheritance and prevented the social dislocation that might otherwise have resulted from the dissipation of the child's assets. Unfortunately, because Süss, Mayer, and Hallwachs served as its three principals, the Pupillenamt immediately became a popular symbol of the government's tyranny and fiscal corruption. Though it is impossible to verify financial impropriety from the documents that came to light at Süss's trial, it does become clear that the Ehrbarkeit despised the board as an unwarranted intrusion by the state into the private affairs of its citizens.

The Württemberg officials objected especially to the crown's unprecedented scrutiny of their personal assets. For in order to standardize and centralize its records, the Pupillenamt claimed the right to evaluate all estates for purposes of death duties and to charge a fee for this task. Moreover, in the case of orphans the board itself took sole responsibility for the investment of the income generated by the principal in the estate. Carl Alexander charged the board with placing this money in capital instruments of its own choosing and authorizing the collection of a management fee as well. The board was empowered to deduct an annual carrying charge of 4 to 5 percent of the testator's net worth and to debit each trust for all expenses incurred in the support and maintenance of the heirs. The fees were to continue until a male child reached majority or a female child married. At that time the board was expected to dissolve the trust and, after collecting a settlement fee of 25 percent of that year's income, to surrender the assets to the heir. Given the carrying charges and the crown's involvement in a series of shaky economic ventures, it is understandable that the officials fought against placing the fortunes of their orphaned relatives in the hands of the state. But additionally their

29. On Mayer, see Stern, *Jud Süss*, 102–103, 111, 156, 287. For popular reaction to the tax, see HSAS, A 53 I: Bü. 25, 41, 43.
30. Wintterlin, *Behördenorganisation*, I, 78.

resistance to the crown's arbitrary fiscal policies reflected their own perception of the Württemberg state. They still regarded the state in corporate rather than unitary terms and endowed each corps with certain inalienable rights. The crown's refusal to recognize these rights thus constituted an attack upon the social as well as the political foundations of the state as they conceived it.[31]

Arbitrary assessments on government officials, the sale of offices, and indirect taxes formed only a part of Carl Alexander's larger fiscal strategy. To obtain a flow of unencumbered cash sufficient to enable him to run the government without dependence upon the estates, he sought to exploit more effectively those properties under the direct control of the crown. These included not only the forests, streams, and pastures of the crown domain (Landschreiberei) but also the holdings of the ducal trust (Kammerschreiberei), which were the farms and woodlands reserved by Eberhard III for the maintenance and support of the House of Württemberg. Eberhard Ludwig had managed these assets in an exceedingly capricious manner. On the occasions when he needed money to stave off pressing creditors or to meet payments on his building projects, he had never hesitated to invade his capital base. Indeed he had pawned the entire property of Weiltingen, one of the largest contiguous holdings in the Landschreiberei, to the estates for 330,000 florins and had lost control over numerous more minor holdings. He let, for example, the great forest of Freudenstadt to the Aemter of Dornstadt, Freudenstadt, and Reichenbach; mortgaged the market properties of Erlsbach, Dürrweiler, and Waldeck; and in exchange for ready cash issued unfavorable long-term leases on the crown houses in the town of Ludwigsburg.[32]

Carl Alexander sought to reverse this trend. Where possible he used the moneys generated by his new taxes to buy up the leases and to pay off the loans.[33] He also forbade further alienation of state property. Equally important, he and Süss reorganized the Rentkammer so as to obtain a better management of these lands. Ignoring the protests of the civil servants who traditionally supervised crown farms, Süss called in adventurous capitalists and allowed competitive bidding for concessions on the management and marketing of the cat-

---

31. HSAS, A 53 I: Bü. 4, 6, 11. H. Tüchle, *Die Kirchenpolitik des Herzogs*, 125f., stresses the positive potential of the board.

32. On Weiltingen, see HSAS, LB: Bü. 376–378; A 203: Bü. 91; A 281: Bü. 596; also E. Lempp, "Philipp Heinrich Weissensee," *BWKG*, 31 (1927), 114–167. For the other properties, see Stern, *Jud Süss*, 50f.

33. K. Müller, "Die Finanzwirtschaft in Württemberg unter Herzog Karl Alexander (1733–1737)," *WVJHLG*, 38 (1932), 289–291.

tle herds and dairies.[34] He published and circulated throughout the duchy standardized price lists on wine, bread, and meat products. With these lists as guidelines, he regulated the procedure used by local officials in accounting to the crown for the income from the ducal properties in the Aemter. Although the Amtmann continued the practice of first deducting his administrative expenses from the gross profits on the crown properties, he now did so on a controlled basis. The new system required each Amtmann to submit a budget to the central treasury, which included precise cost figures and estimates on the cash value of the surpluses from the crown properties in his Amt.[35] In this way the crown obtained a clearer picture of its anticipated income and could arrange its expenses accordingly.

Süss's results were impressive. Reconstructions from Landschreiberei records, which are quite complete for these years, show that crown income increased at a cumulative rate of 52 percent for the reign.[36] Payments from the Aemter provided the principal source for this growth. Whereas in 1733 receipts from the crown lands in the Aemter totaled 138,580 florins and accounted for only 32.4 percent of the duke's income, they had more than doubled by 1736 (299,260 florins) and by that time formed almost one-half (46.1 percent) the total revenue.[37] During that same period contributions from the estates to the crown fell from 20.6 percent (88,340 florins) of the duke's income to 13.1 percent (84,590 florins).[38] It is also interesting to note that very little of the controversial new tax income went into the ducal account: in 1736, for example, only 38,150 florins of the 76,300 florins paid into the Fiskalamt found their way into the Landschreiberei.[39] The remainder apparently went to pay the expenses of the agency and of informers.

District reports indicated that the rise in revenue for the central treasury resulted from the tighter administrative control that Süss introduced in the Aemter rather than from inflation or, more important, from an increase in agricultural production. What Süss and his agents had done was to make expropriation the chief business of gov-

34. W. Söll, "Die staatliche Wirtschaftspolitik in Württemberg im 17. und 18. Jahrhundert (Tübingen: Ph.D. diss., 1934), 97–100.
35. Reyscher, Vollständige Sammlung, XIV, 185ff. (Generalreskript of 2 October 1736).
36. Müller, "Die Finanzwirtschaft in Württemberg," 310, reconstructs income figures as follows: (1733) 427,740 florins; (1734) 482,510 florins; (1735) 581,240 florins; (1736) 649,110 florins.
37. Ibid.
38. Ibid., 303–304.
39. Ibid., 307.

ernment.[40] They did this not by force per se but by a systematic rationalization of the traditional controls over the people. Furthermore they applied these controls without regard to corporate status or traditional privilege, adding something fundamentally new to the concept of the state. At least in financial terms the state now related to the inhabitants as individuals rather than as vested interest groups. It is not surprising therefore that those persons committed to a political system based upon the latter concept responded with almost hysterical rage. And quite apart from constitutional arguments, they justified their opposition by pointing out that, while Süss and the others were skilled at extraction, they were proving decidedly less talented at the accumulation and investment of capital.

Neither Süss nor Carl Alexander concerned himself in any depth with production. In early mercantilist fashion they concentrated more on cash profits than on a systematic program for restructuring the duchy's commercial and industrial base. The Württemberg economy had scarcely changed between the late sixteenth and early eighteenth centuries. By the 1730s the population had virtually recovered its early-seventeenth-century strength and stood somewhere around 428,000 inhabitants, with an approximate density of forty-eight people per square kilometer.[41] These eighteenth-century men and women, like their ancestors, relied primarily upon local markets for the sale of their wine, cattle, and agrarian products. What extraterritorial trade they undertook centered almost exclusively upon wine export, and much of that trade lay in foreign hands.[42] Carl Alexander made only sporadic and largely unsuccessful efforts to change this situation. His primary strategy was to set up manufacturing ventures that he then supported in classic fashion with privileges of tax exemption and monopoly.

On 15 August 1735, for example, he granted rights of monopoly to

40. The fiscalization of government took place elsewhere in Europe, and the implication of this process for the state is drawn in Rudolf Braun, "Taxation, Sociopolitical Structure, and State-Building: Great Britain and Brandenburg-Prussia," in Charles Tilly, ed., *The Formation of National States in Western Europe* (Princeton, 1975), 243–327. In that same volume see also Gabriel Ardant, "Financial Policy and Economic Infrastructure of Modern States and Nations," 164–242.

41. Helen Liebel-Weckowicz, "The Politics of Poverty and Reform: Modernization and Reform in Eighteenth-Century Württemberg," *The Consortium on Revolutionary Europe Proceedings* (Athens, Ga., 1981), 83; cf. Ludwig Elster/Adolf Weber/Friedrich Wieser, *Handwörterbuch der Staatswissenschaften*, II (Jena, 1924), 673.

42. For a contemporary traveler's observations on the early-eighteenth-century Württemberg economy, see Johann Georg Keyssler, *Neüeste Reise durch Teütschland* . . . (Hanover, 1740), 95ff. The notes to Chapter 1 provide a bibliography of the secondary literature on the early modern Württemberg economy.

the Dutch entrepreneur Peter Rigal, who had come to Stuttgart in the last years of Eberhard Ludwig's reign and set up a stocking mill. The patent called for Rigal to undertake domestic mulberry cultivation. To that end the crown leased him thirty Morgens of land between Stuttgart and Maulbronn with rights to import foreign workers (Dutch Calvinists) for planting. The duke also granted a tax-exempt status to the business, its owners, and employees.[43] In 1736 similar privileges went to a linen manufacturer at Urach.[44] Neither project prospered. Additional ventures in salt, leather, and tobacco monopolies likewise foundered. In each instance the duke let contracts to speculators, who in exchange for a lump payment to the crown received exclusive rights to the supply and sale of the commodity. These men either parlayed their concessions into immediate profit through advantageous resale, or they opened for business without an adequate capital foundation. In either event, as the case of the tobacco concession demonstrated, the enterprise suffered.

At the first stage of the tobacco venture, a firm of Palatine Jews, composed of Jacob Bensheim, Koppel Wolf Brühl, and Meyer Wassertrüdingen, obtained concessionary rights. Carl Alexander granted the firm exclusive powers to buy and sell tobacco within the duchy. In exchange the partners guaranteed an annual payment of 8,000 florins to the duke, with the understanding that after two years this sum would be increased to 10,000 florins and remain fixed thereafter at that amount They also promised to establish local plantations and factories for the production and manufacture of tobacco products in Württemberg. But after making an initial payment of 8,000 florins to Stuttgart, the partners sold their privileges for an undisclosed sum, presumably a figure somewhere above the 8,000 florins they had already expended. The purchaser was another speculator active in the Palatinate, a Spaniard with the impressive name of Don Barthelemi Pancorbo d'Ayala et Guerra. He promised the Württemberg crown 12,000 florins a year plus 500 florins in customs revenue and, in addition to approval of the purchase, received authorization to open factories at Ludwigsburg and Stuttgart.

Don Barthelemi typified a particular kind of eighteenth-century fiscal adventurer who flourished at the various German courts in the heady days of cameralistic experimentation. His activities reflected on a smaller scale and in the context of domestic industry the kind of ambitious promotion that the South Sea Company in England and John Law's company of the Indies in France were undertaking. Before

43. Reyscher, *Vollständige Sammlung*, XIV, 161 ff.
44. Stern, *Jud Süss*, 70.

coming to Stuttgart he had persuaded Elector Karl Philipp of the Palatinate to grant him a salt and tobacco monopoly, and he put forward projects for the construction of a highway between Düsseldorf and Mannheim. He had also promoted schemes for an independent Palatine postal service. All these projects had failed, and his plans for Württemberg turned out to be no exception to the pattern.[45] Upon arriving at Stuttgart Don Barthelemi set about raising investment capital from within the Württemberg financial community. He attracted funds, primarily from the recently established territorial bank; but since neither he nor his backers completely understood the imperatives of capital formation, they underfinanced the factories. The plants opened with great fanfare only to close because they lacked capital to continue operations after initial production setbacks had drained current accounts. Those who had invested in the project lost everything.[46]

An attempt to set up a state bank failed for similar reasons. Süss, and Carl Alexander for that matter, accepted completely the emphasis placed on the importance of banking by the two late-seventeenth-century cameralists Johann Joachim Becher and Wilhelm von Schröder. Impressed by the success of the Bank of England, which had been established in 1694, and by the more recent establishment of the Banco del Giro and the Staatsbank in Vienna, the duke on 22 October 1735 ordered the formation of a Württemberg bank. Its official charge was to handle capital deposits, to regulate coinage exchange, and to stimulate industrial growth. Carl Alexander placed the bank under the direction of the governors of the Württemberg mint, of which Süss was chairman, and instructed these men to solicit funds at a guaranteed annual interest rate of 8 percent. They secured the deposits with the gold and silver of the Stuttgart mint and sought to stimulate investment by obtaining a ducal edict that forbid the other moneylenders in the duchy to offer more than a 5 percent return on deposits. Despite its favorable terms the bank could not attract sufficient capital to become stabilized as a permanent institution.[47] Civil

45. On Don Barthelemi's Palatine adventures, see Heinrich von Feder, *Geschichte der Stadt Mannheim* (Mannheim, 1875), 376 ff.
46. O. Linckh, "Das Tabakmonopol in Württemberg," *WJ* (1893), 201 ff.; A. Schott, "Merkantilpolitisches aus Württembergs Herzogszeit," *WJ* (1900), 245 ff. Cf. W. Boelcke, "Ein Herzoglich-Württembergischer Regiebetrieb des ausgehenden 18. Jahrhunderts," *Jahrbücher für Nationalökonomie und Statistik,* 175 (1963), 53–75. Comparative analyses on European problems in money and credit are found in Isser Woloch, *Eighteenth-Century Europe: Tradition and Progress, 1715–1789* (New York, 1982), 119–135; and in chapter 7 of Jan de Vries, *The Economy of Europe in an Age of Crisis, 1600–1715* (New York, 1978).
47. Stern, *Jud Süss,* 78–80. On problems of undercapitalization in these early Württemberg ventures, see W. Boelcke, "Die Wirtschaft in der Zeit des Spätmerkantilismus

servants distrusted the venture; independent moneylenders surreptitiously undercut the bank's rates; and the governors lent unwisely to speculative schemes such as those of Don Barthelemi. Local hostility to these fiscal ventures must not be thought of as unique to Württemberg. Following Law's failure, the French proved reluctant to found a national bank on the English model and thus doomed their state to dependence on private financiers for credit. Prussian merchants withheld support from Frederick the Great's bank, and the Austrian estates steadfastly refused to invest in the Banco del Giro. The Prussian salt monopoly likewise generated bitter hostility in that country.[48] In part, of course, local opposition everywhere was justified in economically rational terms. These enterprises were often ill conceived, unscrupulously managed, and inadequately funded. But at least in Württemberg they failed primarily for political reasons that drew their strength from the widespread outrage within the Ehrbarkeit at what its members perceived as a threat to their very identity.

Most Württembergers with liquid capital belonged to the Ehrbarkeit, and this group quite correctly identified these schemes as aimed at emancipating the crown from the fiscal control of the estates and hence as constituting a princely attack upon the corporate, patrimonial order of the state. They correctly saw that such policies would make them dependent upon a government that they could no longer influence. Government control of the economy undermined not only the unimpeded trade guaranteed by the constitution but also the economic order of the guilds on which the Ehrbarkeit's political power rested. Cultural loyalties compounded the problem; support for these projects demanded a capitalist interest and mentality that ran counter to Martin Luther's strictures against usury and to the traditional Lutheran emphasis upon the just price (*justum pretium*).

Finally, the Württembergers associated the programs with the ambitions of foreigners, particularly of Jews like Süss whom they neither understood nor trusted. And Süss's widely circulated bon mot about the Württembergers—"To make a Swabian anything higher than a transport councilor is to make him too much"—suggests that he at least reciprocated their feelings. Until the time of Carl Alexander, Jews had been permitted to reside officially in only three small towns

---

(1770–1780)," XI, 4, *Historischer Atlas von Baden-Württemberg* (Stuttgart, 1977), 1–15.

48. Herbert Kisch, *Prussian Mercantilism and the Rise of the Prussian Silk Industry* (Philadelphia, 1968); Wilhelm G. F. Roscher, "Oesterreichische Nationalökonomie unter Leopold I," *Jahrbücher für Nationalökonomie und Statistik* (1864); and Erhard Dittrich, *Die deutschen und oesterreichischen Kameralisten* (Darmstadt, 1974).

So prangte Joseph Süss in seinen Eh-
:ren Tagen,
Der als gebohr ner Jud so Herꝛ
als Land betrog,
Den Würtemberg verflucht u: den der Schinderwagen
Nach Urtheil und nach Recht zum eisern Galgen zog.

This posthumous engraving of Süss Oppenheimer shows him in luxurious dress and at the height of his power. But note the instruments of torture hanging just to the left of his head and the drawing depicting his gruesome death in the cartouche below the figure. Photograph courtesy of the Landesbibliothek Stuttgart.

of the duchy: Gochsheim, Aldingen, and Freudenthal.[49] When the duke expanded these privileges to allow greater freedom of settlement at Stuttgart and Ludwigsburg, migration began at once.[50] Increased proximity must have fused with popular resentment over the cameralistic ventures, almost all of which had strong Jewish participation; by the end of the reign anti-Semitic lampoons were featured in virtually all the satirical pamphlets and songs circulating against the government.[51] Mounting prejudice found a particularly nasty expression in the spectacular trial of Süss that followed Carl Alexander's death. A special commission found him guilty of moral corruption and violation of the country's laws, and Süss met his death at a public execution attended by thousands of hostile spectators. His judges ordered him bound in a specially constructed iron cage, which was hoisted to the top of the Stuttgart gallows where Süss, still imprisoned inside, was hanged by the neck until dead.[52]

The public spectacle of the execution harked back to earlier times and reminds us once again of the degree to which the attitudes and values of the Reformation years still pervaded the broader ranks of Württemberg society. Discussions of cosmopolitan royal policies and quasi-modern fiscal problems must not obscure the fact that, outside the palace and the offices of central government, Württemberg remained a preindustrial, overwhelmingly rural society. Even the capital city retained its medieval walls and almost all Stuttgarters—rich as well as poor—lived, worked, and worshiped in fifteenth-, sixteenth-, or early-seventeenth-century buildings. Education for town as well as country remained a virtual monopoly of the established church and in any meaningful sense was confined to the higher social orders. Indeed the village peasants who thronged to Stuttgart to scorn Süss as a devil were scarcely distinguishable from the vast majority of the townsmen whom they jostled there in front of the Gothic Rathaus where Süss hung. And everywhere there flourished that passionate resistance to change and deep-seated hostility to foreign ways which had characterized Württemberg society since the sixteenth century.

49. Hoffaktors appear to have been a major exception to this rule; see Schnee, *Die Hoffinanz*, IV, 87–109.

50. K. von Riecke, *Verfassung, Verwaltung und Staatshaushalt des Königreiches Württemberg* (Stuttgart, 1887), 91 ff.; Carl Alexander's patent is reprinted in Stern, *Jud Süss*, Akten 47 (3 January 1737).

51. H. Hayn, "Süss-Oppenheimer-Bibliographie," *Zeitschrift für Bücherfreunde*, VII (1904/05), 448 ff., provides an index of these lampoons, several of which are reprinted in Elwenspoek, *Jew Süss Oppenheimer, passim*.

52. Eyewitness accounts of the execution are found in *Bericht, umständlicher, von der Execution des Juden Süss Oppenheimers* (Stuttgart, 1738). As part of the anti-

THE MAKING OF A STATE

At least on the surface the regency for the nine-year-old Carl Eugen restored the old political order. It returned the government to its traditional form and dropped most of the economic and fiscal programs that had provoked the Ehrbarkeit to violent rage. The Protestant ascendancy at court also banked the worst of the confessional fears, so that popular unrest quieted as well. Fundamental differences remained, however, and in vital ways the estates and officials found themselves like Humpty Dumpty fallen from the wall—they just could not put themselves back together again. Though sent to Protestant Berlin for his education, the crown prince remained a practicing Roman Catholic. Even more significant from the perspective of the Ehrbarkeit was the fact that Carl Alexander's rationalized fiscal policies had set a precedent that was not to be reversed. The state remained a presence in the Württemberg economy in ways that it had never been before. Government supervision of markets continued, as did the formulation and publication of price indexes and efforts to standardize domestic commerce. By the same token the crown sustained its stricter control over the state domain, by far the largest economic bloc in the duchy. Amt officials now accounted more precisely for these properties and managed them in direct response to the crown's fiscal needs. The leasing of privileged concessions for the herds, dairies, stud farms, timbering, and mining in these holdings became standard practice, so that the crown continued to strengthen such lessees with government assets while protecting them from more sophisticated business competition in the neighboring imperial cities and from the enmity of the town guilds.[53]

In addition Carl Eugen resumed his father's practice of supporting industrial ventures. Throughout his reign he placed state money behind a steady stream of industrial projects, one of which, the Ludwigsburg Porcelain Manufacture, continues to this day. Yet despite the fact that the bulk of these projects yielded only limited re-

Semitic campaign launched in 1939 by the National Socialist government, Oppenheimer became the subject of a film, *Jud Süss* (1940), directed by Veit Harlan. Heinrich Himmler required all SS and Police Corps groups to view the film and had it shown in those regions where Jews were to be sent to concentration camps. For additional information, see Lief Furhmmar and Volke Isaksson, *Politics and Film*, trans. K. French (New York, 1971).

53. This tighter economic control from the center fit into a larger European pattern. See Carl-August Agena, *Der Amtmann im 17. und 18. Jahrhundert: Ein Beitrag zur Geschichte des Richter-und Beamtentums* (Göttingen, 1972); Roland Mousnier, "État et Commissaire," in Roland Mousnier, *La plume, la faucille et le marteau* (Paris, 1970), 179–200; and Otto Hintze, "Der Commissarius und seine Bedeutung in der allgemeinen Verwaltungsgeschichte," in Hintze, *Staat und Verfassung*, ed. G. Oestreich, 2d ed. (Göttingen, 1962), 242–274.

sults, they advanced the principle that economics constituted a legitimate concern of the state.[54] And despite their short-term failures, these eighteenth-century cameralistic efforts laid the foundations for nineteenth-century industrialization. It cannot be an accident that modern industry arose in Baden and Württemberg in the very regions where eighteenth-century enterprises had struggled: the Neckar Basin, the plains of the Upper Rhine, and the foothills of the Alps.[55] Moreover, the experience acquired in earlier experiments undoubtedly increased the economic sophistication of the Württembergers. At least some of them had acquired a dawning appreciation of the potential value of a commercial and industrial production that transcended local guild monopolies and drew upon territorial rather than regional resources and markets. But these industrial ventures produced negative as well as positive effects. There is no doubt that they constituted an assault by the crown upon a social order established on principles of local rather than state monopoly. And the sense of dislocation and social disintegration associated in the municipal magistrates' minds with state industrial development persisted into the nineteenth century. In this larger sense the embittered opposition that vested local interests mounted against Süss set the stage for the struggle between state and community that dominated so large a portion of nineteenth-century domestic politics.[56]

The Ehrbarkeit's sense of social and political disintegration was not without foundation. The magistrates saw in the Aemter, the very cornerstone of their territorial political power, the beginnings of what must have seemed to them a revolution. In seeking popular support to counter the Ehrbarkeit's opposition to his fiscal policies, Carl Alexander had pressured the districts to increase peasant participation in local political affairs. His strategy in this regard appeared to derive entirely from his own political perceptions. That is, the peasants

54. See K. -G. Krauter, "Die Manufakturen im Herzogtum Württemberg und ihre Föderung durch die Wirtembergische Regierung in der zweiten Hälfte des 18. Jahrhunderts" (Tübingen: Ph.D. diss., 1951); Arthur Schott, "Wirtschaftliches Leben," in Albert Pfister, gen. ed., *Herzog Carl Eugen von Württemberg und seine Zeit*, I (Stuttgart, 1906), 313–360; and M. Walker, *Johann Jakob Moser and the Holy Roman Empire of the German Nation* (Chapel Hill, N.C., 1981), 199–208.

55. This point becomes especially evident in W. Zorn, *Handels- und Industriegeschichte Bayerisch-Schwabens, 1648–1870: Wirtschafts-, Sozial- und Kulturgeschichte des Schwäbischen Unternehmertums* (Augsburg, 1961), 12–205; and in Wolfram Fischer, "Ansätze zur Industrialisierung in Baden 1770–1870," VSWG, 47 (1960), 186–231. See also the industrial map with text by W. A. Boelcke in XI, 4, *Historischer Atlas von Baden-Württemberg* (Stuttgart, 1977).

56. M. Walker, *German Home Towns: Community, State, and General Estate, 1648–1871* (Ithaca, 1971), 248–431; also G. A. Hillery, Jr., *Communal Organizations: A Study of Local Societies* (Chicago, 1968).

themselves do not seem to have pressed at this time for an expanded political role. Instead the villages remained comparatively isolated from one another and continued to govern themselves in a virtually autonomous manner. While the upheavals of the Thirty Years War had given peasant leadership a greater participation in the election of Landtag delegates, these rural leaders had been slow to push for a larger role in the most important political decisions.[57] If life in the Amt Nürtingen was at all typical—and there is no reason to assume otherwise—village affairs still proceeded without appreciation of the potential in district government.[58]

Recall that the Amt provided an intermediate organization between the community and the state. Territorial law regarded the Amt as an incorporated political body (*Köperschaft*) with responsibilities both to the state and to local inhabitants. For the former it served as an administrative branch of the central government and as a member of, and hence an electoral district for, the Landtag. But for the persons residing in the area it functioned as a political corporation with its own internal dynamics and administrative autonomy. As in the case of the crown's mortgaging of the great forest of Freudenstadt, an individual Amt could acquire property and contract debts in its own name. Amt officials collected the taxes voted by the Landtag and controlled recruitment for the territorial militia. Each Amt levied its own assessments and provided health care and welfare as well as fire and police services and maintenance for the roads and bridges in its area. As with the affairs of the Landtag, so in these internal matters responsibility rested with the district assembly or a small standing committee. In either case control was vested in the municipal authorities of the *Amtstadt*, the ranking district town.

Carl Alexander sought to weaken the Ehrbarkeit's influence by expanding village participation in the internal management of the districts. Voting rights were crucial to this strategy, and here the crown relied upon an edict of 1702 known as the *Kommunalordnung*.[59] Par-

57. See pp. 105–109 of this book.
58. I am grateful to Prof. David Sabean, then a research fellow at the Max Planck Institute, Göttingen, for sharing his insights on peasant participation in the Amt Nürtingen and more specifically on village life in Neckarhausen, 1750–1850. Recent studies of related, though indirect interest are Günther Franz, *Geschichte des deutschen Bauernstandes von frühen Mittelalter bis zum 19. Jahrhundert* (Stuttgart, 1970); L. K. Berkner, "Inheritance, Land Tenure, and Peasant Family Structure: A German Regional Comparison," in Joan Thirsk, J. Goody, and E. P. Thompson, eds., *Family and Inheritance* (New York, 1976), 71–95; Robert Brenner, "Agrarian Class Structure and Economic Development in pre-Industrial Europe," *PP*, 120 (1976), 30–75; and Heidi Wunder, "Peasant Organization and Class Conflict in East and West Germany," *PP*, 128 (1978), 47–55.
59. Reyscher, *Vollständige Sammlung*, XIII, 755 ff.

agraph 10 of that document stipulated that only six delegates from the Amtstadt could attend a general assembly of the district. Lesser towns could send three delegates each; the larger villages two; and the communities one. But while this arrangement secured an automatic majority of peasant delegates at any assembly, it did not guarantee them control over the meetings. The edict said nothing about voting rights. The result was that, though larger numbers of village officials attended the Amtsversammlungen, local custom continued to regulate the vote and to determine the weight assigned to each ballot. And membership on the standing committees remained firmly in the hands of the *Stadtmagistrat*, the governing elite of the Amtstadt. The importance of these standing committees varied from Amt to Amt. Whereas districts such as Göppingen, Nürtingen, and Stuttgart divided responsibilities between the committees and the assemblies and even allowed for limited peasant participation in both bodies, Aemter such as Tübingen vested all authority in the standing committee. And in the case of Tübingen the city's patricians reserved for themselves exclusive rights of membership on that board.[60]

Carl Alexander and his advisers realized that positions taken in the Amt not only determined local response to crown policies but also governed the Landtag's relations with the central administration. They sought therefore to influence the deliberations of the local standing committees and assemblies. To this end, through a shifting combination of intimidation and parliamentary maneuver, crown agents expanded and then manipulated the district electorate. In parliamentary terms they focused on the issue of representation. Whenever possible they either circumvented the oligarchic standing committees in order to situate deliberations in the expanded plenary assemblies, or they secured peasant participation in the smaller committees. Progress in this latter instance was slow, and victory was not achieved until the nineteenth century. But by the end of Carl Alexander's brief reign even Tübingen, that bastion of the Ehrbarkeit, was allowing limited village participation, whereas in the Stuttgart Amt both the assembly and the standing committee were meeting at least bimonthly with peasant elders contributing in each case. Göppingen, Leonberg, and Nürtingen showed a similar pattern.[61] And at the general Landtag of 1737, the first such meeting in almost forty years,

---

60. Two unpublished Tübingen Ph.D. dissertations contain the most useful general institutional studies of the Aemter: F. Benzing, "Die Vertretung von 'Stadt und Amt' in altwürttembergischen Landtag" (1924) and A. Rieger, "Die Entwicklung des württembergischen Kreisverbands" (1952).

61. W. Grube, "Dorfgemeinde und Amtsversammlung in Altwürttemberg," ZWLG, 13 (1954), 194–219, esp. 205–207; also Grube, *Stuttgarter Landtag*, 403.

village Schultheissen in the majority of the secular Aemter took part not only in the election of delegates but also in the formulation of their voting instructions.[62]

Institutional peculiarities in the great prelacies meant that a slightly different strategy was required for the ecclesiastical establishments. Since the right to participate in territorial politics there rested exclusively with the prelates, the crown contended against the church leaders rather than against groups of municipal officials. A prelate voted at the Landtag without instructions or authorization of any sort from his prelacy. He was bound only by his own sense of duty and conscience (*Amtspflichten und Gewissen*) to represent his peasants' interests. But though they lacked a direct voice in territorial politics, these peasants—who constituted some 10 percent of the total Württemberg population—nonetheless had local assemblies (*Klosterversammlungen*) at which they could discuss internal affairs without interference by any other social order. Both Eberhard Ludwig and Carl Alexander sought to undermine the prelates' territorial influence by encouraging their Klosterversammlungen to regard themselves as legitimately constituted political corporations with rights to instruct their prelates in matters of territorial concern. Carl Alexander infuriated the prelates by making a point of demanding votes of ratification or authorization by the Klosterversammlungen for policies championed at Stuttgart by the prelates on the executive and larger committees of the Landtag. And in 1735, when the peasants of Bebenhausen began demanding their prelate's recognition of their Klosterversammlung's "constitutional right" to share in the administration of the prelacy, the duke backed them in their unavailing struggle.[63]

Of course expanded peasant participation did not in itself mean automatic support for absolutist policies. The peasants resented arbitrary military recruitment just as strongly as the town magistrates did, and they showed themselves no more anxious for increased taxation than anyone else. But corporate solidarity had developed far more slowly among the village leaders than within the politically more experienced Ehrbarkeit. Peasant officials were generally less sophisticated, less well educated than their urban counterparts. They stood in greater awe of their prince and his officials. Carl Alexander attempted to exploit these sociological differences to his advantage. Like his predecessor he steadfastly refused to summon a general Landtag and preferred instead to deal with the executive committee

62. HSAS, A 203: Bü. 106 a–b and 107.
63. Grube, *Stuttgarter Landtag,* 404–406.

of the estates. When this body refused its support, he sought to force the leadership's hand by mobilizing local sentiment on his behalf. His tactics consisted mainly of badgering the standing committees and assemblies of the Aemter. After cajoling or intimidating them into sanctioning his wishes, he then presented the Stuttgart committee with a "popular mandate" from the territorial districts endorsing crown policies.

Franz Josef von Remchigen (1684–1757) orchestrated this campaign to undermine the estates.[64] What Süss did for the fisc, Remchingen worked to achieve in the Aemter and, like his cameralist counterpart, he earned the undying hatred of the territorial Ehrbarkeit. Remchingen too was an outsider, an ardent Roman Catholic from the bishopric of Augsburg, without experience with or regard for Württemberg's religious and cultural traditions. He despised the estates, an institution he referred to as a "hydra," and found utterly intolerable the privy councilors' insistence upon administrative routine. He had followed his brother, a high-ranking commander of the Knights of St. John (an aristocratic German crusading order known as the *Johanniter Orden*) into the military and throughout his life remained first and foremost a soldier, a man accustomed to giving and receiving orders. When he accepted Carl Alexander's invitation to Württemberg, he did so in that spirit. He lived as simply as his ruler, without any of Süss's penchant for personal luxury, and discharged his responsibilities in the fashion of a military officer rather than that of a professional administrator. For him and his subordinates the duke was the state; they did not hesitate to bully or persecute any civil servant who placed constitutional or procedural requirements before the implementation of ducal command. Remchingen was particularly outspoken in his contempt for the estates, and in dealings with the executive committee he made no effort to disguise his views. He informed the delegates to their face: "The duke has only to command; his will can never be circumscribed by his subjects. A wise ruler knows what is best for his land and has no need for estates."[65]

The terms of the Reversalien prohibited Carl Alexander's offering Remchingen a public office. But, as he had with Süss, the duke got around this restriction on non-Lutheran appointments. He made Remchingen governor (*Oberhofmeister*) to the crown prince and, on

64. On the Remchingen family, see Tüchle, *Die Kirchenpolitik des Herzogs Karl Alexander,* 67n69; and O. von Alberti, *Württembergisches Adels- und Wappenbuch* (Neustadt an der Aisch), 629. For analyses of his personality, see E. Schneider, *Württembergische Geschichte* (Stuttgart, 1896), 347–352; and Dizinger, *Beiträge zur Geschichte Württembergs,* 25f. and 95–129.

65. HSAS, A 203: Bü. 104.

the pretext of providing political experience for that infant, ordered the Oberhofmeister to bring the prince to all meetings of the cabinet government. He also commissioned Remchingen, who held the military rank of general, to serve as commander of the Württemberg army and to direct the Kriegsrat, a board technically outside the civil administration and therefore not subject to the restraints of the Reversalien. With Süss running the economic program, Schäffer heading the cabinet, and Remchingen handling military and domestic political strategy, Carl Alexander had diverted the most important government business away from the civil service and into his personal administration. By the end of 1735 he had ceased even to sign the privy council's protocolla, and in the next year he ordered the councilors to forward their reports in bulk rather than as daily accounts.[66] Under this form of government the estates remained virtually the only political force for which an institutional organization provided a possible forum for effective opposition. And when the executive committee balked at commands from the duke, Remchingen threatened military sanctions and worked on the Amtsversammlungen to weaken that body's powers of resistance.

Appealing to local constituencies was a perfectly legal maneuver. The problem lay in the ways in which Remchingen conducted his campaigns. Rather than circularizing the Aemter and thereafter allowing the discussions to take their natural course, he sought to intimidate the provincial deputies. He instructed the ranking official in the Amt to sit in personally on the meetings of the standing committee and assembly. The Amtmann was to attend these sessions with the explicit understanding by those attending that he was under orders to report to the crown on how each man had spoken and voted. Local leaders, especially those from the smaller towns and villages, found it impossible to act independently under this kind of pressure. Outside of Aemter like Tübingen, with a large city and a proud tradition of political independence, few delegates dared to speak out against the crown in the presence of the duke's representative. They tended rather to accept guidance from the Amtmann or to declare themselves in such convoluted circumlocutions that their remarks offered little support to the governing committees at Stuttgart. Without

66. See especially HSAS, A 202: Bü. 67 (letter from Carl Alexander to Schäffer, 21 October 1736); also A 204: Bü. 178 (22 March 1734) and 182–186; A 202: Bü. 29 (17 March 1735 and 11 August 1736). The crown's hostility toward the privy council was reported also in the confidential dispatches to Bishop Friedrich Carl von Schönborn from his resident agent at Stuttgart. These letters for 1737 are published in P. Stark, "Zur Geschichte des Herzogs Karl Alexander von Württemberg und der Streitigkeiten nach seinem Tode," WVJHLG, 11 (1888), 3–25.

a clear mandate from the Aemter the estates' leaders hesitated to defy the duke, especially when Remchingen followed up his local campaigns with threats of physical reprisal against their persons.[67]

By late spring of 1736 Remchingen had bullied the executive committee into accepting a standing army of 12,100 men and the delegates into agreeing to support this force with annual payments of 372,000 florins and the income from a regular levy of the detested Trizesimen. They also consented to exempt all military income and expenditure from accountability to the Landtag.[68] We now know that Remchingen projected the deployment of this armed force throughout the entire duchy. In a position paper that came to light only after the duke's death, Remchingen espoused a scheme that amounted to military rule for Württemberg. According to his plan the principality was to be divided into twelve Obervogteien, or military districts. Like Oliver Cromwell's major generals, each district commander would administer both the civil and military affairs of his area. And since these officers were all to be practicing Roman Catholics, a program of religious conversion could be undertaken at will.[69] To bolster his case with the duke, Remchingen wrote in early 1737 to Franz Ludwig Fichtl, a Würzburg lawyer who had already visited Stuttgart as a representative to Carl Alexander from his old friend Friedrich Carl von Schönborn. Fichtl, an outspoken champion of absolutist government, was to win Schönborn's approval of the plan and persuade him to convince Carl Alexander of what Remchingen flamboyantly described as "the need to cut the Gordian knot [estates and bureaucrats] with Alexander's sword."[70]

Carl Alexander's death put a stop to these dreams. Remchingen was arrested but managed to escape; by fleeing the duchy he was able to avoid the gruesome fate that befell Süss Oppenheimer. Meanwhile the regency government repudiated his military policies and dismantled most of the Württemberg army.[71] But here again the privy

67. Benzing, "Die Vertretung von 'Stadt und Amt'," 102–105.

68. F. Carsten, Princes and Parliaments in Germany from the Fifteenth to the Eighteenth Century (Oxford, 1959), 126–128. Grube, Stuttgarter Landtag, 386f., maintains that a faction of the executive committee had been corrupted by Remchingen. See also Lempp, "Philipp Heinrich Weissensee," 114–167.

69. HSAS, Inquisitionsprozessakten des Generals Remchingen, Bd. 2; also Stern, Jud Süss, 152–155.

70. A copy of Remchingen's letter (3 January 1737) is found in HSAS, Inquisitionsprozessakten des Generals Remchingen, Bd. 2. The letter is reproduced in Elwenspoek, Jew Süss Oppenheimer, 114–118.

71. A. Pfister, Herzog Karl Eugen von Württemberg und seine Zeit, I (Esslingen, 1907), 130, documents a reduction to 1,426 soldiers; cf. Carsten, Princes and Parliaments, 129–130.

councilors and estates found that the crown's political innovations had fostered a movement in the Aemter that could be slowed but not reversed. Even without further stimulation from Stuttgart, peasant participation in Amt affairs continued to grow. By mid-century when Carl Eugen assumed personal rule, the urban magistrates in Aemter such as Leonberg, Neuffen, and Nürtingen had already accepted a more modest district influence. They had begun to send delegates to represent them at the assembly rather than automatically attending in person and as a bloc. This practice grew more widespread under Carl Eugen, who encouraged a standard policy of using the Amtsversammlungen for discussion of instructions for delegations to the Landtag as well as for the election of all Amt officials and delegates. Simple farmers from the village courts, as well as rural Schultheissen, attended these beefed-up assemblies; and in a large Amt like Urach, meetings took place with as many as eighty peasant delegates present. On occasion peasant majorities actually determined the composition of the Landtag delegations.[72]

The greater weight given to district assemblies that peasants were attending in larger numbers by no means implied the triumph of local democracy. Certainly we know that well into the nineteenth century the Württemberg Ehrbarkeit proved remarkably tenacious in preserving its grip over domestic politics. One suspects that, whatever the attendance figures for the assemblies, eighteenth-century peasant influence remained restricted to certain of the more influential villages and within them to the most important families. Similarly, final control over assembly agendas and over the formulation of instructions rested in most instances with the more elitist standing committees.[73] Nevertheless, the ironic fact remains that a drive for princely absolutism in the central administration resulted in an expanded franchise and an increased political activity in the districts. In this sense the prince and his personal advisers stimulated a move toward broader participation in government. They both strengthened the locality and extended its involvement in territorial politics.

One final set of developments from this period needs to be noted, this time in connection with the regency rather than with Carl Alexander's domestic innovations. Some two decades of power under the

72. Grube, "Dorfgemeinde und Amtsversammlung," 209–219; Benzing, "Die Vertretung von 'Stadt und Amt'," 105–159; T. Knapp, "Leibeigene Bauern auf den württembergischen Landtagen," *Jahrbücher für Nationalökonomie*, 118 (1922), 531 ff.

73. W. Grube in vol. XXIII of *Württembergische Archivinventare* (Stuttgart, 1952), 11–18 and in vol. II of *Nürtinger Heimatbuch* (Würzburg, 1953), 13–22, cataloged the archival sources on the Versammlungen.

regency allowed the professional officials and their allies among the estates to regroup their badly shaken forces. They did so but in a manner that distinguished their success from that of the previous century. In the golden period under Eberhard III when estates, officials, and monarch had worked together with such harmony, there had been little discernible social differentiation within the Ehrbarkeit. Certainly as regards its political participation, the group had functioned without internal distinctions of rank, and all the members had contributed to the deliberations and policies of the Landtag. Now there was clearly an inside and an outside faction, with the insiders controlling the small key committees and seeking to vest them with the operative powers of the Landtag. During the regency, this elite tier of magistrates, supported by their cousins in the privy council, achieved two significant political victories: they secured the preservation of committee rule within the Landtag and wrote legislation regulating the Pietist movement within the duchy. Neither one affected the immediate momentum of the crown's initiative in domestic politics. But both played an important role in determining the strength and nature of the opposition that formed in the second half of the eighteenth century against autocratic rule and succeeded finally in reversing the crown's earlier triumphs.

A reorganized privy council took the lead in the regency government. Georg Bernhard Bilfinger (1693–1750), one of the most distinguished of Württemberg's professional officials, guided the board during these years.[74] Bilfinger's leadership reflected both his conservative social orientation and his extraordinarily high intelligence. By birth he belonged to one of the most distinguished families of the territorial Ehrbarkeit—his father was prelate of Lorch and Blaubeuren—and when he took control of the privy council after Carl Alexander's death, he filled the board with men who came primarily from the upper echelons of territorial society. Of the five appointments that he engineered, all but Friedrich August von Hardenberg (1700–1768) were Württembergers or, if born outside the technical borders of the duchy, from families with prominent Württemberg relatives and long-standing ties to the government.[75] All three non-

---

74. E. Schmid, "Geheimrat Georg Bernhard Bilfinger (1693–1750)," *ZWLG*, 3 (1939), 370–422.

75. Dates and places of birth are unknown for the remaining two appointees, Ferdinand Reinhard Wolfgang Freiherr von Wallbrunn (died 1770) and Johann Eberhard Friedrich Freiherr von Wallbrunn (died 1752). Alberti, *Wappenbuch*, 980, ascribes a Rhenish origin to the Wallbrunn family, but members are already in Württemberg service by the second half of the seventeenth century. Pfeilsticker, *Dienerbuch*, 201, lists Georg Reinhard Freiherr von Wallbrunn as Hofmeister to the young princes in 1678.

nobles on the council—Bilfinger himself, Johann Eberhard Georgii (1694–1772) and Philipp Eberhard Zech (1696–1755)—had immediate connections to the Ehrbarkeit. Like the Bilfingers, the Georgiis belonged to the highest ranks of that order, and Zech, whose family members held numerous government posts, had married the daughter of Landschaftskonsulent Sturm.[76]

Bilfinger's appointments confirmed a pattern of recruitment already noted as beginning under Carl Alexander: namely, the tendency to select councilors locally and to draw them from the ranks of the most prominent territorial families. The result was to bring the privy council, at least in terms of its members' social origins, more firmly into the orbit of the upper ranks of the territorial estates. We find, moreover, that the council members shared the attitudes of their upper-class relatives toward the larger body of the estates. Bilfinger himself never hesitated to poke fun at the self-importance of the provincial delegates, the most tiresome of whom he referred to as "such Bürgermeisters," and to deplore their excessive particularism. In April 1742, for example, he wrote in disgust to Georgii, then at Berlin with the young princes: "It is a long-established custom for the estates to work against the common good" (Es ist schon lang üblich, dass die Landschaft dem Guten widerstrebt).[77] Certainly he always maintained a careful separation of powers between his own board and the general Landtag. Especially in territorial politics the privy council could now be expected to side with the governing elite among the estates on any issues involving a challenge to their authority from the wider membership of the territorial assembly.

The privy council took just such a stand in the complicated political jockeying surrounding the Landtag of 1737–1739. The councilors allied themselves with the executive committee and used their powers to assist the most ambitious members of that board in perpetuating an oligarchic control over the business and politics of the Landtag. To follow this maneuver one must return to the weeks immediately following Carl Alexander's death when general confusion prevailed over

Pfeilsticker (403, 404, 1746) also documents intermarriage with the Gemmingen family. See HSAS, A 202: Bü. 80 for F. R. von Wallbrunn's letter of appointment to the privy council (20 April 1739).

76. On Georgii, see Pfeilsticker, Dienerbuch, 1101, 1138, 1217, 1652, 1655, 1659, 2015, 2276; on Zech, see ibid., 21, 1151, 1160, 1161, 1233, 2015; and HSAS, A 202: Bü. 82 (appointment letter of 18 March 1737). Zech received an imperial patent of nobility in 1751.

77. LBS, Q 318 contains 157 letters written by Bilfinger to Georgii between December 1741 and August 1743, while the latter was chaperoning Carl Eugen and his brother at Berlin. The letters are unusually frank in their accounts of privy council business and in their personal assessments of Bilfinger's colleagues in the government.

the organization of the regency. The Württemberg constitution had specifically endowed the privy council with powers equal to those of the regent so that its members were assured of a central role in the new government. But no one was quite certain as to the precise format in which the estates were to participate. In particular there was dispute as to whether or not the Landtag as a body was to share in the government or whether its contribution was better rendered through one of the smaller committees.

Key members of the executive committee held no doubts on that score. Acting on the advice of the privy council, the prelate of Bebenhausen, together with the committee's ranking civil officials, the mayors of Stuttgart and Tübingen, took steps that would secure their leadership over the estates. They fired the Landtag's chief lawyer, Veit Jacob Neuffer (died 1741), whom they suspected of having betrayed their interests during Carl Alexander's reign, and replaced him with Johann Friedrich Stockmayer, the thirty-two-year-old son of the Bebenhausen prelate.[78] They also dissolved the larger council of the estates, by coincidence in session at Stuttgart at the time of the duke's death, and proclaimed themselves "the eternal guardians of the Fatherland" (perpetui procuratores patriae). Under the mandate of this inflated title and supported fully by the privy council, they assumed exclusive rights of supervision over the preparations for the general Landtag that the prince regent and the privy council were convening after a hiatus of thirty-eight years. Their self-proclaimed duties included regulating the rules governing representation from the Aemter, vetting the size and composition of the individual delegations, and helping the privy councilors to draw up the agenda.

The executive committee discharged these responsibilities under a policy of strict legal constructionism calculated to preserve its control. Seventy-six-year-old Christoph Friedrich Stockmayer, the patrician prelate of Bebenhausen, was the only official on either the executive committee or the privy council who could remember the last general assembly.[79] He used his expertise to guard against any procedural innovations in the Aemter which might threaten the Ehrbarkeit's position in the districts. He also saw to it that parliamentary procedure at the diet remained such that political power at the territorial level

---

78. Neuffer, who had served as mayor of Tübingen from 1720 to 1733 and sat on the executive committee of the Landtag, was Konsulent from 1733 to 1737; Pfeilsticker, *Dienerbuch*, 1226, 1310, 1325, 1426, 1448. On Stockmayer, see ibid., 1179, 1227, 1330, 1468, 1884, 2774, 2910, 3027, 3415; and also A. Adam, *Johann Jakob Moser als württembergischer Landschaftskonsulent, 1751–57* (Stuttgart, 1887), 4–5 and 16–18.

79. Pfeilsticker, *Dienerbuch*, 1330, 1433, 1157, 1185, 2910, 3304, 3358.

would continue to be vested in great magisterial families like his own. In this spirit his committee rejected the attempt by rapidly growing towns such as Kornwestheim and Zuffenhausen, not yet incorporated into any of the surrounding Aemter, to send their own delegates to represent them at the assembly.

The executive committee likewise denied the Maulbronn Kloster-versammlung's request that the prelacy be allowed to send a delegate to represent the village component of that prelatal Amt. And on the principle that no man of "unsavory reputation" (*schlechten Rufes*) could attend the Landtag, the committee required each of the Aemter to submit a list of its delegates in advance of the opening of the diet. The understanding was that the executive committee members reserved the right to screen out all undesirables from the delegations. It is unclear from the documents whether or not the executive committee actually denied any delegate his seat, but there is ample evidence that its members refused to allow matters that they regarded as threatening to come up for general discussion. They flatly rejected, for example, a petition signed by forty Stuttgart tradesmen which challenged the legality of that city's election procedure and called for an investigation of the municipal administration by the assembly.[80]

Despite these precautions the assembly proved a turbulent one. The executive committee's negotiations before the opening of the diet had revealed its determination to exclude new social forces from political power. By the same token it was clear to everyone that its members were separating themselves from the rank and file of the estates. A party of radical outsiders formed on the floor of the assembly to protest these policies. Heartened by Carl Alexander's opening up of the lower levels of territorial politics, they sought to reassert the unity of the Ehrbarkeit and to revise the political balance in districts so as to include a broader social representation for the Landtag. The leader of the movement was Christoph Matthäus Pfaff (1686–1760), the chancellor of Tübingen and a scholar of international reputation.[81] When he realized that the elder Stockmayer's committee had excluded all dissonant complaints from the docket, he introduced

80. HSAS, A 203: Bü. 106 a–b.
81. Pfeilsticker, *Dienerbuch*, 2913 and 3437; *Allgemeine Deutsche Biographie*, xxv (Berlin, 1970), 587–590. Pfaff enjoyed a national reputation for his efforts to reunite the Calvinist and Lutheran churches of Germany. On his theology and politics, see H. Lehmann, *Pietismus und weltliche Ordnung in Württemberg vom 17. bis zum 20. Jahrhundert* (Stuttgart, 1969), 88–95; F. Fritz, "Konventikel in Württemberg," *BWKG*, 52 (1952), 28–65; and M. Walker, *Johann Jakob Moser*, 16–26.

from the floor a series of resolutions aimed at ending the system of committee rule. Though a patrician by birth, he objected strenuously to class differences within the Ehrbarkeit and denounced what he called the closed-door policy of the standing committees.

Pfaff resented especially the executive committee's policy of withdrawing from the plenary discussions in order to consider controversial matters in private. This practice, he claimed, violated the principle of open debate. And, since the executive committee formulated the final proposals upon which the assembly voted, it allowed the committee to hammer out in secret a united front and to present business for voting in such a manner as to predetermine the outcome. Pfaff also deplored the oligarchic nature of the committee membership and insisted that the pool of recruitment be widened to include delegates from the less populous and prosperous Aemter. As an extension of this point he called for an end to the local standing committees' control over the districts' instructions for the Landtag. Instead the assemblies were to be opened in greater measure to the peasants and given a more significant voice in drawing up the instructions. Finally he attacked the influence of the estates' legal counsels (*Konsulenten*), whom he described as mere creatures of the duke and his privy council.

Pfaff's fiery radicalism swept through the delegates and resulted in a series of tumultuous assembly meetings and widely subscribed petitions of protest to the prince regent. The most vociferous objection took place late in the year when word reached the floor of the diet that after the Christmas recess only the larger council would be summoned back into session for discussion of unfinished business. Delegates from the historically less influential Aemter of Balingen, Ebingen, Tuttlingen, Rosenfeld, Sulz, Dornstetten, Calw, Zavelstein, and Hornberg organized as a group and complained bitterly about this possibility. They echoed Pfaff's attack on the oligarchic nature of the executive committee, protested their own exclusion from such bodies, and called for a permanent end to the practice of deputizing narrowly constituted boards to speak on behalf of the estates. In this instance, as had been the case with Pfaff's earlier parliamentary ploys, the regent, acting on the advice of the privy council, sided unequivocally with the committees against the reform movement. He ordered an end to the attacks on the parliamentary leadership and instructed the delegates to get on with state business.[82]

82. On the Landtag negotiations, see HSAS, LB: Bü. 406–413; Grube, *Stuttgarter Landtag*, 409–424.

This unqualified support from the regental government ensured the executive's ability to perpetuate committee rule. It also guaranteed that, while the progressives could succeed in certain minor areas such as blocking the reelection to the larger council of two unpopular mayors and expelling a much-hated prelate from the executive committee, the old guard retained its preponderant influence.[83] With the exception of the personnel changes and a reluctant agreement by the executive committee to expand its membership by one prelate and two mayors (and thus the larger council by two prelates and four mayors), the Landtag closed its final session in April 1739 with its system of committee rule firmly in place.[84] Nor did the assembly legislate a restructuring of the political balance in the districts. The Ehrbarkeit's control remained unchallenged by the Landtag, and local reform movements were left to develop as best they could without official endorsement by the diet. The defeat of the reform movement made it plain that, while a broader political consciousness was growing within the duchy, this growth was still in its tender stages. Without direct support from the crown it would advance only with the greatest difficulty.

The close cooperation between crown, privy council, and executive committee continued throughout the regency. It manifested itself most significantly in the united front that the government presented to the Pietist movement. We have seen that beyond the walls of the ducal residence cultural conformity was a salient characteristic of Württemberg society. Certainly no institution had worked with greater effect to promote this uniformity of values than the established church had. It not only organized worship and education in the duchy but also provided the intellectual rationale for the regulation of entry into public office. Except in the court and the army, both of which stood under the direct control of the duke, local and territorial posts could be held only by those who had sworn an oath of loyalty to official church doctrine. And that body of thought prescribed in considerable detail the criteria by which contemporary attitudes were formed. In recent years a threat to this self-contained unanimity had surfaced in the form of a radical religious movement known generally as Pietism. Since the late seventeenth century Pietist teachings had circulated in the duchy without visibly eroding the church's author-

83. Philipp Heinrich Weissensee, prelate of Hirsau, was expelled from the executive committee by a vote from the floor; E. Lempp, "Weissensees Sturz," *BWKG*, 32 (1928), 531 ff. The plenary assembly also refused to ratify the continued appointment to the larger committee of Mayors Sack of Waiblingen and Faber of Sulz.
84. Reyscher, *Vollständige Sammlung*, I, 399–401.

ity. But now it was becoming clear to the defenders of the established order that the movement was gaining ground in the larger cities and towns and that it contained an alarming potential for disruption.

In their milder form Pietist ideas emphasized the importance of a personal spiritual commitment and constituted nothing more than a mandate for a purer Christian life within the framework of orthodox Lutheran doctrine. But what began in some quarters as a spiritual revival gradually acquired radical political overtones. Though these religious activists remained a distinct minority in the general population, consistory reports spoke ominously of declining church attendance, wildcat revival meetings, and defections within the ranks of ordained pastors and prominent families. Certainly the government regarded the threat as serious and, as we shall see, took considerable pains to domesticate the movement. The problem was that the emphasis upon Bible reading and discussion by lay groups, or conventicles as they were called, was leading the Pietists to downgrade the importance of ordination and by extension the established church that the pastors represented. Indeed more extreme elements were beginning to regard the territorial church, with its close ties to crown and government, as an object of scorn and to demand a complete separation from what they deplored as a corrupt, worldly institution. At the same time they attacked the formalism of orthodox doctrine and insisted upon a greater emphasis on visions, prophesies, and inward illumination.[85]

From the government's perspective Bilfinger's political acumen and philosophic disposition made him the ideal man to handle this potentially inflammatory situation. His academic credentials were impeccable: after attending the preparatory schools at Blaubeuren and Bebenhausen, he had entered Tübingen where he studied mathematics, philosophy, and theology until leaving for Halle to work with Christian Wolff. Wolff's lectures on Leibniz won Bilfinger completely to rational philosophy. He began an intensive reading of Leibniz and published his commentaries on Leibniz's philosophic writings in a series of essays that made him one of the leading exponents of German enlightened thinking. The French Academy acknowledged his importance by awarding him a prize for his publications, and the Russian government invited him to a chair at St. Petersburg. After two years in Russia he returned to Tübingen, where in addition to teaching the science of military fortifications—and it was this work that brought

<hr/>

85. Christian Kolb, "Die Anfänge des Pietismus und Separatismus in Württemberg," *WVJHLG*, NF 11 (1902), 65–78; and Lehmann, *Pietismus und weltliche Ordnung*, 22–82.

him to Carl Alexander's attention and earned him a seat on the privy council—he lectured with distinction on the philosophy of the *Aufklärung*.[86] The point is that, while conventional in his religion and conservative in his social outlook, Bilfinger internalized the values of toleration so central to enlightened thinking and presented himself as a man to whom at least the moderate and centrist Pietists could turn with confidence. Under his leadership there was never any question of the government's persecuting the Pietists in such a way as to make martyrs of the radicals or to polarize the church. On the contrary, Bilfinger set out immediately to dampen tension and to accommodate the Pietist insistence upon lay conventicles within the institutional framework of the Württemberg church.

He first moved to secure the established church (*Landeskirche*) and to guarantee the privy council's continued control over that institution. After persuading the regent to issue an edict reaffirming the Augsburg Confession as the basis of the Württemberg church, and hence of official religion in the duchy, he published a collection of legal documents (*Urkunden*) dealing with the incorporation by the Landtag of the Landeskirche (1565) and with its subsequent governing ordinances. These latter documents culminated with the confirmation in 1735 of the Reversalien by the Protestant corps (*corpus evangelicorum*) of the Reichstag.[87] After the publication of these charters Bilfinger next moved to secure their endorsement by the great European powers. In 1742 he obtained official recognition by Emperor Charles VII of all the duchy's laws from the Tübinger Vertrag to the Reversalien. At the same time he persuaded the so-called guarantor states—the crowns of England, Prussia, and Denmark—to pledge themselves to the continuation of the religious settlement.[88] With the church's ordinances now a matter of public record and the Reversalien fortified by official commitments from the emperor, the Reichstag, and three major Protestant powers, Bilfinger turned to the Pietists. Here his strategy was essentially political. He set up a joint committee staffed by members from the executive committee of the

86. On Bilfinger's career prior to entering the privy council in 1735, see E. Schmid, "Geheimrat Georg Bernhard Bilfinger," 370–396; cf. Pfeilsticker, *Dienerbuch*, 1136 and 2015; HSAS, A 202: Bü. 111 and 112 (his private papers); R. Uhland, *Geschichte der Hohen Karlsschule in Stuttgart* (Stuttgart, 1953), 3f.; and E. Marquardt, *Geschichte Württembergs* (Stuttgart, 1961), 183f.

87. *Urkunden, die Religion in dem Herzogthum Würtemberg betreffend* (Stuttgart, 1738); see also HSAS, A 202: Bü. 2375, 2376, 2378, 2379; and Reyscher, *Vollständige Sammlung*, VIII, 601.

88. On these negotiations, see Lehmann, *Pietismus und weltliche Ordnung*, 88–89; R. Rürup, *Johann Jacob Moser: Pietismus und Reform* (Wiesbaden, 1965), 130–131; and Walker, *Johann Jakob Moser*, 122–125.

Landtag and the privy council and charged it with working out a religious accommodation. The result was a series of edicts issued in 1743, just one year before Carl Eugen assumed control over the government, which won Pietist support for the territorial church and guaranteed the institutional unity of religious life in the duchy.[89]

The final settlements—the *Grosse Kirchenordnung*, the *Erneuete Gemeine Land-Recht*, and the *Generalreskript über die Privat-Versammlungen der Pietisten*—asserted the principle that the common weal (*Gemeinwesen*) was not compromised by the conventicles, so long as the members pledged their obedience to the government. Pastors were to be invited to join; and when they could not or did not choose to do so, conventicle members were to inform the parish office (*Pfarramt*) of all meetings. Since women as well as young boys and girls were to be allowed to attend, conventicle meetings were to end before dark lest they should lead to unseemly behavior. Finally the Württemberg Pietists were to repudiate the radical theology preached in the duchy during the preceding years by missionaries from Count Nicholaus Ludwig von Zinzendorf's Herrenhut community.[90] They were also to eschew any excessive stress upon visions or notions of communities of the elect such as might support "we and they" attitudes toward the district and state authorities.[91] The compromise, in other words, was a political one. It ensured the institutional unity of the Landeskirche but allowed an intellectual freedom within that church for those with Pietist inclinations. Theological pluralism, at least of a politically harmless sort, could now flourish within a structure where secular administrative authority continued to reside with the central government and with the social order that staffed the most important of government offices.

Under Bilfinger's guidance the executive committee and the privy council thus co-opted for the established order a movement with a psychological orientation potentially destructive to that system. Nothing better illustrated their success than the career of Johann Albrecht Bengel (1687–1752), the most influential of the early-eighteenth-cen-

89. Reyscher, *Vollständige Sammlung*, VIII, 641–652; also Friedrich Fritz, "Konventikel in Württemberg," *BWKG*, 103 (1953), 82–130 and 104 (1954), 75–122.

90. Robert Geiges, "Zinzendorf und Württemberg," *BWKG*, 17 (1913), 52–78 and 138–152. Also by Geiges, "Die Ansiedlungspläne der Brüdergemeinde in Württemberg," *BWKG*, 25 (1921), 245–263; and "Württemberg und Herrenhut im 18. Jahrhundert," *BWKG*, 42 (1938), 28–88.

91. Here the figures of Jeremias Friedrich Reuss, Friedrich Christoph Steinhofer, and Friedrich Christoph Oetinger were central. See Walker, *Johann Jakob Moser*, 162–172; Lehmann, *Pietismus und weltliche Ordnung*, 68–94; K. C. E. Ehmann, ed., *Friedrich Christoph Oetingers Leben und Briefe* (Stuttgart, 1859), 172–174; and Julius Roessle, *Friedrich Christoph Oetinger* (Metzingen, 1969).

tury Württemberg Pietist theologians.[92] As an instructor *(Kloster-präzeptor)* in the celebrated preparatory school at Denkendorf, he had written and lectured on biblical eschatology and in so doing had won the leadership of the Pietist separatists. His authority proved a difficult burden. For while his visions of the triumphs to be accorded the persecuted children of God made him indifferent to the blandishments of the Herrenhut missionaries and irritated by the excessive moralism of the extreme radicals, he nonetheless insisted on the importance of biblical study for the laity and thus on the necessity of conventicles. Bilfinger's diplomacy gave him an opportunity for reconciliation. Even though he recoiled from the pragmatic rationalism in Bilfinger's philosophic outlook, he could accept the opportunity for the freedom of religious thought implicit in Bilfinger's settlement.[93] He returned to active participation in the territorial church and carried the bulk of the Pietists with him in that commitment. Having secured Bengel's support, Bilfinger consolidated his gains by co-opting the religious leader into the political system. As president of the Württemberg consistory, he secured Bengel's appointment to the prelacy first of Herbrechtingen and then of Alpirsbach. Then in 1747 he engineered Bengel's election to the larger council of the estates. One year later Bengel entered the executive committee and thus assured Pietist support for that inner sanctum of government power.[94]

Indeed, when the estates and bureaucrats went back on the defensive under Carl Eugen, it was with strengths and weaknesses different from the ones that had shaped their abortive struggle against Eberhard Ludwig. Their leadership now formed a united social class, supported by a church in which intense spiritual energy had been marshaled behind its governance. Their constitutional rights to share in the government were now matters of public record; there could be no more talk of their clinging to old, outmoded laws that were no longer recognized. Imperial as well as foreign powers had sanctioned

92. Most recent scholarship on Bengel's life and works includes: H. Hermelink, *Geschichte der evangelischen Kirche in Württemberg von der Reformation bis zur Gegenwart* (Stuttgart, 1949), 215–230; Karl Hermann, *Johann Albrecht Bengel: Der Klosterpräzeptor von Denkendorf* (Stuttgart, 1937); E. Benz, "J. A. Bengel und die Philosophie des deutschen Idealismus," *Deutsche Vierteljahrschrift für Literaturwissenschaft und Geistesgeschichte,* 27 (1953), 528–554; Martin Brecht, "J. A. Bengels Theologie der Schrift," *Zeitschrift für Theologie und Kirche,* 64 (1967), 99–120; and Julius Roessle, *Von Bengel bis Blumhardt* (Metzingen, 1981).

93. On Bilfinger's rationalism, see Heinz Liebing, *Zwischen Orthodoxie und Aufklärung: Das philosophische und theologische Denken Georg Bernhard Bilfingers* (Tübingen, 1961).

94. Pfeilsticker, *Dienerbuch,* 337, 1408, 2018, 2819, 3271, 3363. On Bengel's stance in government politics, see Lehmann, *Pietismus und weltliche Ordnung,* 94–101.

these rights and pledged themselves to uphold them, placing the estates and bureaucrats in a much stronger position. So long as Carl Eugen operated within the established categories of Württemberg politics, they could hope to handle the crown's challenge.

# [7]

# A Return to Course

Carl Eugen took over the government officially in 1744, at the age of sixteen, and ruled until his death in 1793. For the first decade of the reign he left the administration in the hands of his privy councilors. They in turn worked closely with their friends and relatives on the executive committee to carry forward the policies of the regency. But gradually the young prince began to take matters more directly into his own hands. His flamboyant policies set him at loggerheads with the central administration and activated once again the familiar triangle of antagonists: prince, estates, and civil servants. Though the ensuing conflict followed the now classic lines of Württemberg politics, the changing structure of the territorial Ehrbarkeit meant that the resolution carried quite novel implications.

Whereas the earlier municipal magistrates had functioned as a cohesive corps, their eighteenth-century descendants were fracturing into classes. A magisterial elite now controlled the more important state offices, so that in terms of their social composition these governing boards represented only a single relatively small group. The rest of the Ehrbarkeit retrenched in the provincial towns and districts. There the magistrates sought to exercise on the local level the kind of political authority that their more exalted colleagues were wielding at Stuttgart. The result was twofold. First, there emerged a latent tension between the districts and the central administration. Second, any settlement worked out between the crown, the executive committee of the Landtag, and the privy council meant that only the one class of magisterial elite shared with the monarch in the affairs of state.

Given his personality and religion, what were the obstacles that Carl Eugen confronted in his determination to rule without the constraints of estates or bureaucracy? At least in the past these groups had shown themselves unable to withstand on their own a direct assault by the legitimate ruler. But his predecessors, even if initially victorious, had never succeeded in consolidating their gains. They were unable to translate their successes into an institutional structure that could sustain absolute rule. Their efforts in each instance had set in motion a larger set of checks and balances which in the end they could not surmount.

At its most basic level the problem of the Württemberg rulers was a legal one. Territorial law had vested certain sovereign rights in institutions outside the crown: control of taxation in the estates, administration of the church in the privy council. To redirect these responsibilities the monarch would have had to change the law, but he lacked the constitutional authority as well as the material sources to effect such revisions unilaterally; he needed outside support. Yet each of the principal domestic sources from which this support might have come were closed to him. Neither estates nor bureaucrats were prepared to endorse measures aimed explicitly at restricting their influence. Nor could the crown tap more popular levels of strength. Confessional differences between the duke and his subjects still posed a formidable barrier to closer cooperation.

Equally important, the duke lacked the institutional means for generating broader support. The political organization of the duchy left the localities relatively free from domination by the center. Carl Eugen's difficulties in this regard made it plain that the early modern territorial state remained in fact a far weaker force in the general society than legislative rhetoric suggested. Finally the imperial system worked to promote stability in the sense of preserving the status quo. Domestic politics in the secondary German states remained inextricably bound up with those of the Reich. The same checks and balances that ensured the fragmentation of political authority in that larger body prevented a consolidation of power in many territorial states. The result was that the old regime came to a close in those polities, as in the Reich itself, with the problem of authority still unresolved.

In many ways Carl Eugen resembled Eberhard Ludwig more than he did his own father. Like that earlier monarch he had grown up for the most part in the duchy and had known from the beginning that he was destined to rule. Bilfinger had seen to his education as a young prince and provided a plan of study that was wide-ranging in content but honed to local custom.[1] Although Carl Eugen was eventually to

1. F. K. Dizinger, *Beiträge zur Geschichte Württembergs und seines Regentenhauses zur Zeit der Regierung Herzogs Karl Alexander und während der Minder-*

develop exalted ideas of monarchy, he tended to ground his despotism in the traditional categories of Württemberg politics. That is, he
sought to dominate the historical elements in his government, the estates and bureaucracy, and to use his position to create a court that
would make him the envy of the other German princes. Whereas his
father's fiscal ruthlessness had challenged the social as well as constitutional order of the duchy, Carl Eugen's arbitrary behavior, like that
of Eberhard Ludwig, threatened above all the political balance en-
shrined in the charters of the Tübinger Vertrag and the Reversalien.

Even in such areas as religion, where father and son shared a common commitment, there was a discernible difference in orientation.
For Carl Alexander, the convert, reformed Catholicism was linked to
military conquest and authoritarian government. Carl Eugen reveled
more in the ceremony than in the power politics of Catholicism. Indeed his first controversy with the privy council sprang from a lavish
Corpus Christi celebration that he staged in 1749 in the huge courtyard of the Stuttgart castle and then orchestrated on an even grander
scale the following year at Ludwigsburg. The councilors reacted with
indignation when they learned that streams of Catholic monks and
secular clergy had marched with the prince in the Ludwigsburg procession. The centerpiece on that occasion was a brocaded baldachin
with silk tassles and a golden fringe under which the Sacrament was
carried aloft in an elaborate baroque monstrance studded with pre-
cious stones. During the procession cannons roared throughout the
city, sending startled burghers flocking to the palace to gawk. There
they beheld young virgins in white dresses with wreaths of flowers in
their hair scattering petals before the prince, his entourage, and what
the jittery council officials regarded as little better than an idolatrous
golden calf.[2]

Much in Carl Eugen's personality suggested a return of the exaggerated competitiveness that had driven so many of his predecessors
to assault the constitution for greater revenue. The duke made no secret of his determination to create a court that would dazzle his fellow
princes. And in this he succeeded. His fêtes and lavish patronage became the talk of Germany and earned him the reputation in some circles of a Lorenzo de Medici and in others of a wildly extravagant ego-
maniac.[3] Goethe captured the ambivalence in contemporary opinion

---

*jährigkeit seines Erstgeboren*, II (Tübingen, 1834), 65–76; *Politische Korrespondenz
Friedrich des Grossen*, ed. J. G. Droysen, II (Berlin, 1879), 296.

2. Gerhard Storz, *Karl Eugen: Der Fürst und das "alte gute Recht"* (Stuttgart,
1981), 56–57.

3. For a comprehensive sample of contemporary opinion, see *La pure vérité:
Lettres et mémoires sur le duc et le duché de Virtemberg pour servir à fixer l'opinion*

when he wrote to Duke Carl August of Saxe-Weimar, shortly after Carl Eugen's death, concerning his own impressions of life at the Württemberg court:

"Duke Carl [Eugen], to whom one must concede a certain grandeur of vision [*Grossheit*], worked nevertheless to gratify his momentary passions and to act out a series of ever-changing fantasies. But in that he strove for status, show, and effect, he had a particular need for artists. And even when his motives were less than noble, he could not help but further a higher cause."[4]

Various influences fed this almost compulsive obsession with the arts. Carl Eugen had spent two years as a young teenager at Berlin and had been greatly impressed by the cultivated court of Frederick the Great.[5] He subsequently married Frederick's niece, Elisabeth Friederike of Brandenburg-Ansbach (1732–1780), and thereafter found further stimulation in the lively theater and opera that flourished at her parents' capital of Bayreuth. Inspiration came likewise from the two neighboring Wittelsbach courts of Max Joseph of Bavaria and Carl Theodore of the Palatinate. But though these German models doubtless played an important role in shaping Carl Eugen's taste, it was Louis XV of France who provided the ultimate standard against which the duke measured himself. From 1748 on Carl Eugen employed a full-time consultant at Paris whose sole responsibility was to supply the duke with all new French publications, court circulars, and manuals of architecture and decorative style.[6] He read these bulletins and essays avidly and drew heavily upon French models for his own extensive building and artistic programs.

French classical taste influenced the first of his imposing building projects, the horseshoe-shaped palace constructed at Stuttgart to supersede the old castle.[7] Though the original plan derived from Italian models, French standards alone governed the construction and deco-

*publique sur le procès entre le prince et ses sujets* (Augsburg, 1765); also G. Kleemann, *Schloss Solitude bei Stuttgart* (Stuttgart, 1966), 89–113.

4. Goethe's letter of 12 September 1794, written from Tübingen, is reproduced in *Goethe reist durchs Schwabenland: Aus Goethes Tagebüchern und Briefen*, ed. Erika Neuhauser (Stuttgart, 1941).

5. Eugen Schneider, "Herzog Karls Erziehung, Jugend und Persönlichkeit," in *Herzog Karl Eugen von Württemberg und seine Zeit*, I (Esslingen, 1907), 30–39. This two-volume collection of essays, published by the Württembergische Geschichts- und Altertums-Verein, remains the definitive work on Carl Eugen's reign. It is cited hereafter as *HKE*.

6. Storz, *Karl Eugen*, 65.

7. The estates voted 150,000 florins, paid at an annual rate of 30,000 florins, for this construction in the hopes that the prince would then reside permanently in Stuttgart. See A. E. Adam, "Herzog Karl und die Landschaft," *HKE*, I, 195.

ration of the east wing containing the private apartments of the ducal family. For that work Carl Eugen summoned the Parisian architect Philippe de la Guêpière and charged him with creating a setting that would rival Louis's apartments at Versailles.[8] The French king's celebrated redecoration there set the tone for the intimate yet highly refined elegance that Carl Eugen achieved first in Stuttgart and later, with even more stunning success, in the construction and embellishment of his two most famous pleasure retreats, "Solitude" (1763) and "Mon Repos" (1764).[9]

While hammers were still ringing on his building projects, Carl Eugen was busy launching what one can regard only as a series of incredibly diverse, expensive, and distinguished artistic projects. First he reconstituted the court orchestra, an ensemble of full-time musicians that had been established under Eberhard Ludwig but dissolved as an unnecessary expense by Carl Alexander. Then in 1750, to celebrate his wife's eighteenth birthday, he attended the first performance of the court opera company that he had founded and endowed. To ensure the success of the operatic enterprise Carl Eugen had hired from Rome a world-renowned singer and composer named Niccolo Jomelli. Under Jomelli's sixteen-year directorship the opera subsequently became an international attraction and set a widely emulated standard of quality in settings and costume design as well as in musical excellence.[10] Carl Eugen's enthusiasm grew with the opera's reputation, and in 1764 he brought the company to Ludwigsburg, where he had constructed the largest, most sumptuous opera house in Europe.[11]

The duke used the opera house for productions by the French theatrical company that he had founded in 1757 and for the staging of the lavish ballets produced under the directorship of Jean-Georges Noverre (1727–1810).[12] Carl Eugen had brought Noverre from Paris to

8. B. Pfeiffer, "Die bildenden Künste unter Karl Eugen," *HKE*, I, 630–634; also H. A. Klaiber, *Der württembergische Oberbaudirektor Philippe de la Guêpière* (Stuttgart, 1959).

9. W. Fleischhauer, "Solitude und Hohenheim," *Schwäbische Heimat*, 2 (1950) 67ff.; Kleemann, *Schloss Solitude*, 8–22; H. A. Klaiber, *Der württembergische Oberbaudirektor Philippe de la Guêpière*, 81–94 (Mon Repos) and 94–109 (Solitude).

10. Hermann Albert, "Die dramatische Musik," *HKE*, I, 558–611. J. Sittard, *Zur Geschichte der Musik und des Theaters am württembergischen Hofe*, 2 vols. (Stuttgart, 1891).

11. Peter Lahnstein, *Ludwigsburg: Aus der Geschichte einer europäischen Residenz* (Stuttgart, 1968), 31–95.

12. Rudolf Krauss, "Das Theater," *HKE*, I, 485–554; by the same author, *Das Stuttgarter Hoftheater* (Stuttgart, 1908). On Noverre, see his reports from Stuttgart, *Lettres sur la danse, et sur les ballets* (Stuttgart, 1760); and more generally Manfried Krüger, *Jean-Georges Noverre und sein Einfluss auf die Ballettgestaltung* (Endstetten, 1963).

Schloss Solitude. Many consider this elegant pavilion among the finest examples of rococo architecture in Europe. Carl Eugen actually resided in a nearby dependence and used this building only for entertaining.

create a company that to this day ranks among the most celebrated ballets in the world. Noverre also set up a school for the teaching of choreography and dance which attracted students from all over Europe. And the list goes on: Carl Eugen endowed an Academie des Arts to house the crown's collection of pictures, prints, and sculpture and to train young artists.[13] In 1756 he opened his vast collection of books, manuscripts, and engravings to the public as a library at Ludwigsburg, available "to all without distinction of rank or social order, excepting those persons compelled to wear livery in their work."[14] Seventeen seventy saw the creation at the Solitude of an officers' academy, a school that later moved to Stuttgart, where as the Hohen Karlsschule it developed into one of Europe's most famous humanistic colleges.[15]

In addition to the outlays for his extensive musical and artistic pursuits, Carl Eugen demanded considerable sums to purchase additional territory for the duchy. The acquisition of these heretofore independent properties involved more than just princely vanity; these lands rounded out Württemberg's borders and expanded the capital base of the state. By the time of his death Carl Eugen had substantially enlarged the crown domain (Kammergut) by the purchases of one-half the comital principality of Limpurg (1780–1782); the lordships of Justingen (1751), Bönnigheim (1785), and Sterneck (1749); and the properties of the former knights of Stettenfels and Gruppenbach (1747), Schwieberdingen (1773), Hofen (1751), Hochdorf and Hochberg (1783), and Ebersberg (1786). He had also strengthened his family trust, the Landschreiberei, by acquiring the independent properties of Zaberfeld, Michelbach, Ochsenberg, and Leonbrunn (1749), Geisingen (1783), and Mühlhausen (1784).[16] Whatever the merit of these various undertakings—and clearly many of them were of the very highest order—they exceeded the capacities of the Württemberg fisc. Demands of the kind that Carl Eugen levied simply could not be accommodated by a tax system set up to maintain a domestic status quo. When the estates refused to vote the dramatic increase in taxation that eventually became necessary to sustain his projects—and the military adventurism that re-

13. Pfeiffer, "Die bildenden Künste unter Herzog Karl Eugen," 675f.
14. R. Uhland, Geschichte der Hohen Karlsschule in Stuttgart (Stuttgart, 1953), 13.
15. Gustav Hauber, "Die Hohe Karlsschule," HKE, II, 3–114; and more recently, Uhland, Geschichte der Hohen Karlsschule.
16. F. K. Wintterlin, "Landeshoheit," HKE, I, 176. On Stettenfels and Gruppenbach, see H. Lehmann, Pietismus und weltliche Ordnung in Württemberg vom 17. bis zum 20. Jahrhundert (Stuttgart, 1969), 99.

sulted from certain of them—Carl Eugen resorted to arbitrary rule. He reconstituted the cabinet government, impressed native sons into his armies, and used force to collect the taxes that he had imposed. His activities, like those of so many early modern rulers, are best viewed in the context of a drive for money rather than for gains on a constitutional chessboard. Though his actions had profound political implications and violated the legal rights of his subjects, they stemmed initially from a need for money rather than from any coherent vision of kingship. Carl Eugen's ideas on that score were a muddle of personal egoism, old-fashioned paternalism, and high-blown theories of divine right. Even at his most extreme he never sought anything like the totalitarian powers that we associate today with a word like absolutism. Nor did he seek the restructuring of society implicit in his father's colonial authoritarianism.

Like Eberhard Ludwig he looked on the duchy as a personal possession and upon his subjects as children in his own family. But unlike that earlier prince, who had been notoriously lazy in matters of government, Carl Eugen showed an enormous capacity for work. In this regard he resembled his wife's famous uncle. In much the same fashion as Frederick of Prussia he traveled incessantly up and down the principality, inquiring about problems *in situ* and acquainting himself with the most minute concerns of his people. Moreover he maintained a voluminous state correspondence. His secretary estimated that the duke dictated some twelve thousand letters a year, many of which went to his most humble subjects.[17] He also held public audiences each Friday and encouraged the townsfolk and peasants to present themselves on those weekly occasions for personal redress of their grievances. The bureaucrats objected strenuously to the custom. They resented so highly personal a manner of dispensing justice and claimed that it short-circuited due process.[18] Carl Eugen ignored them. He had no intention of subjecting himself to the constraints of bureaucratic routine and rejected the notion of any other authority in his lands. "What Fatherland?" he demanded of a Tübingen deputation claiming to speak for the country, "I am the Fatherland!"[19]

The estates' opposition to the foregoing policies contained its own complexities and unresolved ambiguities. What Carl Eugen sought

17. K. Pfaff, *Geschichte des Fürstenhauses und Landes Wirtemberg*, III (Stuttgart, 1839), 401 f. Pfaff's father served as Carl Eugen's personal secretary.
18. Schneider, "Herzog Karls Erziehung, Jugend und Persönlichkeit," 43–45.
19. Adam, "Herzog Karl und die Landschaft," 240. Also E. Marquardt, *Geschichte Württembergs* (Stuttgart, 1962), 208.

for Württemberg—the transformation of his court into an international cultural center and the ability of the duchy to enter German politics on independent terms—cost money, more money than any of the estates cared to spend. They rejected, or failed to grasp, the sheer size of the revenues that would be required to sustain so competitive a posture. Nor were they geared to provide ordinary taxation on that scale. Most important of all, they found distinctly uncongenial the idea that their duty to the state, as Carl Eugen now defined it, could be so incompatible with their wish to preserve an internal balance of power in the duchy.

The estates themselves were split over the proper definition of that balance. One group sought a return to the Eberhardine years when each of the traditional legs of the Württemberg political triangle had functioned as an entity, endowed with its own individual set of rights and responsibilities. The opposite view departed from this model in two ways. The ranking municipal officials and prelates who now dominated the estates' leadership no longer thought of themselves as one of three discrete legs of a triangle. Rather they allied with their cousins and friends on the privy council to form a unified bloc of upper-class estates and officials. In this connection—and this is the second point—they sought to rule with the duke as a corporate duumvirate.

Until 1756 and the outbreak of the Seven Years War, the various tensions remained muted. Carl Eugen managed to supplement his income by massive outside funding, so that even though he was spending wildly and living far beyond his means, he was able to avoid a fiscal showdown with his estates. They in fact contributed less than their collected tax revenues during these years to the duke. The executive committee made an annual grant of some 500,000 florins, plus an additional 30,000 florins for the construction of the Stuttgart palace. The committee also made occasional gifts such as the 56,700 florins voted in 1748 for the duke's wedding expenses and subsequent travel grants for trips to Bayreuth and then in 1753 to Italy.[20] But remaining tax income went to pay off earlier crown debts and to cover the operating expenses of the estates.

Carl Eugen complained about this division, of course, and never failed to demand more money. But he did so in an inoffensive manner and confined his squabbles with the estates to conventional issues: hunting rights, allowances for trips, household and court expenses, and funds for his miniature, largely decorative army. Negotiations over these differences caused no undue alarm. They involved no

20. F. L. Carsten, *Princes and Parliaments in Germany from the Fifteenth to the Eighteenth Century* (Oxford, 1959), 134; and Storz, *Karl Eugen*, 64–66.

questions of public policy but rather were in line with the irritants that fueled domestic politics in most of the eighteenth-century German states. The executive committee or the privy council could absorb them or bargain over them in time-honored fashion.[21]

Decidedly less conventional, and far more serious in their implications, were Carl Eugen's negotiations for outside funding, the most substantive of which took place with France. Without consulting either his privy councilors or his estates, both of whom claimed consultative rights in foreign affairs, Carl Eugen concluded a six-year treaty with Louis XV. In September 1752 he promised the king to recruit and train 6,000 infantrymen, whom he would quarter in Württemberg until France needed soldiers. For this service Louis agreed to deposit 290,000 florins in Carl Eugen's private account. He also obligated himself for the upkeep of the soldiers at an annual allowance of 387,000 florins in peacetime and 479,000 florins in war.[22]

By Württemberg standards the cash flow represented in this transaction was enormous. Recall that the estates' annual grant to the crown hovered around 500,000 florins. They thought this sum sufficient for the duchy's contribution to the total expenses of central government (monarch, court, bureaucracy, military, and foreign office). And now these French subsidies gave Carl Eugen unrestricted access to 677,000 florins for the first year and a minimum of 387,000 florins for each of the remaining five years of the treaty. Since he had no intention of recruiting the soldiers unless called to account by war, he could spend the money entirely as he pleased. Unencumbered cash on this scale—the French never checked to see whether he was neglecting his part of the bargain—enabled Carl Eugen to inflate his court to unprecedented heights. For in addition to his extensive artistic ventures the duke lived in a manner more appropriate to a major monarch than to the ruler of what was after all a minor European state. By the end of the decade the Württemberg court had swollen to over 1,800 persons, of whom 169 had no other function than to serve as gentlemen-in-waiting to the prince.[23] That lordly figure, moreover, had been giving fêtes where the fireworks alone cost 50,000 florins and where, on at least one occasion, presents for the ladies were reckoned at 75,000 florins.[24]

Less politically sensitive than the subsidy treaty but just as corro-

---

21. Adam, "Herzog Karl und die Landschaft," 193–204; cf. W. Grube, *Stuttgarter Landtag* (Stuttgart, 1957), 425–429.
22. LBS, cod. hist. fol. 647; also E. Schneider, "Regierung," *HKE*, I, 149–150.
23. HSAS, A 202: Bü. 80 (promotion list for 11 February 1763).
24. Albert Pfister, "Hof und Hoffeste," *HKE*, I, 104–118.

sive of the treasury's good health were Carl Eugen's efforts to attract capital investment from outside the duchy. He sought cash deposits which he then secured with crown property—deals that provided the duke with large one-time infusions of cash and no doubt helped make possible his sumptuous style of life. But in that the money went for material consumption rather than industrial production, it generated no subsequent yield. Instead interest payments on the deposit had to come from the mortgaged properties with the result that the crown suffered a long-term reduction in current income. Since Carl Eugen conducted these negotiations privately and sequestered all funds into his secret account, few records of these transactions survive. The privy councilors suspected that enormous sums were involved; and if the one documented case was at all typical, the officials had every reason to worry. In that particular instance the celebrated French philosopher Voltaire, who had accumulated a fortune from his writings, honoraria, and lottery winnings, was casting about for opportunities for capital investment. In 1752 he arranged with Carl Eugen —it is not clear which of the two men initiated the transaction— for two deposits to the duke's account. The first was for 260,000 florins, serviced and secured by the income from the crown's Left Bank lordships of Reichenweiler and Horburg. The value of the second remains unknown. It must have been considerable; Carl Eugen pledged all the income from the lands around the city of Mömpelgard to cover the deposit.[25]

Despite their stunned bewilderment over the extravagant scale of the duke's personal expenditure, government officials had little to say in these financial transactions. The duke kept most of them secret; and so long as he adhered to the constitution neither the estates nor the privy councilors had any legitimate grounds for intervention. An opportunity did present itself when news of the subsidy treaty leaked out; for in matters of foreign alliances the law stipulated that the duke consult with his councilors and estates. Even so, the officials showed themselves surprisingly complacent and slow to react. Executive committee members were especially unresponsive. Carl Eugen's fiscal negotiations cost them nothing. In fact, at least in the short run, subsidies and foreign deposits eased the financial pressure on the estates. At any event they saw no need to stir up trouble over this question. Johann Jakob Moser (1701–1785), who from 1751 to 1770 held

25. Adam, "Herzog Karl und die Landschaft," 246, reckoned the total of Voltaire's deposits at 280,000 livres. Figuring 2.5 florins (guilders) to the livre, the sum stood at 700,000 florins. See also Storz, *Karl Eugen*, 59f. Privy council discussions of the subject are found in HSAS, A 202: Bü. 20 and 29.

the office of counsel to the estates, was virtually alone in trying to muster concerted opposition to the subsidy treaty.[26] He wrote a fiery tract on the subject in which he conjured up visions of young Würt-tembergers being pressed into service for foreign despots. He also appeared before the privy council and alarmed its officials with prophecies of a popular uprising in the event of a forced conscription for foreign service. But though the council supported Moser in a letter to Carl Eugen, the duke pressed ahead with his plans; he departed with his wife to attend the carnival season at Venice and left the councilors to swallow a fait accompli.[27]

The incident revealed a good deal about the inner workings of the government at this time, especially in respect to the executive committee and the privy council. The Landtag had not met in plenary session since 1739, when it had confirmed the system of committee rule for the estates. Since that occasion the executive committee, with its staff of lawyers, secretaries, clerks, and tax officials, had carried on the estates' business.[28] Now Moser's entry as the senior of two active legal counsels brought a dissonant voice into what had otherwise become a harmonious chorus of oligarchs. These magnates were led by Johann Friedrich Stockmayer, who since 1735 had combined the two key posts of legal counsel and chief secretary to the executive committee. Stockmayer, the son of the old Bebenhausen prelate who had led the fight to preserve committee rule at the Landtag of 1737–1739, shared power with two prelates. The first, the abbot of Adelberg Wilhelm Gottlieb Tafinger (1691–1757), served as committee president. He also held the title of court preacher (*Hofprediger*) and sat on the consistory.[29] The other was the new prelate of Bebenhausen, Stockmayer's younger brother Christoph Friedrich (died 1782).[30]

The Stockmayers dominated the executive committee for the remainder of the century; Johann Friedrich's son and then his grandson

---

26. For a comprehensive analysis of Moser's role as counsel, see M. Walker, *Johann Jakob Moser and the Holy Roman Empire of the German Nation* (Chapel Hill, N.C., 1981), 189–279.

27. Adam, "Herzog Karl und die Landschaft," 201–202.

28. Moser defined the executive committee's duties in an essay found in LBS, cod. jur. 4° 239.

29. W. Pfeilsticker, *Neues württembergisches Dienerbuch* (Stuttgart, 1957), 369, 1414, 2020, 3257, 3373; also R. Rürup, *Johann Jacob Moser: Pietismus und Reform* (Wiesbaden, 1965), 156f.

30. On the Stockmayer brothers' careers, see Pfeilsticker, *Dienerbuch*, 1157, 1179, 1185, 1227, 1330, 1433, 1468, 1884, 2774, 2854, 2910, 3027, 3304, 3358, 3415. A. Adam, *Johann Jakob Moser als württembergischer Landschaftskonsulent, 1754–77* (Stuttgart, 1887), 4–5 and 16–18, offers an interesting analysis of their personalities.

succeeded him as counsel-secretary. They held equally vital posts in the administrative branch of the government. Christoph Friedrich's son-in-law Eberhard Friedrich Hochstetter (died 1786) was soon to become chief secretary to the privy council (1766–1786), while Stock-mayer's son Jakob [von] Stockmayer served as resident minister at Vienna and championed committee interests at the imperial court.[31] The ranking secular figures on the committee, the mayors of Tübingen and Stuttgart, had similar links throughout the municipal administrations of those cities as well as in the university and the church.[32] With this kind of inbred control, the executive committee members had no desire for a general Landtag that might result in a curbing of their influence. They therefore turned an indifferent ear to Moser's agitated protests against the subsidies and refused to support his demands for a plenary assembly to debate the matter.[33]

The privy council, as has been noted, acted somewhat more vigorously than the executive committee, but it too was in process of internal restructuring. Since Bilfinger's death in 1750, the council had been dominated by Friedrich August von Hardenberg (1700–1768), a professional civil servant from northern Germany (Mansfeld) who had risen in the Württemberg administration through service first on the Oberrat (reorganized now as the Regierungsrat) and subsequently on the Rentkammer.[34] Hardenberg was a man of balanced judgment and firmly committed to constitutional government. It was he, incidentally, who had commended Moser as counsel to the Württemberg estates; and, so long as he held office, he seconded Moser's insistence upon principles of correlative government.

Frederick the Great, in the Miroir des princes that he prepared for Carl Eugen when the young prince left Berlin in 1744, had warned the duke against both Bilfinger and Hardenberg.[35] Carl Eugen had ignored the warning in both instances. But after Hardenberg encouraged the privy council to support Moser's criticism of his foreign pol-

31. Pfeilsticker, Dienerbuch, 1157, 1185, 1330.
32. Karl Pfaff, Miszellen aus der wirtembergischen Geschichte (Stuttgart, 1824), 104–110.
33. Grube, Stuttgarter Landtag, 426, emphasized the executive committee's fear of a Landtag; cf. Rürup, Johann Jacob Moser, 56–58. On Moser's quarrel with the Stockmayers, see UT: Mh. 267.
34. Pfeilsticker, Dienerbuch, 1113, 1119, 1194, 1195, 1652, 2288, 2565, 2589, 3010. On the Regierungsrat, see F. Wintterlin, Geschichte der Behördenorganisation in Württemberg, I (Stuttgart, 1902), 77–79.
35. That essay is reproduced in L. T. von Spittler, Oeuvres de Frédéric le Grand, IX (Berlin, 1848), 1–7. Schneider, "Regierung," 148, suggested that Frederick regarded the two councilors as pro-Austrian and hence unsympathetic to Prussian influence at Stuttgart.

icy, Carl Eugen recalled Frederick's reservations and shifted his support away from the councilor and his colleagues. By 1753, for example, he was routinely sending his demands for money directly to the executive committee.[36] In so doing he not only bypassed the privy council but denied by implication that board's constitutional role as the official mediator between crown and estates. Matters reached a head in the spring of 1755. On 4 April Carl Eugen appeared unexpectedly at a privy council meeting and began berating the councilors for disobeying his orders and for taking too great an administrative initiative in his government.[37] Two months later, without benefit even of a hearing, he dismissed Hardenberg on trumped-up charges of fiscal impropriety.[38]

With Hardenberg's dramatic fall from office and the death that same year of Philipp Zech, who had supported first Bilfinger and then Hardenberg in the struggle to keep the council at the center of government, the board went into a decline. The patrician Johann Eberhard Georgii, another stalwart from the regency, took over from Zech as director of the consistory and championed old-line politics on the board. His non-noble colleagues—Dr. Günther Albrecht Renz (1705–1767) and Christoph Heinrich Korn (1688–1764)—were Württembergers of similar professional training and social background to his own. That is, they too had studied law at Tübingen and belonged to the upper ranks of the territorial Ehrbarkeit.[39] But though both men supported Georgii's policies, they were new to the board and had no particular access to the duke. Their combined strength could not prevent the council's loss of power.

The noblemen on the board—Ferdinand R. W. Freiherr von Wallbrunn (died 1770), Christoph Dieterich von Keller (1699–1758), Reinhard Freiherr von Gemmingen (1687–1756), and Johann Freiherr von Rotkirch (dates unknown)—were either committed to the court party or were working largely outside the duchy. Wallbrunn moved entirely in court circles where he held the post of Lord High Steward (*Oberhofmeister*), while Gemmingen and Rotkirch served respectively as governor of Mömpelgard and as Württemberg's repre-

---

36. Grube, *Stuttgarter Landtag*, 428–429.
37. L. von Spittler, *Geschichte des wirtembergischen Geheimen-Raths-Collegiums*, in *Sämtliche Werke*, ed. K. Wächter, XIII (Stuttgart and Tübingen, 1837), 430–432.
38. On the dismissal, see HSAS, A 202: Bü. 79 and 82 (esp. papers for 4 April, 24 June, and 23 August).
39. Renz: Pfeilsticker, *Dienerbuch*, 1140, 1227, 1298, 1327, 2036; HSAS, A 202: Bü. 82 (12 May 1751) and 69. Korn: *Dienerbuch*, 1137, 1155, 1210, 1237, 1238, 1297, 1445, 2016, 2024, 2028, 2033, 2041; HSAS, A 202: Bü. 82 (19 and 24 February 1744). See note 42 to this chapter.

sentative to the Reichstag at Regensburg. Keller, who had earlier been personal secretary to Carl Alexander and had then held a post on the delegation to Regensburg, resided mostly in Berlin, where he lobbied for Württemberg interests at Frederick's court.[40]

In terms of their backgrounds and professional abilities the councilors differed little from their predecessors under the regency. Their declining influence did not reflect on their professional qualities but stemmed from the fact that Carl Eugen consulted them with increasing rarity. Though he did not interfere with their administrative duties, he minimized their roles as advisers to the crown. Council minutes show that by the end of 1755 the councilors were already handling only routine crown business.[41] Personal contact with the duke had virtually ceased and their only consultation was with members of the estates' executive committee. Publication the next year of the Court Address Book (*Hofkalendar*) underscored the drop in council prestige. Whereas the directory had customarily listed the privy councilors immediately after the members of the ducal family, the new table of precedence placed the members of the duke's personal secretariat at the head of government and the privy council below that body in a subordinate position.[42]

Personal rule became official policy in 1758. At that time Carl Eugen created the *Staats- und Cabinettsministerium* for the direction of the government.[43] His explanation for the innovation recalled that of Eberhard Ludwig. Once again the duke announced blandly that he was creating a cabinet "in line with the precedent set by the other most illustrious princely governments." He allowed the privy council to continue its deliberations but turned the board into a clerical clearinghouse. In a letter of 11 February 1758 he informed the councilors that they were "to expedite immediately, without correction or

40. Gemmingen: Pfeilsticker, *Dienerbuch*, 1118. Rotkirch: *Dienerbuch*, 1122, 1370, 2136, 2310, 2329, 2640. Keller: *Dienerbuch*, 213, 1136, 1153, 1209, 1235, 1367, 1369, 1381; HSAS, A 202: Bü. 80–82, and A 204: Bü. 188. See note 42 to this chapter.
41. The councilors communicated with the duke through his personal secretariat (*Geheime Kanzlei*); HSAS, A 204: Bü. 1755, 3196–3197.
42. A precedence table of 11 August 1744 (HSAS, A 202: Bü. 73) had assigned three generals precedence over the non-noble councilors. Under Duke Carl Alexander the crown began an annual publication listing all members of the ducal family, the court, and the government. Entries were arranged according to rank and included all titles and offices of those listed. It is therefore possible to reconstruct career patterns from these volumes. Contemporaries referred to them most often by the title of *Hofkalendar*. The most common bibliographic citation down to 1918 is *Württembergische Hof- und Staats-Handbücher*, though actual publication titles changed every few years. The complete series is found in the HSAS library, the LBS, and the UT.
43. Wintterlin, *Behördenorganisation*, I, 72n2. See also his essay, "Landeshoheit," 170–171; and A. Dehlinger, *Württembergisches Staatswesen in seiner geschichtlichen Entwicklung bis Heute*, I (Stuttgart, 1951), 107.

change," all decisions coming from the cabinet. Furthermore the councilors were to refer at once to the new group all items of business requiring ducal approval that reached the privy council from either the districts or the central branches of government.[44]

The cabinet functioned independently of the great bureaucratic offices; it was staffed entirely at the duke's pleasure and accountable only to him. Three prominent courtiers composed the group: Count Friedrich Samuel von Montmartin (1712–1778), Baron Johann Christoph von Pflug (1705–1772), and Baron F. R. W. von Wallbrunn.[45] The aforementioned letter to the privy council made it plain that each of the courtiers would exercise certain specified responsibilities. The councilors were to send imperial and Kreis matters to Montmartin, who held the title of *premier ministre*, or cabinet president; domestic, court, and confessional business was to be assigned to Wallbrunn; and administrative, judicial, feudal, and Polizei questions to Pflug, who also served as president of the Regierungsrat. In turn these three men, though their spheres were separate, worked together as the cabinet. They set up a chancellery and a cluster of subcommittees to implement their policies. Each of them also held a seat on the privy council. But as had been the case in Eberhard Ludwig's cabinet ministry, none of them took an active role in its affairs. Not even Wallbrunn, who had been on the council since 1739, thought the title of privy councilor of sufficient importance to list in his biographical sketch for a succeeding edition of the *Hofkalendar*.

Montmartin appears to have masterminded the new system. A Prussian by birth, he had made a successful career in the politics of the smaller German courts and in the process had become a strong supporter of princely absolutism. Carl Eugen first encountered him at Bayreuth as a privy councilor to the Ansbach government. At that time Montmartin had upheld the duke's courtship of Princess Friederike and in addition had used his influence as an imperial councilor (*Hofrat*) to persuade Emperor Charles VII to declare the sixteen-year-old Carl Eugen of sufficient age to rule. For these services the duke had named him an honorary Württemberg privy councilor and granted him a stipend of 1,200 florins.[46] Montmartin later left Bayreuth and took a position at Saxe-Weimar, where, as ambassador

44. HSAS, A 202: Bü. 78.

45. Pflug, a Saxon nobleman, married Louise von Bernerdin, the sister of Carl Eugen's morganatic wife Franziska von Hohenheim. On his Württemberg career, see Pfeilsticker, *Dienerbuch*, 1115, 1121, 1190, 1198, 1294, 1296, 2603, 2985, 3245; also *Hofkalendar*, 1736–1772. Montmartin: *Hofkalendar*, 1758–1766; *Dienerbuch*, 538, 1113, 1120, 1168, 1381, 1479, 3188; HSAS, A 202: Bü. 70 and 73. Also A 74 alt: Bü. 125 alt (correspondence between Montmartin and Baron von Thun).

46. HSAS, A 202: Bü. 73 (24 February 1744).

to the Reichstag, he violated his master's Protestant scruples by allying the Thuringian duchy with Catholic Austria in the declaration against Prussia that began the Seven Years War. For this service Maria Theresa, who was anxious to build an Austrian party at Stuttgart, recommended Montmartin for a full-time position as chief minister in the Württemberg government.[47]

Montmartin's arrival at Stuttgart coincided with the beginning of a long period of domestic upheaval in the duchy. His leadership in the cabinet government, his unqualified commitment to the unpopular Franco-Austrian alliance, and his open bias toward absolute rule have earned him the reputation of an arch-villain in Württemberg history.[48] The estates and the old guard on the privy council regarded him as little better than a cutpurse, a man contemptuous of law who sought only to batten off his master's despotic power. And certainly Montmartin did not hestitate to pander to the most over-charged of Carl Eugen's conceptions of monarchy. One of his first acts upon arrival at Stuttgart was to change the straightforward wording in the *Hofkalendar* announcing the date of the sovereign's birth. He substituted for "was born on" the preposterous euphemism, "has increased the number of mighty in the world on."[49]

Montmartin most certainly held a highly individual view of the state, rejecting the balance of power inherent in Württemberg's constitutional tradition. But one should note that his notions of absolutism were of the old-fashioned sort. They carried none of the implications of social reconstruction implicit in Carl Alexander's authoritarian fiscal and military policies. He accepted without question the idea of a corporate society and jockeyed for a leading role in the established categories of Württemberg political life. He insisted only that the monarch knew best and therefore must rule without being held accountable by any group in his territory. His attitude toward the estates recalled that of his late-seventeenth-century predecessor Baron Staffhorst. In words similar to those used by Staffhorst in dealing with Landschaftskonsulent Sturm, he informed the executive committee that the estates had no responsibility beyond "unconditional obedience" to the ruler's "absolute command."[50]

47. On Montmartin's earlier career, see Eugen Schneider, "Montmartin," in *Allgemeine Deutsche Biographie*, XXII (Leipzig, 1885), 204. Spittler, *Geheimen-Raths-Collegiums*, 435, attributes Montmartin's appointment to Maria Theresa.

48. Spittler, Geheimen-Raths-Collegiums, 437–438; cf. Marquardt, *Geschichte Württembergs*, 204; and Walker, *Johann Jakob Moser*, 228–229. A study in progress by Wolfgang Böhm, "Baron Ulrich von Thun: Ein deutscher Diplomat und Prinzenerzieher am französischen Hof, 1707–88," promises a more favorable assessment of Montmartin's statesmanship.

49. *Württembergisches Hof- und Staats-Handbuch*, 1759.

50. Paul von Stälin, "Karl Eugen, Herzog von Württemberg," *Allgemeine Deutsche*

Montmartin's rhetoric met with no more favor from the Württembergers than had that of Staffhorst. But once again the estates and officials found it difficult to hold their own against concerted pressure from their ruler. As they contended with the duke for their continued share in the direction of government, it became increasingly obvious that both sides were circumscribed by forces outside their control. For all their sovereign independence the secondary German states still functioned as separate but indivisible parts of a larger whole. They were subject finally to built-in limitations that operated outside their sphere of influence. And though the duke appeared for a time to be more independent than his opposition, he ultimately discovered that he too was checkmated. The same forces that constrained his estates reassembled in a different configuration to frustrate his bid for absolute rule.

The battle had been joined before Montmartin arrived in the duchy, having begun in June 1756 when war broke out between France and England. At that point Louis XV sent an agent to Stuttgart to supervise transport for the six thousand mercenary soldiers who the king assumed had been assembled and trained with his subsidies. But the agent found nothing at Stuttgart beyond an elaborately dressed palace guard and a top-heavy officer corps used to impart an aura of military grandeur to Carl Eugen's overblown court. Since he had done nothing to fulfill his contract, the duke now faced the immediate necessity of raising an army in a country whose constitution expressly forbade impressment and authorized recruitment only in the event of a military danger to the duchy. Moreover, he was supposed to fund this enterprise out of a purse that he had long since depleted. To make matters worse, in August of that same year his wife's Prussian uncle invaded Saxony. The imperial government, now allied to France as a result of the so-called diplomatic revolution, was mobilizing the Reichstag for a declaration of war against Prussia and thus against England and Denmark, Berlin's principal allies.

Carl Eugen withheld his support for a declaration of war against his in-laws. But once the Reichstag had voted such an action, he entered the conflict as an estate of the empire and as an ally of the House of Austria.[51] This commitment meant that in addition to the troops for

---

*Biographie,* xv (Leipzig, 1882), 378–379; Adam, *Johann Jakob Moser,* 39–40; Walker, *Johann Jakob Moser,* 229. On Staffhorst, see pages 169, 189–192 of this book.

51. The *corpus evangelicorum* had blocked a formal vote to place the king under an imperial ban, so that questions of constitutional legality clouded the Reichstag's final declaration of war. Those opposed to the decision, such as the privy councilors and estates of Württemberg, could argue that the individual states remained free to use their discretion in entering the alliance with Austria. On the declaration, see J. S. Pütter, *Historische Entwicklung der heutigen Staatsverfassung des Teutschen Reichs,* 3d ed.,

France, he had to raise an army for the Reich. Since his personal finances were utterly exhausted at this point, he could turn for money, men, and supply only to the public resources of the duchy. The problem here, of course, was that most of those resources remained tied to the ecclesiastical trust (Kirchengut) and to the revenues of the estates. The Reversalien had invested the privy council with responsibility for the former and the executive committee of the Landtag with control of the latter.

If he was to stay within the limits imposed by the constitution of the duchy, Carl Eugen thus had to secure the active approval of these two institutional bodies, neither of which he had consulted before signing the subsidy treaty that now imposed such heavy military obligations. The councilors and executive committeemen refused to endorse an alliance that placed the duchy so squarely in the Catholic camp and at war with its long-trusted Protestant allies in the Reich.[52] Moreover, these latter states—Schleswig-Holstein (Denmark), Brandenburg (Prussia), and Hanover (England)—were the very forces that stood as guarantors for the Reversalien. The Württembergers feared that, if they cut themselves off from such allies, there would be no outside force to secure the territorial church and the patterns of influence and constitutional settlements that were tied to its structure. And their anxiety mounted when they discovered that Friederike, herself a Protestant, had returned to her parents at Bayreuth and announced her intention to remain there, separated from her husband.[53]

Short of revolution or decisive backing from outside the duchy, there was little that the estates and councilors could do to prevent the duke from ignoring the constitution and acting on his own initiative to obtain what he needed. They could, and did, refuse to vote him the money and supplies that he demanded in order to satisfy the French. But when he raised these by force they could only protest and declare him in violation of the Reversalien. Their problem of course was that such a declaration lacked teeth. The duke was already at war with the three royal guarantors and so had nothing to fear from their further displeasure. And the imperial crown, the principal constitutional force within the Reich to recognize the Reversalien, needed the very material that Carl Eugen was seeking to secure by violation of the constitutional settlement.

---

III (Göttingen, 1799), 87–113; and Von denen Teutschen Reichs-Tags-Geschäften, VI (Frankfurt am Main, 1768), 206–220.

52. Lehmann, Pietismus und weltliche Ordnung, 101 f. On popular response to the Catholic alliance, see also HSAS, A 8: Bü. 390.

53. On Friederike's departure, see Storz, Karl Eugen, 78–81; and P. von Stälin, "Die beiden Ehen des Herzogs. Friederike," HKE, I, 55–78.

The result was that by the time of Montmartin's arrival—and indeed for the duration of the Seven Years War—Carl Eugen exercised a more or less free hand over the duchy. Even before the institution of cabinet government he had begun a program of compulsory conscription that bears upon this study because of its subsequent implications for relations between the crown and the localities. The chief figure in this enterprise was Friedrich Philipp Rieger (1722–1782), whom the duke appointed as his personal military adviser (*Geheimer Kriegsrat*).[54] Rieger served his master in much the way that General von Remchingen had served the duke's father; that is, as a military henchman ready to carry out ducal orders by force. But whereas Remchingen came from outside the duchy, Rieger was a native-born Württemberger with intimate ties to the highest echelon of Württemberg society. His father Georg Conrad was a celebrated Stuttgart pastor; his brother Carl Heinrich occupied the post of suffragan court chaplain (*Hofkaplan*); his nephew Gottlob Heinrich, also a Stuttgart pastor, took a leading role in Pietist circles; and his father-in-law Ludwig Eberhard Fischer, prelate of Adelberg, presided as ranking Protestant preacher over the court chapel.[55] More important, in 1757 Fischer succeeded Tafinger as chief prelate on the executive committee of the Landtag and at once began to exercise substantial influence on its deliberations.[56]

Although family connections did not prevent Rieger from serving his master with single-minded devotion, they nonetheless shaped his political views. Unlike his counterpart Remchingen, he always confined his aggression to the traditional categories of Württemberg governmental affairs. He had none of Remchingen's reformed Catholic zeal. Instead he accepted as natural the idea of a territorial church geared to the social and economic organization of the duchy. And he conceived of that organization in terms that endowed each corporate group with distinct privileges and obligations. His harsh military policies, his brutal use of force against the estates, and his heavy trafficking in the sale of offices (*Diensthandel*)—all aimed at the domination not the destruction of the established institutions of Württemberg political life.[57]

By the end of the summer of 1757 Rieger had recruited some six

54. HSAS, A 202: Bü. 92 (appointment papers of 8 December 1757); Pfeilsticker, *Dienerbuch*, 1989, 2434, 2682.
55. On the role of the Rieger family in the territorial church, see Lehmann, *Pietismus und weltliche Ordnung*, 75–149.
59. Fischer also held a seat on the consistory; see Pfeilsticker, *Dienerbuch*, 365, 1137, 1319, 1417, 2019, 2130, 3257, 3390.
57. Receipts and letters in HSAS, A 202: Bü. 2739 show Rieger to have been far more heavily involved in Diensthandel than Württemberg historians have heretofore

thousand peasants and artisans into the Württemberg corps destined for French service. To accomplish this feat he had ridden roughshod over the Württembergers' civil liberties. His agents had raided local taverns and even surrounded villages to impress into service any unattached young men they could find. They stood guard outside the churches and abducted healthy males as they came out of Sunday worship. Then they took these men to local recruiting stations where they held them without bread or water until they consented to enlist "voluntarily" in the mercenary army. Having once signed, the rustics received almost no training. Instead, undisciplined and completely ignorant of military tactics, they were herded off to join the Austrian army in Saxony. They arrived just in time to take part in the Battle of Leuthen (5 December 1757) and to suffer a crushing defeat by Frederick the Great. Only 1,900 of the original six thousand recruits survived that winter to return to Württemberg.[58]

This military debacle placed the crown in an even more awkward position. In the first instance the troops' poor performance and notoriously low morale made the French disinclined to renew the subsidy treaty, so that it looked as though that funding would cease. To sustain the lavish style of life that the subsidies had underwritten, Carl Eugen would have had not only to raise another mercenary army by force but also to find a new client for these raw conscripts. Second, Württemberg still faced the problem of fielding its imperial contingent, and its resolution inevitably involved the duke in acrimonious negotiations with the outraged estates over grants of supply. Finally the staggering loss of Württemberg life at Leuthen, together with the popular outcry over Rieger's impressment tactics, made voluntary local recruiting, even for the imperial obligation, extremely difficult.

Under these circumstances the duke was scarcely in a position to return to constitutional behavior. Having once embarked on an illegal course, he had lost his hold over events. He had committed himself first to a court and then to a military involvement beyond his means. Only a yet more autocratic response could rescue his princely *gloire*. By the end of the first year of the war, Rieger was organizing manhunts up and down the duchy for the hordes of peasants who had run away from compulsory service. Even worse, he had persuaded Carl Eugen to issue for the duchy a code of military punishment that vio-

---

supposed. For an interesting account of his philosophy, see F. Nicholai, *Beschreibung einer Reise durch Deutschland und die Schweiz im Jahr 1781*, X (Berlin, 1795), 162.

58. Carsten, *Princes and Parliaments*, 137f.; Albert Pfister, "Militärwesen," *HKE*, I, 121–127; Adam, "Herzog Karl und die Landschaft," 211–213; and E. Schneider, *Württembergische Geschichte* (Stuttgart, 1896), 357f.

lated territorial liberties. The code decreed the most severe penalties for those who fled service, and it denied runaways recourse in the civil courts. Anyone who deserted on the battlefield was to be shot on the spot, defections while on guard duty earned thirty-six laps through the gauntlet, and any soldier found at a distance of more than a quarter mile from his unit during a march was to be hanged then and there. Furthermore, the state assumed the right to confiscate all property of deserters.[59]

These measures were classic ones. They differed very little from those employed by the eighteenth-century Prussian and English monarchs in raising troops for their own military establishments. But they aroused bitter protests from the Württemberg estates and provided the executive committee with a constitutional justification for refusing the duke's demands for money and supply. Relations between the two political camps deteriorated steadily. But with the privy council now shorn of influence and exterior forces unable to intervene, the executive committee could do no more than refuse its vote and then stand by helplessly when the crown took steps to raise tax revenue on its own. And Carl Eugen did just that.[60] He resorted to all the shortcuts open to precapitalist governments in the quest for ready money. He pawned crown properties, invaded the ecclesiastical trust, forced loans from government officials, debased the coinage, and reinstated the tobacco and salt monopolies—in the latter instance forcing every inhabitant in the duchy to purchase fifteen pounds of state salt. Similar tactics were used in the state lottery that Carl Eugen established. The government allotted tickets on a compulsory basis, like a tax, so that virtually everyone had to purchase them regardless of personal preferences. In the end the duke resorted to the selling of offices (Diensthandel). He set up an agency for the sale of government jobs and vested its control in a creature of Montmartin, an unscrupulous Expeditionsrat from Thuringia named Kaspar Laurentius Wittleder (died 1769).[61]

Rieger saw to the enforcement of these arbitrary measures. He

59. A. L. Reyscher, Vollständige, historisch und kritisch bearbeitete Sammlung der württembergischen Gesetze, XIX (Stuttgart and Tübingen, 1849), 667; W. Kohlhaas, "Die Meuterei der Württemberger anno 1757," Beiträge zur Landeskunde, 5 (1971), 11–16.

60. The most complete account of these arbitrary policies is found in Adam, "Herzog Karl und die Landschaft," 209–233; cf. the collection of documents published by the estates' executive committee, Verhandlungen zwischen des regierenden Herrn Herzogens zu Württemberg Hoch-Fürstl. Durchlaut und dero treu-gehorsamsten Prälaten und Landschafft in den Jahren 1757 und 1758 (Stuttgart, 1758).

61. Pfeilsticker, Dienerbuch, 2032, 2039, 2053, 2356, 3407, 3505; HSAS, A 202: Bü. 2738–2739 and 2743–2758.

backed up crown demands with soldiers and did not hesitate to use force wherever necessary. He operated in the Aemter as well as at the capital. His most spectacular ploy at the capital came in January 1759. On that occasion he surrounded the estates' office buildings with soldiers from the Stuttgart garrison and compelled the tax officials inside to empty their chests for inventory by crown agents and to hand over 30,000 florins which he claimed was owed the duke. In June of that year he repeated the maneuver, this time without the troops, and collected another 30,000 florins.[62] His district strategy was equally aggressive and recalled that of Eberhard Ludwig. After the executive committee had refused Carl Eugen's request for extraordinary taxes, Rieger and his officers went to the local assemblies where they intimidated the small-town officials and village elders into supporting the crown. On one occasion Rieger went even further and, in flagrant violation of the Tübinger Vertrag, confiscated the grain reserves (Fruchtvorräte) of several districts for a forced sale on behalf of the crown.[63]

Rieger fell from power in 1762, an apparent victim of Montmartin's jealous intrigues.[64] But his fall did not end crown activity in the districts. On the contrary Carl Eugen stepped up pressure on local institutions. In that the political reorientation after the end of the Seven Years War forced the duke to abandon his aggressive policies, we can only speculate as to their long-term purposes. Certainly Carl Eugen's preliminary moves indicated that he envisioned a dramatic restructuring of the Aemter which would have brought the districts under the thumb of the central government. The essence of his policy lay in the establishment throughout the duchy of a series of subdistricts that were then attached to the historic Aemter on terms that would benefit the crown. These new units were composed of the villages that had sprung up in the area since the creation of the Amt or villages that for one reason or another had escaped incorporation in earlier days. Since the crown assumed sole administration of the new units—there were no elections for local officials—the duke claimed the right to send his agents to the Amt assemblies to represent these new vil-

62. HSAS, A 34: Bü. 86–87; Eugen Schneider, "Zur Charakteristik des Oberst Rieger," Staatsanzeiger: Literarische Beilage (1888), 293–296.

63. Grube, Stuttgarter Landtag, 430.

64. Versions vary as to details, but historians agree that Montmartin engineered Rieger's fall. Cf. Pfister, "Militärwesen," 136f.; Schneider, "Regierung," 156; Lehmann, Pietismus und weltliche Ordnung, 170; and Walker, Johann Jakob Moser, 226f. Rieger spent four years in the fortress at Hohentwiel but upon release was restored to favor, promoted to general, and given the lifetime command over the Hohen Asperg Citadel, just outside Ludwigsburg.

lages. In this way, for the first time since the early seventeenth century, the crown could obtain open access to the Amtsversammlung.[65] There the duke's officials might challenge the Ehrbarkeit's supervision of the various standing conmittees and make it impossible for the municipal magistrates to be any longer assured of dominating district policies. Indeed their presence would undermine the Ehrbarkeit's control over the appointment to local offices, a patronage network that heretofore had insured the magistrates' regional political influence.

This network rested on the ancient right of the localities to make their own appointments to district offices. As early as 1758 the executive committee had sought to bolster that custom by the publication of a communal ordinance based upon the research of the committee's chief legal counsel, J. J. Moser.[66] He documented some thousand rescripts and privileges that over the years had vested communal offices in local hands. This custom of course meant that the crown was restricted to an indirect role at the district level of territorial government, and Carl Eugen's subdistricts aimed at remedying that situation. An incident in 1765 demonstrated how this challenge might have unfolded had the subdistricts been allowed to develop. At that time the Ehrbarkeit of the Amt Lauffen protested that a ducal commissioner, supported by crown agents in the subdistrict, had deposed the local Amt treasurer (*Amtspfleger*) and installed his own man, an agent called Pfeilsticker, in that office. The executive committee managed to block the appointment by a court injunction. Then in the postwar negotiations before the emperor the committee succeeded in obtaining a final ruling forbidding such practice.[67] But the incident remained an ominous portent—an indication to the Ehrbarkeit of the direction Carl Eugen's district strategy might take.

Whatever the fate of his subdistricts, Carl Eugen's other arbitrary measures yielded prodigious immediate results. Between 1758 and 1764 the government collected nearly 10,000,000 florins from the duchy, only 3,117,000 florins (31 percent) of which had been voted by the executive committee.[68] That body's financial credit suffered accordingly. Investors from outside the duchy who had placed funds with the Landschaften now began calling in their deposits. The only way the committee could attract new funds was by raising its interest

65. W. Grube, "Dorfgemeinde und Amtsversammlung in Altwürttemberg," ZWLG, 13 (1954), 194–219.
66. Reyscher, *Vollständige Sammlung*, XIV, 537–777.
67. HSAS, A 202: Bü. 3204 (case of 14 August 1765).
68. Carsten, *Princes and Parliaments*, 140.

rates and thus making it increasingly difficult for the estates to realize any profit on these investments.[69] Meanwhile court life continued to flourish on a scale of unprecedented luxury. In the winter of 1763, to give but one example, two weeks of uninterrupted celebration—hunts, balls, operas, pageants, parades, fêtes, dinners—marked Carl Eugen's thirty-fifth birthday. Princes from throughout the southern part of the empire flocked into Stuttgart for the festivities. And each brought a retinue of courtiers and servants, all of whom, like the monarchs themselves, were housed at Württemberg expense.[70]

Under such trying circumstances one might well wonder why the estates never considered getting rid of their ruler through some act of violence. That they did not do so testified to the deep-seated loyalty that eighteenth-century Germans still felt for their hereditary rulers. This sentiment was to surface again in the early nineteenth century when reformers such as Baron Karl Friedrich vom Stein found the territorial princes an indispensable element in the Wars of Liberation. Though he himself despised the "princelets" for their personal failings, Stein acknowledged that they alone had the capacity to inspire the populace to a general uprising against Napoleonic rule.[71]

In this present instance, however, more than pious sentiment restrained the territorial elite from a violent resolution of their difficulties. The brunt of Carl Eugen's arbitrary tax measures were falling upon the peasantry and the urban masses, not upon the municipal magistrates. There is no question that the estates were hard-pressed by the forced loans and assessments imposed upon them by the duke and that they were anxious over the constitutional implications of Carl Eugen's despotic levies. But since the bulk of the taxes derived from repeated doublings of the traditional assessments that they allocated, the magistrates of the Ehrbarkeit could afford to wait until an alteration in the European balance of power offered a chance to seek legal redress for their legitimate grievances. Meanwhile the Württemberg crown conducted the war effort, guaranteed the Ehrbarkeit's municipal status, and secured the magistrates against interference by neighboring states such as Bavaria in which authoritarian monarchs governed without constitutional restraints.

Again, internal divisions made it difficult for the Ehrbarkeit to un-

69. Grube, *Stuttgarter Landtag,* 430.

70. LBS, AH 1021: *Description des fêtes données pendant quatorze jours à l'occasion du jour de naissance de son altesse Serenissime Monseigneur le Duc Regnant de Württemberg et Teck* (Stuttgart, 1763).

71. English readers should see especially chapter eight in the forthcoming edition of Franz Schnabel, *Freiherr vom Stein,* by Jefferson Adams.

dertake a concentrated attack upon the monarchy. Most upper-class executive committee members still resisted the idea of a general Landtag at which they would be outnumbered by the provincial delegates. Nor could the leadership agree upon a political strategy. Whereas Moser pushed for active resistance, the Stockmayers and Fischer—the latter inevitably influenced by his ties with Rieger—felt temporization to be the wiser course. Once peace returned, they hoped that the imperial organization, working at this time to favor their sovereign's cause, would provide the structure for a successful legal counterattack against the duke. Such a possibility would then allow them to reassert the constitutional balance without surrendering their own control over the remaining two legs of the domestic political triangle.[72]

At any event the forces favoring delay prevailed throughout the war. Moser fell victim to Carl Eugen's displeasure in 1759 and spent the next five years in the fortress at Hohentwiel.[73] In his absence the executive committee managed only sporadic, inevitably ineffective resistance. The privy council fared even worse. By the middle of the war the old guard on the board—Georgii, Renz, and Korn—had lost all contact with the duke and become nothing more than glorified secretaries to the cabinet. Their one outstanding moment came in 1758 when they sided openly with the executive committee by refusing Montmartin's command for a council declaration forbidding the executive committee to assemble without the monarch's permission.[74] Korn retired after that incident, however, leaving Georgii and Renz an isolated minority on a board committed to rubber-stamping crown policy.[75] The new appointments went to men who backed Montmartin on every issue: Tobias Conrad Renz (1704–1779), Johann Christian Commerell (1714–1781), and Ernest Ludwig von Volgstädt.[76] Their relations with the two older men grew so acrimonious that Georgii and G. A. Renz finally resigned. Georgii went quietly, claiming poor health, but old Renz created something of a scandal. He flatly refused to endorse a property tax that the crown was consider-

---

72. Adam, *Johann Jakob Moser*, 49–60; also UT: Mh. 267 on the 1758 clash between Moser and the Stockmayers.
73. Walker, *Johann Jakob Moser*, 226–245.
74. HSAS, A 202: Bü. 2834 (esp. papers for July).
75. HSAS, A 202: Bü. 3201 (1762).
76. T. C. Renz: Pfeilsticker, *Dienerbuch*, 1140, 1156, 1227, 1298, 1306, 1330, 1385; Commerell: *Dienerbuch*, 1137, 1150, 1210, 1318, 1344, 1649, 2015, 2490, 2495, 2567; Volgstädt, a Thuringian nobleman: *Dienerbuch*, 1118, 1193. On the reorganization of the privy council, see HSAS, A 202: Bü. 80 (6 August 1763) and 70 (Revers of Graf Montmartin).

ing for the Ehrbarkeit. Instead, he sent a written protest to Carl Eugen branding the plan as illegal and requesting to be released from the duke's service "because no law is sacred any longer [in the duchy]." Carl Eugen fired him immediately.[77]

Just as the privy council was passing under cabinet control, the executive committee began to rally. Whereas uncooperative councilors such as G. A. Renz could be weeded out by an aggressive monarch, the executive committee membership was relatively immune from outside interference. These men could dig in and wait for better times in ways not available to the more vulnerable councilors. Carl Eugen had sought to change this situation by restructuring the Aemter so as to give the crown a more decisive voice in the internal structure of the estates. But the changes had not yet begun to take effect by the time that the Treaty of Hubertusburg (15 Feburary 1763) ended the war between Austria and Prussia. As a result, peace found the old guard still firmly in place on the executive committee. And once the configurations of European power shifted, the members found that forces within the empire were beginning to work in their favor. The emperor no longer needed Carl Eugen, whose high-handed territorial politics and wildly extravagant court had become something of a European scandal. Equally important, Prussia, Denmark, and England were now in a position to assume their roles as guarantors of the Reversalien and to press for compliance with that constitutional settlement. Under these circumstances the estates' leadership felt emboldened to assume a more defiant posture toward the duke.

For the next seven years Carl Eugen battled with his estates. The struggle followed the customary outlines of domestic controversy; it began with a dispute over the military and then moved quickly into a struggle over taxation. At issue was Carl Eugen's refusal to dismantle his army. Unwilling to dismiss the soldiers, he demanded a grant of 1,622,000 florins with which to maintain a standing force of 10,000 men.[78] The executive committee retorted that it could not commit the estates to an obligation four times as large as the amount agreed upon for peacetime in the 1739 settlement between the prince regent and the diet. Thereupon Carl Eugen decided to summon a general assembly, hoping no doubt to fare better with a new group of provincial delegates than he had with the entrenched warriors on the

77. Spittler, *Geheimen-Raths-Collegiums*, 440–442.
78. Carsten, *Princes and Parliaments*, 139f. and 139n2. The sum averaged to 3.5 florins per head of the Württemberg population, a ratio similar to that of Prussia's (2.5 Reichsthaler per inhabitant).

The *corps de logis* at Ludwigsburg. Carl Eugen occupied this wing of the palace, where he maintained a magnificent suite of apartments that he had redecorated entirely in the French manner.

executive committee. His calculations misfired. The Landtag that he opened on 19 September 1763, the only diet of his whole reign, proved the longest in the history of the duchy. With only brief recesses it lasted seven years and closed with the signing of the famous compromise known as the *Erbvergleich*.

Any possibility that Carl Eugen would be able to drive a wedge between the leadership on the executive committee and the general members vanished in the spring of 1764. At that time the duke, who seemed remarkably slow to appreciate the extent to which peace had altered his domestic political position, presented the estates with a revolutionary revenue plan. The proposal recalled Eberhard Ludwig's earlier attempts to reform the tax structure and contained certain of the leveling tendencies that had so alarmed the Ehrbarkeit in Carl Alexander's fiscal programs. It produced a similar reaction; differences between the estates lost their edge, and a frayed corporate solidarity reasserted itself in defense of privilege.

Carl Eugen's plan called for what amounted to a graduated property tax. The crown was to make an inventory of each citizen's capital assets and on that basis divide the population into twelve categories. The lowest category, a group made up of laborers, apprentices, and servants, would pay a quarter of a florin a year; whereas the municipal magistrates in the highest group were assessed twenty-five florins a year. In addition, taxes would be levied upon the schools, charitable homes, woodlands, and farms of the ecclesiastical trust, a body of capital that the Reversalien had placed under the control of the privy council and estates and had specifically exempted from interference by a Catholic monarch. This general tax, estimated to yield 1,621,000 florins a year, would replace the complicated and often discriminatory assessments computed and controlled by the estates. Moreover the money would be collected by crown officials and go directly into the military chest, bypassing the estates' treasury completely.[79]

It is unclear whether the new system would actually have reduced the tax burden on the general public. But there can be no doubt about its effect upon the Ehrbarkeit. That group not only challenged the constitutionality of so large a peacetime army; it also objected to the fact that the plan freed the monarchy from dependence upon the estates in matters of military supply. But most serious of all, the magistrates saw that the Ehrbarkeit, sheltered heretofore by virtue of its own control over the assessment rolls, would be brought unequivo-

79. Reyscher, *Vollständige Sammlung*, XVII, 597–627; Adam, "Herzog Karl und die Landschaft," 241–246.

cally into the tax structure.[80] The private finances of the magisterial families would now be open to crown scrutiny. Account books could be read, real estate transactions made public, investments analyzed for profits. Finally, by asserting the crown's rights of attachment on the Kirchengut, it challenged the network of patronage that sustained all levels of magistrates as well as their brothers and cousins in the civil service. Its effect, in other words, would be to strip the Ehrbarkeit of its supervision of the purse, to subject it to government regulation, and to vest the crown with an absolutely free hand over the most substantial part of the state's financial administration.

The estates took up the challenge on three fronts. The municipal magistrates, especially those in the two great cities of the duchy, rallied their forces in the Aemter and blocked ratification of the duke's proposal by the district assemblies. Their stand encouraged the more provincial districts, some of which had succumbed at first, to hold fast and even sometimes to rescind earlier votes of approval. Under these circumstances Carl Eugen could not muster a clear mandate for reform, and he felt it best to drop the proposal.[81] But though he substituted a more conventional levy that once again shifted the burden away from the Ehrbarkeit, the now thoroughly antagonized estates pressed ahead in an effort to seek redress for their wartime grievances. The executive committee, fortified by an unqualified vote of confidence from the floor of the Landtag, filed a formal complaint against Carl Eugen before the Imperial Aulic Council *(Reichshofrat)* at Vienna.[82] At the same time the Württembergers sought active help from the three guarantor kings.

In this endeavor the estates found Frederick the Great an especially sympathetic ally. The king deeply resented Carl Eugen's support of the Catholic powers in the Seven Years War and, on a more personal front, felt that the duke had mistreated his wife and that the collapse of their marriage was entirely Carl Eugen's fault. In fulfilling

80. Grube, *Stuttgarter Landtag,* 436–437, points out that the poor man paid no more under this system than he had under the Monatssteuer.
81. On the campaign in the Aemter, see Adam, "Herzog Karl und die Landschaft," 241–246; Grube, *Stuttgarter Landtag,* 436–438; Adam, *Johann Jakob Moser,* 74–75. Johann Ludwig Huber, Oberamtmann of the Tübingen Versammlung, led the opposition and subsequently suffered imprisonment on the Hohen Asperg. For his account of the events, see J. L. Huber, *Etwas von meinem Lebenslauf und Etwas von meiner Muse auf der Festung: Ein kleiner Beitrag zu der selbst erlebten Geschichte meines Vaterlands* (Stuttgart, 1798). It was over this tax proposal that Renz and Georgii left the privy council.
82. Court action was filed on 30 July 1764. The prelates supported the suit. They claimed that violations of the Reversalien had released them from any restriction on their rights to appeal outside the duchy.

his confessional obligations he thus found a legitimate pretext for disciplining an unreliable fellow sovereign and a profligate in-law. He strongly encouraged the emperor to side with the Württembergers and orchestrated a series of public dispatches from the guarantor powers endorsing the estates' suit before the Reichshofrat.[83] He also organized an official delegation from the kings to investigate Carl Eugen's conduct as a ruler. To the duke's utter fury, these "outsiders" bustled about his duchy taking depositions, demanding to see records and inventories of church properties, and tampering generally with what Carl Eugen insisted were the domestic affairs of a sovereign state.[84]

Undeniably these developments demonstrated once again that curious intermixture of religion and politics characteristic of German history. At Carl Alexander's accession confessionalism had shown itself a sufficiently overriding force to secure a constitutional settlement such as the Reversalien. Now it mustered international support in defense of that earlier arrangement. In the name of religious particularism lofty kingdoms intervened to obtain imperial sanctions against the duke. In the end the Imperial Aulic Council decided in favor of the estates, and the emperor negotiated a settlement that secured the liberties of a people under attack from their sovereign ruler. But note that once the legal process had begun, confessional interests faded as a motive force and the empire demonstrated yet another time its capacity to neutralize single-issue politics. In deciding the case and in forcing Carl Eugen to an accommodation, the imperial machinery took no account of religion per se. At issue was the question of constitutional law, and that resolution placed a Catholic emperor behind a Protestant settlement at the expense of a Catholic monarch. The empire also revealed its capacity to discipline a monarch and to preserve the civil liberties of his subjects. Far more was at stake than just the duke's power; the settlement secured the historic rights of the Württemberg people—even though the exercise of those rights was restricted for the moment to a narrow territorial elite.

Under the auspices of the emperor and the Reichshofrat, representatives of the concerned parties negotiated the final settlement.[85]

83. The Prussian dispatch is reproduced in Robert von Mohl, *Beiträge zur Geschichte Württembergs*, I (Tübingen, 1828), 38–42. For the others, see J. J. Moser, *Abhandlungen verschiedener besonderer Rechts-Materien*, IV (Frankfurt am Main, 1774), 431–440.
84. The delegation consisted of Gebhard Werner Graf von der Schulenburg-Wolfsburg (Prussia); Ludwig Eberhard Freiherr von Gemmingen-Hornberg (England); and Achaz Ferdinand von der Asselburg (Denmark).
85. The text of the Erbvergleich is printed in Reyscher, *Vollständige Sammlung*, II, 550–609. A useful summary is found in Mohl, *Beiträge zur Geschichte Württembergs*, I, 54–58.

In the winter of 1770 they forwarded the summation of their six years of labor to Stuttgart for ratification by the duke and his estates. By any standards the terms of the Erbvergleich constituted a defeat for the monarchy. For almost a century the Württemberg dukes had sought control over the tax system, free access to ecclesiastical revenue, and the unrestricted right to regulate military expenditure. In each instance they had come within close reach of their goals only to find that death, outside intervention, or a realignment of domestic interests had frustrated a final consolidation. Now the imperial government, backed by Prussia and Austria, the two mightiest German states, resolved these matters once and for all. The settlement fixed the annual military budget at 460,000 florins, a sum that could support a standing army of no more than about 3,000 soldiers.[86] The duke had to agree that, if an emergency necessitated a larger force, he would request the funding through the executive committee rather than through the Aemter. In other words the crown was to make no further effort to circumvent the estates' leadership in military matters. Finally, the duke had to surrender his exclusive supervision over military accounts. He acknowledged the estates' rights in this area by consenting to create an audit committee for military affairs with seats on that board reserved for officials from the executive committee. His capitulation on the ecclesiastical question was equally complete. He recognized formally that control over church property rested in the exclusive joint management of the privy council and the estates. He removed himself from any role whatsoever in the territorial church.

The Erbvergleich likewise spelled out the constitutional responsibilities of the estates, the privy council, and the Aemter. In this last area the duke recognized the autonomy of the Amtsversammlungen and accepted restrictions on his participation in the appointments to district offices. From now on he was to do no more than confirm local officials such as the tax receivers, who were to be elected in the first instance by their district assemblies. Furthermore crown agents were excluded from these assemblies. The notion of subdistricts was simply dropped. Instead the settlement restored the earlier electoral procedures that had confined voting rights to municipal and village delegates. It is interesting to note here that the Erbvergleich made no effort to turn back the clock by restoring the Aemter to the exclusive management of the urban magistrates. Instead it recognized the assembly as the centerpiece of district political life and accepted the fact that over the previous century the crown had built up these bod-

86. From this sum 70,000 florins went each year to amortize the duke's debts.

ies to include more substantial peasant representation. The policy of electing the Landtag delegates in the Amtsversammlungen rather than in closed committees was now confirmed, and full village representation at these meetings was recognized as standard procedure. True, the Erbvergleich left unresolved the question of supervision over the assemblies. In many cases the shaping of final instructions for the diet remained a closed preserve of the Ehrbarkeit, and everywhere representation at the level of territorial politics continued to be the exclusive monopoly of the municipal magistrates. But the settlement guaranteed at least a limited regional political expression for village leadership. Accordingly Württemberg would confront the upheavals of the French Revolution without a totally disfranchised peasantry.

At the level of state politics the Erbvergleich reaffirmed the Eberhardine principal of correlative sovereignty for the duchy. The duke was obliged to acknowledge his estates and their executive committee as the *"corpus representativum* of the whole beloved fatherland" and to promise that he would deal with them "in the time-honored ways of negotiation" *(in altüblichen modus tractandi)*. Moreover, the duke agreed to make no changes in the constitution or the legal code *(Allgemeinene Landesgesetze und Ordnungen)* without the approval of the estates. In this way the estates (or their representatives) were guaranteed consultative rights in and veto powers over any reorganization of the duchy's administrative or legislative structure. Furthermore the executive committee received the right to assemble at will, with the sole proviso that the Landschaftskonsulent notify the privy council of all meetings.

Rights of free assembly ensured that it would be the executive committee rather than any larger body which carried on estates' business in the central government. Such an arrangement meant the virtual institutionalization of territorial influence for the prelates, Bürgermeisters, and lawyers who sat on that governing committee. In the course of the eighteenth century they had become an increasingly inbred group and by the time of the settlement were functioning much like an exclusive extended family. Preponderant influence resided with the Stockmayers, by far the most conspicuous political clan in the duchy. Friedrich Amandus, who had succeeded both his father and grandfather as legal counsel and chief secretary, ran the committee with an iron hand,[87] He presented the agenda and presided over all deliberations. In 1786 his son Friedrich Amandus, Jr.

87. Pfeilsticker, *Dienerbuch*, 1449, 1452; *WVJHLG* (1905), 36–63.

(1760–1837), followed him in office and thus became the fourth consecutive generation of his family to serve as chief secretary to the committee.[88] A few years later in 1791 his brother-in-law Konradin Abel (1750–1823), who had been an under secretary since 1774, became head legal counsel.[89] In this way the family managed for over three-quarters of a century to influence appointments to all major offices under the estates' control. The Stockmayers staffed these posts with their friends and relatives so that by the time of Carl Eugen's death people had begun to refer to the central government as a Stockmayer family enterprise.[90]

It is curious that the broader body of estates accepted this condition with only a half-hearted protest. The most obvious explanation for their indifference stems from the fact that some seventy years of committee rule had accustomed the provincial estates to a local rather than a territorial political orientation. Then too the Stockmayer clique had succeeded in forging a settlement with the duke that guaranteed estates' rights, and there was no need to repudiate a successful leadership. Frequent Landtags meant considerable expense to the districts and high personal costs for the individual delegates. Most of them obviously preferred to leave matters of state government in the hands of the executive committee and to concentrate their own attention upon the districts in which they held offices and owned properties. Certainly their localism helps to account for the difficulties that the nineteenth-century state was to encounter in its efforts to bring the municipalities under central control. The towns constituted the preserve of that sector of the Ehrbarkeit represented in the estates but removed from the daily workings of the state. These officials had no desire to subordinate themselves to an enterprise in which they exercised only theoretical powers.

A brief opposition to executive committee leadership did in fact surface during the debates over ratification at the diet; its failure pointed to all the conditions discussed above. It called attention as well to the enormous influence exerted by outside forces over the final resolution for the Württemberg duchy. Those opposed to the Stockmayers—and the group included the chancellor of Tübingen Jeremias Reuss as well as that city's Bürgermeister, Johann Dann—

88. Pfeilsticker, Dienerbuch, 12ξ3, 1453.
89. Ibid., 1444, 1450.
90. E. Hölzle, Das alte Recht und die Revolution: Eine politische Geschichte Württembergs in der Revolutionszeit 1789–1805 (Munich and Berlin, 1931), 4–43; Grube, Stuttgarter Landtag, 447–449. On popular attitudes toward the Stockmayers, see Nicolai, Beschreibung einer Reise durch Deutschland und die Schweiz, x, 24–32.

opened a campaign for the appointment to the executive committee of J. J. Moser, now released from prison and an articulate champion of estates' rights in their broadest sense. Just a year before the conclusion of the negotiations at Vienna, Moser had published the thirteenth volume of his *Neues Teutsches Staats-Recht*, in which he insisted that the estates' powers resided only in plenary diets and could not be exercised by special committees or officers. Now, faced with a virtual Stockmayer dictatorship, he returned to the point with a vengeance and circulated an impassioned appeal for reform of the assembly.[91]

Moser's position was that the Erbvergleich, in its present construction, meant the end of Württemberg's constitutional system. Indeed, he described that tradition as in its last stages of decay, arguing that in accepting a settlement that placed the executive committee before the diet, the estates had reduced themselves to "an empty name." The Landtag had become "a mere shadow of what diets mean elsewhere and were once in Württemberg itself." To revitalize the constitution the executive committee must be curbed and its responsibilities returned to the diet. However eloquent Moser's prose or sound his logic, neither the emperor nor the guarantor kings shared these sympathies. Their agents made this point plain to the delegates and warned them against disrupting ratification. And when Carl Eugen sought to exploit their internal divisions and to introduce terms more favorable to himself into the settlement, the majority of delegates grew fearful that they might be jeopardizing their victory. They repudiated the Moser faction and voted to uphold the executive committee. The diet recessed on 25 June 1770, having vested that board with the full constitutional powers of the estates.[92]

In effect, the Landtag did not meet again until the French invasions had brought an end to the old regime in Germany.[93] In the intervening years, the last in the history of the duchy, the Stockmayers and their relatives and friends joined with the monarchy in what amounted to a duumvirate. There was no longer any question of a major confrontation with the duke. To be sure, differences surfaced,

---

91. For an analysis of both works, see Walker, *Johann Jakob Moser*, 265–276. Volume XIII, entitled *Von der Teutschen Reichs-Stände Landen, deren Landständen, Unterthanen, Landes-Freyheiten, Beschwerden und Zusammenkünfften*, appeared in 1769 (Frankfurt am Main). Moser's subsequent appeal is reproduced in Adam, *Johann Jakob Moser*, 117–143.

92. UT: Mh. 677: "Consulent Mosers Readmission zum Landtag, acta 1770." Also, Grube, *Stuttgarter Landtag*, 446f.; and Adam, "Herzog Karl Eugen und die Landschaft," 272–281.

93. The four diets held between 1793 and 1810 dissolved without an Abschied.

but they centered on three relatively conventional issues: court expenditure; the duke's occasional efforts to wiggle around the military settlement; and debates over financial underwriting and university accreditation for the Hohen Karlsschule, a pet project of the duke that challenged the Ehrbar-dominated University of Tübingen's monopoly over higher education in the duchy.[94] All were settled by negotiation. Since neither duke nor executive committee wanted another Landtag, both sides took care to avoid a final deadlock.

The privy council played its part in this cozy arrangement. The Erbvergleich had restored the council to its position as the administrative head of the central government and thus the highest authority under the duke. But as with the executive committee, the nature of the council's membership gave a curious twist to constitutional victory. Here again social connections secured the highest positions for families like the Stockmayers who now dominated the estates through their control over the executive committee. Some four years before the Erbvergleich, Carl Eugen had sought to win over the guarantor powers by abolishing the cabinet government. He dismissed the pro-French Montmartin as prime minister, sent Pflug into retirement, and brought the privy council membership back up to full strength.[95] These changes did not produce an immediate effect. Council records indicate that Montmartin continued to participate ex officio in privy council business and that two of his closest backers—T. C. Renz and E. L. von Volgstädt—remained active on the board.[96] The new members came directly from the Regierungsrat. Although they were professionally trained and skilled in territorial law, they had entered the council with no previous experience in the give-and-take of government politics. The result was that, although council business began to increase once more in size and scope, the council members tended to steer a cautious course and to avoid antagonizing the monarch during the negotiations before the Reichshofrat.[97]

94. Adam, "Herzog Karl und die Landschaft," 281–310; Uhland, *Geschichte der Hohen Karlsschule in Stuttgart*, 129–138; A. Pfister, "Hof und Hoffeste," 116f.; Kleemann, *Schloss Solitude*, 143–146; LBS, cod. his. Q243e; HSAS, A 202: Bü. 348. At Carl Eugen's death, his army stood at 2,600 men, including the 1,400 Württemberg soldiers on duty with the Kreis army. He had an additional troop of 2,000 mercenaries serving with the Dutch India Company.

95. On Montmartin's dismissal, see HSAS, A 202: Bü. 70 (esp. 10 May 1766). New members added were F. E. J. von Uxkull, F. K. E. von Kniestedt, A. H. Weikersreuter, and J. C. Commerell.

96. HSAS, A 202: Bü. 73 (e.g., 25 December 1769); A 74 alt: Bü. 125 alt (letters to Baron von Thun at Paris: 20 March, 21 July, 9 August 1771).

97. HSAS, A 202: Bü. 3205, 3207, 3208; also Spittler, *Geheimen-Raths-Collegiums*, 443f.

The signing of the Erbvergleich changed this situation. The settlement endowed the councilors with control over all central agencies except the war council and military commissariat and made them once again the indispensable link between monarch and executive committee. Under these circumstances the councilors gradually assumed a more vital role in the formation of government policy. And since Carl Eugen needed men on the privy council who could work well with the executive committee, he turned for council recruitment to the duchy's ranking magisterial families. Indeed the eight non-noble councilors who sat on the board from 1770 to the end of the reign were all native-born Württembergers.[98] Furthermore, each of them belonged to the leading sector of the Ehrbarkeit; and at least six of the eight had in-laws or close relations serving terms concurrent with their own on the executive committee of the estates. Two of the group, in fact, were Stockmayer in-laws.[99] Given these family ties, it is not surprising that the operative distinctions between privy council and executive committee began to blur and that the two boards worked in the closest harmony.

This fusion of interests was reinforced by the fact that, as the council drew closer in social orientation to the estates' leadership, the noble element on the board declined in importance. For the remaining years of the reign only four noblemen entered the privy council. Two of them—Ludwig Karl Eckbrecht von Dürckheim (died 1774), son-in-law to Montmartin, and Gottlieb Christian von Mossheim (died 1787)—filled only brief terms and spent most of their time outside the duchy on diplomatic missions.[100] The others, Friedrich Emich Johann Baron von Uxkull (1724–1810) and Friedrich Karl Eberhard Freiherr von Kniestedt (1725–1794), served throughout the entire period. They provided an important liaison between the monarch and the other councilors and their relatives on the executive committee. Uxkull, who served from 1766 to 1799, was a consummate courtier, extremely adroit at flattering Carl Eugen into thinking that he was in fact ruling as he pleased. His presence provided balance in moments of disagreement between the duke and his government.[101]

98. A. J. [von] Bühler (1722–1794); J. C. Commerell (1714–1781); J. F. Faber (died 1790); L. E. Fischer (1728–1809); Dr. J. D. Hoffmann (1743–1814); T. C. Renz (1704–1779); I. [von] Rieger (1727–1798); A. H. Weickersreuter (1713–1783).

99. Bühler married the daughter of the Stuttgart Stadtvogt J. J. Gross and through his own daughter became an in-law of the Stockmayers. T. C. Renz was brother-in-law to J. F. and uncle to F. A. Stockmayer. Faber, Fischer, Rieger, and Weickersreuter each had relatives who served on the executive committee.

100. Pfeilsticker, *Dienerbuch*, 1117, 1121, 2015.

101. Ibid., 1114, 1123, 1202, 1383, 1400; *Hofkalendar*, 1766–1799; HSAS, A 202: Bü. 2749 (esp. the report of 8 November 1794 to Duke Ludwig Eugen). For an exam-

CAROLUS D:G:                    WIRTEMBERGIÆ
   AC TECCIÆ                        DUX,
ALMÆ CAROLINÆ                  STUTTGARDIANÆ
   STATOR                          AC PATER.

Carl Eugen is painted here in 1782 as the protector of the Hohen Karlsschule. By this time his relations with the estates and officials had stabilized,
and he was casting himself more in the role of a grand seigneur than a self-
indulgent despot. Photograph courtesy of the Hauptstaatsarchiv Stuttgart.

[293]

Kniestedt, who married the daughter of the ranking Stuttgart municipal official Johann Jakob Gross (and was thus brother-in-law to the most influential of his non-noble colleagues on the council, A. J. [v] Bühler), also enjoyed close relations with Carl Eugen. By training he belonged to neither the court nor the government; he had worked earlier as business manager for various of Carl Eugen's construction projects.[102] He had entered the council under the patronage of Franziska von Hohenheim (1748–1811), then the duke's mistress and later his morganatic wife. Countess Hohenheim was a woman widely admired for her piety, her personal modesty, and her general amiability.[103] The two of them handled Carl Eugen with enormous skill, so that from the perspective of the crown, relations with the privy council became exceedingly cordial.[104] Here too of course these relations were not always harmonious. As late as 1791, while on a trip to the Low Countries that included a visit to revolutionary France, Carl Eugen wrote to Uxkull complaining about his officials. He announced that he could not return to the duchy without assurance that he would never again suffer the disobedience and impertinence of his privy councilors and estates.[105] But such moments passed and, as in his disputes with the executive committee, they never escalated into confrontation. With rare exceptions the duke seemed content for the rest of his reign to play the role of the patriarch—a serious-minded, hard-working if incorrigibly extravagant Landesvater.

The Erbvergleich had divided the reins of government between the prince and the leaders of his estates and civil service in what turned out to be the final such division in the history of the duchy. With Carl Eugen's death Würtemberg was thrown into a period of acute turmoil. When the dust settled after twenty years of French invasion and Napoleonic hegemony, the old duchy had vanished. In

ple of his ability to deal with Carl Eugen, see HSAS, A 202: Bü. 113 (correspondence for February and March 1784).

102. Pfeilsticker, *Dienerbuch*, 1116, 1192, 1649; *Hofkalendar*, 1761–1792; HSAS, A 202: Bü. 80 (5 December 1767).

103. E. Veln's study of Franziska's personality and influence remains useful, *Herzog Karl von Württemberg und Franziska von Hohenheim* (Stuttgart, 1876). See also, A. Osterberg, *Tagbuch der Gräfin Franziska von Hohenheim* (Stuttgart, 1913); and Paul von Stälin, "Die beiden Ehe des Herzogs. Franziska," *HKE*, I, 79–101. A recent, though highly romanticized interpretation is Utta Kepler's, *Franziska von Hohenheim* (Stuttgart, 1969).

104. See HSAS, A 202: Bü. 113 (Kniestedt correspondence, 1786–1788); Bü. 2973 (New Year reports, 1767–1787); Bü. 68 (policy advice for 1793); Bü. 3236 (negotiations, 1791). Kniestedt resigned in 1792 under charges of financial impropriety in connection with the sale of wine (A 204: Bü. 1792).

105. HSAS, A 202: Bü. 113 (29 March and 2, 3, 13, 19 April).

its place stood a kingdom, more than double the size of the old duchy, in which new forces jostled old interests for a share in the government. Questions of political authority required different formulation; for the state now included a substantial Catholic population as well as a strong hereditary aristocracy, both of which had arrived with the numerous abbeys, city-states, lordships, and principalities that had been annexed to form the new kingdom. Equally important, the Holy Roman Empire had vanished; national politics now took place within a looser, less cohesive system of confederation.[106]

What then are the generalizations that can be extracted from the events surrounding this final step in the making of the ducal monarchy? First we have seen that it was ultimately the Holy Roman Empire that operated to preserve the traditional forms of power in the duchy. Whatever the developments in a major state like Prussia, monarchs in the secondary German principalities, no matter how aggressive, lacked the strength to break through the constraints in the imperial system to pursue an independent direction. In this sense German territorial politics can be studied only in the context of the old Reich. Second, even on those occasions when outside forces remained in abeyance, the Württemberg duke was contained by institutions and social barriers that he could not fully surmount.

Strong-willed sovereigns could bully the most provincial of their district assemblies. But as long as the central government stopped at the gates of the towns, the crown could not legally dislodge the Ehrbarkeit from its most substantial political base. And since the imperial system held the monarch within at least the broader confines of territorial law, the estates could always retrench and wait until his death or a shift in outside forces brought them relief. Religious differences between the duke and his subjects worked against absolute monarchy. Without direct access to the revenues and the psychological resources of the church, the duke was denied two indispensable ingredients for undivided strength—money and propaganda. Furthermore he was shut off from the network of patronage embraced by the territorial church. He could neither appoint his own men nor exclude his opponents from that lucrative and pervasive organization.

Finally, the question of motivation and goals emerges. Sociologists lay particular emphasis on the concept of control; economic determinists stress the primacy of financial pressure. Both elements loomed

106. Hölzle, *Das alte Recht und die Revolution*; Max Miller, "Die Organisation und Verwaltung von Neuwürttemberg unter Herzog und Kurfürst Friedrich," *WVJHLG*, 37 (1931), 130–144, 302 ff.; 39 (1933), 232–247—subsequently published as *Neuwürttemberg unter Herzog und Kurfürst Friedrich* (Stuttgart, 1934).

large in the development of Württemberg. But they have emerged as secondary rather than as initiating forces of motivation. Instead, social competition—whether the self-indulgent extravagances of Eberhard Ludwig or the inflated notions of grandeur that obsessed Carl Eugen —has surfaced as the primary impulse behind the dukes' attacks upon their government. And one must note in this regard that, despite their profligacy, the princes were demanding money not just to keep the wine flowing but to fund the army, to purchase new territories, and to cut the figure expected of an eighteenth-century monarch. The point is that their demands for money escalated rapidly into struggles over social, economic, and military issues, which in turn must be seen as debates over the question of where authority was to reside in the new state. For though the opposition framed its refusal in moral terms, in reality prince, estates, and bureaucrats were all waging a contest as to where the crux of decision making would lie.

The resolution offered by the Erbvergleich operated on two levels. In strictly constitutional terms it restored the mid-seventeenth-century triangle of Landtag, privy council, and crown. But the social configurations underlying these reconstituted institutions imparted a novel direction to two of them. In this sense—that is, in social rather than formal institutional terms—the settlement affirmed a triangle that no longer operated. The upper echelons of the Ehrbarkeit had separated themselves from the lesser magistrates and had taken over both the privy council and the executive committee of the estates. The high civil bureaucrats as well as the estates' leadership came now from this exclusive corps. As a result, the distinctions between the privy council and executive committee lost their sharpness. An official distribution of authority between three distinct socio-institutional forces translated into an operative system of government in which power was shared between two groups. Two of the three legs in the classic triangle had merged into one. But note that this merger was of a particular sort. It was not the professional, socially mobile bureaucrat who captured the leadership of the estates. It was rather the influential old-line families of the Ehrbarkeit who were directing the administration of government in the duchy.

The Erbvergleich constituted the final twist in the corkscrew pattern of Württemberg's growth. It looked back, as we have seen, to earlier developments in the making of that state. But it also looked forward and in another sociopolitical climate would provide the basis for a new kind of government. Students of nineteenth-century Germany will find in these last days of the old order, as in the settlement itself, plentiful sources of energy for later developments. There are two points to notice. First, there was the discernible growth in the political maturity of the Württembergers. For the preceding century peasant participation had steadily increased in the assemblies. Although this expanded franchise had not yet produced major political change, it nonetheless provided the old order in the duchy with something of a safety valve against the immediate pressures of the Revolution. By the same token, we leave the state at a moment when both bureaucrats and estates have access to an active political life: the more prominent participated at the level of the state; the others in the towns and districts. But one way or another, the most articulate elements of the society were included in the established system and thus had a stake in its survival.

A second point is closely related; prevailing conditions forecast change rather than political stability. In 1734 the population of the duchy stood at about 428,000 inhabitants; by 1790 that figure had risen by 44.85 percent to a total of 620,000 Württembergers. Population density, in other words, rose from forty-eight to sixty-seven persons per square kilometer.[107] Meanwhile town government, like that of the church and state, remained firmly in the hands of established elites, elites who were divided against themselves, with the upper tier co-opted into the state and the lower group based in the communities. An acute observer might well have anticipated two kinds of trouble: demands by a rapidly growing population for wider participation in the localities (towns and districts) where oligarchic rule still persisted; and a struggle by the state to bring the towns and communities under complete domination.

The Erbvergleich had provided for a triangular distribution of political power, but late-eighteenth-century social divisions had created a de facto duumvirate. This duumvirate would shatter under the pressures of the French invasions. What is fascinating is that, having shattered, the old social alliances coalesced again in an expanded but still vigorous form. And the constitutional framework that we have seen evolving over the previous two hundred years proved sufficiently resilient to accommodate these new social groupings without a fundamental disruption of the by then classic channels of power within Württemberg.

107. Helen Liebel-Weckowicz, "The Politics of Poverty and Reform: Modernization and Reform in Eighteenth-Century Württemberg," *The Consortium on Revolutionary Europe Proceedings* (Athens, Ga., 1981), 83n1. Lehmann, *Pietismus und weltliche Ordnung*, 116–135, offers an interesting analysis on the implications for radical Pietism of this demographic increase. The number of pastors remained fixed throughout the century, so that by the 1790s large numbers of less-educated Württembergers were going into conventicles for lack of an alternative in the territorial church. These new elements were receptive to more extreme ideas, and the conventicles became seedbeds for nineteenth-century radicalism.

# APPENDIX. *Social and Geographic Makeup of the Württemberg Privy Council*

The following two tables chart changes in the social and geographic make-up of the Württemberg privy council. For convenience the percentages are reckoned in terms of decades. In that specific trends discussed in the body of the text followed a chronology tied to crown policy rather than to periodization by decades, the percentage figures computed in such instances can differ from those given for the entire decade in which the events occurred. These broader calculations simply provide a perspective for the entire period of the study. The reader should note that councilors whose terms of office spanned several decades appear in the totals for each decade in which they served.

*Württemberg Privy Councilors, Geographic Origins*

| decade | born in Württemberg as ducal subjects | born within the Swabian Kreis but not ducal subjects | born elsewhere | number |
|---|---|---|---|---|
| before council constituted | | | | |
| 1593–99 | 41.7% | 16.6% | 41.7% | 12 |
| 1600–09 | 45.8 | 16.7 | 37.5 | 24 |
| 1610–19 | 40.0 | 20.0 | 40.0 | 15 |
| 1620–29 | 41.7 | 16.6 | 41.7 | 12 |
| after council constituted | | | | |
| 1630–39 | 66.7 | 33.3 | 0.0 | 9 |
| 1640–49 | 42.9 | 14.2 | 42.9 | 7 |
| 1650–59 | 70.0 | 10.0 | 20.0 | 10 |
| 1660–69 | 50.0 | 16.7 | 33.3 | 6 |
| 1670–79 | 36.4 | 9.0 | 54.6 | 11 |
| 1680–89 | 33.3 | 16.7 | 50.0 | 6 |
| 1690–99 | 11.1 | 22.2 | 66.7 | 9 |
| 1700–09 | 0.0 | 27.3 | 72.7 | 11 |
| 1710–19 | 7.1 | 28.6 | 64.3 | 14 |
| 1720–29 | 7.1 | 21.4 | 71.5 | 14 |
| 1730–39 | 39.1 | 4.4 | 56.5 | 23 |
| 1740–49 | 54.6 | 9.0 | 36.4 | 11 |
| 1750–59 | 42.9 | 7.1 | 50.0 | 14 |
| 1760–69 | 30.8 | 23.1 | 46.1 | 13 |
| 1770–79 | 42.9 | 42.9 | 14.2 | 7 |
| 1780–89 | 50.0 | 25.0 | 25.0 | 8 |
| 1790–93 | 71.4 | 14.3 | 14.3 | 7 |

*Württemberg Privy Councilors, Social Status*

| years | entered ducal service with noble status | ennobled while in service | never obtained noble status | number |
|---|---|---|---|---|
| before council constituted | | | | |
| 1593–99 | 58.4% | 8.3% | 33.3% | 12 |
| 1600–09 | 54.2 | 4.1 | 41.7 | 24 |
| 1610–19 | 60.0 | 6.7 | 33.3 | 15 |
| 1620–29 | 66.7 | 0.0 | 33.3 | 12 |
| after council constituted | | | | |
| 1630–39 | 44.5 | 11.0 | 44.5 | 9 |
| 1640–49 | 57.1 | 28.6 | 14.3 | 7 |
| 1650–59 | 40.0 | 30.0 | 30.0 | 10 |
| 1660–69 | 50.0 | 16.7 | 33.3 | 6 |
| 1670–79 | 45.4 | 18.2 | 36.4 | 11 |
| 1680–89 | 66.7 | 16.7 | 16.7 | 6 |
| 1690–99 | 55.6 | 22.2 | 22.2 | 9 |
| 1700–09 | 72.7 | 18.2 | 9.1 | 11 |
| 1710–19 | 64.3 | 21.4 | 14.3 | 14 |
| 1720–29 | 57.1 | 14.3 | 28.6 | 14 |
| 1730–39 | 47.8 | 13.1 | 39.1 | 23 |
| 1740–49 | 54.5 | 18.2 | 27.3 | 11 |
| 1750–59 | 57.1 | 14.3 | 28.6 | 14 |
| 1760–69 | 61.5 | 0.0 | 38.5 | 13 |
| 1770–79 | 42.9 | 14.2 | 42.9 | 7 |
| 1780–89 | 37.5 | 25.0 | 37.5 | 8 |
| 1790–93 | 28.6 | 28.6 | 42.9 | 7 |

# Bibliography

## I. Primary Sources:

My research rests primarily upon materials in the Württemberg-isches Haupt-Staatsarchiv, known generally as the Hauptstaatsarchiv Stuttgart. The collection includes virtually all extant records on the central administration, the court, the estates, and the ducal monarchy. Footnote references indicate the file box, or *Büschel*, in which the documentation for each particular point is located. Whenever possible a specific document has been identified, usually by date or subject heading. But in a great number of cases, my generalizations have come from analyses of a series of reports, memoranda, letters, and records, so that no one document can be cited as central. In such instances I have simply noted the Büschel and referred the reader to its general contents.

Three divisional holdings *(Bestände)* proved especially significant for my research: A 202, A 203, and A 204. Of these, the A 202 section is the most extensive. It contains over three thousand Büschel, each of which holds several hundred pages of records. In this series are found the working papers of the most important central agencies: the chancellery, the privy council, the judiciary, the consistory, and the Rentkammer. Also included are reports to the crown from the Aemter; an extensive collection of diaries, memoirs, and letters belonging to various important officials; and the correspondence between the dukes and the privy council.

A 203 is comprised of the papers from negotiations between the privy council and the Landschaft. Büschel 8 through 192 cover the period 1660–1792. A 204 includes the minutes of all privy council meetings, together with the research materials assembled for those occasions. The reader should note a peculiarity in the cataloging of this material. Büschel 27 through 188 cover the years from 1648 to 1738 and contain draft copies of the minutes as well as final versions. These editions are then separated for the years 1726–1738, with one set filed as A 204: Bü. 1726–1738 and the other A 204: Bü. 153–188. After that all papers are grouped according to year and cataloged by that year.

Two other series deal with the estates, their committees, and the Landtag: LB are the *Konventsakten* and contain the business records for the plenary diets and for the meetings of the executive committee and the larger council. The TA, *tomi actorum provincialium Wirtembergicorum (Abschriften von Landschaftsakten im Hauptstaatsarchiv Stuttgart)*, are volumes of minutes and summary extracts from these meetings.

Finally the archives of the House of Württemberg are preserved in the Hauptstaatsarchiv. These papers have their own register and are cataloged as Bestand G 2–8. Each family member has been assigned a Roman numeral, so that the citation is always G 2–8, followed by the number for that prince or princess and then by the appropriate Büschel number.

## II. Printed Sources

A list follows of those printed sources that have been consistently useful for this study. Travel accounts, journals, and collections of more limited importance appear at appropriate moments in the footnotes.

Adam, Albert E., ed. *Württembergische Landtagsakten,* Württembergische Kommission für Landesgeschichte, 2 Reihe, vols. 1–3 (1593–1620). Stuttgart, 1910–1919.

Alberti, Otto von. *Württembergisches Adels- und Wappenbuch,* 2 vols. Stuttgart, 1889. Reprint (in one volume). Neustadt an der Aisch, 1975.

Bernhardt, Walter. *Die Zentralbehörden des Herzogtums Württemberg und ihre Beamten, 1520–1629.* Veröffentlichungen der Kommission für geschichtliche Landeskunde in Baden-Württemberg, Reihe B, Forschungen, Bände 70 and 71. Stuttgart, 1972.

Blessing, Elmar. "Die territoriale Entwicklung von Württemberg bis 1796, einschliesslich der linksrheinischen Besitzungen," Beiwort zur Karte VI, 2. In *Historischer Atlas von Baden-Württemberg,* Kommission für geschichtliche Landeskunde in Baden-Württemberg, 1–4. Stuttgart, 1972.

————. "Einteilung Württembergs in Ämter um 1525," Beiwort zur Karte VI, 10. In *Historischer Atlas von Baden-Württemberg,* Kommission für geschichtliche Landeskunde in Baden-Württemberg, 1–4. Stuttgart, 1972.

de Bourgeauville, Sieur. "Mémoire envoyé au Sieur de Juvigny touchant la Cour de Virtemberg," Bibliothèque Nationale de Paris, manuscrits fonds français 17070 f. 138ff. [date 1686].

Bull, K. -O. "Die durchschnittlichen Vermögen in den altwürttembergischen Städten und Dörfern um 1545 nach den Türkensteuerlisten," Beiwort zur Karte XII, In *Historischer Atlas von Baden-Württemberg*, Kommission für geschichtliche Landeskunde in Baden-Württemberg, 1–15. Stuttgart, 1975.

Bürck, Albrecht and Wilhelm Wille. *Die Matrikeln der Universität Tübingen, 1600–1710.* Stuttgart, 1955.

Decker-Hauff, Hans Martin. "Die Entstehung der altwürttembergischen Ehrbarkeit, 1250–1534." Erlangen: Ph.D. diss., 1946.

Denk, E. *Das württembergische Finanzarchiv: Die Aktensammlung der herzoglichen Rentkammer.* Stuttgart, 1907.

Einsle, Hans. *Baden-Württemberg von A–Z.* Tübingen, 1979.

Faber, Ferdinand F. *Die württembergischen Familienstiftungen.* Stuttgart, 1853–1858. Reprint of Hefte 9–24. Stuttgart, 1940.

Fischer, Hermann, ed. *Schwäbisches Wörterbuch*, 6 vols. Tübingen, 1904–1936.

Fischlin, Ludwig. *Vitae praecipuorum cancellariorum et procancellariorum ducatus wirtembergici.* Stuttgart, 1712.

Gaisberg-Schöckingen, Friedrich Freiherr von. *Das Königshaus und der Adel von Württemberg.* Pforzheim, 1908.

Georgii-Georgenau, Eberhard Emil von. *Fürstlich-Württembergisches Dienerbuch vom IX bis zum XIX Jahrhundert.* Stuttgart, 1877.

Hanack, Ingrid, ed. *Die Tagebücher des Herzogs Johann Friedrich von Württemberg aus den Jahren 1615–17.* Göppingen, 1972.

Hirsching, Friedrich Carl Gottlob. *Historisch-Geographisch-Topographisches Stifts- und Klosterlexikon.* Leipzig, 1792. Reprint. Hildesheim and New York, 1972.

*Historischer Atlas zu Baden-Württemberg*, Kommission für geschichtliche Landeskunde in Baden-Württemberg. Stuttgart, 1975– .

Huber, Johann L. *Etwas von meinem Lebenslauf und etwas von meiner Muse auf der Vestung.* Stuttgart, 1798.

*Das Königreich Württemberg: Eine Beschreibung nach Kreisen, Oberaemtern und Gemeinden*, K.-Statistisches Landesamt, 4 vols. Stuttgart, 1904–1907.

Krapf, Ludwig and Christian Wagenknecht, eds. *Stuttgarter Hoffeste*, 2 vols. Tübingen, 1970.

Maier, Christian. *Die Bezirkskörperschaften und Amtsversammlungen in Württemberg mit Andeutung und Vorschlägen für ihre zeitgemässe Neugestaltung und volkstümliche Erweiterung.* Stuttgart, 1848.

Mosapp, Hermann. *Die württembergischen Religionsreversalien: Sammlung der Originalurkunden samt einer Abhandlung über die Geschichte und die zeitgemässe Neuregelung der Religionsreversalien.* Tübingen, 1894.

Moser, Rudolf. *Vollständige Beschreibung von Württemberg*, 2 vols. Stuttgart, 1843.

Nägele, Paul. *Bürgerbuch der Stadt Stuttgart*, 3 vols. Stuttgart, 1956.

Nicholai, Ferdinand Friedrich. *Beschreibung einer Reise durch Deutschland und die Schweiz im Jahr 1781*, x. Berlin, 1795.

Osterberg, Adolf. *Tagbuch der Gräfin Franziska v. Hohenheim, späteren Herzogin von Württemberg*. Stuttgart, 1913.

Pfaff, Karl, ed. *Sammlung von Briefen gewechselt zwischen J. E. Pfaff und Herzog Carl von Württemberg*. Leipzig, 1853.

Pfeilsticker, Walther. *Neues württembergisches Dienerbuch*, 3 vols. Stuttgart, 1957.

Pöllnitz, C. L. von. *Lettres et mémoires*, 1. Frankfurt am Main, 1738.

*La pure vérité: Lettres et mémoires sur le duc et le duché de Virtemberg pour servir à fixer l'opinion publique sur le procès entre le prince et ses sujets*. Augsburg, 1765.

Rath, Hans W. "Stuttgarter Familienregister," 4 vols. (deposited in Stadtarchiv Stuttgart).

Reyscher, A. L. *Vollständige, historisch und kritisch bearbeitete Sammlung der württembergischen Gesetze*, 19 vols. Stuttgart and Tübingen, 1828–1851.

Röder, Philipp L. H. *Geographisches statistisch-topographisches Lexikon von Schwaben*, 2 vols. Ulm, 1791.

Schefold, Max. *Alte Ansichten aus Württemberg*, 2 vols. Stuttgart, 1956.

Schneider, Eugen. *Ausgewählte Urkunden zur württembergischen Geschichte*. Stuttgart, 1911.

Siebmacher, Johann. *J. Siebmacher's Grosses Wappenbuch*, Bd. 23, *Die Wappen des Adels in Württemberg*. Neustadt an der Aisch, 1982. Reprint of 1856 edition.

*Staatshandbuch für Baden-Württemberg, Wohnplatzverzeichnis 1961*, Statistisches Landesamt Baden-Württemberg. Stuttgart, 1964.

Steiff, K. and Gebhard Mehring, eds. *Geschichtliche Lieder und Sprüche Württembergs*. Stuttgart, 1912.

*Tabellen zur Verwandung der alten württembergischen Masse in das Metermass*, Württembergisches Innenministerium. Stuttgart, 1952.

Taube, M. Freiherr von. *Die von Uxkull: Genealogische Geschichte des uradeligen Geschlechts der Herren, Freiherren und Grafen von Uxkull 1229–1929*. Berlin, 1930.

*Verhandlungen zwischen des regierenden Herrn Herzogens zu Württemberg Hoch-Fürstl: Durchlaut dero treu-gehorsamsten Prälaten und Landschafft in den Jahren 1757 und 1758*. Stuttgart, 1758.

Wais, Gustav. *Alt-Stuttgarts Bauten im Bild*. Frankfurt am Main, 1977.

*Württembergische Hof- und Staats-Handbücher*. Stuttgart, 1736–1918. Title varied in eighteenth century: *Hof- und Staatsbuch; Hofkalender; Hof- und Staatskalender*.

Zedler, Johann Heinrich, ed. *Grosses vollständiges Universal-Lexikon aller Wissenschaften und Künste*, 32 vols. Halle and Leipzig, 1735.

ARTICLES AND MONOGRAPHS

Again, what follows is not a complete bibliography but a reference guide to key articles and monographs dealing with Württemberg in the period 1593 to 1793.

Adam, Albert E. "Das Unteilbarkeitsgesetz im württembergischen Fürstenhause nach seiner geschichtlichen Entwicklung." *WVJSLG*, 6 (1883), 161–222.

——. *Johann Jakob Moser als württembergischer Landschaftskonsulent, 1751–77*. Stuttgart, 1887.

——. "Württemberg vor dem siebenjährigen Krieg, geschildert in einen Gutachten Johann Jakob Mosers vom 9 November 1752." *WVJHLG*, NF 12 (1903), 205–226.

Andler, D. von. "Die württembergischen Regimenter in Griechenland, 1687–89." *WVJHLG*, NF 31 (1922–1924), 217–279.

Bader, Karl Siegfried. *Der deutsche Südwesten in seiner territorialstaatlichen Entwicklung*. Stuttgart, 1950.

Bätzner, von. "Die Amtskörperschaftsverbände in Württemberg, ihre Entstehung und Ausbildung; ihre Aufgaben und Leistungen und die auf die Erreichung ihrer Zwecke verwendeten Mittel." *Amtsblatt des Kgl. württ. Ministeriums des Innern*, 8 (1878).

Beaver, Edward. "Witchcraft and Magic in Altwürttemberg." Princeton: Ph.D. diss., 1983.

"Beiträge zur Statistik der Vermögensverwaltung der Amtskörperschaften, Gemeinden und Stiftungen in Württemberg und der Besteuerung für Amtskörperschafts-und Gemeindezwecke." *WJ* (1883), 187–229.

Benzing, Fritz. "Die Vertretung von 'Stadt und Amt' im altwürttembergischen Landtag unter besonderer Berücksichtigung des Amts Nürtingen." Tübingen: Ph.D. diss., 1924.

*Beschreibung des Oberamts Münsingen*, K.-Statisches Landesamt. Stuttgart, 1912.

Binder, M. Christian. *Wirtembergs Kirchen- und Lehraemter*, 2 vols. Tübingen, 1798.

Binder, M. C. *Württembergische Münz- und Medaillen-Kunde*. Stuttgart, 1910.

Boelcke, Willi A. "Bäuerlicher Wohlstand in Württemberg Ende des 16. Jahrhunderts." *Jahrbücher für Nationalökonomie und Statistik*, 176 (1964), 241–280.

——. "Die Wirtschaft in der Zeit des Spätmerkantilismus (1770–1780)," Beiwort zur Karte XI, 4. In *Historischer Atlas von Baden-Württemberg*, Kommission für geschichtliche Landeskunde in Baden-Württemberg, 1–15. Stuttgart, 1977.

——. "Ein Herzoglich-Württembergischer Regiebetrieb des ausgehenden 18. Jahrhunderts." *Jahrbücher für Nationalökonomie und Statistik*, 175 (1963), 53–75.

————. "Zur Entwicklung des bäuerlichen Kreditwesens in Württemberg vom späten Mittelalter bis Anfang des 17. Jahrhunderts." *Jahrbücher für Nationalökonomie und Statistik*, 176 (1964), 319–358.

Bofinger, Wilhelm. "Kirche und werdender Territorialstaat." *BWKG*, 55 (1965), 75–149.

Borst, Otto. *Stuttgart: Die Geschichte der Stadt*. Stuttgart, 1973.

Brändle, W. "Ein württembergisches Hugenottenprivileg aus dem Jahr 1685." *ZWLG*, 29 (1970), 351–359.

Bull, K. -O. "Zur Wirtschafts- und Sozialgeschichte der württembergischen Amtstadt Vaihingen an der Enz bis zum Dreissigjährigen Krieg." *ZWLG*, 38 (1979), 97–140.

Bütterlin, Rudolf. *Der württembergische Staatshaushalt in der Zeit zwischen 1483 und 1648*. Stuttgart, 1977.

————. *Die merkantilistische Geldpolitik im Herzogtum Württemberg von der Reformation bis Napoleon*. Urach, 1966.

Carsten, Francis L. "The German Estates in the Eighteenth Century," *Recueils de la Société Jean Bodin pour l'Histoire Comparative des Institutions*, 25 (1965).

————. *Princes and Parliaments in Germany from the Fifteenth to the Eighteenth Century*. Oxford, 1959.

Decker-Hauff, Hans Martin. *Geschichte der Stadt Stuttgart: Von der Frühzeit bis zur Reformation*, 1. Stuttgart, 1966.

Dehlinger, Alfred. *Württembergisches Staatswesen in seiner geschichtlichen Entwicklung bis Heute*, 2 vols. Stuttgart, 1951 and 1953.

Dizinger, Karl Friedrich. *Beiträge zur Geschichte Württembergs und seines Regentenhauses zur Zeit der Regierung Herzogs Karl Alexander und während der Minderjährigkeit seines Erstgeboren*, 2 vols. Tübingen, 1834.

Eimer, Manfred. *Konrad Breuning, Vogt zu Tübingen, Mitglied der Landschaft und des Regimentsrats*. Stuttgart, 1948.

Elwenspoek, Curt. *Jud Süss Oppenheimer: Der grosse Finanzier und galante Abenteurer des 18. Jahrhunderts*. Stuttgart, 1926. Translated by E. Cattle, *Jew Süss Oppenheimer*. London, 1931.

Ernst, Fritz. "Fünfhundert Jahre Stuttgarter Landtag 1457–1957." *ZWLG*, 17 (1958), i-xvi.

Ernst, Hans-Joachim, "Das württembergische Armenwesen im 18. Jahrhundert." Tübingen: Ph.D. diss., 1951.

Ernst, Viktor. "Die Entstehung des württembergischen Kirchenguts." *WJSL* (1911), 377–424.

Fink, Hubert. "Probleme und Aufbau einer wissenschaftlichen Untersuchung der kommunalen Selbstverwaltung Altwürttembergs." Typewritten manuscript on deposit in SAL, 1958.

————. "Zusammenstellung über das Landtagswahlrecht der altwürttembergischen Städte und Aemter." Typewritten manuscript on deposit in SAL, 1957.

Fleischhauer, Werner. *Barock im Herzogtum Württemberg*. Stuttgart, 1958.

————. *Renaissance im Herzogtum Württemberg*. Stuttgart, 1971.

Fleischhauer, Werner, Walter Grube, and Paul Zinsmaier, eds. *Neue Beiträge zur südwestdeutschen Landesgeschichte: Festschrift für Max Miller*. Stuttgart, 1962.

Gmelin, H. *Ueber Herzog Friedrich I. und seine Stände* (Stuttgart, 1885).

Gothein, Eberhard. *Wirtschaftsgeschichte des Schwarzwaldes und der angrenzenden Landschaften*. New York, 1970. Reprint of 1892 edition.

Grabinger, Christine. *Bernhausen*. Bernhausen, 1974.

Graner, Ferdinand. "Zur Geschichte des Hofgerichts zu Tübingen." *WVJHLG*, 32 (1925), 36ff.

Griffith, Eugene J. "Political Writing and Enlightened Monarchy in Württemberg during the Reign of Duke Carl Eugen, 1744–93." University of Illinois: Ph.D. diss., 1979.

Grube, Georg. *Die Verfassung des Rottweiler Hofgerichts*, Veröffentlichungen der Kommission für geschichtliche Landeskunde in Baden-Württemberg, Reihe B, Forschungen, Bd. 55. Stuttgart, 1969.

Grube, Walter. *Der Stuttgarter Landtag, 1457–1957*. Stuttgart, 1957.

———. "Dorfgemeinde und Amtsversammlung in Altwürttemberg." *ZWLG*, 13 (1954), 194–219.

———. *Geschichtliche Grundlagen: Vogteien, Aemter, Landkreise in Baden-Württemberg*. Stuttgart, 1975.

———. *Vogteien, Aemter, Landkreise in der Geschichte Südwestdeutschlands* (Stuttgart, 1960).

Günter, Heinrich. *Das Restitutionsedikt von 1629 und die katholische Restauration Altwürttembergs*. Stuttgart, 1901.

Hamburger, Hans. *Der Staatsbankrott des Herzogtum Wirtemberg nach Herzog Ulrichs Vertreibung und die Reorganisation des Finanzwesens*. Schwäbisch Hall, 1909.

Hammer, Otto. *Schwäbisches Beamtentum*. Stuttgart, 1923.

Hasselhorn, Martin. *Der altwürttembergische Pfarrstand im 18. Jahrhundert*. Stuttgart, 1958.

Haug, F. "Die Einwanderung in die Herrschaft Friedberg-Scheer nach dem Dreissigjährigen Krieg." *ZWLG*, 5 (1941), 284–301.

Heine, Anton. *Geschichte der katholischen Gemeinde Ludwigsburg*. Ludwigsburg, 1932.

Hellstern, Dieter. *Der Ritterkanton Neckar-Schwarzwald, 1560–1805*, Veröffentlichungen des Stadtarchivs Tübingen, v. Tübingen, 1971.

Hermelink, Heinrich. "Geschichte des allgemeinen Kirchenguts in Württemberg." *WJSL* (1903), I, 79–101; II, 1–81.

———. *Geschichte der evangelischen Kirche in Württemberg von der Reformation bis zur Gegenwart*. Stuttgart, 1949.

*Herzog Karl Eugen v. Württemberg und seine Zeit*, Württembergischer Geschichts- und Altertums-Verein, 2 vols. Esslingen, 1907–1909. Volume I is published in two parts.

Heyd, Ludwig Friedrich. *Ulrich, Herzog zu Württemberg*, 3 vols. Tübingen, 1841–1844.

Hippel, Wolfgang von. "Bevölkerung und Wirtschaft im Zeitalter des Dreissigjährigen Krieges: Das Beispiel Württemberg," *Zeitschrift für Historische Forschung*, 5 (1978), 413–448.

Hoffmann, Leo. *Des württembergische Zunftwesen und die Politik der herzoglichen Regierung gegenüber den Zünften im 18. Jahrhundert*. Tübingen, 1906.

Hölzle, Erwin. *Das alte Recht und die Revolution: Eine politische Geschichte Württembergs in der Revolutionszeit 1789–1805*. Munich and Berlin, 1931.

Jänichen, Hans. *Beiträge zur Wirtschaftsgeschichte des schwäbischen Dorfes*. Stuttgart, 1970.

Jungel, Julius. "Der Begriff der Polizei im württembergischen Recht." Stuttgart: Ph.D. diss., 1912.

Keppler, Utta. *Franziska von Hohenheim*. Stuttgart, 1969.

Kleemann, Gotthilf. *Schloss Solitude bei Stuttgart*. Stuttgart, 1966.

Knapp, Theodor. "Leibeigene Bauern auf den württembergischen Landtagen." *Jahrbücher für Nationalökonomie und Statistik*, 118 (1922), 531–532.

Kohlhaas, Wilhelm. "Die Meuterei der Württemberger anno 1757." *Beiträge zur Landeskunde*, 5 (1971), 11–16.

Kolb, Christian. "Die Anfänge des Pietismus und Separatismus in Württemberg." *WVJHLG*, NF 9, 10, 11 (1903–1904).

Kothe, Irmgard. *Der fürstliche Rat in Württemberg im 15. und 16. Jahrhundert*, Darstellungen aus der württembergischen Geschichte, XIX. Stuttgart, 1938.

Krauter, Karl-Gunther. "Die Manufakturen im Herzogtum Württemberg und ihre Förderung durch die Wirtembergische Regierung in der zweiten Hälfte des 18. Jahrhunderts." Tübingen: Ph.D. diss., 1951.

Lahnstein, Peter. *Ludwigsburg: Aus der Geschichte einer europäischen Residenz*. Stuttgart, 1968.

Lange-Kothe, Irmgard. "Zur Sozialgeschichte des fürstlichen Rates in Würt-Jahrbuch, 50, (1882).

Lange-Kothe, Irmgard. "Zur Socialgeschichte des fürstlichen Rates in Württemberg." *VSWG* (1940).

Lehmann, Hartmut. "Die württembergischen Landstände im 17. und 18. Jahrhundert." In Dietrich Gerhard, ed., *Ständische Vertretungen in Europa im 17. und 18. Jahrhundert*, Veröffentlichungen der Max-Planck-Instituts für Geschichte, 27, 183–207. Göttingen, 1969.

———. *Pietismus und weltliche Ordnung in Württemberg vom 17. bis zum 20. Jahrhundert*. Stuttgart, 1969.

Lempp, Eduard. "Philipp Heinrich Weissensee." *BWKG*, 31 (1927), 114–167.

———. "Weissensees Sturz." *BWKG*, 32 (1928), 531 ff.

Leube, Martin. "Die fremden Ausgaben des altwürttembergischen Kirchenguts." *BWKG*, 29 (1925), 168–199.

Liebel, Helen. "Der Beamte als Unternehmertyp in den Anfangstadien der Industrialisierung: Johann Friedrich Müller und die Staats- und Wirtschaftsreform Württembergs, 1750–80." In G. A. Ritter, ed., *Entstehung und Wandel der modernen Gesellschaft, Festschrift für Hans Rosenberg zum 65. Geburtstag*, 221–260. Berlin, 1970.

Liebel-Weckowicz, Helen. "The Politics of Poverty and Reform: Modernization and Depotism in Eighteenth-Century Württemberg." In *The Consortium on Revolutionary Europe Proceedings*, 76–85. Athens, Ga., 1981.

Lindner, Otto. *Die Entstehung der Verwaltungsrechtpflege des Geheimen Rats in Württemberg*. Berlin, 1940.

Marquardt, Ernst. *Geschichte Württembergs*. Stuttgart, 1962.

Martini, Eduard C. *Geschichte des Klosters und der Pfarrei St. Georgen*. St. Georgen, 1859.

Maschke, E. and J. Sydow, eds. *Verwaltung und Gesellschaft in der südwestdeutschen Stadt des 17. und 18. Jahrhunderts*, Veröffentlichungen der Kommission für geschichtliche Landeskunde in Baden-Württemberg, Reihe B, Band 58. Stuttgart, 1969.

Mehring, Gebhard. "Schädigungen durch den Dreissigjährigen Krieg in Altwürttemberg." *WVJSLG*, 19 (1910), 447–452.

———. "Wirtschaftliche Schäden durch den Dreissigjährigen Krieg im Herzogtum Württemberg." *WVJHLG*, 30 (1921), 58–89.

———. "Württembergische Volkszählungen im 17. Jahrhundert." *WJSL*, 1919/20, 313–318. Stuttgart, 1922.

Mohl, Robert von. *Beiträge zur Geschichte Württembergs*, I. Tübingen, 1828.

———. *Das Staatsrecht des Königsreichs Württemberg*. Tübingen, 1840.

Moser, Friedrich K. "Leben und Ende des Herzogs Carl Alexander von Württemberg." *Patriotisches Archiv* (1784), 105–220.

Müller, Karl O. "Die Finanzwirtschaft in Württemberg unter Herzog Karl Alexander (1733–1737)." *WVJHLG*, 38 (1932), 276–317.

Naujoks, Eberhard. *Obrigkeitsgedanke, Zunftverfassung und Reformation; Studien zur Verfassungsgeschichte von Ulm, Esslingen, und Schwäb. Gmünd.*, Veröffentlichungen der Kommission für geschichtliche Landeskunde in Baden-Wüttemberg, Reihe B: Forschungen, 3 Bde. Stuttgart, 1958.

Niethammer, Hermann. "Ludwig Friedrich von Stockmayer." *ZWLG*, 3 (1939), 449–474.

Oehme, Ruthardt. "Ein Bericht zum Tod des Herzogs Eberhard Ludwig." *ZWLG*, 30 (1971), 241–243.

———. *Geschichte der Kartographie des deutschen Südwestens*. Constance and Stuttgart, 1961.

Overdick, Renate. *Die rechtliche und wirtschaftliche Stellung der Juden in Südwestdeutschland im 15. und 16. Jahrhundert*. Constance, 1965.

Pfaff, D. "Geschichte des Münzwesens in Württemberg in seiner Verbindung mit dem Schwäbischen und Reichsmünzwesen." *Württembergische Jahrbücher für Vaterländische Geschichte, Geographie, Statistik, und Topographie*, 2 (1858), 44–216.

Pfaff, Karl. "Die Verhandlungen des Herzogs Karl Eugen wegen und mit der Reichsritterschaft." *WJ* (1851).

―――. *Geschichte des Fürstenhauses und Landes Wirtemberg*, 3 vols. Stuttgart, 1839.

―――. *Geschichte des Militärwesens in Württemberg von der ältesten bis auf unsere Zeit und der Verhandlungen darüber zwischen der Regierung und den Landständen*. Stuttgart, 1842.

―――. "Württembergische Zustände zu Ende des 16. und zu Anfang des 17. Jahrhunderts." *WJ* (1841), 312ff.

―――. *Württembergs geliebte Herren*, edited by Peter Lahnstein. Stuttgart, 1965.

Pfister, J. C. *Herzog Christoph zu Wirtemberg*, 2 vols. Tübingen, 1819–1820.

Puchta, Hans. "Die Habsburgische Herrschaft in Württemberg, 1520–34." Munich: Ph.D. diss., 1967.

Rauch, Moritz von. "Salz- und Weinhandel zwischen Bayern und Württemberg im 18. Jahrhundert." *WVJHLG*, 33 (1927), 208–250.

Rauscher, Julius. *Württembergische Reformationsgeschichte*, 3 vols. Stuttgart, 1934.

Rieger, Alfred. "Die Entwicklung des württembergischen Kreisverband." Tübingen: Ph.D. diss., 1952.

Rössger, A. "Die Herkunft der württembergischen Waldenser und ihre Verteilung im Lande 1698 bis 1732." *WJSL* (1873), 259–300.

Rothenhäusler, Konrad. *Die Abteien und Stifte des Herzogtums Württemberg im Zeitalter der Reformation*. Stuttgart, 1886.

Rürup, Reinhard. *Johann Jacob Moser: Pietismus und Reform*. Wiesbaden, 1965.

Sabean, David W. *Landbesitz und Gesellschaft am Vorabend des Bauernkriegs*. Stuttgart, 1972.

Sattler, Christian F. *Geschichte des Herzogtums Wirtenberg unter der Regierung der Grafen*, 4 vols. Tübingen, 1773–1777.

―――. *Geschichte des Herzogtums Wirtenberg unter der Regierung der Herzogen*, 13 vols. Ulm, 1769–1783.

Schäfer, Gerhard. *Kleine württembergische Kirchengeschichte*. Stuttgart, 1964.

Schall, J. "Zur kirchlichen Lage unter Herzog Karl Alexander." *BWKG*, 4 (1900), 123–143.

Schmid, Eugen. "Geheimrat Georg Bilfinger (1693–1750)." *ZWLG*, 3 (1939), 370–422.

Schmucker, Heinz. *Das Polizeiwesen im Herzogtum Württemberg*. Tübingen, 1958.

Schnee, Heinrich. *Die Hoffinanz und der Moderne Staat: Geschichte und System der Hoffaktoren an den deutschen Fürstenhöfen im Zeitalter des Absolutismus*, 6 vols. Berlin, 1953–1967.

Schneider, Eugen. "Das Tübinger collegium illustre." *WVJHLG* (1898), 217ff.

————. "Der Tod des Herzogs Karl Alexander von Württemberg." *Besondere Beilage des Staatsanzeigers für Württemberg* (1900).

————. *Württembergische Geschichte*. Stuttgart, 1896.

Schnürlen, Matthew. "Geschichte des württ. Kupfer- und Silbererzbergbaus." Tübingen: Ph.D. diss., 1921.

Schott, Arthur. "Merkantilpolitisches aus Württembergs Herzogszeit." *WJ* (1900), 245 ff.

Schott, Theodor. "Die württembergische Geiseln in Strassburg und Metz, 1693–1696." *Zeitschrift für allgemeine Geschichte*, 3 (1886), 583–602.

Schöttle, G. "Verfassung und Verwaltung der Stadt Tübingen am Ausgang des Mittelalters." *Tübinger Blätter*, 8 (1905), 1–34.

Schulte, Aloys. *Geschichte der grossen Ravensburger Handelsgesellschaft, 1380–1530*, 3 vols. Stuttgart, 1923.

Siegler, Karl G. *Stuttgart*. Munich and Berlin, 1968.

Söll, Wilhelm. "Die staatliche Wirtschaftspolitik in Württemberg im 17. und 18. Jahrhundert." Tübingen: Ph.D. diss., 1934.

Specker, H. E. "Die Verfassung und Verwaltung der württembergischen Amtstädte im 17. und 18. Jahrhundert." In E. Maschke and J. Sydow, eds., *Verwaltung und Gesellschaft in der südwestdeutschen Stadt des 17. und 18. Jahrhunderts*, 1–22. Stuttgart, 1969.

Spittler, L. T. von. *Geschichte des wirtembergischen Geheimen-Raths-Collegiums*. In *Sämtliche Werke*, edited by K. Wächter XIII. Stuttgart and Tübingen, 1837.

————. "Herzog Eberhard Ludwig und Wilhelmine von Grävenitz." In *Sämtliche Werke*, edited by K. Wächter, XII. Stuttgart and Tübingen, 1837.

Stadlinger, L. I. von. *Geschichte des Württembergischen Kriegswesens von der frühesten bis zur neuesten Zeit*. Stuttgart, 1856.

Stälin, Christoph F. von. *Wirtembergische Geschichte*, 4 vols. Stuttgart and Tübingen, 1841–1873.

————. "Württembergische Kriegsschäden im Dreissigjährigen Krieg." *WVJHLG*, 7 (1899), 54 ff.

Stark, P. "Zur Geschichte des Herzogs Karl Alexander von Württemberg und der Streitigkeiten nach seinem Tode." *WVJHLG*, 11 (1888).

Stern, Selma. *Jud Süss. Ein Beitrag zur deutschen und zur jüdischen Geschichte*. Berlin, 1929.

Stolz, Otto. "Die Bauernbefreiung in Süddeutschland im Zusammenhang der Geschichte." *VSWG*, 33 (1940), 1–68.

Storm, Peter-Christoph. *Der Schwäbische Kreis als Feldherr*. Berlin, 1974.

Storz, Gerhard. *Karl Eugen: Der Fürst und das "alte gute Recht."* Stuttgart, 1981.

Tröltsch, Walter. *Die Calwer Zeughandlungskompagnie und ihre Arbeiter*. Jena, 1897.

Tüchle, Hermann. *Die Kirchenpolitik des Herzogs Karl Alexander von Württemberg, 1733–1737*. Würzburg, 1937.

Uhland, Robert. *Geschichte der Hohen Karlsschule in Stuttgart*. Stuttgart, 1953.

Vann, James A. *The Swabian Kreis: Institutional Growth in the Holy Roman Empire, 1648–1715*. Brussels, 1975.

Walker, Mack. *German Home Towns: Community, State, and General Estate, 1648–1871*. Ithaca, 1971.

———. *Johann Jakob Moser and the Holy Roman Empire of the German Nation*. Chapel Hill, N.C., 1981.

———. "Rights and Functions: The Social Categories of Eighteenth-Century German Jurists and Cameralists." *JMH*, 50 (1978), 234–251.

Weidner, Karl. *Die Anfänge einer staatlichen Wirtschaftspolitik in Württemberg*. Stuttgart, 1931.

Weller, Karl. *Württembergische Geschichte*. Stuttgart, 1963.

Weller, Karl and A. Weller. *Württembergische Geschichte im südwestdeutschen Raum*. Stuttgart, 1971.

Wintterlin, Friedrich. "Beamtentum und Verfassung im Herzogtum Württemberg." *WVJHLG*, NF 32 (1925/26), 1–20.

———. "Die altwürttembergische Verfassung am Ende des 18. Jahrhunderts." *WVJHLG*, NF 23 (1914), 195–210.

———. *Geschichte der Behördenorganisation in Württemberg*, 2 vols. Stuttgart, 1902–1906.

———. "Wehrverfassung und Landesverfassung im Herzogtum Württemberg." *WVJHLG*, 34 (1928), 239–256.

———. "Zur Geschichte des herzoglichen Kommerzienrats." *WVJHLG*, NF 20 (1911), 310–327.

Wunder, Bernd. "Der Administrator Herzog Friedrich Karl von Württemberg." *ZWLG*, 30 (1971), 117–163.

———. "Die Sozialstruktur der Geheimratskollegien in den süddeutschen protestantischen Fürstentümern (1660–1720)." *VSWG*, 58 (1971), 145–220.

———. *Frankreich, Württemberg und der Schwäbische Kreis während der Auseinandersetzungen über die Reunionen, 1679–1697*. In *Veröffentlichungen der Kommission für geschichtliche Landeskunde in Baden-Württemberg*, LXIV. Stuttgart, 1971.

———. *Privilegierung und Disziplinierung: Die Entstehung des Berufsbeamtentums in Bayern und Württemberg, 1780–1825*. Munich, 1978.

"Württembergs Bevölkerung in früheren Zeiten." *Württemburgische Jahrbücher für Vaterländische Geschichte, Geographie, Statistik und Topographie*. Stuttgart, 1847.

Zimmermann, Karl. *Der Vogt in Altwürttemberg: Ein Beitrag zur Geschichte des württembergischen Staats- und Verwaltungsrechtes*. Marbach a.N., 1935.

Zorn, Wolfgang. *Handels- und Industriegeschichte Bayerisch-Schwabens, 1648–1870: Wirtschafts-, Sozial- und Kulturgeschichte des Schwäbischen Unternehmertums*. Augsburg, 1961.

# Index

*Library of Congress Cataloging in Publication Data*

Vann, James Allen, 1939–
  The making of a state.

  Bibliography: p.
  Includes index.
  1. Württemberg (Kingdom)—Politics and government. 2. Holy Roman Empire—
Politics and government. I. Title.
JN4920.V36 1984        943'.47        83-18841
ISBN 0-8014-1553-5